Vol. 22 No. 1
February 1980

JOURNAL OF INTERAMERICAN STUDIES and WORLD AFFAIRS

A Publication of the Center for Advanced International Studies,

The University of Miami

SAGE PUBLICATIONS

Journal of INTERAMERICAN STUDIES and WORLD AFFAIRS

The editors and publisher wish to acknowledge with gratitude the assistance and encouragement of the Center for Advanced International Studies, University of Miami, in providing ancillary services and support for this journal.

Journal of
INTERAMERICAN
STUDIES
and WORLD AFFAIRS

Vol. 22
No. 1
February
1980

CONTENTS

Cuba's Involvement in Africa: An Interpretation of Objectives, Reactions, and Limitations
WOLF GRABENDORFF 3

U.S.-Mexican Groundwater Problems: Bilateral Prospects and Implications
STEPHEN P. MUMME 31

Perspectives on the Mid-Vargas Years: 1934-1937
ROBERT M. LEVINE 57

From Jew to Basque: Ethnic Myths and Antioqueno Entrepreneurship
ANN TWINAM 81

REVIEW ESSAY

German-Latin American Relations: The First Half of the Twentieth Century
WARREN SCHIFF 109

BOOKS RECEIVED 119

SAGE PUBLICATIONS / *Beverly Hills* *London*

Policy: The **JOURNAL OF INTERAMERICAN STUDIES AND WORLD AFFAIRS** reflects the interests of the scholarly community and interested public concerned with the social, economic, political, and cultural aspects of life in Latin America (including the Caribbean), particularly in those instances where the subject is of concern to more than one of the traditional disciplines. As these concerns change, so will the content of the journal.

Articles which have special relevance for interrelationships between American nations and of those nations with the rest of the world will be given special consideration. An effort will be made to include occasional articles that state an unusual or even discordant position on a subject of broad interest to be supplemented by critical comments of authorities representing differing positions on the topic. The editors continue to welcome articles by scholars from all parts of the world.

Manuscripts should be submitted in duplicate to: Editor, **JOURNAL OF INTERAMERICAN STUDIES AND WORLD AFFAIRS,** Box 24-8134, University of Miami, Coral Gables, Florida 33124. Manuscripts should be typewritten, double-spaced, with footnotes, references, tables, and charts on separate pages, and should follow the current journal style. A brief biographical paragraph describing each author's current affiliation, research interests, and recent publications should accompany the manuscript.

Correspondence regarding book reviews should be sent directly to: Book Review Editor, **JOURNAL OF INTERAMERICAN STUDIES AND WORLD AFFAIRS,** Box 24-8134, University of Miami, Coral Gables, Florida 33124.

JOURNAL OF INTERAMERICAN STUDIES AND WORLD AFFAIRS is published four times annually—in February, May, August, and November.

Subscriptions: Regular institutional rate $32.00 per year. Individuals may subscribe at a one-year rate of $16.50. Add $1.00 for subscriptions outside the United States. Orders from the U.K., Europe, the Middle East, and Africa should be sent to the London office (address below). Noninstitutional orders **must** be paid by personal check.

Second class postage paid at Beverly Hills, California. ISSN 0022-1937

This journal is abstracted or indexed in **Historical Abstracts, Human Resources Abstracts, Sage Urban Studies Abstracts, International Political Science Abstracts, Public Affairs Information Service, Current Contents, Social Sciences Citation Index, Social Sciences Index, ABC POL SCI,** and **United States Political Science Documents.**

Back Issues: Information about availability and prices of back issues may be obtained from the publisher's order department (address below). Write to London office for sterling prices.

Inquiries: Address all correspondence and permissions requests to SAGE PUBLICATIONS, Inc., 275 South Beverly Drive, Beverly Hills, California 90212. Inquiries and subscriptions from the U.K., Europe, the Middle East, and Africa should be sent to SAGE PUBLICATIONS Ltd, 28 Banner Street, London EC1Y 8QE, England. Other orders should be sent to the Beverly Hills office.

Advertising: Current rates and specifications may be obtained by writing to the Advertising Manager at the Beverly Hills office (address above).

Claims: Claims for undelivered copies must be made no later than three months following month of publication. The publisher will supply missing copies when losses have been sustained in transit and when the reserve stock will permit.

Change of Address: Six weeks' advance notice must be given when notifying of change of address. Please send old address label along with the new address to insure proper identification. Please specify name of journal. Send change of address to: Journal name, c/o 275 South Beverly Drive, Beverly Hills, CA 90212.

WOLF GRABENDORFF
Stiftung Wissenschaft und Politick
Forschungsinstitut für Internationale Politik und Sicherheit
D-8026 Ebenhausen, Federal Republic of Germany

CUBA'S INVOLVEMENT IN AFRICA

An Interpretation of Objectives, Reactions, and Limitations

Any examination of the Cuban involvement in Africa should take into consideration the political conditions surrounding such involvement. Only by analyzing the objectives and motivations of those involved, while disregarding any arguments in justification, can one adequately demonstrate the complexity of the relations between Cuba and its African allies. An analysis of Cuba's assessment of its own political and ideological function in Africa or of the objectives of the Soviet Union in Africa is not as important as an examination of the African expectations arising from Cuban military and development aid.

Expectations in Africa

In spite of the fact that each African state has developed independently, one can identify certain universal interests common to all African states except those with white minority governments. These universal interests certainly include a sustained alienation from the former colonial powers. They also include the desire for an end to European influence even in areas where a certain interdependence with Europe would not necessarily have negative implications for further development. In addition,

Journal of Interamerican Studies and World Affairs, Vol. 22 No. 1, February 1980 3-29

continuing structural distortions which are either a direct consequence of colonialism or of undesirable trends since Africa's independence have led many African states to take a generally negative stance towards the West. Since African nations have had their say in international issues, this anti-Western attitude has grown noticeably.

Despite their structural differences and divergent interests, the desire for early independence demonstrated by those states still under white minority rule is strong evidence of a common denominator in African politics. Indeed, these liberation movements, which the West all too easily tends to equate with terrorism, play an important role in the self-perception of most African states. Any nation supporting such liberation movements is considered to demonstrate a generally pro-African attitude. Moreover, the Africans, with their strong emotional, political, and ideological antiracist attitudes, consider support for an end to white government in Africa an essential condition for any further relations with a foreign country.

As in all countries of the Third World, the achievement of formal independence in Africa by no means puts an end to actual dependence. On the contrary, this dependence continues to exist, due in part to the processes inherent in economic development and in part to the severe economic exploitation by indigenous elites. Therefore, the African nations express a common concern in demanding stricter control over African resources and the greatest possible latitude in forming their own foreign policy. Since the West appears to identify with white minority regimes and to display strong economic interest in those regions, many African states have turned to the nonaligned movement as an instrument of their foreign policy objectives.

These are, in brief, the political preconditons upon which Cuba bases its African activities. It is easy to see that in many respects Cuba's policy blends conveniently with Africa's aspirations. Yet one should not underrate the criticism voiced by some African states at the presence of this foreign power. Because of their continuing dependence and the resulting trauma about colonial interference, the majority of African states want to prevent any foreign nation or group of nations from gaining dominating influence. Undoubtedly, most African states view Cuban intervention in Africa as help in achieving independence through self-help rather than as a step toward the type of dependence which would result from a similar commitment by the superpowers.

The specific African expectations vis-à-vis Cuba and the justifications given by certain African states for their positive reaction to Cuba's involvement can best be illustrated by three different, though typical, case studies.

ALGERIA AS THE TEST CASE

When Algeria became involved in a border conflict with Morocco in 1963, shortly after its independence, it sought help everywhere, particularly since it feared that the former colonial power, France, might support Morocco's demands that Algeria cede part of its territory. Since the Front de libération nationale (FLN), as a liberation movement, had enjoyed Cuban support since 1960, Algeria also turned to the Cubans for help. These appear to have been the first military South-South contacts based on the foresight of two revolutionary governments fearing destabilization of their countries by external influence. Despite these contacts, relations between the two states were later often tense. This early revolutionary support for a state facing external attack is, however, a good example of the type of South-South cooperation which Africa has come to expect from Cuba.

ANGOLA AS THE IDEAL CASE

Military support and training for a country involved in a struggle for liberation was considered an ideal example of relations among revolutionary countries and provided a perfect model for Cuban demonstrations of solidarity with African nations. The Movimento Popular de Libertação de Angola (MPLA) received massive assistance from Cuba beginning in the early 1960s. Its cadres were partly trained in Cuba, training camps were set up in

Africa, and arms and funds were made available. After Angola achieved independence, the external invasions and the continuing conflict between externally supported guerilla factions—the Frente Nacional de Libertação de Angola (FNLA) and the União Nacional de Independência Total de Angola (UNITA)—resulted in unexpected intensification of Cuban military activity. However, Angola insists that Cuban development aid played a more important role in its bilateral relations than did Cuban military aid either before or after liberation. The development aid is considered by most African states to be the most positive indication of Cuban support. It includes not only improvements to the educational system and medical welfare, but also the establishment of a national infrastructure to implement development objectives. Thus, Cuban cooperation with Third World countries ideally comprises three elements:

(1) assistance in gaining liberation or independence,
(2) assistance in the defense against external aggressors seeking to destabilize revolutionary regimes,
(3) assistance for self-help toward internal stabilization.

The long-standing cooperation with the MPLA leadership and probably the good personal relationship between Castro and Neto had created a special atmosphere of mutual confidence between Angola and Cuba. Furthermore, the MPLA maintains that Cuba, lacking a sufficient power base and in spite of any friction which is bound to arise from such close cooperation, would never claim or pursue imperialistic interests. Moreover, the Cubans, critical of their own experience with the Soviet Union, understand the fears of the Angolans. The fears in this case are surely typical of all of Africa, and Cuba accepts Angola's insistence on its own sovereignty. From an African viewpoint, this special relationship with Cuba could not be duplicated by any type of cooperation offered by European powers, China, the Soviet Union, or the United States.

THE HORN OF AFRICA AS THE PROBLEM CASE

The exceedingly difficult ethnic and geopolitical situation at the Horn of Africa, though giving Cuba the opportunity to demonstrate its honest intentions, has considerably restricted its freedom to act. Originally, Cuba had supported only part of the Eritrean independence movement and Somalia. The rapid shift toward Ethiopia, with which there had hardly been any relationship, was probably more in the Soviet than in the Cuban interest. On the other hand, the Cubans were undoubtedly convinced that the Ethiopian revolution was a revolution sui generis. At first the Marxist-oriented liberation movement Eritrean People's Liberation Front (EPLF) had placed high hopes on Cuba, only to be disappointed. Somalia, too, had expected major support from Cuba, particularly in the field of development. Cuba's rapid reversal caused confusion in Africa despite the Organization of African Unity's (OAU) condemnation of Somalian aggression in the Ogaden conflict. Due to the unbridgeable antagonism between Ethiopia and Somalia, Castro's efforts to bring about a socialist federation at the Horn of Africa have so far failed. But since the internal stability of both states seems highly fragile, Cuban mediation efforts, which have Soviet support, may yet prove successful. Cuba's past activities, however, have been restricted to resisting external invasion, which it viewed as an attempt to destabilize a revolutionary regime. On the Eritrea issue, Havana preferred to remain aloof, considering this an internal affair of Ethiopia.

The Horn of Africa thus has proved to be a problem case for Cuba, since the expectations of all involved could not be met—a situation contrary to the experience in Angola. Cuba had to drop the liberation movement EPLF from its list of political priorities, and because Havana adheres strictly to the OAU maxim of the inviolability of the postcolonial borders, it was forced to take Ethiopia's side against Somalia's territorial claims. The disappointment in the lack of Cuban solidarity with a liberation movement and an African country will probably have an impact on how Africa assesses Cuba's reliability. After following

Havana's conduct at the Horn of Africa, those African states involved in border conflicts or fighting secessionist movements will in all likelihood harbor some doubts about Cuban support.

Africa expects Cuba to recognize certain limits to its involvement, such as the toleration of national peculiarities and the maintenance of African economic independence. Cuba has successfully stressed the former in its relations with the Soviet Union but has been unable to retain its economic independence. Unlike all other developing countries supplying development aid, Cuba has the advantage of not wanting to promote any economic interests of its own. Yet another Cuban advantage is its policy of providing support without trying to dictate to the recipients. In this context Cuba's insistence that every nation fight for its own independence without external inducement has been of particular importance to the liberation movements.[1] This recognition of the primacy of the liberation movements in national issues has been instrumental in building the confidence which Cuba today enjoys in many parts of Africa.

Cuba's Self-Assessment

Cuba's African relations can be understood only if one takes into consideration its perception of self and its own concept of those relations. One must start with an understanding of Cuba's perception of revolution, a perception determined to a large extent by its experience since 1959 with the United States, which continually attempted to influence the course of its revolution. The period of internal consolidation of the revolution lasted for a decade after Castro's seizure of power, followed by a period of external consolidation beginning early in the 1970s. The Cubans are convinced that the Soviet security guarantees alone cannot insure their survival. Rather, they believe that one way to protect their own revolution is for other Third World states to follow a similar revolutionary path.[2] Hence, Cuba's active role in foreign relations not only stems from Fidel Castro's revolutionary élan; it is above all a continued effort to protect the Cuban model for the future. In this process, because of Cuba's real interests, the North-South conflict plays a much greater role than the East-West conflict.

An additional element in Cuba's self-perception, one too easily ignored by Western analysts, is the Afro-Cuban tradition. The strong historical retrospective which has developed in Cuba since its revolution is part of its attempt to establish a national identity. This retrospection includes recognition of a cultural tradition arising from Cuba's experiences as a slave society and a victim of colonial exploitation. Particularly in the areas of music and religion but also in literature, the African elements introduced by migrating slaves have survived. Parallel to the decline of American influence, they have grown. The feeling of belonging with the nonwhite have-nots of the world, of having only gained a certain independence during the last twenty years, and not without a painful struggle, has greatly contributed to the Cubans' willingness to help other black and poor nations in their struggle to advance.

The strongest element of Cuba's perception of its role in Africa is the emphasis it places on proletarian internationalism. Here the revolutionary ideology is clearly foremost, with Cuba's own experience again becoming the yardstick for its external conduct. The Cubans are well aware that without the Soviet Union or the socialist camp their revolution would not have had the slightest chance of survival in a generally hostile environment. This is a central argument for Cuba in turn would like to give other Third World countries a similar chance at survival in such an environment. Since such support surely cannot be given in the form of material aid, proletarian internationalism, as Cuba sees it, can best be expressed in the form of development aid and temporary military aid.

Cuba's exemplary method of practicing antiimperialism dates back to Che Guevara's concept of South-South cooperation among oppressed peoples. Guevara had always held that Africa was the weakest link in the imperialistic chain. During the last 15 years, therefore, Cuba has given its support primarily to African liberation movements and to ruling parties emerging from these movements. Its goal is not so much to support revolutions akin to its own, but to provide proletarian aid to all progressive or revolutionary regimes threatened by external forces.

The typically nationalist character of the Cuban revolution is also evident in the defense of its objectives in Africa. Cuba has time and again warned revolutionary regimes like those in Angola and Ethiopia not to accept territorial losses in order to remain in power. That would deprive every revolution of its patriotic justification. Thus, the proletarian internationalism cannot be interpreted as a supranational system of socialist preferences. Rather, it has to be understood as assistance for national self-help—here as well, the Cuban intentions coincide with the African expectations—and as mutual assistance by proletarian states in the international economic system.

The moral starting point of Cuban foreign policy in Africa is the fight against racism. Cuba feels that the West not only has failed to honor this moral position, but has even criticized it. A second assumption made by Cuba is that it should provide assistance even when material interests would not be affected. This willingness to provide moral and military support for the establishment and stabilization of a just social system was pointed out in Castro's rhetorical question as to how much property and how many investments the Cubans had after all defended in Africa. It is this kind of moral support which the Cubans received from the Soviet Union and which they now wish to pass on to the African states. A third moral assumption which Cuba, more than many other nations, can justify is that it must assist in improving the standard of living of the peoples of the Third World. Castro believes this is a task which capitalism is incapable of performing, one which only socialism can accomplish.[3]

Another major factor in the Cuban's moral stand is the legal base of their cooperation with African liberation movements and states. Indeed, Cuba has responded only to calls for help made by a legitimate government or a liberation movement legally recognized by the OAU. Consequently, massive support for the Katanga rebels and a Shaba invasion as well as a destruction of the Eritrean liberation movement would have been incompatible with Cuban policy.

Finally, the Cubans argue that they are by no means mercenaries, since they stand to gain nothing by waging war. On the contrary, they have always urged negotiations, especially in conflicts between states of the Third World. Castro's personal attempts at mediation on the Horn of Africa are a good example.

From the point of view of both Cuba and Africa, these arguments are highly convincing, mainly because these countries see the world less in terms of an East-West division than of a division between developed and developing states. Hence, the task of overcoming mass misery must take precedence over questions of political influence or regional stability. The Cubans, therefore, believe that the overwhelmingly positive response to their policy in black Africa will endure, provided Soviet superpower interests do not force it to compromise on its moral ideals.

Soviet Objectives

An analysis of the Soviet Union's objectives in Africa and its motives for cooperating with Cuba is not an explanation of Soviet strategy in black or southern Africa. Rather, it is an attempt to separate its ideological interests, which are probably largely identical with those of Cuba, from its strategic interests, in which Cuba takes no part. In view of the sparse information emanating from the Soviet Union about its goals and strategies, it is difficult to outline actual Soviet interests. The triangle among African partner states, Cuba, and the Soviet Union is extremely complex and in many areas still difficult to comprehend. It can be assumed that the Soviet Union is pursuing long-term goals in accordance with its international position and intentions in Africa, whereas Cuba, which is pursuing its own long-term objectives, may be interested in completely different developments.

Any study of Soviet strategy in Africa cannot ignore the fact that the present harmony between Cuba and the Soviet Union, and their broad agreement on African policies rest on a generally difficult alliance between two very differently structured actors in the international system. During the 1960s, when the conflict between a small Cuba and a powerful United States was making headlines, the West tended to ignore the numerous disagreements between Cuba and its new superpower ally. Only in the early 1970s, after a number of internal changes had taken place which were by no means prompted solely by Soviet pressure, did the relationship improve sufficiently for the Soviet Union to consider Cuba a useful experiment. Since then, despite occasional ideological differences, both partners in the unequal alliance seem to have balanced their expectations and are able to depend on each other as a relatively stable and reliable factor in the pursuit of their policy objectives (Blasier, 1978).

The generally identifiable course of Cuban foreign policy in Africa from 1975 to 1978, with its apparent division of labor with the Soviet Union, would seem to have been the result of changing political circumstances rather than of a structural understanding which one could use to make straightforward projections into the future. Historically, the relationship between Cuba and the socialist camp, in particular the Soviet Union, has so often been subject to political fluctuations that it seems unlikely that the present division of labor in Africa will become permanent (Fontaine, 1978: 19).

The often-quoted "proxy theory" can hardly be corroborated given the multifaceted nature of Cuban-Soviet relations. It would be very difficult to prove that Cuba actually acts as a proxy for the Soviet Union in Africa. On the contrary, there are several indications that, at least in the case of Angola, it was Cuba which urged the Soviet Union to act instead of vice versa. Conversely, in the Ethiopian conflict it was obviously the Soviet Union which, for strategic reasons, was the driving force. If the Soviet Union wishes to continue to pursue a policy of détente, making Cuba its instrument could hardly serve that purpose. In individual cases, however, the idea of using the Cubans "to pull the chestnuts out of the fire" may be tempting to the Soviets, above all for logistical reasons. Soviet recognition that Third World countries experiencing progressive internal development could be put under political pressure by the West has evidently led the Soviet Union to consider how it could either neutralize these destabilizing forces or turn them to its own advantage.

Angola has become the model for the socialist camp's support of a Third World nation based on both legalistic justifications and international law. The Soviet Union likes to point out the success of this intervention, but given the specific international situation, this success should not be overrated. The problem of decolonization faced by this former Portuguese colony, the Vietnam trauma which the United States was experiencing, and South Africa's military intervention all created a favorable environment for Cuban-Soviet intervention in Angola.

Of course, should the Soviet Union choose to use Cuba as its agent in Africa or eventually in other parts of the Third World, it must also be in a position to disavow Cuba at least partially should such a course of action fail. This, however, seems unlikely since the Soviet Union would then have to jeopardize its long-term success in giving socialist development aid, notably in Cuba, in favor of a relatively minor foreign policy objective.

Brezhnev's statement that the Third World would not remain passive in the East-West discussion (International Herald Tribune, 1977b) reveals the politically decisive factor of cooperation between the Soviet Union and Cuba in Africa. The Soviet Union evidently wants to utilize the Cuban Third World image in order to make its own system more attractive to Africa. It likes to use Africa's strong fascination with the relatively autonomous socialist state in Cuba as a supplement, but not an alternative, to its own orthodox road to socialism.

The Soviet Union's inability, never admitted but at least suspected, to act as an example for the future development of the Third World should be offset by the fact that Cuba, with the help of its own purely national revolution, has been able to contribute to worldwide recognition of the socialist camp. Therefore, the Soviet Union prefers to refer to its international responsibilities in Africa (International Herald Tribune, 1977b) in connection with the overthrow of white minority governments in southern Africa. The visits of Podgorny and Castro to Africa in 1977, however, showed that this growing influence of the socialist camp did not necessarily benefit only the Soviet Union. The different receptions enjoyed by Cuban and Soviet personalities and activities in Africa was noticeable in almost all states. It is indeed much easier for the Soviet Union to contain both Western and Chinese influence in Africa with Cuba than without it. Yet it is doubtful whether the Soviet Union rejoices in this fact. It is more likely that Soviet satisfaction over developments in Africa stems from the fact that Soviet and Cuban policies of anticolonialism and antiracism, launched at a very early stage, are now beginning to pay off. Both the Soviets and the Cubans consider the military defeat of the "reactionary forces" as confirmation of their own long-term political strategy, although they each interpret this strategy differently.

Reactions of the United States

The United States and Cuba have a specific bilateral problem resulting not only from the enormous contrast between their differing political capabilities and their close historical ties, but above all from the United States' lack of political restraint in any question concerning Cuba (Bender, 1975). The U.S. reaction to Cuba's involvement in Africa may easily be considered the second "Cuban trauma" of American foreign policy. The first "Cuban trauma," starting in 1959 with the seizure of power by the guerilla leader Castro, whom the United States refused at first to take seriously, and ending in 1962 with a direct threat to the U.S. mainland during the missile crisis, left deep wounds in the political consciousness of both the general public and the foreign policy elite of the country. Accordingly, the reaction of the United States to Cuba's African policy during the last few years could not help but be prejudiced. The almost 20-year-old conflict with the thoroughly despised regime just 90 miles off Florida's coast has had a decisive impact on the United States' assessment of Cuba's leverage in foreign affairs. In almost every respect, the United States refuses to accept the fact that the

Cubans are capable of pursuing an independent foreign policy. This fact cannot be explained solely by Cuba's objective dependence on the Soviet Union. It is also rooted in the assumption of the United States that any state the size of Cuba and within its own political sphere of influence must naturally consider American interests when forming domestic or foreign policy. This refusal to recognize any independence in Cuba's ability to make political decisions makes it difficult for the United States to take a rational view of the background and problems of Cuba's foreign policy in Africa.

The United States sees Cuban African policy from four different aspects:

(1) Domestically, the relationship with Cuba is extremely difficult, particularly for the Carter administration which has declared its intention of pursuing a less arrogant policy toward the Third World. The Panama Canal debate, however, demonstrated to Carter the present lack of domestic support for such an approach. Similar controversies arise in the debate on Cuba's African policy. The host of overlapping political and economic interests, aggravated by the influential minority of Cubans living in exile in the United States, has precluded a coherent, balanced reaction to Cuban policy.

(2) Former UN Ambassador Andrew Young's varying reactions to the Cuban presence in Africa are a clear illustration of the ideological debate being carried on in the United States.[4] On the one hand, one can hardly criticize Cuba's consistent support for self-determination and an end to minority rule in Africa. On the other hand, acceptance necessarily implies support for progressive and essentially anti-Western elites. It therefore seems relatively unimportant to the United States if Cuban activities in support of liberation movements or governing African elites are of a different character from the aid offered by the Soviet Union. Ideologically, the United States sees as the main threat posed to the West the fact that in both cases socialist regimes, not representing Western interests, are being established and stabilized through outside forces.

(3) Since for many years the United States has regarded the socialist regime in Cuba as the gravest regional problem in the Western

Hemisphere, it is particularly displeased that Cubans are actively encouraging the establishment of ideologically similar regimes in other parts of the world. In this sense, Cuba's African policy is an important factor in the U.S. interpretation of Cuba's role in the Western Hemisphere. The United States could not fail to realize that at least in the eyes of some of the states of the region, Cuba's reputation was enhanced by its support for Angola and Ethiopia. In particular, the United States sees developments in the Caribbean as cause for great concern. The political instability and economic underdevelopment of Central America and the Caribbean, for which surely the United States is partly to blame, makes Cuban support for revolutionary governments, as in Nicaragua or Grenada, quite understandable.

(4) Of vital importance to the United States is the security question. On the one hand, the United States is concerned about the possible implications of the Cuban-Soviet influence in Africa for the security of the Western oil routes. On the other hand, the United States is especially concerned about the Cuban's ability to use its military strength in crisis areas of the Third World. The implicit consequences of Cuba's financial, technological, and military dependence on the Soviet Union are turning this ability into a largely incalculable factor. Cuba's revolutionary readiness for action combined with the resources of a superpower such as the Soviet Union constitute a high security risk for the United States as far as its global interests are concerned.

It is not these basic political problems alone, however, which complicate the relationship between the United States and Cuba with regard to Africa. In the course of the last few years, four additional internal barriers have arisen to aggravate further any successful U.S. response to the increasing Cuban presence in Africa.

(1) Above all, the United States lacks any means of exerting political pressure in Africa to promote its own interests in contrast to Cuba's. At first, the United States had hoped to establish a linkage between the withdrawal or reduction of Cuban troops in Africa and the establishment of diplomatic relations with

Cuba. But the Cubans, who had stressed their interest in a resumption of diplomatic relations since about 1974, rejected this linkage decisively.[5] Instead, Cuba tried to demonstrate a policy of strength by demanding the lifting of the U.S. trade embargo as a major precondition for resuming diplomatic relations. At the same time, it emphasized that its policy of proletarian internationalism would take priority over a rapprochement with the United States, which would have been so promising economically.

(2) The second barrier is the U.S. government's apparent lack of resolve in developing a conduct appropriate for dealing with Cuban African policy. This certainly is due not only to the Vietnam experience but also to the obvious change of policy of the Carter Administration. The extent of the differences of opinion within the administration on Cuba's African policy are personified by Zbigniew Brzezinski and former UN Ambassador Andrew Young.

(3) The third barrier is the U.S. government's lack of information about actual Cuban involvement in Africa, which probably results from its lack of experience with the revolutionary self-perception of Cuba and the African liberation movements. This shortcoming has led not only to obvious errors in assessing the Shaba invasion, but also to a virtually neurotic statistical registration of almost every individual Cuban in Africa.[6]

(4) This information gap results in the fourth barrier, namely a lack of differentiation in the assessment of individual Cuban measures or generally of the Cuban strategy in Africa. For contrary to the U.S. reaction to French, Soviet, or even Chinese activities in Africa, a certain hysteria over Cuban involvement, particularly in public opinion, has been unmistakable (Bender, 1978). This is unfortunate, since a differentiation between the various elements and intentions of Cuba's African policy would have permitted a more flexible reaction while at the same time making American criticism internationally more credible and effective. These negative aspects, however, cannot be attributed solely to domestic and foreign policy difficulties of the Carter Administration. They are also rooted in the inability of American foreign policy makers to come to grips with a 20-year-old revolutionary socialist system in their immediate vicinity.

In addition to these problems, Cuba's own position in the international system has further precluded a balanced U.S. reaction to Cuba's African policy. Cuba's simultaneous membership in the community of Latin American nations, in the socialist camp, and in the nonaligned movement made it necessary for the United States to exert pressure simultaneously on friendly governments in the region, on the Soviet Union, and on nonaligned countries. Such a concept obviously put considerable strain on the Carter Administration, which in addition had attempted to convince some African governments to form a more critical attitudc toward Cuba. This turned out to be an almost hopeless undertaking. Carter's policy of open diplomacy was bound to cause additional difficulties. Military or secret counteractions would only have further strengthened Cuba's position, at least within the socialist camp and nonaligned movement.[7]

Evidently because of this dilemma, the United States, apart from attempting to influence discussions within the nonaligned movement, has refrained from effectively counteracting. The Carter Admnistration, by adhering to the "proxy theory," deprived itself of any means of influencing Cuba directly. In public debate at least, any critique of Cuba had to be interpreted as being directed at the Soviet Union.

Doubts Within Africa and the Third World

Africa's attitude toward Cuba's policy is determined by the respective interests of various groups. The Western-oriented states mainly fear direct or indirect destabilization of their own positions by neighboring states under Cuban influence. Moreover, many of these states do not rule out the danger that a majority of relatively radical Cuban-oriented regimes seizing power in Africa could eventually have a kind of spillover effect upon their own regimes.

Within the OAU, open criticism of the Cuban presence was in fact voiced only by those countries directly affected by the Cuban policy, in this case mainly Somalia. The reactions of other OAU members were more reserved. They stressed the right of all African states to decide for themselves which non-African states to ask for assistance in protecting their sovereignty. This phraseology was meant to enable Cuba's African allies, as well as the francophile states, to justify politically the presence of foreign troops in their respective countries.

Those states feeling threatened by a growing Cuban support of counterelites have reacted particularly violently. South Africa has openly accused the West of having brought about a rapid decline of the anti-Communist bloc of Africa because of its lack of readiness to counter Cuban-Soviet influence in Africa. In the case of the South West African People's Organization (SWAPO) in Namibia and the Patriotic Front in Zimbabwe, Castro's offers to help[8] have obviously substantiated this argument.

Because of the chronic political instability of African states, offers of foreign assistance to seize and stabilize power cannot be refused. In fact, only after the states concerned have become so consolidated as to be able to decide for themselves how much and what kind of help to seek from Cuba, will they know whether Cuba's offer of assistance for self-help was in fact the only goal of its "proletarian internationalism." Angola's recent interest in the West could be an indication that a growing domestic stability in revolutionary states is directly proportional to their efforts to diversify their foreign relations. At the same time, the hysteria of some African states over Cuban involvement is also likely to diminish. From the viewpoint of power politics, Cuba's presence offers much less cause for criticism than the presence of other foreign powers, such as France or the Soviet Union, because of its position as a developing country.

All Arab and African doubts about and objections to Cuban activities have a common denominator. They are not against the military presence and ideological influence of an extra-regional power in principle, but will attack this presence if it contravenes their respective national interests.

Within the Third World surprisingly, it is Latin America, where an anti-Cuban mood prevailed years after the Cuban revolution, which has not been overly harsh in its criticism of the Cuban presence in Africa. This is due primarily to a basically contradictory attitude of military regimes in Latin America: On the one hand, they feel threatened by Cuban socialism and are relieved that present Cuban activity is focusing on another continent. On the other hand, some of them feel a kind of pride over the foreign policy achievements and the international importance of such a small country from their own region.

Castro was quick to explain that no regime in Latin America had anything to fear from Cuban activities.[9] It was Cuba's policy, he said, to support only legal governments and only if they asked for aid officially. This reassurance by Castro, who incidentally had warned Panama against any premature steps during the last phase of the Canal negotiations, obviously stifled debate in Latin America over Cuba's African policy. Instead, it appears that Cuba is pursuing a completely different policy toward Latin America than toward Africa, where it can evidently count on greater political success because it is able to meet expectations of a different nature from those in Latin America.

Within the Third World it is undoubtedly the nonaligned movement which is most preoccupied with Cuba's presence in Africa. Cuba's role in this movement, of which it has been the only Latin American member since 1961, has always been controversial. Whereas initially Cuba needed the nonaligned movement in its search for international political support, its successful internal stabilization has made it a very self-confident member of this group. Since the Algiers conference in 1973, when Fidel Castro countered the theory of the two imperialisms, Cuba—or rather Castro—has come to embody the general political problem of the orientation of the nonaligned movement. The question, therefore, is less the extent to which Cuba remains nonaligned following its African involvement, but rather which future political trend is going to prevail within the movement.

The policy of détente certainly weakened the policy of the nonaligned movement, so important during the Cold War, of maintaining an equal distance from both of the superpowers. Meanwhile, economic and political reasons have rendered cooperation with one or the other attractive for individual members (Mattes, 1978).

From the very beginning the nonaligned nations tailored their definition of the enemy to fit Israel and South Africa. Apart from India and Yugoslavia, it has been the Arab and black African states which in this respect have set the tone for the movement since its inception. The fact that Castro is now not only claiming a very personal leadership role in this Third World forum, but also is permitting Soviet access to the movement has led to misgivings about Cuba's role in Africa. While the number of direct conflicts between the superpowers has decreased, the number of indirect conflicts in their spheres of influence, including conflicts between members of the nonaligned movement, has increased remarkably. Some members, therefore, fear that the Cuban form of South-South cooperation could not only set a precedent but also give rise to or aggravate a host of conflict situations in the Third World resulting from this indirect intervention by the superpowers.

The greatest concern about Cuba's African policy, voiced by many major and powerful Third World states, is the fear that Cuba's excessive influence within both the nonaligned and international systems is apt to threaten their own position. This threat seems substantiated by the fact that Cuba was granted a privileged position at the 1979 summit meeting of nonaligned nations, thus enabling it to play a crucial role in determining the political course of the movement in a critical situation. Some nonaligned states fear that the Soviet Union, in view of the growing importance of the North-South conflict to the international system, might try to use Cuba's leading role in the nonaligned movement for its own purposes.

Cuba's Options and Limitations

Although Cuba's revolutionary self-perception has provided the basis for its influence in Africa, at the same time it has set the limitations for its future involvement. The government of

Cuba will surely be unable to risk the consolidation and institutionalization of its own revolution in favor of certain foreign policy objectives. Cuba will therefore continue to restrict massive intervention to those areas where it hopes to achieve a maximum of prestige with relatively limited means while at the same time protecting the interests of the Cuban revolution (Grabendorff, 1977).

The possibilities for future Cuban involvement in Africa can be predicted from its record of military intervention over the past four years. Following the failure of the so-called internal solution in Zimbabwe and Namibia, increased Cuban involvement could be expected in both of these countries. By contrast, the number of military units in Angola are likely to be reduced in order to be deployed to other crisis areas. Because of the favorable political constellation and its contacts with the SWAPO, Cuba is likely to give increasing support to the revolutionary struggle in Namibia. However, diminishing Cuban contacts with Mozambique and competition between the Zimbabwe African People's Union (ZAPU) and the Zimbabwe African National Union (ZANU) which form the Patriotic Front will cause the Cubans to be more cautious in Zimbabwe. Cuba's involvement in Ethiopia, which it does recognize unofficially as being problematic, is also unlikely to increase.

The emphasis Cuba places on its involvement in the so-called front-line states in southern Africa is completely in line with the past logic of Cuban decisions. The Cuban military contingent of 40,000 troops in Africa, roughly a quarter of Cuba's armed forces, will probably not be enlarged in the future. However, the number of civilian advisers in all fields of development politics, presently about 10,000, will probably increase.

In order to assess Cuba's options, it is useful to work out the political constellation which would be the ideal prerequisite for Cuban military involvement. Such a constellation should, according to the Cuban concept, contain the following features:

—a clearly defined and uncontested enemy, for example South Africa or Israel, which morally justifies the participation of a foreign state in the conflict

—the existence of established internal forces whose virtues, political backbone, and prospects for success are beyond dispute
—indications of an autochthonous, mostly collectivist concept for development which insures popular support for the liberation movement
—the coincidence of racist, nationalist, and ideological conflicts
—a history of long-standing informal contacts which can later form the basis for an official request for support
—OAU or UN recognition of the to-be-supported liberation movement

Cuba's past military activity in Africa suggests that the foreign policy decision-making process in Cuba is the result of a well-conceived calculation (Dominguez, 1978). The objective is not only to achieve optimum success with as limited means as possible, but also to capitalize on the weaknesses of the potential adversary (Lowenthal, 1977).

Military success in Africa is expected to fulfill three Cuban political objectives:

(1) *Regaining the position of revolutionary vanguard* of the Third World, which it had lost because of the consolidation process and increased Soviet influence over Cuba's indigenous development. Cuba hopes to convince those countries of the Third World which had at first considered Cuba's successful revolution to be a model that it was just this comprehensive Soviet support which made Cuba's present self-confident and independent foreign policy possible. On the other hand, the recovery of international status can be put to good use domestically, since the process of institutionalization has produced a certain wear in the revolutionary consciousness of the Cuban population. The Cuban leadership obviously believes that an offensive external defense of the revolution encourages additional domestic legitimization.[10]
(2) The possibility of *guiding socialism in Africa to victory.* Since Africa lacks a bourgeois middle class as found in Latin America, Castro believes that the future social development of Africa must incorporate the social systems of the various tribes, which

already display some collectivist characteristics, into a system of national socialism.[11] One will have to await developments in Angola, Mozambique, or Ethiopia to know how realistic this concept is. Certainly a short-term disadvantage is that the post colonial elites, most of whom are Europe-oriented, will be unwilling to accept this concept, although it may well be the only way to satisfy the needs of the general population. Also, the Cuban solution of having the Soviets finance the transition period is probably unacceptable. Thus, although some aspects of the Cuban model are transferable, there is no certainty that developments in Africa will follow precisely the same pattern. The only means for Africa to realize the kind of socialism which Cuba envisages is to use the extraordinary African economic resources, like those in Namibia, to finance such a development.

(3) Cuba's greatest expectation is the possibility of gaining a *two-fold bargaining power* from its African involvement. On the one hand, it could enhance its position vis-à-vis the hegemonic USSR (Ronfeldt, 1978: 19), since the Soviet Union is probably well aware of the fact that the military, organizational, and developmental achievements of Cuba could also serve antithetical interests in the Third World. On the other hand, Cuba also could gain bargaining power vis-à-vis the United States. Its African card could become a useful trump in overcoming problems and resuming diplomatic relations with the United States. In either case, Cuba, because of its military commitment to liberation movements, can count on the support of many Third World countries in solving its own problems of independence. Concretely, this would mean that after the current financial agreements with the Soviet Union expire in 1986, Cuba could negotiate similar new favorable accords with the Soviet Union and simultaneously resume trade relations with the United States, thus ending its exclusive dependence on the Soviet Union.

Examination of the limits of Cuban influence in Africa reveals that inner-African developments could have a direct impact on the future success of Cuban intervention. One particular problem could be to what extent a pragmatic approach, for example to the confusing situation at the Horn of Africa, could undermine Cuban credibility in the eyes of the liberation movements or newly established regimes. Whenever more is at stake than defending against foreign invasion, achieving national independence, or establishing a regime similar to Cuba's, the Cuban policy will encounter substantial difficulties. This will be particularly true if border conflicts or elites competing for power force a clear division between Cuba's long-term intentions and the partner country's short-term objectives.

Given the extent of Cuba's involvement, for example in Angola and Ethiopia, one cannot rule out friction with the friendly governments, especially if Cuban troops are employed not only to fend off external invasion but also to counter indigenous guerilla forces (Segal, 1978: 5). The limits to Cuban influence become visible where consolidation of power has been accomplished and discussions start about divergent concepts of the political and economic systems. Though Cuba stresses repeatedly that it wants to supply aid without any political strings attached, conflicts cannot be avoided altogether in view of the close connections between Cuban experts and African governmental institutions.

Another restricting factor for Cuba is its unavoidable collaboration with the Soviet Union. Since relatively few critical comments by either side have leaked out, one can only speculate about possible conflicts of interest. It is not clear to what extent the differing Soviet and Cuban interests or the differences found in the means they employ, particularly in the economic sphere, could cause friction. Especially apparent, also to its African partners, is Cuba's dependence on Soviet weapons and armament deliveries and transcontinental troop transport.

Two further factors clearly limit Cuba's political maneuverability: the reactions of the West and of the nonaligned. There are a great number of indications that Cuban intervention in Angola or Ethiopia would not have taken the form it did if the West had demonstrated massive opposition. In any case, Cuba is willing to respect to a certain extent those limitations to its military involvement which the West attempts to impose only because it is well aware of the limits of such pressure.

Cuba, however, must take much more seriously any criticism emanating from the Third World, and in particular from the nonaligned movement. Cuba's rather conciliatory conduct during the Conference of Foreign Ministers in Belgrade in 1978, as well as its partial interest at the 1979 summit in Havana, followed by a concomitant adjustment to its foreign policy illustrate the importance it attaches to the opinion of the nonaligned. This limitation to its political leverage makes it all the more necessary for Cuba to pursue an uncompromising straight-line policy, particularly concerning those questions which remain unsettled within the nonaligned movement. An example is the support of liberation movements, as it is primarily in this area that Cuba can expect acceptance rather than rejection from the nonaligned movement, whose criticism has been concentrated on the difficult case of the Horn of Africa.

Besides those limitations imposed on Cuban commitments by external influences, domestic factors also play a major role despite the one-party rule in Cuba. The restrictions on Cuba's external activity imposed by internal factors do not stem from political opposition groups, but rather from the conflicts of interest of its elites who cannot agree on the degree to which Cuba should cooperate in East-South or South-South relationships. Should Cuba make a long-term commitment, the domestic strain imposed by the unavoidable sacrifices which the general populace would be called upon to make for a war being waged far from Cuba's own shore would become increasingly important. The consequences for Cuba would be inevitable: growing dissatisfaction in the population and the need to relegate Cuba's own development to a back burner, thus prolonging its dependence on the Soviet Union and putting objective limitations upon Cuba's future involvement. At the same time that Cuban civilian experts are being employed by foreign governments, there is a shortage of such expertise, particularly in the technical professions, in their own country. Teachers, doctors, and social workers can be exported more easily because they are trained at a higher rate and have largely saturated the country's infrastructure.

In addition, since the military plays a decisive role in Cuban politics (Dominguez and Mitchell, 1978), it will be unwilling to increase further its involvement in Africa, thereby limiting its own domestic presence. Although it is unlikely that the military will demand a reduction of Cuban involvement because of its losses in Africa, unofficial statements would seem to indicate that the internal limits have been reached. This would mean that any additional military activities in Africa would have to be achieved by transferring existing troops with the help of Soviet transport equipment, rather than by sending new expedition forces.

Despite all conceivable drawbacks, Cuba will presumably carry on its African activities and continue to try to justify them. Its hinge function between the socialist camp and the Third World, however, will hardly suffice to justify its activities, at least on an international level. Domestically, it will always have to retain the possibility of putting the emphasis back on its own development, while at the same time stressing the political and social aspects of its involvement in Africa over the military aspect.

It is an asset to Cuba that even in its own revolutionary history, its political and social consolidation was preceded by a long military phase. It is easy for Cuba to emphasize that because of the very success of its own revolution, it is necessary to continue to provide development and military aid to the Third World. As long as no one can offer a viable alternative to the liberation movements in southern Africa, the Cuban troops and advisers will be welcomed even by those regimes in Africa which do not a priori consider the Cuban experience to be the perfect solution. Compared to the interests of the superpowers, however, many African states regard Cuban cooperation not only as the lesser of two evils but also as the most effective in both form and substance.

NOTES

1. Fidel Castro made this very clear while visiting various African states in 1977: "That is, independence is not brought from abroad. It is conquered from inside with the support of the people of progressive countries" (Daily News, 1977).

2. This is an argument that has been used by Fidel Castro as well in his interview with Afrique-Asie (1977).

3. "After all, socialism is the only solution for all underdeveloped countries. For with capitalism they will not be able to solve any problems" (Daily News, 1977).

4. "It is a kind of new colonialism" (International Herald Tribune, 1977a) and "I don't believe that Cuba is in Africa because they were ordered there by the Russians. I believe Cuba is in Africa because it really has shared a sense of colonial oppression and domination, and is dedicated to fighting against it" (Newsweek, 1978).

5. Fidel Castro: "It has nothing to do with Carter, it has nothing to do with the United States. Our relations with Africa, that we can't discuss, that we can't negotiate" (Washington Post, 1977).

6. Very revealing in that respect is Abraham F. Lowenthal's commentary in International Herald Tribune (1978a).

7. See Cole Blasier's plea for caution in his commentary in International Herald Tribune (1978c).

8. "Castro quite openly and explicitly acknowledged the fact that Cuba was providing advice and training and logistical assistance to the liberation forces in Zimbabwe, Namibia and South Africa" (International Herald Tribune, 1978c).

9. "No Latin American country, whatever its social system, will have anything to fear from the Armed Forces of Cuba" (Latin American Report, 1976).

10. "For many Cubans the ability to send doctors, technicians and troops abroad is perhaps the clearest sign that the revolution has succeeded at home" (International Herald Tribune, 1978d).

11. He used this argument in his interview with Afrique-Asie (1977): "C'est là qu'existent des perspectives excellentes pour pouvoir passer presque du tribalisme au socialisme sans avoir a traverser les diverses étappes qu'ont dû parcourir quelques autres régions du monde."

REFERENCES

Afrique-Asie [Paris] (1977) May 16.

BENDER, G. F. (1978) "Angola, the Cubans and American anxieties." Foreign Policy 31 (Summer): 3-30.

BENDER, L. D. (1975) The Politics of Hostility: Castro's Revolution and United States Policy. Hato Rey: Inter-American Univ. Press.

BLASIER, C. (1978) "The Cuban-U.S.-Soviet triangle, changing angles." Cuban Studies/Estudios Cubanos 8 (January): 1-9.

Daily News [Tanzania] (1977) March 23.

DOMINGUEZ, J. I. (1978) "Cuban foreign policy." Foreign Affairs 57 (Fall): 83-108.

——— and C. N. MITCHELL (1978) "The Cuban operation in Angola: costs and benefits for the armed forces." Cuban Studies/Estudios Cubanos 8 (January): 10-21.
FONTAINE, R. W. (1978) "Cuban strategy in Africa: the long road of ambition." Strategic Review 6 (Summer): 18-27.
GRABENDORFF, W. (1977) "Die kubanische aussenpolitik nach der intervention in Angola." Berichte zur entwicklung in Spanien, Portugal und Lateinamerika 2 (July/August): 10-20.
International Herald Tribune (1978a) July 19.
——— (1978b) June 24, 25.
——— (1978c) June 15.
——— (1978d) February 16.
——— (1977a) December 6.
——— (1977b) April 6.
Latin American Report (1976) 4 (April 9): 4.
LOWENTHAL, A. F. (1977) "Warum ist Kuba in Angola?" Berichte zur entwicklung in Spanien, Portugal und Lateinamerika 2 (July/August): 3-9.
MATTES, L. (1978) "The nonaligned countries between Colombo and Havana." Pacific Community (April): 291-301.
Newsweek (1978) March 20: 56.
RONFELDT, D. F. (1978) Superclients and Superpowers: Cuba-Soviet Union, Iran-United States. Santa Monica: Rand.
SEGAL, A. (1978) "Cubans in Africa." Caribbean Rev. 7 (July/September): 4-10.
Washington Post (1977) Dec. 7.

Wolf Grabendorff is a Senior Research Associate for Latin American Affairs at Stiftung Wissenschaft und Politik at Ebenhausen near Munich. The author of Kubas Engagement in Afrika, *he is presently completing a study on Argentine foreign policy and has written numerous articles on contemporary foreign policy of Latin American nations.*

STEPHEN P. MUMME
Department of Political Science
315 Social Sciences
University of Arizona
Tucson, Arizona 85721

U.S.-MEXICAN GROUNDWATER PROBLEMS
Bilateral Prospects and Implications

Introduction

Obscured amid the headline issues of illegal aliens, drug smuggling, and the Mexican petroleum bonanza, yet another controversy is nascent in U.S.-Mexican relations—the dispute over common groundwaters underlying the frontier zone. This dispute, with roots in the recent salinity accords of 1973, emerges as the latest phase in the long history of water resource controversies exacerbating problems between the two nations.

Until recently, the history of U.S.-Mexican water relations had been one of preoccupation with the capture and distribution of shared surface waters. The present dispute thus marks a distinctive evolution in bilateral relations. Moreover, just as the groundwater issue is new, it also points to the complexity of the transboundary ecology and the special problems of interdependence. Only since World War II, for instance, have the full implications of the area's groundwater hydrology been appreciated with respect to such matters as quality, distribution, and movement. Rapid agricultural development, human settle-

AUTHOR'S NOTE: An earlier version of this article was read at the twenty-seventh Annual Meeting of the Rocky Mountain Council on Latin American Studies held May 3-5, 1979, at El Paso, Texas.

Journal of Interamerican Studies and World Affairs, Vol. 22 No. 1, Feburary 1980 31-55 ment, and increased exploitative potential have accentuated the economic and political importance of groundwaters in the border region and lie at the roots of the present conflict.

The groundwater conflict has emerged most visibly in the vicinity of the Colorado river, though it is by no means dormant elsewhere. In that rich agricultural region embracing the important San Luis and Mexicali valleys of Mexico and the Yuma and Imperial valleys of the United States, groundwater has been increasingly relied upon by Mexico as an adjunct to scarce surface waters and as a substitute for waters contaminated by salinization.

Recently, these needs prompted Mexico to increase its exploitation of groundwater through the initiation of massive pumping operations. Exploitation began in 1972 with an anticipated withdrawal of 160,000 acre feet annually, approximately one-tenth of Mexico's current allocation of Colorado river water under treaty. Mexico's tapping of the vast underground water reserve in the region raised immediate fears in the United States. Given the hydrological characteristics of the area, U.S. Geological Survey studies indicated that Mexican exploitation of the shared aquifer would siphon off a total of 465,000 acre feet within a decade, and more thereafter. This threatened to deplete the availability of U.S. drainage waters currently being used to fulfill treaty obligations pertaining to surface water deliveries to Mexico, in addition to depriving the United States of groundwater reserves. Subsequently, the United States initiated a program of "protective pumping" in proportion to the 160,000 acre feet withdrawn annually by Mexico to establish equilibrium in the groundwater table and prevent unnecessary loss of groundwater reserves to Mexico (Bradley and DeCook, 1978).[1]

Although the groundwater conflict has been most intense in the Colorado river zone, at least six other border zones, ranging from San Diego-Tijuana in the west to Brownsville-Matamoros in the east, harbor potential for conflict in the short and medium term (Bittenger, 1972). Conflicting claims over the "percolating" waters of the Hueco Bolson aquifer underlying the important adjoining border cities of El Paso and Juárez, as well as disputes concerning Mexican utilization of the U.S. portion of the groundwaters underneath the Yuha Desert basin in the vicinity of Calexico, California, underscore the range of potential conflicts along the border. In the case of the Hueco Bolson, the potential for conflict emerges from an almost exclusive dependence on groundwater for municipal and agricultural purposes. Rapid depletion of groundwater reserves, at the rate of nearly 1% per annum in the aquifer, threatens valley farmers with both drought and saline contamination and circumscribes the prospects for growth in this rapidly developing metropolitan area (Day, 1978). Already, Mexican *ejiditarios* in the vicinity of Juárez have been beset by the rapid desertification of their croplands and are clamoring for a revision of extant bilateral treaty arrangements (Meraz, 1979). In the Mexicali-Calexico region, the source of the controversy is less a function of scarcity and more one of location. The Mexican municipality of Mexicali has increasingly come to rely upon the fresh groundwaters of the U.S. sector of the Yuha Desert basin for its drinking water and kindled the resentment of basin dependent U.S. settlers in the process (Rempel, 1979).

As the latest issue in the unfolding of bilateral conflict, the groundwater issue presents both nations with thorny and complex problems, technical and political in nature. This article will examine the groundwater issue as it is presently emerging in U.S.-Mexican relations. The analysis places particular emphasis on the structural elements conditioning the prospects for settling the issue as viewed from a historical, economic, political, and diplomatic perspective.

The Ground Problem and the Prospect for Settlement

Within the context of U.S.-Mexican relations, both the conflict over water resources and the manner in which these disputes have been resolved demonstrate the historic importance of water in the structure of bilateral relations. Both nations rely heavily on common water resources and the conflicts engendered thereby are among the most visible manifestations of physical interdependency. In a similar sense, the resolution of water conflicts has historically recognized interdependence with a gradual evolution towards cooperative resource management along the frontier. Among the principal bilateral cooperative agreements are the Convention of 1906, the Treaty of 1944, and a series of joint resolutions under the auspices of the International Boundary and Water Commission (IBWC). The most important are Minutes 218, 241, and 242, the most recent.[2] The IBWC itself, evolving in response to bilateral questions of surface water distribution and a host of minor water and boundary disputes, exemplifies the capacity of Mexico and the United States to institutionalize conflict resolving procedures.[3] Indeed, the management of water resources is depicted by some as the quintessential example of the putative "special relationship" between the two nations. Within this context, the groundwater issue appears as another stage in a scenario featuring the progressive development of cordial bilateral relations.

This hopeful perspective of the significance of the groundwater conflict in the web of U.S.-Mexican affairs stems in good measure from the relative success of past negotiations and a growing understanding of the complexity of the hydrological frontier. Of special moment to the United States, the major water disputes have been settled on terms which have not seriously hampered its domestic patterns of utilization and growth. From the standpoint of the United States, the treaties may be interpreted as tokens of commitment to equity and comity in relations with Mexico. From the Mexican vantage, the treaties and agreements have achieved and regularized the recognition of its national interest in common waterways by its powerful upstream neighbor and have secured certain of its claims to the resource vital to the development of its northern border region.

Reinforcing these views is a heightened awareness of the ecological interface implicit in the nature of groundwaters. This ecological consciousness is evident in an increasing body of international water law accepting the concept of "international drainage basins" requiring functionally integrated international management (Caponera and Alhéritière, 1978). Collectively, these factors contribute to the present optimism in predicting the eventual integration of U.S.-Mexican water management functions, or at least an increasing level of cooperation and convergence in the performance of these functions along the frontier.

The potential for integration of water management functions ranges from the limited form of administrative consultation which is presently practiced to the hypothetical form of complete functional integration within an autonomous supranational agency. At this time, few observers foresee the amalgamation of the respective national water management functions within a supranational agency, although such a scenario has been hypothesized. However, current discussion does generally foresee the amicable settlement of this problem, implying some degree of integration or convergence. In this modest form, the argument suggests that the IBWC be authorized to expand its jurisdiction to accommodate groundwater as well as surface water resources. Such an elaboration of IBWC powers entails at minimum the negotiation of a bilateral treaty encompassing the full range of potential water resources problems.[4]

It is important to note that the scenario traced above is not exclusively an American perspective. A prominent Mexican legal scholar has also commented on the integrative possibilities of the groundwater issue in U.S.-Mexican relations (Sepúlveda, 1975: 215-221). Nevertheless, scholars in the United States are more optimistic about the resolution of bilateral groundwater conflict than their Mexican counterparts. In some respects, this optimism reflects their mutual differences of interpretation of the state of bilateral relations generally. It is worth considering these relations more carefully, therefore, in terms of the structure of U.S.-Mexican affairs and the context of present diplomacy.

The Historical Setting

The pattern of bilateral relations is conditioned by the experiences of past and recent history. Particularly salient to contemporary water relations is the fact that negotiations over water resources have invariably forced Mexico to acknowledge water poverty in the borderlands. In the major disputes, Mexico played the role of petitioner for the redress of grievance.[5] Rarely have the roles been reversed, with the possible exception of the U.S. interest in the apportionment of the waters of the lower Rio Grande. Moreover, Mexico has been forced to acknowledge its inferior strength and economic dependency in these negotiations. Seldom, for instance, has Mexico been able to employ strategic or economic sanctions as a bargaining chip in bilateral negotiations. In a similar vein, Mexico has found expedient the resort to the moral force of international law and the process of arbitration to pursue its claims, whereas the United States has historically eschewed such universal appeals and arbitral forums.[6]

These facts admittedly constitute the darker side of U.S.-Mexican relations, revealing Mexico's vulnerability to the United States. Yet, it is frequently the darker side of such affairs that the aggrieved party finds most germane to an interpretation of an unsatisfactory relationship. It remains significant in the Mexican view that the United States refused to accept the arbitral judgment of the International Boundary Commission in 1911 in the El Chamizal controversy and that subsequently, the United States only reluctantly chose to acknowledge the Mexican claim to Colorado river water. More recently, Mexican statesmen were offended by U.S. procrastination on the salinity issue, which led to widespread damage to Mexican agriculture and development in the San Luis and Mexicali valleys.

The formal settlement of surface water disputes notwithstanding, the historical record thus fosters a Mexican posture of suspicion and hesitancy in bilateral water relations. From the Mexican standpoint, the United States has not always negotiated in good faith. Although the outstanding issues have been resolved, the social and economic costs of postponing the solution of outstanding problems seems to have been inordinately borne by Mexico.[7] Moreover, settlements achieved, such as the treaties of 1906 and 1944, carried the weight of U.S. pressure and insensitivity to Mexico's problems (Hundley, 1966: 28-30, 97-99, 163-169). The terms of the treaties themselves have acted to restrain Mexican development, while other unanticipated crises like the salinity problem have emerged to complicate water resource relations. Thus, Mexican observers have speculated that the terms of extant treaty arrangements might not be regarded by the United States in instances of "extraordinary drought" or "serious injury to the U.S. irrigation system" (Sepúlveda, 1978: 132-134).

Given such reservations, it is understandable that the Mexican government maintains a certain distance in its water relations with the United States. In this respect, the Mexican posture resembles its general stance in bilateral relations. Historically, such distance or independence has been crucial to the nationalist symbolism cultivated by the regime and to the preservation of an untarnished image of Mexican sovereignty in its conduct of foreign relations. This sovereign image—and its reality—conditions the practical realization of the government's uppermost priorities. In the arena of water relations, this image function is especially magnified due to the pivotal role of water as an instrument of development in the borderlands.

The Environment of Mexican Development in the Borderlands

The current bilateral controversy over groundwater derives largely from the national development policy of the Mexican government and the development of the borderlands region within that broadly conceived developmental strategy. Within this developmental context, the disparity between U.S. and Mexican economic development looms as an obstacle to an understanding on the appropriation and use of groundwaters. In the borderlands, water is the essential resource governing developmental potentialities, and its present allocation is evidence of the economic asymmetry between the two nations. With water defining the limits to growth, Mexican developmental initiatives in the region have largely focused on the appropriation and distribution of this scarce fluid resource.

As the most crucial structural element determining the consumption of water, the general import of agriculture within the Mexican economy should be noted. Since the mid-1940s, developmental strategy in Mexico has emphasized industrialization as first priority. This strategy has been pursued with calculated cost to the agricultural sector, impacting most adversely upon the *ejidal* and smallholder economy. Nevertheless, industrialization is contingent upon the steady development of agricultural production for export and domestic consumption. As the structural foundation for economic development, the promotion of agricultural production is a central element in Mexican development policy and planning, historically superseding other priorities within the agricultural sector in its importance.

It is significant that the Mexican government has recently chosen to reemphasize its investment in the countryside in light of population growth and setbacks in agricultural production. Although some of this investment will be directed toward the development of *ejidos* and small private commercial units, a larger share will contribute to the development of cultivation of scale with a continuing focus on production (Bath, 1978a: 20).

In this context, the economic role of the Mexican border states is pivotal. Historically, at least since the mid-1940s, the border states have made contributions to the national economy in excess of national norms. Major sources of this regional economic prosperity have been the commercial trades, tourism, and agricultural and mineral production. The borderland has developed rapidly into the most productive and affluent region of the nation outside the Federal District, and hence has become an important source of income and exchange in the national economy (Urquidi and Méndez Villareal, 1978: 145-151; Navarette, 1971: 60-61).

While the developmental goals and dynamics of the nation at large are germane to a consideration of the groundwater problem, developments in the borderlands are most directly relevant to the issue. Several major trends imply an increasing demand for water resources in this area. Most critical, of course, is the pressure to develop further Mexican agriculture in the borderlands. In no other region of the country has the development of water resources been so controlling in the expansion of agricultural production. Largely a consequence of past appropriation of surface water resources and, more recently, of the new emphasis on groundwater mining, the border states together have the lion's share of the irrigated acreage in the nation and produce a disproportionate amount of the nation's staples and export crops (Hansen, 1971: 60-61). Pressures to expand agricultural development in the region include (1) the transformation of the border agricultural structure from an internal to an external market orientation, (2) the desire to expand the scope of production, and (3) the increasing burden of underemployed and unemployed persons in need of agricultural employment in the border area.

While the expansion of agricultural cultivation exerts the greatest single influence on the consumption of water in the Mexican borderlands, other factors are also important. The rapid expansion of urban settings, by far the single most dramatic indicator of growth on the border, implies an ever-increasing need to service the demands of the border region. There is also discussion and potential for the expansion of the extractive industries in the frontier (Cortner et al., forthcoming; Ríos, 1977; Goodsell, 1975). The development of the industrial sector in the border economy, though currently at the incipient stage, has been fostered by the Border Industries Program (BIP), and will feature a larger role in the economic development of the border zone with a concomitant requirement for water.

It is impossible to estimate the actual impact of these disparate trends on the consumption of water, but consumption will develop rapidly on the Mexican side of the frontier. That groundwater will figure prominently in the development is already evident in the important Mexicali-San Luis and Juárez regions of the northern frontier. Moreover, groundwater is a particularly propitious source of water for promoting the regime's developmental objectives. It affords both a degree of independence from U.S. pressure or unilateral action in the allocation—or contamination—of shared water resources as well as more flexibility in the utilization of water resources as a whole.[8] As recent government initiatives to encourage groundwater development in Sonora indicate, the economic and strategic importance of groundwater as an adjunct to the fixed surface water reserve (established by treaty) will exert pressure for its further exploitation (Latin American Commodity Report, 1978: 147).

The economic and developmental trends which foster the development of groundwater on the Mexican side of the border are the consequence of public policies pursued by the Mexican government in response to demographic and social trends. In both the United States and Mexico, however, such policy is formed and shaped by political institutions, whose uniqueness determines the content of policy as well as the manner in which it is pursued. Insofar as a cooperative accommodation of bilateral interests hinges on these policy structures, they deserve consideration as they bear on the groundwater issues.

Water Resources Policymaking: Bilateral Approaches

Discussions of U.S.-Mexican bilateral relations must necessarily take into account the manner in which each nation formulates and administers public policy. In the case of water resources, the political structures of the respective governments have a significant impact on the way such issues are perceived and pursued. Within the United States, the nature of federal-state relations determines that water resource policy will be formulated in a highly decentralized manner. Water resources issues tend to emerge locally, to be defined at that level in terms of the particular developmental objectives of the sponsor, and to be resolved through a system of partition and reward via the "distributive" mechanisms of the federal government.

The distributive pattern of domestic water resource policy in the United States is reinforced in legal structures pertaining to water appropriation and use. The emphasis on private ownership and state-level determination of statutes governing the appropriation of water conditions the decentralized patterns of interest aggregation and adjudication. The power to regulate in water resource matters is therefore left largely to the individual states, where most often that function devolves upon the courts (Hayton, 1978: 202-204).

In matters of foreign policy, these characteristics of the U.S. domestic environment tend to impede the development of an active and cohesive policy stance. Repeatedly, for example, the United States has sought to avoid linking water resource discussions in one area with those in other areas. Rather, water resource issues tend to be treated as unique problems, reflecting particularized conflicts affecting the domain of specific localities within the border states.

Within this fragmented domestic policy milieu, foreign policy, as Lowi (1964) has observed with respect to tariff policy, tends to take the form of protectionism. The common interest dictates the protection of extant private, hence local, water resource consumption from the encroachments of foreign neighbors. U.S. policy is conserving, seeking to maximize and defend its perceived natural endowment in the manner of all sovereign states.

Conversely, the centralistic authoritarian political pattern in Mexico insures that the national government will pursue definite lines of policy and act assuredly in the determination of objectives for the nation and its constituent parts. The systemic features of Mexican public administration are reflected in the legal and administrative environment bearing on water resources. Under the far-reaching powers of Article 27 of the Mexican constitution, all subsoil and mineral rights are vested in the state. This fundamental power of the federal government to control the national patrimony is further elaborated in the 1947 Health Engineering Act, which invests the central government with exclusive power to plan and operate water delivery systems throughout the nation. Furthermore, the 1934 National Waters Act specifies clearly the priority whereby water is to be utilized and, in essence, constitutes a national plan—in a broad sense.[9]

Within the constitutional setting, administration of water policy is centrally vested in one superagency, the Ministry of Agriculture and Hydraulic Resources (SARH). Although SARH does not exclusively occupy this domain, it presently represents the incumbent López Portillo administration's initiative to integrate the agricultural functions of the major agencies of the Mexican government, and is in fact at the center of the government's vast irrigation and agricultural development program. The structure of SARH insures that policy formation will adhere to a consensus on the political objectives of the regime, while permitting the water resource agency nearly an exclusive role in influencing what are perceived to be the technical aspects of policy. Coupled with its representational role (e.g., the ministry functions as the basic mechanism for aggregating and articulating water resource demands), the influence of SARH is apt to be considerably greater than that exerted by federal water-related agencies in the United States.

Nevertheless, the most important set of policy determinants in Mexico are the ideological priorities of the regime at the symbolic level and the way these priorities are given concrete emphasis by an incumbent administration (Anderson and Cockcroft, 1972: 221-222). Within the set of priorities both domestic and foreign, water policy is traditionally accorded a high status. Domestically, water is the keystone of the development of the agricultural sector's capacity to feed a burgeoning population, to provide a surplus for export and foreign capital exchange, and to accommodate an ever-enlarging employment burden in rural areas. In both ideological and practical terms, the legitimacy of the government is partly derived from its capacity to develop the agricultural sector within the larger development strategy. The public furor over the United States' salinization of Mexican treaty waters dramatizes the importance of agricultural development and rural interests to the political stability of the regime (Gonzáles-de-León, 1975: 109; Hundley, 1966: 176-177).

In bilateral relations, water is considered as a precious national resource to be jealously developed and protected from foreign encroachment. Since the Treaty of Guadalupe Hidalgo, water has been an ideological measure of Mexican sovereignty and independence from the North American colossus. U.S. appropriation of what Mexico regards as a part of its historic patrimony is seen as a blot on the national sovereignty which present treaty arrangements have insufficiently compensated.

Thus, interdependency in water resources may be perceived in Mexico as dependency and constraint.

The Mexican government, therefore, has a strong interest in the expansion of its water resource base. Insofar as its developmental goals in the borderlands are limited by access to surface water resources, the Mexican government is cognizant that the development of groundwater affords a means of skirting the de facto limitations imposed by U.S.-Mexican surface water agreements.[10] Internally, the development of such resources are presently of great concern within the SARH which itself has been an active proponent of groundwater development and, importantly, has an institutionally vested interest in the development of groundwaters (Greenberg, 1970: 41, 54-55).

Groundwater, then, is a trump card facilitating Mexican development. It is a resource amenable to the sovereign control of the Mexican government, exclusive (or nearly so) of U.S. interference. It contributes to the net physical resources available for exploitation as well as to the independence of actions which the Mexican government can employ in developing its water resources apart from the limitations historically imposed by the United States. The political structures and priorities of the regime strongly enhance the prospects for the unilateral development of groundwater as a means of satisfying its economic and political needs in the borderlands.

Finally, the political differences between the United States and Mexico are manifest in the style with which each nation approaches its water resources policy-making. The previous discussion demonstrates the infusion of political meaning into the process of policy-making in Mexico. At issue in all water resource policy and related decisions is the potential of that action either to enhance or diminish the image of the regime. National periodicals which regularly lampoon the government's propensity to indulge in self-glorification or monumentalism attest to the fact that this highly symbolic function of policy is one of the characteristic features of Mexican public policy behavior. It is particularly relevant in the water policy arena where irrigation projects and hydraulic developments have been the stock-in-trade of Mexican politicians seeking to promote their own and the regime's image. The lampooning notwithstanding, monumentalism in Mexican politics is indicative of the fact that the symbolic content of a policy figures most prominently in the structuring of the government's schedule of priorities.

This domestic policy trait is even more pronounced in the area of foreign policy, especially in bilateral relations with the United States. The Mexican government is as attentive to the political capital to be obtained through its bilateral relations as it is to the substantive content of its diplomatic achievements. In a very real sense, the political meaning may be far more significant in the short run than the actual national advantages or consequences of its relations with the United States.

The dramaturgical importance of politics in the Mexican political system is practically the converse of the role of politics in the water policy-making system of the United States. As seen previously, the U.S. policy system encourages the reconcilation of contending interests in a distributive fashion. This system fosters a tendency to effect technical—apolitical—solutions which diminish the deprivation effect of a given policy, thereby reducing the potential for conflict. As in the case of Mexico, this technical approach to domestic water resource policy-making spills over into the arena of foreign relations. In order to minimize the potential for a politically unsatisfactory solution or an injury to interests at the local level, the United States prefers to treat bilateral water resource issues as amenable to solution through such devices as study projects, water treatment facilities, construction of dams and aqueducts, and other public works, rather than redefining the existing claims to water resources in terms of legal standards and principles of equity.

In their respective approaches to the achievement of national water policy objectives, in sum, the two nations are prone to adopt conflicting perspectives. This conflict, however, is influenced by the state of international relations between Mexico and the United States and by their respective negotiating styles. To these factors the article will now turn in order to take account of the larger context of bilateral relations shaping U.S.-Mexican groundwater relations.

The Diplomatic Context: Implications for the Groundwater Issue

Though it would be presumptuous to attempt a comprehensive analysis of the state of U.S-Mexican relations, it is necessary to place the groundwater issue against the backdrop of bilateral issues and attitudes to assess the forces impinging on the prospects for settlement. Currently, such contextual analysis has special relevance in view of the structural flux in relations wrought by the recent Mexican petroleum discoveries and new initiatives in the illegal alien area. Inasmuch as water relations have historically been the paradigm of the "special relationship" between Mexico and the United States, the alterations in bilateral relations, particulary in their respective styles of negotiation, have imminent significance for the groundwater issue.

In the larger sweep, relationships between the two nations have been marred by historical infringements—actual or felt—of Mexican sovereignty by the United States. Since World War II, however, relationships between the two countries have been described in terms of "good feelings," "partnership," and "special relations." These sanguine notions of contemporary bilateral relations take note not only of the obvious structural facilitators of bilateral amity and cooperation (e.g., geographic proximity and sociocultural interface), but also a pattern of policy based on preferential relations in trade, collaboration in the settlement of water and boundary issues, several well-publicized instances of joint participation in the eradication of infectious diseases affecting livestock, the increasing level of social intercourse (e.g., tourism and intercultural exchanges), and other matters.

More currently, however, this favorable perspective of U.S.-Mexican relations has been called into question as a variety of new problems have emerged to complicate bilateral affairs. For instance, in matters of trade, traditionally the mainstay of the special relationship, the United States has increasingly become less exclusive in its preferential commercial relationships on both global and hemispheric levels. Naturally, this redounds to the disadvantage of Mexico, which has persistently pursued favorable access to U.S. markets. Furthermore, although the United States is the overwhelmingly dominant participant in Mexico's foreign economic relations, the terms of trade have historically favored the United States, and an expanding balance of payments deficit has frustrated the developmental intentions of Mexican policy makers in the 1960s and 1970s. Under these circumstances, Mexican officials have had reason to suspect the benefits of partnership with the United States.[11]

Other issues outstanding in bilateral relations stem from socially disruptive forces internal to both nations. A structural problem of enormous magnitude, the illegal alien issue percolated for over a decade after the termination of the bracero treaty, finally emerging as a crisis issue on the agenda of the Carter Administration in 1977. For its part, prior to the Mexico City summit conference in February, 1979, the Mexican government sought to sidestep the issue in bilateral relations (Mumme, 1978: 85-86). Even with bilateral recognition, the issue promises to elude solution and continues to provoke ill will between the two nations. Similarly, in the various aspects of illicit trade (e.g., smuggling of drugs, arms, and antiquities), social problems in both countries have interfaced in an exacerbating manner dramatizing the incapacity of the respective governments to cope with pressing domestic problems (Brown, 1976: 482-483; Craig, 1978).

Undoubtedly the most significant of the recent alterations in the structural relationship between Mexico and the United States is the recently discovered petroleum reserves in the Mexican Southeast. These petroleum reserves provide a symbolic and powerful bargaining vehicle upon which Mexico can predicate its general interests vis-a-vis the United States. This, in turn, as it signifies independence, also suggests the possibility that Mexico may link negotiations on the petroleum issue to other issues of national concern. The linkage potential in the petroleum bonanza has already been made clear by President López Portillo and promises a change in the previous pattern of Mexican negotiations with the United States, heretofore one of isolating issues and treating them discretely (Williams, 1978a: 212-214).

Accompanying the trend toward issue linkage is a more forceful and independent international posture in general. The administration of Luis Echeverría, 1971-1976, is credited with creating a new style of Mexican diplomacy defined by its growing independence of the United States in international affairs and the development and strengthening of its ties to third world countries (Poitras, 1974: 65-67). Though Echeverría's personal "radicalism" and troublesome domestic policies partially explained his aggressive foreign policy, his policy innovations have largely been continued by the incumbent government (El Sol de México, 1976; Waters, 1979).

As these matters signifying substantial modifications in the "special relationship" impact upon the groundwater issue, they are likely to be felt in an insistent emphasis on sovereignty in the utilization of groundwater resources and in the integration of groundwater issues with related matters of bilateral concern. Moreover, these developments are apt to sharpen rather than diminish existing differences in policy-making style between the two nations. Two aspects of policy-making style are salient here; the Mexican interest in emphasizing the political element in bilateral relations, and its preference for a pattern of secrecy in the conduct of bilateral negotiations.[12] These factors are established features of Mexican diplomacy which conflict with the U.S. preference for technical solutions and the structural linkage of U.S. foreign policy to domestic pressures.

The differences in policy-making style stem from what is, in effect, a structural bottleneck between the two systems. The pattern of diplomacy typical of each nation reflects the unique stage of the policy process at which an issue tends to become politicized in foreign relations. Mexican foreign policy, as seen previously, is calculated for political effect, while politicization in the United States tends to occur at the stage of policy formation, the very point at which the Mexican negotiators enjoy the greatest latitude in policy development. The different political requirements exacted by this structural dissimilarity are evident at the level of the IBWC, which given its primary technical role, should be well insulated from the political aspects of the conflict. Yet, as Tilden (1975: 77-78) has shown in his study of the 1944 treaty decision, the approaches and interests of the IBWC negotiators conformed neatly to this general pattern of style and interest.

The relational changes now occuring are likely to promote an even greater emphasis on the secrecy of negotiations while simultaneously infusing the particular content of water policy issues with enhanced political effect. In a sense, one is the cause of the other; the greater latitude and leverage stemming from its new energy importance is likely to impose new issues of a political nature and dramatize the nationalistic importance of old ones. The politicization of oil in the Mexican domestic environment constrains Mexican politicians to behave cautiously and to maximize their flexibility in international economic relations—especially with the United States—and, to the extent that this has an effect on negotiating style, it is likely to push that style in the directions outlined above.

If the issue context and trends in U.S.-Mexican relations yield slight prospect for closer U.S.-Mexican relations in the management of common aquifers, at least one other contextual issue needs to be addressed. As seen earlier, the historical basis for Mexico's water resource claims is vested in the concept of equity and the adjudication of the concept through bilateral diplomacy and international arbitration. The negotiation of water resource conflicts on the basis of moral principle and Mexico's long-standing emphasis on equitable sharing of common water resources might well be expected to incline that nation toward the prospect of equitable administration under supranational auspices. Certainly, the logic behind the development of such institutions rests upon the importance of "depoliticizing" the current state of bilateral relations in view of the higher interests of both nations in equitable apportionment, rational management, and conservation of a scarce and vital resource.

However, while the fact of Mexican reliance upon abstract juridical principles in the past is indisputable, the changing bilateral environment may modify the extent to which Mexico is willing to depend on such mechanisms in the future. It is important to note that though the concepts of juridical equality and equitable apportionment have served well in lieu of other forms of influence in the past, such mechanisms are now made less exclusive as instruments of diplomacy. Particularly in the case of groundwater, the control over the resource enables Mexico to adopt a more forceful and diversified bargaining stance. In essence, this means that the political elements in the resolution of the groundwater issue will be magnified in relation to the technical and strictly legal elements of the question, though the latter will surely be an important avenue of negotiation and treaty management as they have been in the past.

The heightened politicization bearing on the groundwater issue draws attention to the enduring importance of politics in water resource deliberations. As one scholarly observer of the IBWC points out, settlement of issues through the IBWC, despite that institution's overtly technical and apolitical role, has never been divorced of political influences. Instead, political interests have been most prominent in determining the IBWC's functions and role (Bath, 1978b: 190-193). This point is also made by Sepúlveda (1978: 140-141) who observes that the national sections of the IBWC function under the supervision of their respective governments and do not exercise a true policy-making function independent of the political authorities they represent. In this sense, the IBWC may illustrate the limits rather than the possibilities of technical cooperation in U.S.-Mexican relations. Such political constraints reflect the enduring salience of structural and procedural differences between the United States and Mexico in their bilateral relations.

Groundwater: Its Bilateral Significance

Viewed in the context of U.S.-Mexican relations, the groundwater issue is unlikely to facilitate a more intimate level of cooperation in water resource relations than that which presently exists. It is more probable that the groundwater issue will tend—surely in the short run—to exacerbate relations between the two nations and elude an easy solution. The major lesson to be digested from the preceding analysis is that, by itself, the groundwater issue is not of sufficient moment to alter or to cause a significant change in the existing patterns of political intercourse between the United States and Mexico. Rather, the groundwater conflict is very much contingent on existing structures and processes as they impact on the competition for limited and vital resources, thereby contributing to the divisive potential between the two neighbor states.

Fundamentally, the groundwater conflict is symptomatic of intersystemic disparities and conflicting national interests. The weight of scholarly judgment on the potential for international integration suggests that the differences of economic development, political systems, national culture, and national history tend to diminish the prospects for successful integration of authoritative decision-making in the management of water resources shared by the two nations, nothwithstanding the fact that an institutionalized pattern of management and consultation in the form of the IBWC already exists and has been successful in reconciling such conflicts (Cobb and Elder, 1970: 133-139; Jacob and Teune, 1969: 458-479). Generally, the analysis of the groundwater conflict in this article lends support to the difficulty of integration between such dissimilar national systems.

Still, the groundwater conflict is a significant and emerging issue in bilateral relations which demonstrates again U.S. and Mexican interdependence. As the demands for water increase, as they must on both sides of the border, the need for a settlement of conflicting demands will become more acute. Within the parameters of recent bilateral experience, the prospects for an eventual treaty or series of treaties resolving the specific distribution of groundwaters are good and have already been indicated in the willingness of each nation to acknowledge the existence of the problem and to consider a degree of regulation within the context of Minute 242 (Day, 1978: 163-180). While such a treaty is bound to spark controversy on both sides of the border, the existence of an international forum and consultative procedure for initiating such proceedings, as well as the historic reliance upon diplomatic devices to resolve water resource disputes, lends confidence to the prospect for an eventual settlement. What is new in this situation is that Mexico will be capable of engaging in more aggressive bargaining with the United States with great potential for escalating the "political" relevance of the issue in the bargaining process. While this change in the Mexican position is partly dictated by its new energy importance and its more aggressive foreign policy posture, it is very much affected by its enhanced control over groundwater resources within its territorial limits. Taken together, these factors signal a relatively new era in the conduct of bilateral water relations which should be of great interest to political scientists and legal scholars concerned with evolving trends in U.S.-Mexican affairs.

NOTES

1. A discussion of "protective pumping" is found in U.S. Departments of Interior and State (1974).

2. The Convention of 1906 refers to the settlement of conflict over the upper basin waters of the Rio Grande. The Treaty of 1944 dealt principally with the distribution of the Colorado river waters, though it also partitioned waters of the lower Rio Grande and Tijuana rivers. Minutes 218, 241, and 242 pertain to the settlement of the salinity problem resulting from the U.S. delivery of saline treaty waters to Mexico.

3. The background and development of IBWC is treated in Timm (1941) and Friedkin (1968).

4. A discussion of the range of water resource management options is given in Utton (1978: 640-654). For various views favoring the elaboration of the powers of the IBWC with reference to the groundwater problem, see Bradley and DeCook (1978); Dworsky (1978: 146-149); Burman and Cornish (1975: 396-400); Sepúlveda (1975: 215-221); Day (1978: 177-179); Hayton (1978: 201-211).

5. For a discussion of Mexico's role as plaintiff in the major water resource negotiations with the United States, see Hundley Jr. (1966).

6. Sepúlveda (1978: 140-141) observes that the Mexican experience with arbitration has shown it to be a generally unsatisfactory method of resolving differences with the United States. He argues that Mexico would be reluctant to employ such methods in the future.

7. President Luis Echeverría took note of the damage caused to Mexican interests through procrastination of settlement by the United States in his address to the United States Congress in June, 1972. Echeverría stated, with special reference to the salinity problem, "The damage is enormous and Mexican public opinion is becoming increasingly impatient about this important matter that has been going on for more than a decade without any satisfactory solution." Echeverría's comments as quoted in the Congressional Record in Brown (1976: 492).

8. Mexican planners have long been acquainted with the "flexibility" afforded by groundwaters for agricultural development. See Salas (1972: 132-133) and Cummings (1972: 38, 45-50).

9. In practice, however, Mexican water resource planning has evolved more recently. National planning in the important sphere of irrigation policy, for instance, began with the six-year irrigation plan introduced by President Avila Camacho in 1941 (Orive Alba, 1960: 79). According to Manuel Anaya (1967), there was no real central control of water resources until the 1946 advent of the Ministry of Water Resources. On these matters see also Orive Alba (1974: 149-150) and González Villarreal (1973: 1008-1009).

10. J. C. Day (1978: 171-174) notes in the case of the Hueco Bolson that the Mexican government pursued a strategy of groundwater development in response to the U.S. failure to deliver specified treaty waters during drought years. Similarly, the development of groundwater in the San Luis-Mexicali region is, in part, a response to limitations imposed by salinization of Mexican treaty waters (Furnish and Ladman, 1975: 83-108).

11. On the waning of the special relationship, see Pellicer de Brody (1974: 332-333) and Shapira (1978: 40-41).

12. The recent hue and cry brought against the Mexican government by opposition leftists regarding the proposed gas line and sale to the United States suggests the extreme delicacy of such matters and the importance of minimizing public knowledge of the substance of negotiations with the United States. The advantage of the government in response to the protest was precisely its monopoly of information concerning the proposed arrangement (Williams, 1978b: 14-18).

REFERENCES

ANAYA, M. (1967) "Mexico and its water resources policy," pp. 682-691 in International Conference on Water for Peace 8. Washington, DC: Department of Interior.

ANDERSON, B. and J. D. COCKCROFT (1972) "Control and cooptation in Mexican politics," pp. 219-244 in J. D. Cockcroft et al. (eds.) Dependence and Underdevelopment. Garden City, NY: Doubleday Anchor.

BATH, C. R. (1978a) "A review of Mexico's water policy." Proceedings of the Rocky Mountain Council on Latin American Studies (May): 18-23.

——— (1978b) "Alternative cooperative arrangements for managing transboundary air resources along the border." Natural Resources J. 18 (January): 181-200.

BITTINGER, M. W. (1972) "Survey of interstate and international aquifer problems." Ground Water 10 (March/April): 44-54.

BRADLEY, M. D. and K. J. DECOOK (1978) "Ground water occurrence and utilization in the Arizona-Sonora border region." Natural Resources J. 18 (January): 29-48.

BROWN, L. C. (1976) "The politics of United States-Mexican relations." pp. 471-493 in J. W. Wilke et al. (eds.) Contemporary Mexico. Berkeley: Univ. of California Press.

BURMAN, B. G. and T. G. CORNISH (1975) "Needed: a ground-water treaty between the United States and Mexico." Natural Resources J. 15 (April): 384-404.

CAPONERA, D. A. and D. ALHERITIERE (1978) "Principles for international groundwater law II." Natural Resources Forum 2: 359-371.

COBB, R. W. and C. ELDER (1970) International Community. New York: Holt, Rinehart & Winston.

CORTNER, H. J., S. P. MUMME, and E. J. WILLIAMS (forthcoming) "Energy in the border region," in E. R. Stoddard (ed.) The United States-Mexico Borderlands Sourcebook. El Paso: Texas Western Press.

CRAIG, R. (1978) "La Campaña Permanente: Mexico's antidrug campaign." J. of Interamerican Studies and World Affairs 20 (May): 107-132.

CUMMINGS, R. (1972) Water Resource Management in Northern Mexico. Baltimore: Resources for the Future and Johns Hopkins University.

DAY, J. C. (1978) "International aquifer management: the case of the Hueco Bolson on the Rio Grande River." Natural Resources J. 18 (January): 163-180.

DWORSKY, L. B. (1978) "The management of water-land-environmental resources at international boundary regions." Natural Resources J. 18 (January): 143-152.

El Sol de México (1976) "JLP: I will continue Echeverría's foreign policy." February 19. (English translation in Transdex, JPRS Translations on Latin America, 67109 [1976].)

FRIEDKIN, J. F. (1968) "History and functions of joint Mexican-American public bodies regulating and allocating water resources along the Rio Grande (Bravo)," pp. 1-7 in C. S. Knowlton (ed.) International Water Law Along the Mexican-American Border. El Paso: Univ. of Texas Press.

FURNISH, D. B. and J. R. LADMAN (1975) "The Colorado river salinity agreement of 1973 and the Mexicali valley." Natural Resources J. 15 (January): 83-107.

GONZALES-DE-LEON, A. (1975) "The Mexican position: national and international considerations." Natural Resources J. 15 (January): 109-113.

GONZALEZ VILLARREAL, F. J. (1973) "Mexican national water plan: organization and preliminary assessment." J. of Agricultural Economics 55 (December): 1008-1016.

GOODSELL, J. N. (1975) "Mexico gets a second go—at oil boom." Christian Science Monitor (January 14).

GREENBERG, M. (1970) Bureaucracy and Development: A Mexican Case Study. Lexington, MA: Lexington Heath.

HANSEN, R. D. (1971) The Politics of Mexican Development. Baltimore: Johns Hopkins Univ. Press.

HAYTON, R. D. (1978) "Institutional alternatives for Mexico-U.S. groundwater management." Natural Resources J. 18 (January): 201-212.

HUNDLEY, N. Jr., (1966) Dividing the Waters. Berkeley: Univ. of California Press.

JACOB, P. E. and H. TEUNE (1969) "The integrative process," pp. 458-479 in R. L. Pfaltzgraff, Jr. (ed.) Politics and the International System. Philadelphia: J. B. Lippincott.

Latin American Commodity Report (1978) "Mexico heads for serious food shortage." September 22.

LOWI, T. J. (1964) "American business, public policy, case studies, and political theory." World Politics 16 (July): 677-715.

MERAZ, F. (1979) "Texas acapara el agua del Rio Bravo." Excelsior (July 3).

MUMME, S. P. (1978) "Mexican politics and the prospects for emigration policy: a policy perspective." Inter-American Economic Affairs 32 (Summer): 67-94.

NAVARETTE, I. M. (1971) "La distribución de ingreso en México: tendencias y perspectives," pp. 15-71 in El Perfil de México en 1980, vol. 1. México, DF: Siglo Veintiuno.

ORIVE ALBA, A. (1960) La política de irrigación en México. México, DF: Fondo de Cultura Económica.

——— (1974) "Water resource administration in Mexico," pp. 142-165 in A. Lepawsky (ed.) National Systems of Water Adminstration. New York: United Nations, ST/ESA/17.

PELLICER DE BRODY, O. (1974) "Mexico in the 1970's and its relations with the United States," pp. 314-333 in J. Cotler and R. Fagen (eds.) Latin America and the United States: The Changing Political Realities. Stanford: Stanford Univ. Press.

POITRAS, G. E. (1974) "Mexico's 'new' foreign policy." Inter-American Economic Affairs 28 (Winter): 59-77.

REMPEL, W. C. (1979) "Water sales bitterly fought." Los Angeles Times (November 5).

RIOS, S. (1977) "Enormes yacimientos de petróleo y gas en 3 estados: Pemex." Excelsior (August 31).

SALAS, G. P. (1972) "Aprovechamiento de los recursos naturales de las zonas desérticas. Solución para su problema socio-económica," pp. 131-136 in Memoria del coloquio sobre planificación regional. México, DF: Universidad Nacional Autonoma de México, Instituto de Geográfica.

SEPULVEDA, C. (1978) "Instituciones para la solución de problemas de aguas de superficie entre México y los Estados Unidos." Natural Resources J. 18 (January): 131-142.

——— (1975) "Implications for the future: design of viable international institutions." Natural Resources J. 15 (January): 215-222.

SHAPIRA, Y. (1978) Mexican Foreign Policy Under Echeverría. Beverly Hills, CA: Sage.

TILDEN, W. (1975) The Politics of Salt: Background and Implications of the American Mexican Treaty of 1944. Tucson: University of Arizona, Institute for Government Research.

TIMM, C. A. (1941) The International Boundary Commission: United States and Mexico. Austin: Univ. of Texas Press.

URQUIDI, V. and S. MENDEZ VILLAREAL (1978) "Economic importance of Mexico's northern border region," pp. 141-162 in S. R. Ross (ed.) Views Across the Border. Alburquerque: Univ. of New Mexico Press.

U.S. Departments of the Interior and State (1974) Draft Environmental Statement: Colorado River International Salinity Control Project. Int. Des. 74-39. Washington, DC: Author.

UTTON, A. E. (1978) "International groundwater management: the case of the U.S. Mexican frontier." Nebraska Law Rev. 57 (3): 633-664.

WATERS, B. (1979) "López Portillo's jabs mar cordial welcome for Carter." Arizona Daily Star (February 15).

WILLIAMS, E. J. (1978a) "Oil in Mexican-U.S. relations: analysis and bargaining scenario." Orbis 22 (Spring): 201-216.

——— (1978b) "Petroleum policy and Mexican domestic politics: left opposition, regional dissidence, and official apostasy." Presented at the annual meeting of the Southern Economic Association, Washington, D.C., November.

Stephen P. Mumme, a Ph.D. candidate in political science at the University of Arizona, is the author of a number of papers and articles dealing with Mexican politics and U.S.-Mexican affairs. His research activities focus upon U.S.-Mexican relations and the ecology of the borderlands.

ROBERT M. LEVINE
Department of History
State University of New York at Stony Brook
Stony Brook, New York 11794

PERSPECTIVES ON THE MID-VARGAS YEARS 1934-1937

In the period following Brazil's 1964 military coup, many historians turned their attention to the Vargas years, especially the 1930s. For one thing, the period had not been thoroughly examined. For another, factors common to both "revolutions" intrigued them: interplay among civilians and military officers in the respective *golpes*; repression of dissent and the use of nationalistic propaganda; concern over Brazil's place in the international order; social mobilization to neutralize class conflict and promote growth; tension between liberalism and corporatism; and efforts to promote national integration. Many of the historical actors, as well, were the same. Although Vargas died by his own hand in 1954, many of his early contemporaries returned to prominence after the 1964 coup: Francisco Campos, Oswaldo Cordeiro de Farias, Juarez Távora, Juracy Magalhães, Olímpio Mourão Filho, Felinto Mueller, Plínio Salgado, Helder Câmara, Miguel Reale, Alceu Amoroso Lima, and others. Most reemerged at centerstage as if a page in history had been turned back, leapfrogging the record of the populist years of the 1950s and early 1960s.

AUTHOR'S NOTE: The author thanks Frank D. McCann, Kenneth P. Erickson, John D. Wirth, Carolyn Eisenberg, and Joseph L. Love for their comments on early versions of this essay.

Journal of Interamerican Studies and World Affairs, Vol. 22 No. 1, February 1980 57-80

A further reason for the awakened interest in the period was the silent treatment given to Vargas by the image makers of the military regime. This fact, together with the normal passage of time, prompted the Vargas family to open Getúlio Vargas's papers in the mid-1960s. In addition, unprecedented access to the Oswaldo Aranha archive, the post-1930 files of the *Presidência da República* collection of the National Archives in Rio de Janeiro, and the availability of other smaller but invaluable repositories offered new incentives to researchers and paved the way for a spate of dissertations, articles, and monographs.

The first wave of these studies appeared in the late 1960s and early 1970s (Silva, 1969a, 1969b, 1970; McCann, 1973).[1] Since then, published works have focused, for the most part, on specialized topics and have not brought to light substantially new documentation. This task belongs to the next generations of researchers, most of whom will be Brazilian, who will benefit from the work of Rio de Janeiro's Centro de Pesquisa e Documentação de História Contemporânea do Brasil (CPDOC), which has tackled the enormous task of organizing and coordinating the Vargas-era papers, including extensive oral history depositions. What may change is what Carlos Bakota (1979) calls the "time warp" in which Vargas-era studies have been caught. Coming studies will want to examine Vargas the "master politician" more closely—his motivation, methods, and the larger rationale behind the dramatic shift in policy from the ad hoc provisional government in 1930 to the relatively sophisticated police state imposed in the form of the Estado Nôvo in 1937 (Bakota, 1979: 206).

Since the author's own monograph, *The Vargas Regime*, appeared in 1970,[2] new material has become available in diplomatic and military archives of the United States and Great Britain. These collections—to some degree open, on the United States side, to the period almost up to the present day by virtue of the Freedom of Information Act (Zweiben, 1978)—offer rich and detailed data on all aspects of Brazilian life seen through foreign eyes.

This article will look at some of the historiographical themes of the 1930s from the perspectives of British and American observers, information heretofore unexplored by students of the subject. It will conclude by briefly summarizing scholarly views of the mid-Vargas era.

I

The Vargas Regime examines the ideological polarization which Brazil's 1930 revolution created against the wider backdrop of the international conflict between fascism and communism. Mobilization by the left in the form of the popular-front Aliança Nacional Libertadora (ANL) in mid-1935 and the clandestine return from exile of *tenente*-hero Luis Carlos Prestes as the titular head of the Brazilian Communist Party (PCB) led to futile and poorly coordinated uprisings by soldiers, noncommissioned officers, and a few civilians in three cities in late November. The insurrections gave Vargas a convenient excuse to submerge liberal opinion beneath a wave of anticommunist hysteria and to govern under successive states of national emergency until the eve of the promulgation of the corporatist/authoritarian Estado Nôvo in late 1937, imposed to some extent to allow the regime to pursue sustained domestic industrialization. Allowing the right to flex its muscles (and unleashing powerful currents of reaction under which many of the social and cultural innovations of the mid-1920s and early 1930s were overturned), Vargas consolidated his power with the backing of the military. Moderates were driven from influence and replaced by a cadre of bureaucrats not dissimilar in outlook and origin from those who came to power after the 1964 military coup.

As the decade of the 1930s progressed, the major issue both for foreign and domestic observers was the changing role of the Brazilian state. Despite continuing rivalry over influence within Brazil, commercial as well as diplomatic, the British and American positions converged. Brazil watchers from both countries tended to view Vargas in the same way, generally endorsing liberal measures in the Brazilian political arena and bristling at moves to strengthen the state's interventionist apparatus, since this was perceived as nationalist and consequently harmful to the economic interests of both powers. Their analysis, for the most part, treated Brazil patronizingly, dwelling on partisan factionalism and the fragile nature of Brazilian democracy (FO, 1933, 1934a, 1934e, 1935m, 1935q).

British and American intelligence networks were well informed, principally through the Brazilian Foreign Ministry and to some degree through the federal police; they not only anticipated the major political events of the decade (including the 1935 insurrections) but understood the dynamics of Brazilian social unrest sufficiently to know that such outbreaks posed little serious danger to established order.

Military commentators at both embassies worried that Brazil's police apparatus was too weak and corrupt to guard against Communist infiltration, especially in urban centers. They also distrusted Vargas's tacit return to constitutionality in 1933-1934 after the unsuccessful São Paulo revolt, finding the 1934 federal charter filled with "numerous advanced ideas popular with communists" including "complete freedom of expression" and "guarantees to the citizen [of] his rights to move about and to carry on practically any brand of propaganda he chooses (NADW, 1934a; 1934c). Foreign military observers clearly held the Brazilian citizenry in as little regard as their counterparts in the Brazilian elite.

The Brazil watchers agreed that the strikes gripping urban centers in 1934 and 1935 reflected the new Labor Ministry's weakness and the "ineptitude" of its first incumbent minister, Lindolfo Collor. They also reported that the soaring cost of living was driving workers to desperation. The United States military attaché's office warned that São Paulo was a powder keg, given the city's large Italian population as well as widespread animosity toward the federal government.[3] Granting wage concessions, it was contended, would backfire, since labor militancy would only be fueled. Since 80% of the population was illiterate, the report concluded, public gatherings posed the greatest menace, since

Communist propaganda could be spread by word of mouth (NADW, 1934a, 1934b).

Intelligence agents carefully monitored the political disturbances linked to the return of constitutional rule after 1933 and the accompanying efforts by old-line politicians to regain their hegemony, lost in the 1930 *tenente* victory. From mid-1934 on, confidential reports from the British Consulate in Recife related day-to-day details of the badly deteriorating situation in Paraíba, Pernambuco, and Bahia, and in the region's worst trouble spots, Rio Grande do Norte and Pará (FO 1934f). As early as August 1934, thc British consul in Recife blamed the Natal-based Twenty-First Light Infantry Battalion (B.C.) with trying to depose Interventor Mário Câmara. This was the same battalion which had rioted in Recife when it was located there in 1931 (FO, 1934g).

Commentators also noted "serious unrest" in the region's rural interior, where the old *coronel*-political machine alliance had revived. Most of the northeastern states were considered vulnerable to anti-Vargas electoral victory, in part because of the stubborn unwillingness of the *tenente* interventors to cooperate with the ousted elites and in part because of the general malaise afflicting the region in spite of rising agricultural exports. Strikes plagued the Northeast, especially among transport and utility workers, and officials responded by sending armed troops against the strikers. In Bahia, a coordinated work stoppage in late August 1934 brought the state capital to a standstill until the young Interventor Juracy Magalhães—probably the most politically astute of the *tenente* governors—received union leaders and submitted their wage grievances to federal arbitration (FO, 1934d). The British Vice Consul in Maceió warned of a climate of anarchy in Alagoas, citing instances of intimidated juries blatantly absolving political murderers (FO, 1934c).

United States officials focused their attention on the Vargas regime's seeming inability to maintain order in urban centers, especially in São Paulo, where socialists and labor militants clashed frequently with the fascist Integralists. A report listed 28 strikes which lasted one day or more, including 8 by textile operatives and 5 by bakers, all attributed, at least in part, to

"Communist machinations." The reports were accurate enough in listing the work stoppages, although they tended to exaggerate the role of the "foreign agitators" responsible, who were described by the American Consul General in São Paulo as "Lithuanians, Hungarians, Poles, and to a lesser extent Spaniards, Uruguayans, Argentines, Italians, Portuguese, and Jews (NADS, 1934).[4]

After the state elections on October 14, 1934, fears of politically motivated violence seemed to recede, since government-backed parties fared better than predicted, but the foreign Brazil watchers found a new source of worry: The newly elected state administrations were edging closer to open hostility against foreign-owned companies, especially railroad lines and public utilities. Newspaper editors began to ridicule the British managers for their intransigence against strikes when workers in England, they pointed out, regularly struck as a matter of right. "Brazilians are treated as if they were goods and not worthy of having their necessities considered," the conservative *Diário da Bahia* editorialized (1934).[5] The British diplomats duly noted the complaints and transmitted them back to the Foreign Office without additional comment.

Internal grumbling within the army reached a new peak during the first months of 1935 over salaries, promotion policy, and internal discipline. Colonels Dutra and Silva Pessôa, close to Vargas, were passed over older officers to become the youngest two-star generals in Brazilian history, and General Guedes da Fontoura threatened to parade his brigade in front of Congress if pay raises were not granted as demanded. Major strikes again broke out across the country, including a week-long work stoppage by postal and telegraph employees and other strikes by maritime transport pilots, stevedores, packinghouse employees, taxi drivers, and railway workers. Sergipe's federal interventor was defeated at the polls; the old crisis in Pará over control of the state machine heated up again; War Minister Góes Monteiro's two brothers were involved in an armed attack on the gubernatorial palace in Alagoas in which several men were killed or seriously wounded. In Rio Grande do Norte the murder by federal troops of Octávio Lamartine, a leading member of the opposition, was interpreted as a desperate show of power by the unpopular interventor. A general strike purportedly instigated by "socialist" deputy João Café Filho paralyzed Natal for several days, and another clash between state police and federal troops, this time on the last day of Carnival, killed six; again the Brazil watchers blamed Vargas's interventor, Mário Câmara (FO, 1935o; NADS 1935c).[6] British officials sympathized with Vargas's decision to promulgate a draconic National Security Law as a consequence of "the strikes, the fears of Communism, and the criticisms levelled at the Administration (FO, 1935l).

In late March 1935, at the time the popular-front ANL was taking shape, the American interim chargé d'affaires summarized the deteriorating political situation by pointing to the government's fiscal confusion, its incapacity to deal with stubborn state officials, and the incompetence of the minister of justice, Vicente Ráo (NADS, 1935c). The British ambassador shrugged off any specific prognosis for immediate upheaval, quoting Góes Monteiro's laconic statement that most of the Brazilian people live "like vegetables" and that the rest are "given to indiscipline and anarchy." Ambassador Seeds added:

> The General's strictures on the behavior of the politically-minded Brazilians, in the more civilized regions as distinct from the vegetating interior, are fully justified by what has been in progress for many weeks in the North and Northeast of the country. It is the custom here in Rio de Janeiro government circles to pay small attention to those turbulent States whose local politics—petty, as seen from here—always seem to demand arbitrary action by the official in power, responded to by shootings on the part of the oppressed. . . . I must confess to viewing with some alarm the possible effects of politics, discontent, agitation . . . on the army, which is the ultimate guarantee of national security [FO, 1935k].

Consul-General Abbott in São Paulo, an old Brazil hand, offered a more cynical view about the way the Brazilians were handling threats to order, remarking:

> I remember quite well when Washington Luiz [Pereira de Souza] was Prefeito here in 1918. . . . Rioters were shot down by machine guns and rifle fire and given no quarter whatsoever [FO, 1935p].

In April, Seeds notified the Foreign Office that the ANL had been organized and that Luis Carlos Prestes was "still in exile," although a handwritten comment added to the transcript of his confidential report noted that the consul general in São Paulo in January had advised London that Prestes was planning to return to Brazil from the Soviet Union if he had not done so secretly already (FO, 1935n). Both embassies worried that the Brazilians were insufficiently concerned with potential subversion and watched the growth of the ANL with great care; the British seemed almost relieved when the conservative afternoon tabloid, *O Globo*, warned its *carioca* readers that Prestes was either in Brazil or Argentina and that the Communists planned a "political take over." Rio's *Correio da Manhã* corroborated the report the next day, and claimed that Vargas's cabinet had secretly met to decide on appropriate steps. In the ensuing vitriolic debate between *O Globo* and the ANL's *A Manhã*, the left-wing paper tacitly admitted that Prestes was in Rio de Janeiro (FO, 1935j). The government, in turn, prohibited the ANL's "monster" rally scheduled for July 5, prompting Prestes to issue his inflammatory manifesto on July 6, in turn giving authorities convenient justification to close the ANL organization for six months under the National Security Law. The United States embassy noted:

> A measure of Communism is perhaps inevitable in a country in which ignorant and poverty-striken masses live in juxtaposition with an indolent and parasitical moneyed class. But in spite of the undisciplined character of the people it is difficult to believe that with their happy-go-lucky temperament they would be much inclined to accept communistic dogmas [NADS, 1935b].

The British claimed later in their internal correspondence that the Brazilian police did not know of Prestes's specific whereabouts, nor had they known of the existence of the Comintern's chief agent, Arthur Ernest Ewert (Harry Berger). In August, however, the British suggested that plans for the PCB-led uprisings were known to Brazilian authorities. Once the revolts erupted, and were subdued, a member of the Foreign Office's American Division commented that "it will be noticed that *we* are accused of having warned the Government Authorities in advance—though it is declared [by the Brazilian Communists] that the Japanese, United States, German [and] Italian representatives also had a finger in the pie" (FO, 1936g).

The comment referred to one of the *A Manhã* diatribes accusing the British Intelligence Service of aiding and abetting the drive to close the ANL by feeding Brazilian officials false information about plans for revolt. The allegation is corroborated in a general way by Mr. Edward Coote's report to London on August 9, 1935, confirming that the police were on the track of the "secret and acknowledged leaders of the Alliança, who were known both to themselves and to the police of other countries with whom they exchanged information" (FO, 1935i). Coote also warned: "The fight is not over; but the first round is the Government's (FO, 1935j).

In August, the Procurator-General of Brazil responded to an ANL legal challenge to its closing by releasing documents revealing a link between the ANL and PCB, Comintern direction from Montevideo, and plans adopted at the plenum of the PCB Central Committee meeting in May outlining revolutionary activity. This (presumably authentic) document, "The Revolutionary Popular National Government and the Tasks of the Party," outlined the ANL's role to mobilize the proletariat and the necessity to sieze power under the leadership of Prestes. The document created a sensation, and the Supreme Court unanimously rejected the ANL's appeal as well as a similar one from its women's auxiliary, the *União Feminina do Brasil.* On the matter, Mr. Coote observed:

> The future is uncertain. It is doubtful if the Government, by closing the offices of the ANL, have scotched the snake; they have certainly not killed it. I learn on good authority that the ANL are by no means worried . . . their influence is growing not only among the men but also among the officers of the armed forces [FO, 1935i].

Judging from what we now know about the ineffectiveness of the ANL during the short span of its institutional life, it seems apparent that the foreign diplomats were as anxious as their Brazilian peers to locate Communistic influence and exaggerate its strength. Other reports were more specific, and revealed bits of evidence which later would be fitted together to show that officials did in fact anticipate a rebellion in the military: In October, Sir Hugh Gurney, the new British ambassador, warned that General Manoel Rabello, the military commander of the Recife region, was holding his insurrection-prone officers "in check for the moment" but that trouble loomed on the horizon (FO, 1935h).

The end of the month of October saw the contested election of the opposition candidate for governor of Rio Grande do Norte, Raphael Fernandes, culminating in the flight of Interventor Câmara to Rio de Janeiro. This suggested sharply that the administration's willingness to return to formal democracy was backfiring: Anti-Vargas candidates and blocs had now won in Pará, Maranhão, Ceará, Sergipe, Santa Catarina, and Mato Grosso as well as in Rio Grande do Norte. Foreign reports emphasized that the last of the discretionary powers vested in officials by revolutionary decree now seemed to be extinguished and that the Vargas administration seemed vulnerable, mildly unpopular, and dependent upon the loyalty of the armed forces (NADS, 1935a; NADW, 1934b, 1934c).

II

The outbreak of the barracks' revolts in late November 1935 prompted predictable response. The British consul in Recife remarked that the general assumption was that inquiry into the causes of the uprisings "will attribute the disaffection in the ranks to Communist propaganda" (FO, 1935d). Noting the absence from Pernambuco of both Governor Carlos de Lima Cavalcanti and General Rabello as a likely factor in the timing of the insurrection, the consul added further that two state cabinet members, Nelson Coutinho and Sylvio Granville, had "declared themselves neutral in the struggle between the rebels and government" and had been summarily dismissed, along with Paulo Carneiro, the secretary of agriculture, also suspected of Communist sympathies. He warned that reaction to the revolts would exacerbate nationalistic feelings and antiforeign sentiments. "At no post in my career," he averred, "have I felt less welcome than at Pernambuco" (FO, 1935d).[7]

When the revolt in Recife erupted, the British Admiralty advised Ambassador Gurney in Rio de Janeiro that H.M.S. Dragon was available at Montevideo and could reach Pernambuco in four days at high speed (FO, 1935g). Gurney advised the Foreign Office, in turn, that a coup in the federal capital was likely within 48 hours led by "certain sections of the army who are supporters of Prestes with assistance of the Prefect of Rio de Janeiro (FO, 1935f). The prediction, of course, was accurate, although *prefeito* (major) Pedro Ernesto was never linked concretely to the Praia Vermelha uprising and, as Michael Conniff has shown (1976), was positively cleared of participation in the revolt. British intelligence agents reported a "large sum of money . . . recently received by [a] Russian organization at Montevideo to finance the uprising," and ventured that the failed revolt would bolster Vargas's shaky domestic position (FO, 1935f; NADW, 1935).[8]

The British consular advisor, Mr. Troutbeck, told the ambassador not to congratulate Vargas publicly for having suppressed the uprising, as did the French, since if the revolutionaries "happened to win the second round and took over the government, it might be a little awkward if they found our message of congratulations in the archives." Also, given the roundup of leftists which followed the restoration of order, "there might possibly be questions in Parliament demanding why His Majesty's government had thought fit to applaud acts of brutality" (FO, 1935e). For its part, the Brazilian embassy in London sent a communique to the Foreign Office assuring that English property had not been harmed, that the labor syndicates in Recife and Rio de Janeiro had remained loyal to the government, and that during the entire insurrection all factories had worked "with perfect regularity" (FO, 1935c). The Brazilians, probably more than the British, in this case knew perfectly what their opposite numbers wanted to hear.

Assessing the impact of the revolutionary movement, Ambassador Gurney advised his superiors that the Comintern had counseled delay but that the Brazilian Communists had set their own timetable (FO, 1935b).[9] He summarized the current state of affairs with insight:

> I should like to emphasize . . . that this outburst was of an entirely different character from the ordinary revolt so familiar in Brazilian and indeed all South American history. The normal Brazilian revolution is an attempt by the "outs" to oust the "ins," and owing to the peculiarities of the Constitution it is almost the only effective method of achieving that object. This outburst . . . inspired and directed by the Comintern . . . inspired real fear in the hearts not only of the politicians in power, but also of the propertied classes and bourgeoisie; it was dealt with by the Government with unusual energy; and it has induced that Government to consider the advisability of inflicting really severe punishment on the revolutionaries [FO, 1935a].

Both the British and the Americans reported the insurrectionary events in elaborate detail, noting without comment the Brazilian government's position but adding, when appropriate, further explanations based on their own observations and prejudices. Gurney dutifully reported the death of American Communist Victor Allan Baron in prison but left room for doubt as to whether he had been a suicide. He also suggested broadly that allegations by Arthur Ewert and his wife that they had been tortured were probably true, given the "notorious" reputation of Felinto Müeller's police and the length of their incarceration before being brought before a judge (FO, 1936c). A Foreign Office analyst remarked that anti-Communism would likely become a "profitable racket in Brazil on the lines of 'protection' afforded by gangsters in the United States" (FO, 1936d). Other reports labeled official claims and rumors of impending Communist risings "alarmist and exaggerated" (FO, 1936e).

Once the excitment subsided, the British and American analysts turned their attention to prospects for stability under the state of siege, a condition which they openly and anxiously sought. The observers measured the Vargas administration against the "normal" standard of the ousted pre-1930 political climate, invariably praising measures which produced domestic tranquility. British Consul White, in March 1936, cast aspersions on the new Seventh Military Region commander, General

Newton Cavalcanti, mocking his right-wing alarmism (FO, 1936e).[10] The American military attaché drew attention to Vargas's 1936 New Year's address, the first national radio broadcast in Brazilian history, in which he railed at the Communist menace and its "threat to Christian civilization" (NADW, 1936b). Ambassador Hugh Gibson blamed Vargas for not having been "responsive" to the expectations raised by his taking power in 1930, and labeled his social measures half-hearted, insufficiently enforced, and premature (NADS, 1936). If Vargas was the "man of the hour," as the English called him, he still had to prove himself as a leader who could guarantee order, control the armed forces, and honor Brazil's fiscal and diplomatic responsibilities.

Observers took increasing note of the "clouds on the horizon in the shape of the Integralist party" and predicted that the Fascists might spoil their chances for attaining power through the electoral route by prematurely attempting a coup d'état (FO, 1936f). This premonition was borne out in a minor way with police discovery of Integralist plots to overthrow state administrations in Bahia, Espírito Santo, and Rio de Janeiro State during September and October 1936 (FO, 1936b). With the presidential elections approaching, the British began to write warmly of São Paulo's Armando de Sales Oliveira, the conservative, anti-Vargas candidate, praising his "elegant" defense of the role of foreigners in Brazil's economy and of democracy as the best defense against extremism (FO, 1936a).

Concern about the political trend to the right extended even to reporting the rather flimsy rumors that Vargas himself might assume leadership of the Integralists, on the grounds that greenshirt chief Plínio Salgado was "not a person of any great distinction." The British reported Deputy Café Filho's poignant speech to the Chamber of Deputies describing the inhuman treatment of political prisoners (censors banned mention of the speech in the press) and warned about Vargas's flirtations with the Fascists (FO, 1937b, 1937c). United States Embassy Counsellor R. M. Scotten noted that the Army General Staff was carefully directing the anti-Communist drive (NADS, 1937c). By late October 1937, U.S. intelligence agents were predicting a coup on the right, and the British reported that the elections would probably be canceled and that "known Fascists" like Francisco Campos were moving into positions of strength (FO, 1937a; NADS, 1937a, 1937b).

Through the remainder of the prewar years, British and American diplomats continued to monitor Brazilian events with the same balance of reporting and speculative analysis, oriented toward the center-right of the Brazilian political spectrum. The British embassy noted the defection from the PCB in late 1937 of the "Leninist Workers' Party," a Trotskyist faction, oriented around labor union militancy, and called attention to the activity of its chief organizer in Rio de Janeiro, a woman named Patricia Galvão. The abortive Integralist *putsch* against Vargas in 1938 was described in close detail without undue alarm, although the British commented on the fact that the army had waited three hours before sending relief "because the military leaders wanted to see how things were going" (FO, 1938). Both embassies increased their surveillance of German and Italian activities in Brazil as the war neared (NADS, 1939; Hilton, 1977).[11] The growing tension in Europe brought British and American diplomats even closer together in outlook than before. Internal British correspondence, traditionally cool to U.S. hemispheric initiatives, praised Roosevelt's Good Neighbor Policy, noting that "though this policy may at first sight appear somewhat timid, there would seem to be little doubt that it will pay in the long run, and that by 'parallel action' British interests will also stand to gain" (FO, 1939).

III

Some of the other historiographical themes which bear reexamination include the controversial fate of Prestes's wife, Olga Benário, the reasons for the November 1935 uprisings, and the view of Vargas as chief of state during the middle years of his regime. Based on research done in 1964-1965, I felt that allegations in the Communist press that Olga Benário Prestes had perished in a German concentration camp had never been satisfactorily documented and noted that some Brazilians maintained that she had died in a Swiss hospital of tuberculosis (Levine, 1970:

121-122). Sadly, a combination of old and new evidence suggests more convincingly that the allegations were true. First jailed in Berlin, where she was tortured to extract information on Comintern activities, she was ultimately transferred to Ravensbrück, where it is known that she remained at least through mid-1941. After that time communications with her family were broken (previously they had been able to send money and letters through the Berlin branch of the Bank of Mexico), and she was reported to have been transported with 560 other Jewish women either to Auschwitz or to an extermination compound within Ravensbrück itself (Wainer, 1946). Margarete Buber-Neumann locates Olga's death at Ravensbrück in 1942, and a camp inmate, Ruth Eberle, later claimed to have witnessed her execution by machine gun fire in March of that year (Buber-Neumann, 1967: 430; Chilcote, 1974: 295).

Modest revelations have also been disclosed of Axis financial support for the movements on the right and left. The Italian Fascists sent at least 50 contos a month (U.S. $4,320) to the Integralists, and the Germans subsidized Nazi activities among the 100,000 German nationalists and more than 800,000 Brazilians of German origin, mostly in the southern states. Polish fascists under Pilsudski aided organizational work among youth in Paraná through its religious Junak society and allegedly sent a few young men to Poland for training as pilots (Rodrigues, 1970: 8; Hilton, 1975: 172-174; Levine, 1970: 20-101, 212-213).

The degree to which the Comintern orchestrated the 1935 revolts is for the most part of less importance than the reasons that militants loyal to Prestes so badly misgauged Brazil's ripeness for revolution. The handful of Comintern operatives who accompanied Prestes when he clandestinely entered Brazil in 1935 (Ewert, Baron, Rodolfo Ghioldi) knew little if anything about the country, although one memoir asserts that some agents were trained in the Soviet Union in civil warfare tactics in carly 1935 for use with Prestes (Cheston, 1972: 141).[12]

It is highly improbable that the Comintern model of grassroots insurrection could ever have succeeded in Brazil. The Russians may have seen Prestes as a more controllable Chaing-kai-shek, but he never revealed much ability to organize his followers even during his famous guerrilla march of the 1920s, nor did he seem to understand the outlook of the Brazilian lower classes. Not that the working-class population lacked consciousness—Peter Flynn has convincingly demonstrated the extent to which the strikes of the mid-1930s penetrated working-class society—but the distance between ANL/PCB organizers and the masses was too great to be bridged by rhetoric. Leôncio Basbaum, then connected to the inner circle of the Communist party, reveals in his memoirs that Communist agents often exaggerated local militancy in order to earn their comrades' adulation. The agent assigned to Salvador, Lauro Reginaldo (Bangú), sent a stream of messages to the Central Committee in Rio de Janeiro assuring his comrades of readiness when in fact little or no organizing had been done (Basbaum, 1976: 158-159).

Of the leaders of the left, only Carlos Marighella, Gregório Bezerra, and a handful of others, as Flynn notes (1978: 74-88), had roots among the people.[13] Others, like Robert Sissón and Agildo Barata, were romantic visionaries of middle-class origin, and as far out of touch with reality as Belmiro Valverde and his green-shirted Integralist putschists. The PCB failed to trust even its own labor union cadres: When the revolts broke out in November, PCB agents were unable to mobilize their own subordinates to strike, and in at least one instance, had to blow up a section of railroad track in order to disrupt communications.[14]

On one hand, the ANL did stir sufficient interest among opportunistic, populist-minded politicians, some of whom negotiated privately with ANL leaders and who may have pledged financial support. But the left's plans for insurrection ignored soundings that the masses were not responding to its propaganda. The Brazilian popular front seems to have been betrayed from without and from within. Most of the thousands who joined the ANL were liberals of Anti-Fascist sentiments who knew nothing about the planned-for revolts, and at least some of the ANL-PCB inner circle doubled as police *agents provocateurs*. Moscow, which sought to label Vargas a Fascist dictator, used the insurrection as much for the repression which failure guaranteed as for the victory idealists sought. Vargas, for his part, played a similar cynical game: Had the revolts not materialized he could have used any of a number of strikes or incidents to justify his seizure of power in the name of national security. His use of the fraudulent Cohen Plan in 1937, an Integralist forgery, and his tacit permission for officials to spread the lie that Communist rebels had systematically "murdered their loyal comrades" in their beds illustrates his willingness to invent a threat if legitimate ones were unavailable (Alves, 1973: 95).

IV

What of Getúlio Vargas's role in the course of events? José Honório Rodrigues (1970: 8) reflects the orthodox school of historiography which emphasizes his calculated political opportunism—"como todo gaúcho"—painting Vargas as a believer in the existence of the state to conciliate conflicting demands rather than to mirror class interests. Others, including Frank D. McCann (1973: 105), see Getúlio as a nationalist, "more interested in establishing a personalist government that would advance Brazilian development than in any form of fixed ideology." Rodrigues concurs that Vargas, identifying Brazil's future with industrialization (he cites John D. Wirth here), crushed liberalism and tolerated repression, relying on the Gestapo as his "primary anti-Communist informant in Brazil," and, in 1938, inviting Sumner Wells to send FBI agents to train and work with the Brazilian Secret Service (Rodrigues, 1970: 8).

Other scholars have emphasized different sides of Vargas's political personality. Conniff's studies (1976, 1978) of urban populism in Rio de Janeiro show Pedro Ernesto's Partido Autonomista to have been a precursor of Vargas's postwar populism. John W.F. Dulles (1967: 342-344) stresses Vargas's independence from the currents which "were powerful and ambitious," and emphasizes the tug-of-war between politicians and *tenentes*, the right and the left, the Dutra wing and the Aranha wing. Dulles tends to rationalize Vargas's use of authoritarian power, arguing that the purpose of the Liberal Alliance dictatorship and the assault on civil liberties was "not the practice of vindictiveness." Stanley Hilton (1975: 174) attributes Vargas's political motivations to the leader's need to remove challenges to his own authority and to foreign policy considerations which prompted him to suppress the far right in order to assuage United States sensitivity about the Estado Novo and German trade penetration of Brazil.

John D. Wirth (1970: 217-224) emphasizes the fact that the decision of Brazilian planners in the 1930s to follow a course of developmental nationalism led Vargas to aggregate personal power and notes that "his decision-making load increased simultaneously with a more complex political system." By the mid- and late-1930s, unresolved political conflicts took more and more of Vargas's attention. Irritated, he turned to nationalism as a vehicle for political mobilization to free himself from the frustrations of political infighting. Never terribly popular among the electorate, he devised the showy framework of the Estado Novo dictatorship as a stage upon which to recast his image and build a national following. Kenneth P. Erickson (1977: 2) emphasizes the same on the economic side: Vargas deplored the class conflict which accompanied industrialization and embraced corporatism to rid himself of competing interests. In so doing, Vargas had to abandon the *tenentes*, civilian and military, with whom he had risen to power in 1930, but in a way the Estado Novo and his later political directions coopted the nationalistic *tenente* goals (Conniff, 1978: 61-82).

One of the best of the new analyses to date is Bóris Fausto's essay (1969) on the 1930 Revolution. Viewing 1930 as no true break with the past, Fausto sees Vargas as having had to deal with the rising expectations of the urban population—workers, the middle class, small employees, professionals, military officers—who in turn posed a "grave problem for the new and old oligarchies" (Fausto, 1969: 260). The ANL's capacity to mobilize nationalist sentiments, even under flawed conditions, heightened pressure on Vargas to eliminate reformist voices from the political arena. The post-November 1935 repression, then, represented a significant victory for Vargas, allowing him to consolidate power, isolate moderates and potential rivals, and to maintain control over the military while using anti-Communism to suffocate the reformist impulses cultivated successfully by such politicians as the Federal District's Pedro Ernesto and less successfully by others.

Neither *tenentismo*, the ANL, nor the PCB were able to forge viable constituencies, either broadly or among the civilian and military ruling elites. State-directed corporatism held greater usefulness for the powerful. Even when such *paulista* industrialists as Roberto Simonsen and Francisco Matarrazo "preached the virtues of interclass harmony and consensus," employers used force and intimidation to prevent any attempt at strikes, as Peter Flynn shows us (1978: 101, citing Dean, 1969: 164). Trade unions under Vargas were absorbed into the state apparatus, and civil service reform, modified to soothe vested interests, was adopted, providing the base for the postwar emergence of Vargas's new political machine.

An earlier view of Vargas is provided in a 1938 memorandum prepared by Norbert A. Bogdan of the J. Henry Schroder Banking Corporation for his company. Bogdan's portrait of Vargas was shared by foreign diplomatic contemporaries and, to some degree, reflects the interpretation still held by scholars:

> Of all living statesmen of the world today, [Vargas] is without a doubt the coldest, most rational, and cynical one. Emotion of any kind he does not know. . . . He is a man for whom the words "loyalty" and "consideration" have no meaning. . . . What we today see in Brazil is a dictatorship which is naturally a highly [authoritarian] one but which is neither truly Fascist nor totalitarian. . . . In fact it is no system at all and there is no clear or preconceived ideology or doctrine back of it. Vargas had none and still doesn't have any. It is simply Getúlio Vargasism supported by the armed forces and now engaged in picking from the various forms of government at present practiced in different parts of the world, whatever he and the Army together believe is useful [NADS, 1938].

What was the impact of the diplomats' perceptions on their home governments? From 1934 to 1939, both Washington and

London continued to view Brazil as a badly governed country, always on the verge of anarchy and subversive rebelliousness, under the thinly veiled control of the armed forces. Few if any of the changing diplomatic observers gave Vargas credit for his not inconsiderable ability to manipulate competing interest groups and to isolate threatening currents on the far left and the far right. The diplomats tended to measure Brazilian events on a continuum ranging from stability at one end of the scale to instability at the other. As a result, they provided detailed data to their superiors but often failed to appreciate the underlying effort by the Vargas administration to gain greater independence in the international arena and to achieve a greater degree of national integration. In this sense, Vargas, by 1939, had achieved significant progress, which was acknowledged only grudgingly by the professional Brazil watchers of the 1930s.

NOTES

1. Among the first studies to use the Vargas papers were Helio Silva's *Ciclo de Vargas* volumes (1969a, 1969b, 1970), essentially collections of documents selected by the author from the Vargas archive and elsewhere.

2. In 1973 it was revised and translated under the title *Os vinhos da liberdade: a politica no brasil, 1934-1938*, but it was criticized by censors and its publication canceled.

3. The military attaché during this period, Major William Sackville, was absent. Observations were forwarded to Washington by the Quartermaster Clerk, Harry W. Brown.

4. From the U.S. Department of State Archives Record Group (RG) 59, 832.00/916. All subsequent citations will omit the 832.00 file number, which designated political affairs.

5. Translated and quoted (NADW, 1934c). For their part, the English took these attacks in stride, noting that Brazil "as viewed from Rio de Janeiro and São Paulo is no longer a backwoods State . . . and her educated public—apart from political and professional agitators—can hardly be blamed for resenting the Leopoldina Railway, for instance. What would be the British attitude to a German-owned Southern Railway" (FO, 1934b)? Seeds also commented on American bankers "who are children—and not particularly nice children—in matters of high international finance."

6. Outbreaks between local police and federal troops also occurred during Carnival in the states of Ceara and Amazonas.

7. For a detailed analysis of the events in Pernambuco accompanying the shift to the right in the period between 1935 and 1937, see Levine (1978).

8. The American military attaché named the Russian legation and the "Yumtorg" (Iamtorg) Trading Association.

9. Gurney added: "It has been long known that the Communists were preparing a revolutionary outbreak, to start probably in the North, towards the end of the year."

10. See also NADW, 1936a, 1936b.

11. This is an excellent source for research on Italian life in prewar Brazil.

12. See also Collotti-Pischel (1968).

13. Both were Brazilian Communists who surfaced politically in the 1930s and who played more prominent roles in the 1950s. See also Hilton (1975: 121), citing German diplomatic correspondence on Comintern activity.

14. Related by Timothy Harding. This was the "Barra de Pirai" incident.

REFERENCES

ALVES, H. (1973) "Brazil: martial mythologies." Latin Amer. Rev. of Books 1 (Spring): 95.

BAKOTA, L. S. (1979) "Getúlio Vargas and the estado nôvo." Latin Amer. Research Rev. 14, I: 205-210.

BASBAUM, L. (1976) Uma vida em seis tempos (memórias). São Paulo: Ed. Alfa-Omega.

BUBER-NEUMANN, M. (1967) Kriegsschauplaetze der Weltrevolution. Stuttgart: Seewald Verlag.

CHESTON, T. S. (1972) "Review." Americas (January): 141.

CHILCOTE, R. H. (1974) The Brazilian Communist Party. New York: Oxford Univ. Press.

COLLOTTI-PISCHEL, E. (1968) L'Internationale Communiste et les problèmes coloniaux, 1919-1935. Paris: La Haya, Mouton.

CONNIFF, M. (1978) "The *tenentes* in power: a new perspective on the Brazilian revolution." J. of Latin Amer. Studies 10 (May): 61-82.

——— (1967) "Rio de Janeiro during the great depression, 1928-1937." Ph.D. dissertation, Stanford University.

DEAN W. (1969) The Industrialization of São Paulo, 1880-1945. Austin: Univ. of Texas Press.

Diário da Bahia (1934) December 9.

DULLES, J.W.F. (1967) Vargas of Brazil: A Political Biography. Austin: Univ. of Texas Press.

ERICKSON, K. P. (1977) The Brazilian Corporative State and Working-Class Politics. Berkeley: Univ. of California Press.

FAUSTO, B. (1969) "A revolução de 1930," in Brasil em perspectiva. São Paulo: DIFEL.

FLYNN, P. (1978) Brazil: A Political Analysis. London: Ernest Benn.

FO [Great Britain Foreign Office, London, Public Records Office] (1939) British Embassy, Rio de Janeiro, to Lord Halifax. Report 72E, March 9. 2369/371/22725/3990.

——— (1938) (Illegible), Rio de Janeiro, to J. Balfour. June 4. 4853/371/21422/3984.

——— (1937a) Sir Hugh Gurney to Foreign Office. November 8. 371/20603/3910.

——— (1937b) Sir Hugh Gurney to Anthony Eden. Report 212, June 21. 4858/371/20603/3910.

——— (1937c) Sir Hugh Gurney to Anthony Eden. Report 195, April 17. 3332/41/6/371/20603/3910.

——— (1936a) Sir Hugh Gurney to Anthony Eden. Report 347, November 10. 8892/68/3/371/19767/3903.
——— (1936b) Edward Coote, Rio de Janeiro, to Anthony Eden. Report 323, October 3. 8431/68/6/371/19765/3903.
——— (1936c) Sir Hugh Gurney to Sir Samuel Hoare. March 31. 2694/68/8/382/371/18649/3877.
——— (1936d) Notation by H. Hohler on memorandum from Sir Hugh Gurney to Foreign Office, March 13. 2118/68/8/371/19765/3910.
——— (1936e) K.J.M. White, Recife, to Sir Hugh Gurney. March 12. 302/1936/371/19765/3910.
——— (1936f) Sir Hugh Gurney to Sir Samuel Hoare. Report 28, February 4. 1660/68/8/371/19765/3910.
——— (1936g) "W.R.G." (no other identification) to Foreign Office, late January. 371/18649/3877/350.
——— (1935a) Sir Hugh Gurney to Sir Samuel Hoare. December 17. 10851/120/6/480/371/18649/3877.
——— (1935b) Sir Hugh Gurney to Sir Samuel Hoare. December 4. 10160/120/6/371/18649/3877.
——— (1935c) Sir Hugh Gurney, Rio de Janeiro, to Foreign Office. Early December. 371/18649/3877/416.
——— (1935d) K.J.M. White, H. M. Consul, Recife, to Sir Hugh Gurney, Rio de Janeiro. Report 59, November 29. 371/19765/3910.
——— (1935e) Memorandum, Sir William Troutbeck, Rio de Janeiro, to Foreign Office. November 29. 371/18649/3877/439.
——— (1935f) Coded telegram, Sir Hugh Gurney, Rio de Janeiro, to Foreign Office. November 26. 9910/120/6/371/18649/3877.
——— (1935g) Notation by H. Hohler on memorandum from Sir Hugh Gurney to Foreign Office. November 25. 9883/120/6/153/371/18649/3877.
——— (1935h) Sir Hugh Gurney, Rio de Janeiro, to Sir Samuel Hoare. October 18. 9358/120/6/371/18649/3877.
——— (1935i) Edward Coote, Rio de Janeiro, to Sir Samuel Hoare. August 9. 7553/371/18649/3877.
——— (1935j) Edward Coote, British Embassy, Rio de Janeiro to Sir Samuel Hoare. August 1. 6807/126/6/371/18649/3877.
——— (1935k) Confidential report, Sir William Seeds, Petrópolis, to Sir John Simon. March 1. 2002/371/18655/3893.
——— (1935l) Sir William Seeds, Petrópolis, to Sir John Simon. March 1. 2002/371/18655/3893.
——— (1935m) Telegram, Sir William Seeds, Rio de Janeiro, to Foreign Office. February 28. 1948/371/18648/3877.
——— (1935n) Note signed "M.T." São Paulo Consulate, Report to Foreign Office, citing Sir William Seeds's "2nd enclosure in 2002." February 28. 1948/371/18648/3877/3834/12016.
——— (1935o) M.A.B. Denton-Thompson, Recife, to British Embassy, Rio de Janeiro. February 28. 371/18648/3877/119-126.
——— (1935p) A. Abbott, H. M. Consul General, São Paulo, Report 5, to Sir W. Seeds. February 4. 371/18655/3893/219.
——— (1935q) Sir William Seeds, Rio de Janeiro, to Foreign Office. January 14. 371/18648/3877/407.

——— (1934a) Ambassador Sir William Seeds, Petrópolis, to Sir John Simon. December 26. 404/371/18651/3885.

——— (1934b) British Consulate, Salvador (Bahia), to Ambassador Sir William Seeds, Petrópolis. Consular Report 43, December 13. 404/371/18651/3885.

——— (1934c) Vice Consul Maceió (Alagoas) to Chargé d'Affaires, Rio de Janeiro. September 22. 371/17487/4454/358-359.

——— (1934d) C. R. Girwood, Acting British Consul, Bahia, to Chargé d'Affaires, Rio de Janeiro. Confidential Report 30, September 14. 7702/371/17486/3884.

——— (1934e) J. M. Troutbeck, Rio de Janeiro, to Sir John Simon. August 29. 371/17486/3884a.

——— (1934f) J. M. Troutbeck, Rio de Janeiro, to Sir John Simon. August 23. 371/17486/3884.

——— (1934g) M.A.B. Denton-Thompson, Recife, to Chargé d'Affaires, Rio de Janeiro. Confidential Report 29, August 21. 7702/371/17486/3884.

——— (1933) H. M. Consul, Pernambuco, to British Embassy, Rio de Janeiro. September 25. 7671/371/16549/3807.

HILTON, S. E. (1977) Suastica sôbre o Brasil, a história de espionagem alemã no Brasil. Rio de Janeiro: Civilização Brasileira.

——— (1975) Brazil and the Great Powers, 1930-1939: The Politics of Trade Rivalry. Austin: Univ. of Texas Press.

LEVINE, R. M. (1978) Pernambuco in the Brazilian Federation, 1889-1937. Stanford: Stanford Univ. Press.

——— (1970) The Vargas Regime: The Critical Years, 1934-1938. New York: Columbia Univ. Press.

McCANN, F. D., Jr. (1973) The Brazilian-American Alliance, 1937-1945. Princeton: Princeton Univ. Press.

NADS [U.S. National Archives, Department of State, Washington, D.C. Record Group 59] (1939) "Italian activities in Brazil (a basic report)." William C. Burdett, General Consul, U.S. Embassy, Rio de Janeiro. February 6. F/19/LH.

——— (1938) Norbert A. Bogdan to U.S. Embassy, Rio de Janeiro. Copy sent to Dr. Herbet Feis and Secretary of State Sumner Welles. No date. 1168.

——— (1937a) Carol H. Foster, Consul General, São Paulo, to Ambassador Jefferson Caffery, Rio de Janeiro. Political Report 92, November 5. 1064.

——— (1937b) R. M. Scotten to Secretary of State. No report number. October 20. 1964.

——— (1937c) "Political developments." R. M. Scotten to Secretary of State. Report 58, October 2. 1053.

——— (1936) Hugh Gibson to Secretary of State. Report 997, April 2. 972.

——— (1935a) Wesley Frost, Chargé d'Affaires ad interim, Rio de Janeiro, to Secretary of State. Report 835. November 1. 972.

——— (1935b) George A. Gordon, Rio de Janeiro, to Secretary of State. Report 730, July 11. 958.

——— (1935c) George A. Gordon, Rio de Janeiro, to Secretary of State. No report number. March 13. 930.

——— (1934) Carol H. Foster, Consul General, São Paulo, to Ambassador Hugh S. Gibson, Rio de Janeiro. Political Report 2, October 22. 916.

NADW [U.S. National Archives, Department of War Military Intelligence Division, Washington, D. C.] (1936a) Major William Sackville. G-2 Report 1584. January 8. WD 2657-K-70-23.

——— (1936b) Major William Sackville. G-2 Report 1582. January 2. WD 2657-K-70-23.

——— (1935) Major William Sackville. G-2 Report 1579. December 24. WD-2657-K-70-22.

——— (1934a) "Brazil: population and social; labor riot in Rio de Janeiro." Harry W. Brown, Quartermaster Clerk. G-2 Report 1335, October 11. 2-1-2657-K-70.

——— (1934b) Harry W. Brown. G-2 Report 1319. August 29. 6-4-2657-K-103.

——— (1934c) "Communist disorder." Harry W. Brown. G-2 Report 1318. August 24. 2-1-2657-K-70.

RODRIGUES, J. R. (1970) "Getúlio Vargas: uma revisão histórica." Jornal do Brasil. October 25-26, caderno especial 8.

SILVA, H. (1970) 1937: Todos os golpes se parecem. Rio de Janeiro: Civilização Brasileira.

——— (1969a) 1935: A revolta vermelha. Rio de Janeiro: Civilização Brasileira.

——— (1969b) 1934: A constituinte. Rio de Janeiro: Civilização Brasileira.

WAINER, S. (1946) "Article on Olga Benário Prestes." Folha da Noite, Rio de Janeiro. (January 7): 1.

WIRTH, J. D. (1970) The Politics of Brazilian Development, 1930-1954. Stanford: Stanford Univ. Press.

ZWEIBEN, B. (1978) "Summary, executive order 12065." Newsletter, Society for Historians of Amer. Foreign Relations 9 (December): 18-20.

Robert M. Levine is Professor of History at State University of New York at Stony Brook. He has written two monographs and three other books on Brazilian political and social history, and is currently writing a social history of Brazil since 1889. He is past chairman of the National Committee on Brazilian Studies and the Columbia University Seminar on Brazil.

ANN TWINAM
Fundación Antioqueño para los Estudios Sociales (FAES)
Apartado Aereo 8650
Medellín, Colombia

FROM JEW TO BASQUE
Ethnic Myths and Antioqueño Entrepreneurship

Twenty minutes by jet or fifteen hours by bus northwest of Bogotá lies the department of Antioquia, with its capital, Medellín, second largest of Colombia's cities. Although the Andes serve as divider and incubator of a diversity of *patrias chicas*, each with characteristic accent, folklore, and regional identity, the country of the Antioqueño, or *paisa*, remains one of the most distinctive. Unlike Colombians from other regions, the Antioqueño has typically been stereotyped as the alien. Whether he has been reviled as a Jew, lauded as a "New Breed," portrayed as a Basque, a Swiss, a Yankee, or a Protestant, writers have used ethnic interpretations which minimize the Latin, the Catholic, and even the Colombian image of the paisa (Lipset, 1967: 27, 28).

Antioqueños have been seen as a strange breed because their department forms a conspicuous entrepreneurial enclave in Latin America. Tracing the link between the historic development of Antioqueño entrepreneurship and the evolution of associated ethnic myths reveals a provocative interplay between the mythmakers and the mythicized. Such analysis not only uncovers

---

AUTHOR'S NOTE: The author thanks Professors Zane Miller, Roger Daniels, and Henry D. Shapiro of the University of Cincinnati for their comments on this article and also acknowledges research support from the Foreign Area Fellowship Foundation and the Brodie and Taft Funds of the University of Cincinnati.

Journal of Interamerican Studies and World Affairs, Vol. 22 No. 1, February 1980 81-107

formative stages in the development of a self-conscious Antioqueño mentality, but it provides pertinent commentary on one variant of entrepreneurial development in Latin America.

Antioqueño Economic Development

Although debate continues as to the origin, timing, and particularity of Antioqueño entrepreneurship, there is general agreement that paisas have played a special role in Colombia's economic history (McGreevey, 1971: 12; Safford, 1965a: 503-526). From the first days of conquest, Antioquia lured colonists to its mountain-locked valleys as the province's rivers literally ran with gold. Utilizing Indian and then African slave labor, Spaniards placer-mined the Cauca and Nechi rivers, bored tunnels into the gold lode mine of Buriticá, and acquired a wealth which made Antioquia famous throughout the Indies. By the early seventeenth century the lowland placers were exhausted, both Indian and black slave gangs were decimated by tropical diseases, and the colonial economy entered more than a century of depression.[2]

A gradual reorganization of both economy and society characterized the late seventeenth and eighteenth centuries. Itinerant panners, called *mazamorreros*, became the most common kind of miner, producing two-thirds of Antioquia's gold, although sluice miners continued to operate on a much reduced scale. Mining sites shifted from lowland to highland placers where a scarcity of water limited production to only six months a year. As a result population gradually concentrated in the fertile valleys of Medellín, Rionegro, and Marinilla, where both miners and mazamorreros operated family farms which they left in the rainy season to mine in the highland camps. In the late colonial years, Antioquia's population doubled (growing from 46,366 in 1788 to 110,662 in 1808), and gold production doubled and then doubled again. The widespread distribution of gold dust created a lively demand for imports, and a diverse merchant community evolved to supply both mining camps and valley settlements. Late colonial Medellín was governed by an elite which attached high status to wealth, particularly if acquired through mining or commerce as opposed to land. This encouraged multiple investments and flexible use of capital, with those attitudes passed on to succeeding generations (Twinam, 1979: 444-475; 1976: 22-165).

Changing conditions after independence provided Antioqueños with favorable opportunities to expand beyond their provincial base. Waves of Antioqueño colonists now struck out from the heavily populated temperate valleys to found strings of new towns which reached to the Cauca Valley in the South (Parsons, 1968: 60-101; Christie, 1978: 260-283). With them went merchant sons who established branch stores from the parent companies in the Antioqueño heartland. Paisa merchants became distributors to national markets, and the most prosperous firms established European branches as well. In alliance with foreign capital, Antioqueños took advantage of advances in mining technology to move from placer to lode operations, thereby greatly expanding production potential (Safford, 1965b: 323-324, 334, 341; Brew, 1973: 128-154).

As the nineteenth century proceeded, Antioqueño expansion and growth was not limited to the traditional colonial occupations of mining and commerce. Antioqueños with excess capital established subsidiary offices in Bogotá; they negotiated the 1824 British loan to Colombia; in the 1840s they organized and controlled the Ambalema tobacco export trade. In the 1880s Antioqueños embarked on coffee production and financed and constructed their own railroad to carry this harvest to market (Safford, 1965a: 521-523).

By the twentieth century, Antioqueño entrepreneurs decided that it was time to industrialize. Since the railroad linking Medellín to its Magdalena port was not totally completed, mules carried the first mechanical loom over the high *cordilleras*. A combination of crushed machinery and a 1904 bank failure doomed this first effort, but the second loom was already on order and in production by 1906. By 1915 there were 150 mechanical looms in Medellín, and within the decade their number increased to 650. By 1945 Antioqueños contributed 24% of the value of national industrial production, although the department contained 14% of Colombia's population (Ospina Vásavez, 1955:

339-342, 390-393).[3] By the 1960s Medellín was the center of a dynamic textile industry which included South America's largest producer, Coltejer. Expanding beyond their textile base, Medellinenses invested in food processing, metal goods, precision machinery, and the other usual products of a diversified and modernizing economy.

Since the 1960s Medellín's early lead has diminished as other Colombian cities have also industrialized (Instituto Geográfico "Agustín Codazzi," 1970: 52). The requirements of high capitalization and high technology have encouraged the multinational corporation as much in Medellín as elsewhere in Colombia and Latin America. Still, Antioqueños retain a reputation as entrepreneurs, and whether allied with outsiders or on their own, they continue to expand their industrial base. Their departmental slogan, "For Colombia, We the Antioqueños can do more," is not only a boast, but a self-conscious expression of a "can-do" mentality more than a century in the making. Significantly, it is the ethnic myth that provides the earliest indication that outsiders perceived Antioqueños as particularly talented entrepreneurs.

The Jewish Myth

If it were possible to conjure up a mid-nineteenth century Bogotano and ask him why Antioqueños such as the Montoyas and the Arrublas had become prominent businessmen in the national capital, there would be a very good chance that he would respond, "because they are Jews." Such an evaluation would be most unflattering; indeed, it would constitute an insult to the Antioqueños. In nineteenth century Colombia, as throughout Spanish America, anti-Semitism prevailed as the product of two historical traditions. One was religious and Catholic, and depicted Jews as "betrayers" and "murderers" of the Savior; the other was Spanish and cultural and added that "honor" and "racial purity" (*limpieza de sangre*, literally, "clean blood") was not compatible with Jewish or Moorish ancestry (Castro, 1954: 521-570).

While the Bogotano might be the first to concede that his Antioqueño contemporaries were true and faithful Catholics and that Antioquia had a reputation as one of the most traditional and most devout regions of Colombia, he might argue that paisas were descended from immigrant *conversos*, Spanish Jews forcibly converted in the fifteenth and sixteenth centuries who then migrated to the colonies. Although a few typical Antioqueño family names such as Correa and Santamaría are possibly of converso origin, a closer study of the evolution of the Jewish myth reveals it is based more on a perception that Antioqueños acted "differently" than on any concrete evidence that they actually were Jewish (Parsons, 1968: 63).

The first known linkage of Antioqueños with Jews occurs in an 1808 *Compendio historial* written by a Colombian, Campo y Rivas. This publication originated during the transitional years from colony to republic when Antioqueños were becoming conspicuous, not only because they were colonizing outside their original pattern of settlement but also because their merchants were extending commercial operations beyond the home province. Indeed, it was the purposeful settlement of Antioquia's hinterland that initially attracted the attention of Campo y Rivas. He posited an extraordinary explanation for the phenomenon by transforming the wandering Antioqueño into the "Wandering Jew." The Antioqueños of his day, he asserted, were seekers of new land because they had failed to reach the Promised Land. Their ancestors had rejected Moses' call to flee their Egyptian bondage, had remained under the pharaohs, and only later had migrated to Algiers, to Spain and finally to Antioquia. Their New World descendants were men suffering under an eternal punishment which drove them to quest compulsively beyond the next horizon in a vain attempt to compensate for the paradise they had lost.

Campo y Rivas also asserted that Antioquia's native dish, mazamorra, was of suspicious origin. Pointing to its slight resemblance to *cush cush*, he charged that its very name, *masa de moros* (dough of Moors), was a sign of its crypto-Jewish heritage. He concluded that since Antioqueños looked like Jews, and acted like Jews, they clearly were Jews (Robledo, 1922: 566).

It might be sufficient to assign Campo y Rivas's admittedly fertile imagination as the source of this bizarre interpretation of Antioqueño colonization. An analysis of his career does suggest an alternative explanation. Although Campo y Rivas ended his days as an *oidor*, or judge, on the Guatemala and Mexico City courts, he had been born in Cartago, Colombia, and had served as a professor in the Bogotá *colegio* of San Bartolomé. The *Compendio historial*, written after he had left his homeland, no doubt reflected the impressions he had formed while in Bogotá. If this is so, perhaps the connection between Antioqueños and Jews was a common one among the Bogotanos of his day (Zuleta, 1929: 12-13). In any case, it is clear that Antioqueños were perceived, possibly by many, not only as deviating significantly from the norm, but as doing so by the end of the colonial period.[4]

Although an exhaustive scrutiny of Colombian newspapers might find intermediary cases, the next linkage of Antioqueño to Jew appears in the 1840s. In July 1844, Bogotá newspaper *El Día* stormed:

> Look at these diligent and active usurers of Jewish face and hardened heart, friends of their own profit and enemies of anyone else's, incapable of accommodating anyone, even their own family. Guard well against . . . one of those who, decended by direct line from the members of that race persecuted by Phillip II, came as parasites to America, hiding their true name and origin, and whose descendants are today the torment of so many individuals [Zuleta, 1929: 19, 20].

Although *El Día* named no names, Eduardo Zuleta (1929: 19-20) argued that this passage was a clear reference to the Antioqueños, as they were the only Colombians associated with Jews. He concluded that the financial success of such paisa families as the Montoyas, the Arrublas, and the Aranzazus, then prominent in Bogotá business circles, prompted these accusations and that this reference reflected the growing tension between the expansionist investments of the Antioqueños and those of the Bogotanos.

Although Zuleta correctly noted that Antioqueños such as the Montoyas and Arrublas had invested beyond their home province in commercial and agricultural enterprises, his assertion that these men were the direct targets of *El Día's* wrath is far from certain. As Frank Safford (1956: 148-149) has noted, none of these Antioqueños were known as moneylenders much less as usurers. *El Día's* remarks, which were paralleled by similar comments in competing newspapers, may rather have reflected the resentments engendered by numerous bankruptcies, the product of a boom-and-bust cycle in the 1840s which dissipated more than one prominent Bogotano family fortune. Even if there is no direct link, the economic difficulties of many Bogotanos may well have promoted an undercurrent of resentment against Antioqueños whose access to their departmentally produced gold dust made them less vulnerable, more quick to recover and to profit from such crises. But six years later, Antioqueños were clearly linked with Jews.

It was in poetry that the next reference to the Semitic origin of the Antioqueños was expressed. In 1851 Gregorio Gutiérrez Gonzales published *Felipe* which contained the following lines:

In this enchanted land lives
The infamous race cursed by God
A race of merchants who speculate
With everything and about everything. An impious race
Through whose cold-blooded veins run
The vile blood of the Jewish nation.
Let pesos upon pesos accumulate
The price of his honor, his goods
And only the interest is considered
Everything is bought here, everything is sold.
There the wife, slave of her husband
Receives neither love nor enjoys pleasures
And subject to her greedy father
Is the innocent daughter [Otero D'Costa, 1924: 264].

When queried as to his inspiration for these lines, Gonzales Gutiérrez recounted the no doubt allegorical, but very pertinent tale of the woes of his friend, Felipe. Felipe, a Bogotano, visited

Medellín where he fell deeply in love with an Antioqueña named Rosa. After a month's acquaintance Felipe knew he had found his heart's desire and pressed his poet friend into forwarding his suit with Rosa's father. Upon hearing that Felipe was "given to literature," the enraged parent summarily rejected him as a candidate for his daughter's hand:

> These studious men are not worth anything. Do you understand? Worth nothing. They would be incapable of investing two hundred pesos if by chance they were able to earn it. [Otero D'Costa, 1924: 264; Restrepo, 1924: 262-279].

The Medellinense announced that his daughter would be reserved to someone who had the means to support her. Felipe fled from Medellín and according to Gonzales Gutiérrez, bitterly penned the lines quoted above in an abandoned house overlooking the valley. Here again, it is instructive to note than although the poem directly connects Antioqueños with Jews, the supposed origin of these lines stems from the mercenary, or the entrepreneurial attitude of Rosa's father.[5]

The 1860s to the 1880s saw yet further references to the supposed Jewish background of the Antioqueño. In 1868 Don José Vergara y Vergara noted in his Historia de la literatura that the state of Antioquia had been settled by a colony of Jews. He confirmed this by showing the similarity between certain Antioqueño and Jewish surnames, by commenting on the particularly "Jewish" beauty of paisa women, and by noting the innate "commercial" character of the inhabitants. In 1875 the Jewish myth entered the political arena when in a newspaper article Don José María Samper sneered that the governor of Antioquia was served by "political Jews." By then the repeated association of Antioqueños with Jews had extended beyond a Medellín-Bogotá dialogue, for it had attracted the attention of at least one foreigner resident in Colombia. When French geographer Elisée Reclus, who had lived for some time on the Santa Marta coast, published his *L'Homme et la terre*, he noted that there was a tradition in Colombia that Antioquia had been settled by Jews (Robledo, 1922: 568-569).

In the 1890s the conspicuous economic activities of the Antioqueños as manifested in their dominance of coffee exports and their construction of a railroad to transport this product to market produced another highpoint in the Jewish legend. In 1892 Colombian novelist Jorge Isaacs, the author of *María*, wrote a poem called *La tierra de Córdoba*, the title of which referred to one of Antioquia's independence heroes. In the poem Isaacs, himself of Jewish ancestry, asked the question: "From what race are you descended, energetic people,/Titan worker[?]" His answer was meant to be laudatory; the Jews.

> You have rejected the ominous inheritance of the cruel Iberian:
> . . . .
> Your daughters are beautiful and the pride of Israel [Isaacs, 1938: 236].

Isaacs's reputation as the foremost Romanticist of nineteenth century Colombian letters insured that the poem received widespread circulation throughout the country.[6]

The year 1892 also marked the internationalization of the Jewish myth when Doña Soledad Acosta de Samper, the Colombian delegate to a meeting celebrating the four-hundredth anniversary of the discovery of America, presented a paper which announced that Antioqueños were indeed descended from one of the lost tribes of Israel (Robledo, 1922: 569-570).

The Rebuttal

Whether out of ignorance or indifference, Antioqueños were slow to counteract these charges of Semitic ancestry. While the 1808 reference no doubt had limited circulation, the 1844 newspaper attack, the 1851 poem, and the 1868 history certainly reached wide audiences. Perhaps the hope that the legend might die a natural death, or the fear that it might be exacerbated by a vigorous response, quelled the pens of potential defenders. Whatever the cause, one of the earliest rebutters was not an Antioqueño but a Barranquilla Jew, who, roused by the 1875 newspaper diatribe that Antioqueños were "political Jews," roundly flayed Bogotanos, first for their anti-Semitism and then for their false identification of Antioqueños. In that same year Dr. Mariano Ospina took up the gauntlet, prefacing his article with the remark that twenty or thirty years of whisperings against his fellow Antioqueños needed to be laid to rest. His 1875 effort was followed in 1882 by two more articles debunking the connection of Antioqueño and Jew. It was the 1892 poem and paper, however, that opened the gate to a veritable flood of articles protesting this association. Emotions ran high. Even Carlos E. Restrepo, an Antioqueño and later president of Colombia (1910-1914), penned a poetic rejoinder:

> Neither in body nor in spirit: there is nothing
> That marks our origin as Jewish
> What is here, is from Spain [Robledo, 1922: 568-570].

Antioqueño rejoinders typically fell into three categories. One response was pseudo-historical and racist, the New Breed of *mestizo* thesis. A second, more reasoned reaction led Antioqueño historians back to their local archives for evidence to disprove the Semetic charge. A third approach traced the origin of the Semitic interpretation. Although the first aim of all authors was to reject the Jewish charge, the very process of research led to a self-conscious questioning why Antioqueños had demonstrated such conspicuous success in business enterprises.

The theory that Antioqueños formed a New Breed of mestizo was one brief episode in the paisa response to the Jewish myth. Stung by late nineteenth century charges that the paisa was descended from "the race which had murdered the Savior," the Antioqueños responded in kind. They attacked the Bogotanos at their most vulnerable point by asserting that although both groups were products of mixed blood, the Antioqueños had evolved into a superior race. This accounted for the more successful development of the department.

The foremost exponent of this theory was Tulio Ospina (1915: 714-716) who suggested that the Antioqueño combined the best characteristics of the Caucasian and Negro races. The Spaniards who emigrated to Antioquia were from the Basque country, thus contributing entrepreneurial talents to the mixture. Antioquia's black slaves were well treated by their masters and imitated their acquisitive habits. The local Indians were Caucasian rather than Mongoloid, with independent and lively characters and a sophisticated native tongue. This mixture of Basque, entrepreneurial slave, and white Indian led to the superior breed known as the Antioqueño!

The implication of this interpretation was not spelled out, but it was clear. Antioqueños were superior because their ancestors had mingled with the best of the Negro and Caucasian races, while the Bogotanos were inferior and "unstable types" because their forefathers had mixed with the stocky, darker natives of the *sabana.* Those were "fighting words" in the heightened racial consciousness characteristic of a post-Darwinian and positivist Colombia. Although the New Breed thesis does not figure prominently in the Antioqueño-Bogotano debate, it does epitomize the conflict at its most bitter.

Another response of Antioqueño writers was to counter the Jewish legend with a great deal of logic and a modicum of historical data. In the enemy's own camp, at least in his own historical journal, the *Boletín de Historia y Antiqüedades*, published in Bogotá, paisa authors mounted an attack. Articles published in 1905 and 1909 noted that colonial travelers to the Americas underwent a screening process specifically designed to eliminate colonists with "impure blood," and argued that royal officials would have speedily investigated if there had been any rumor of a Jewish settlement in Antioquia. The Cartagena inquisition maintained a continual vigilance over the colony and would have persecuted suspected Semites with a relentless zeal. These rebutters concluded that a lack of opportunity combined with a lack of persecution proved that Jews had not settled in Antioquia (Arango Mejía, 1909: 656-658; Ospina Rodriguez, 1905: 511-512).[7]

Such arguments were not totally convincing. Overwhelming documentation proved that Jews had migrated to Spanish

America, and only circumstantial evidence suggested that some had not settled in Antioquia (Marcus, 1970: Vol. 1, 35-84; Liebman, 1970). During the 1920s, as Antioqueño industrialization made impressive strides, references linking Antioqueños to Jews continued, and Antioqueño intellectuals searched for more plausible responses.

In 1922 a North American, in 1925 a Bogotano, and in 1929 even an Antioqueño added new embellishments to the Jewish myth. An annual report submitted by Dr. F. Miller to the International Health Board of the Rockefeller Institution contained the following entry:

> Department of Antioquia
>
> The department of Antioquia has the greatest surface and population and is the most important in the Republic of Colombia. It derives its name from the town of Antioch, in Syria.
>
> Its population is almost all of Jewish origin, for it was here that they established themselves when they fled from Spain. Owing to the disposition inherited from this race, the Antioqueños have succeeded such that their department is the first in finance and in industry in all the country [Robledo, 1922: 565].

Three years later Raimundo Rivas (Rivas, 1925: 137-138) speculated in a Medellín historical journal that the Santamarías, an old, wealthy, and highly respected Antioqueño family, were descendants of Rabbi Salemon Ha Levi, who had taken that Christian name upon conversion. Finally, Antioqueño Eduardo Zuleta related the following personal experience which made him wonder if myth might be reality:

> One day when my Madrid-bound train stopped at Bayona, a woman who looked very much like a friend of mine in Medellín entered my car. As the woman noticed my surprise, she looked at me more closely and after a few minutes said, "I believe that we share a similar religion, for you appear to be Jewish." I told her that I had been born in a town in Colombia whose inhabitants were believed to be of Jewish origin, but that no one had decisively proved this. "When you return to Madrid," she said, "Go to

> Bayona and visit the Jewish barrio, it might interest you." I did so and was astonished to note the incredible resemblance of those Jews with Antioqueños, and even more so when I learned that many of them had the same family names common to Antioquia [Zuleta, 1929: 26].

As part of both a continuing response and a specific attack on the Rockefeller report, Antioqueño authors Emilio Robledo, Enrique Otero D'Costa and A. J. Restrepo identified nineteenth century linkages of Antioqueño and Jew and exposed their vague proof (Robledo, 1922; Otero D'Costa, 1924; Restrepo, 1924). The Santamaría family hired their detractor, Raimundo Rivas, and commissioned him to write their family history, which, not coincidentally, disproved his earlier charge (Rivas, 1933). The final blow to any substantive support for an Antioqueño-Jewish link came from Gabriel Arango Mejía's life work (1924a), *Genealogías de Antioquia y de Caldas.* The product of decades of research in Antioqueño archives, this exhaustive chronicling of paisa family roots proved, to those willing to be convinced by historical evidence, that there was no reason to associate Antioqueño and Jew.

Although the Arango Mejía genealogy disproved, it could not defeat a popular, or folk belief that Antioqueño business acumen derived from Jewish descent. As Emilio Robledo (1922: 570) wryly commented: "They [Colombians] would prefer the invasion of a real Jew, or even the Yankee, to that of the Antioqueño."

In any case, if the 1920s and the 1930s now figure as those decades when Antioqueños substantively discredited the myth, the 1940s were when they came to terms with it. By then Medellín had become conspicuous not only within Colombia but within Latin America as an industrial center, and with the charge disproved and with anti-Semitism on the decline, Antioqueños began to see it as a kind of compliment, even if a left-handed one. As Antioqueños celebrated the four-hundredth anniversary of the discovery of their department (1541-1941), a deluge of publications lauded past accomplishments, and, in the process, they institutionalized a counter-myth of their own.

A 1942 article by Arango Mejía succinctly illustrates a paisa shift from the defensive to the offensive. After commenting that Antioqueños were still rumored to be Jews, Arango Mejía chanted the litany of authors who had debunked this linkage, reviewed their arguments, and ruefully commented:

> And given this, and that, and the rest, the only sure thing is that they will continue to call us Jews, convicts sentenced by the Inquisition, *mestizos, mulatos*, and every other kind of so-and-so, and continue to pester us today as they have in the past [Arango Mejía, 1942b: 304].

He then continued:

> That is their problem. Let us, with pride and confidence, with fear of nothing and hating no one, continue carrying wherever the prolific seed of "this people and this race." We will celebrate its fourth century with almost three million descendants of those four or five hundred sons of Spain who, good or bad, noble or commoner, but in all cases free, independent, hard-headed, and hardworking, passed to these mountains [Aragno Mejía, 1942b: 304].

This upbeat note typifies Antioqueño writings on "La Raza." Eclectically blending regional history, literature, geography, anthropology, folk legend, sociology, economics, and psychology, proponents of "La Raza" argue that Antioqueños form a special race, a distinct culture, and a probably superior people within Colombia. Whether deadly serious or tongue-in-cheek, variations of this "ethnological heresy" (Parsons, 1968: 3) reflect an Antioqueño self-image enduring even today (Franco, 1941-1943: 183-196; Posada, 1965: 5-8).

The Basque Hypothesis

Although "alien" comparisons of Antioqueños with Swiss, Yankees, or Protestants persist, the only ethnic interpretation given any serious consideration today links paisa enterprise to a

Basque heritage.[9] A comparison of the historic and contemporary image of the Antioqueño and the Basque uncovers some intriguing similarities. Like the Basques, Antioqueños manage to be aggressively progressive and sternly conservative at the same time. Both have militantly propounded regional identities and long-term traditions of entrepreneurial behavior (Payne, 1975: 27). In the Spanish colonies the economic success of Basque migrants aroused the enmity of their competitors and led, in one extreme case, to civil war. In the late sixteenth and throughout the seventeenth centuries the silver boom town of Potosí reverberated with verbal and physical attacks against a Basque clique which controlled the mines, commerce, and government. Basques were even equated with Jews:

> Many of the anti-Basque statements that appear in the debates over the incidents at Potosí are reminiscent of the characterizations of Jews by anti-Semites. The analogy is not far-fetched. In one denunciation an effort was made to demonstrate that the Basques were, in fact, disguised Jews, descendents of a lost tribe of Israel [Douglas and Bilbao, 1975: 81-83].

Given these similarities, as well as the fact that a number of typical Antioqueño family surnames are Basque, the linkage of paisa enterprise and Basque ancestry was an obvious temptation. Although late nineteenth century Antioqueños had commented on the congruities between paisa and Basque culture, and Tulio Ospina had injected Basques into his New Breed thesis, contemporary social scientists such as Everett Hagen (1962: 372) and Leonard Kasdan (1971: 225-239) added some embellishments of their own.

Researching in Antioquia in the late 1950s, Everett Hagen was struck by the number of Antioqueño surnames of Basque origin. To test the relationship between Basque ancestry and entrepreneurship, Hagen attempted to compare the number of Antioqueños with Basque names who were entrepreneurs to those with non-Basque names who were entrepreneurs as well. His base was the 1957 Medellín telephone directory, which showed that 15% of the city's population was Basque. Hagen then drew up a detailed list of leading Medellín industrialists in 1957 and found that 20 to 25% of these persons were Basque. Hagen cautioned that these percentages were suggestive rather than definitive: Medellín's phone book might not be representative of the city's total population, nor did the percentage of successful Antioqueños of Basque origin account for the substantial percentage of non-Basque paisas who were also entrepreneurs. Still, Hagen argued that his statistics were impressive, for they demonstrated that Antioqueños of Basque ancestry were nearly twice as numerous among the entepreneurial class than they were in the population as a whole (Hagen, 1962: 380-383).

Hagen's conclusion was conceptually important to students of developmental theory who were examining possible relationships between the personality of individual entrepreneurs and the personalities of the social groups to which they belong. In a follow-up article, Leonard Kasdan (1971: 228) explored these potential links between Antioqueño entrepreneurship and Basque heritage.

Kasdan first challenged Hagen's assertion that Basque culture was necessarily compatible with an entrepreneurial life style:

> The rugged, hard working, culturally separate nature of these mountain people does not constitute a set of characteristics which make for entrepreneurial skills. Quite the contrary these characteristics are conservative traits which are hard to associate with risk-taking and change. . . . The Basques, in fact, are a classic example of a peasant group which has used every means to resist change, including force [Kasdan, 1971: 228].

Although unwilling to assign any particular entrepreneurial psychology to Basques as a group, Kasdan did make a key exception. In an analysis of Basque landholding and inheritance practices, he suggested that nonheirs in that society were forced to develop a flexibility that might have promoted entrepreneurship. Since Basque plots or *caserios* were small, division among heirs was impossible. Basques therefore developed institutionalized means to relieve their population of disinherited males through cash payments in lieu of land, through encouragement of the pursuit of religious, artisan, or naval careers, or, pertinent for Antioquia, through the promotion of emigration (Kasdan, 1971: 230-232).

These disinherited Basques, Kasdan asserted, formed a particular subgroup within their society, one in which an entrepreneurial personality might well have developed: "Non-heirs are forced into situations which give status only for achievement on the basis of individual initiative" (Kasdan, 1971: 233). Thus, although Kasdan did take exception to Hagen's broad generalization that Basque personality characteristics were generally contributory to the formation of an entrepreneurial personality, he tentatively assigned such a potential role to those Basque subgroups who migrated to Antioquia. In his conclusion, Kasdan called for further genealogical study to determine if those Basques who settled Antioquia were "highly biased in the direction of entrepreneurial personality types (Kasdan, 1971: 233).

Hagen's use of Medellín's telephone directory and Kasdan's follow-up unleashed a veritable Basque-o-mania among scholars of Antioquia in particular and of economic development in general. Whether they agreed with them or not, authors James Payne (1968: 97), Luis H. Fajardo (1966: 68-69), Albert Hirschman (1968: 186), and Peter Kilby (1971: 21) felt compelled to mention this linkage. This also figured in the Stanley Brandes (1973: 299-300), William Douglas (1973: 300-302), Leonard Kasdan (and Brandes, 1973: 304-306) debate on Basque migrant entrepreneurs.

A reexamination of Hagen's original proposition, starting with his use of the 1957 phone book, suggests that Bogotanos were not the only perpetuators of ethnic myths concerning the Antioqueño! A first impression might be that Medellín's 1957 telephone directory was not very large, for although the first telephones were installed in 1891 and services had doubled every decade since 1900, by the late 1950s these were only 20 telephones, whether for business or for pleasure, for every 100 inhabitants (Livardo Ospina, 1966: 362; Instituto Georgráfico "Agustín Codazzi," 1969: 50).[9] As the pollsters in the U.S. presidential election of 1936 (Roosevelt vs. Landon) learned to their chagrin, telephones must be widely and fairly evenly distributed among differing income groups before a representative sample can be obtained (Babbie, 1973: 74-75). It is highly probable, with Medellín's telephone service in an early stage, that the 1957 telephone book was selectively biased toward the more affluent Medellinenses.

If this is so, it could be argued that Basques might form an even higher percentage of entrepreneurial Medellinenses than Hagen's survey has indicated. If Antioqueños with Basque names were better businessmen, and therefore more affluent, they would be more likely to have telephones in 1957 than Antioqueños with other Spanish surnames. Therefore, there would be a higher proportion of Basque names in the phone book than actual Basques in Medellín's population. Hagen's estimate of 15% Basques as a base figure, which is taken from the telephone book, would overrepresent their real presence. If Basques actually composed a smaller percentage of the population, for example 5%, when this figure is compared to the percentage of Basques who are prominent industrialists (20-25%), Hagen's case would be statistically even more impressive.

This is a hypothetical argument, for Hagen has not yet proved that Antioqueños with Basque surnames were more entrepreneurial than Antioqueños with non-Basque names. For example, what if the large majority of Antioqueños with Basque surnames were not entrepreneurs, did not have the financial resources to buy telephones, and were therefore underrepresented in Hagen's base figure of 15%? If this were so, and Basques formed perhaps 40% of the actual Medellín population, then they would be conspicuous underachievers as entrepreneurs. On the face of his own evidence, Hagen can neither prove nor disprove his Basque thesis, for his telephone directory source is too problematical to yield a reliable baseline.

What then if Leonard Kasdan's assertion that those Basques who did migrate to Antioquia might have had, at least from a psychological viewpoint, a marked entrepreneurial potential? First of all, those "institutional mechanisms" that Kasdan describes were operational not only in the Basque country, but throughout Spain. This is especially true of the emigration escape valve. New World settlers were often known as *segund-*

ones, that is, second sons unable to inherit familial holdings. There is no reason to assume on these grounds alone that Basque migrants were any more entrepreneurial than any other disinherited Spaniards.

Some data do exist to support Kasdan's thesis. In his massive study of Spanish migration to the Americas, Peter Boyd-Bowman (1973: 24) has found that from 1520 to 1539 Basques sent only 4.5% of total colonists but an impressive 14% of migrating merchants. In the next period (1540-1559), Basque merchants are represented proportionally to Basque colonists (4.2% merchants, 4.4% colonists); while from 1560 to 1579, Basque merchants form a slightly higher percentage than Basque colonists (5.2% merchants, 2.9% colonists). Table 1 compares these percentages with with similar data from Andalusia and Old Castile. These figures suggest that some Spanish regions, for example Old Castile, did not send a representative percentage of merchants to the Americas, while other regions, such as Andalusia, equaled or surpassed the Basques in entrepreneurial potential. Unfortunately Boyd-Bowman's study does not extend to the seventeenth and eighteenth centuries, when Antioquia received the bulk of its emigration.

My own admittedly rough analysis of the Spanish surnames of eighteenth-century Medellinenses suggests that *vecinos* with Basque names were no more entrepreneurial than those from other regions of Spain. Two percentages were needed in this study: an estimate of the percentage of Antioqueños in Medellín who were of Basque origin, and the percentage of those who were also entrepreneurs. To determine the first percentage, a tabluation was made of the dates of arrival and Spanish provinces of origin of all Antioqueño family names appearing in Gabriel Arango Mejía's *Genealogías de Antioquia y de Caldas.* By 1800 the period of migration into colonial Antioquia was almost at an end, for 96% of all Antioqueño families listed in the genealogy had arrived. On the basis of this count from Arango Mejía, 22% of this migration was Basque (Twinam, 1973: 184-207).

Hagen's twentieth century entrepreneurs, the Medellín industrialists, were then compared with their eighteenth century counterparts, Medellín's miners and merchants. These latter

TABLE 1

A Comparison of Basque, Andalusian, and Old Castilian Emigration to the New World, 1520-1579

Years covered	A. Basque		B. Old Castile		C. Andalusia[a]	
	Basques as % Total migrants to New World	% Basque merchants of Total merchant Migration to New World	Old Castilian as % Total Migrants to New World	% Old Castilian Merchants of Total Merchant Migration to New World	Andalusians as % Total Migrants to New World	% Andalusian Merchants of Total Merchant Migration to New World
1520–1539	4.5	14.0	17.6	14.0	32.0	49.7
1540–1559	4.4	4.2	15.4	9.9	36.1	67.4
1560–1579	2.9	5.2	11.3	10.2	37.2	60.5

SOURCE: Peter Boyd-Bowman, *Patterns of Spanish Emigration to the New World (1493-1580)*, Special Studies 34, Council on International Studies, State University of New York at Buffalo (Buffalo, 1973), pp. 17, 24, 25, 44, 47, 48, 72, 74, 76, 77.

a. There may be some bias in the Andalusian data as Seville was the departure point for emigration to the New World. Thus colonists may have given Andalusia as their native province even though they may have been born in another region. Boyd-Bowman analyzes this problem (pp. 22-23) and concludes that approximately 70% of Seville's emigrants were *vecinos* of that city. It is impossible to determine how this might alter the percentages of Andalusian emigrants and merchants.

occupations were the principal economic activities in eighteenth century Medellín: occupations that called for certain amounts of risk-taking, initiative, and manipulation of capital. A first step involved a compilation of the most complete list possible of all miners and merchants in Medellín from 1780 to 1800. These names included small as well as large-scale miners and merchants (Twinam, 1976: 206-238). To narrow the sample to represent an economic elite, *cabildo*, or city council membership was added as a further determinant of status, for in Medellín, as in other eighteenth century Spanish colonies, the economic and political elites were complementary (Twinam, 1979: 444-475; Wibel, 1975: 195; Brading, 1971: 303-328).

As Table 2 demonstrates, of those remaining Medellinenses who were cabildo members as well as miners and merchants, 23.7% were of Basque origin. Since according to Arango Mejía, Basques accounted for 22% of Antioqueño migration, Basque origin does not appear as a significant criterion of entrepreneurship. Nor, as these figures indicate, does there appear to be any correlation between province of origin and entrepreneurial ability, as migrants from Asturias, Extremadura, Andalusia, and Castilla are represented similarly in the entrepreneurial elite and in the emigrant population as a whole. In eighteenth century Antioquia, Basques were no more entrepreneurial than Spaniards from other provinces. Unlike Basque emigrants to other regions of the Americas such as Mexico and Rio de la Plata, Antioquia's *vascos* retained neither language nor distinctive customs, nor did they form ethnic organizations which promoted a self-conscious apartness (Douglas and Bilbao, 1975: 94-97; 161-165). Interpreters of Antioqueño entrepreneurship cannot look to the Basques, for like the Jews, the New Breed, or La Raza, they are as much an ethnic myth as an ethnic reality.

Conclusion

This examination of ethnic images concludes with some closing comments on the role of myth and countermyth in the evolution

TABLE 2

A Comparison of the Province of Origin of Antioquia's Family Founders and the Province of Origin of Medellín's elite, 1780-1800[1]

1. Province of Origin of Family Name	2. Number of Antioqueño Family Names[2]	3. Percent Antioqueño Family Names	4. Number of Medellinenses in Elite 1780-1800	5. Percent in Elite 1780-1800	6. Difference Column 3 and 5
Asturias	22	10.3	16	21.1	+ 10.8
Extremadura	15	7.0	7	9.2	+ 2.2
Basque	46	21.6	18	23.7	+ 2.1
Anadulusia	45	21.1	15	19.7	- 1.4
Castile	59	27.7	12	15.8	- 11.9
Others	26	12.2	8	10.5	- 1.7
Total	213	99.9	76	100.0	

SOURCE: The following runs of information provide this data base: for family names: Arango Mejía (1942a: 2 vols.); for miners, Antioquia's smelting house records 1780-1800 (for complete archival reference see Twinam, 1976: 29); for merchants, Antioquia's commercial registers 1780-1800 (for complete archival reference see Twinam, 1976: 92-93); for Medellín's municipal officers 1780-1800, the cabildo records (for complete archival reference see Twinam, 1976: 221).

1. An earlier version of this table with explanation appears in Twinam (1973: 187-189).
2. Arango Mejía's genealogy (1942a) gives the province of origin of 213 of the 296 families listed.

of an Antioqueño identity and with a comparison of some other Latin American cases.

The Antioqueños, it appears, owe a particular debt to their detractors, for the evolution of a paisa self-image responded as much to attacks from without as to their own business accomplishments. While nineteenth century Antioqueños had single-mindedly and unselfconsciously invested and profited in their traditional manner, they formulated no conscious ideology to legitimize these actions. Those bench marks in the evolution of an Antioqueño entrepreneurial identity—the first articles in 1875, the 1894-1915 cycle of logical historical rebuttal, and the New Breed hypothesis, the substantive archival researches of the 1920s and 1930s and the idea of "La Raza"—developed as responses to the stimulus of the Jewish charge. In the process of denial, Antioqueños learned more than that they lacked any Jewish heritage, for this tracing of their roots gave birth to an ongoing mythology which continues to promote a positive, aggressive regional self-image. This is the link between earlier self-images of Antioqueños as the "New Breed" or "La Raza" and the contemporary slogan "For Colombia, We the Antioqueños can do more."

Although it was not Jewish or Basque ancestry, but business successes than marked Antioqueños as "alien," the timing of these ethnic myths emphasizes that generations of entrepreneurial behavior preceded the locally inspired industrialization of Medellín. While the Antioqueño case is rare, it is not unique within Latin America. Although the historic mixes of human and natural resources which led to the economic development of São Paulo, Brazil and Monterrey, Mexico differ as much from each other as from the mix in Medellín, both Paulistas and Regiomontanos share with Antioqueños histories of long-term entrepreneurial behavior, indigenous industrialization, and ethnic myth. Elites in São Paulo and in Monterrey had to contend, for example, with charges that their financial success derived from Jewish ancestry (Lipset, 1967: 28). Like the Antioqueños, they countered ethnic myth with consciously crafted, aggressively positive regional identities. The Paulistas, for example, proudly harken back to their *bandeirante* tradition as they see the industrialists of this century as worthy followers of those adventurous seekers of slaves and gold who opened up the interior of seventeenth and eighteenth century Brazil. The Regiomontanos take some glory in a nineteenth century stereotype that portrays them as "Shylocks," as they recognize that the careful hoarding of capital in the last century made possible the early industrialization of Monterrey (Twinam, 1976: 6-9). In these cases, as in the case of Antioquia, myth has been succeeded by countermyth to buttress and sustain continuing entrepreneurial enterprise.

NOTES

1. Lipset (1967: 27-28) comments on the Antioqueño "alien" image and Fajardo (1966) on an Antioqueño "Protestant Ethic." The image of Antioqueño as deviant is particularly significant given that, with the exception of their economic activities, Antioqueños are generally conceded to be among the most conservative of Colombians in religious observances, politics (until quite recently), and in maintenance of traditional family life (Safford, 1974: 70-111; Fajardo, 1966: 54-55, 60-62).

2. West (1952) and Restrepo (1952) are standard on Antioquia's mining history.

3. Data from the 1945 industrial census comes from Ospina Vásquez (1955: cuadro 5). Demographic data from the closest year (1951) shows Antioquia's population to be 1,570,197 compared to Colombia's 11,548,172 (Instituto Georgráfico "Agustín Codazzi," 1969: 48; López Toro, 1968: 11).

4. Such a link between colonization and presumed Jewish origin was not unique to Antioquia. Wibel (1975: 377) notes that Arequipeño migration in the 1830s led at least one observer to comment: "You seem like Jews, dispersed to every settlement." In this Peruvian case, the Arquipeños did not distinguish themselves as businessmen and the speculation as to a possible Jewish heritage did not continue.

5. This episode additionally introduces what will later become a main theme in the sometimes serious, sometimes lighthearted, debate between Bogotá and Medellín intellectuals as to their particular regional virtues. The birthplace of the participating authors would determine whether the Bogotano figured as "cultured" or as "ineffectual," the Antioqueño as "enterprising" or as "stingy." See Betancur (1942: 343-377).

6. According to McGrady (1972: 55), Isaacs made an earlier, indirect reference to the Jewish origin of Antioqueños in chapter 9 of *María* (published 1867), which describes the "biblical" appearance of the Antioqueño, José (Isaacs, 1938: 16-17). McGrady (1972: 21-22, 29, 31, 55) traces Isaacs's political activities in Antioquia as well as his request, fulfilled in 1904, that he be buried in that department among those he erroneously believed to be of his "race."

7. Otero D'Costa (1924: 261) calculated that of the 767 sentenced by the Cartagena inquisition, 68 were Jews. None had a typical Antioqueño surname.

8. The Swiss reference is in García Ortiz (1938: 1). Parsons (1968: 1) mentions the Yankee image, and Fajardo (1966) the Protestant one.

9. Livardo Ospina (1966: 362) notes that Medellín had 35,052 telephones in 1957. Medellín's urban population in 1964 (closest census year) was 717,865 (Instituto Geográfico "Agustín Codazzi" 1970: 50).

REFERENCES

ARANGO, MEJÍA, G. (1942a) Genealogías de Antioquia y de Caldas. Medellín: Imprenta Departamental.

——— (1942b) "Algo sobre origenes de los Antioqueños." Repertórico Histórico (Medellín) 15 (January): 297-304.

——— (1909) "Origen de la raza Antioqueña." Boletín de Historia y Antigüedades (Bogotá) 5 (January): 656-658.

BABBIE, E. (1973) Survey Research Methods. Belmont, CA: Wadsworth.

BETANCUR, C. (1942) "Autenticidad y simulación, las virtudes y los vicios, Antioquia y Bogotá." Universidad de Antioquia (Medellín) 13: 343-377.

BOYD-BOWMAN, P. (1973) Patterns of Spanish Emigration to the New World (1493-1580). Special Studies 34. Buffalo: Council on International Studies, State University of New York at Buffalo.

BRADING, D. A. (1971) Miners and Merchants in Bourbon Mexico 1763-1810. Cambridge, England: Cambridge Univ. Press.

BRANDES, S. (1973) "On Basque migration." Amer. Anthropologist 75: 299-300.

BREW, R. (1973) "The economic development of Antioquia from 1750 to 1920." Ph.D. dissertation, Oxford University.

CASTRO, A. (1954) The Structure of Spanish History. Princeton, NJ: Princeton Univ. Press.

CHRISTIE, K. (1978) "Antioqueño colonization in western Colombia: a reappraisal." Hispanic Amer. Historical Rev. 58 (May): 260-83.

DOUGLAS, W. A. (1973) "Reply to Brandes." Amer. Anthropologist 73: 300-302.

——— and J. BILBAO (1975) Amerikanuak: Basques in the New World. Reno: Univ. of Nevada Press.

FAJARDO, L. H. (1966) The Protestant Ethic of the Antioqueños? Social Structure and Personality. Cali: Universidad del Valle.

FRANCO, H. (1941-1943) "Sinopsis de Antioquia." Universidad de Antioquia (Medellín) 14: 183-196.

GARCIA ORTIZ, L. (1938) "En la Antioquia del Ataño." Boletín de Historia y Antigüedades (Bogotá) 23 (January): 1-19.

HAGEN, E. (1962) On the Theory of Social Change: How Economic Growth Begins. Homewood, IL: Irwin.

HIRSCHMAN, A. (1968) The Strategy of Economic Development. New Haven: Yale Univ. Press.

Instituto Geográfico "Agustín Codazzi" (1970) Atlas Básico de Colombia. Bogotá: Editorial Andes.

——— (1969) Monografía del Departamento de Antioquia. Bogotá: Editorial Bedout.

ISAACS, J. (1938) María, Novela Americana, seguida de las Poesías Completas, Buenos Aires: Editorial Sopena.

KASDAN, L. (1971) "Family structure, migration and the entrepreneur," pp. 225-239 in P. Kilby (ed.) Entrepreneurship and Economic Development. New York: Free Press.

——— and S. BRANDES (1973) "Basque migration again." Amer. Anthropologist 75: 303-306.

KILBY, P. (1971) "Hunting the heffalump," pp. 1-40 in P. Kilby (ed.) Entrepreneurship and Economic Development. New York: Free Press.

LIEBMAN, S. B. (1970) The Jews in New Spain, Faith, Flame, and the Inquisition. Coral Gables: Univ. of Miami Press.

LIPSET, S. M. (1967) "Values, education, and entrepreneurship," pp. 3-60 in S. M. Lipset and A. Solari (eds.) Elites in Latin America. New York: Oxford Univ. Press.

LIVARDO OSPINA, E. (1966) Una Vida, una Lucha, una Victoria, Monografía Histórica de las Empresas y Servicios Públicos de Antioquia. Medellín: Editorial Colina.

LOPEZ TORO, A. (1968) Análsis Demográfico de los Censos Colombianos: 1951 y 1964. Bogotá: Italgraf.

MARCUS, J. R. (1970) The Colonial America Jew 1492-1776. Detroit: Wayne State Univ. Press.

McGRADY, D. (1972) Jorge Isaacs. New York: Twayne.

McGREEVEY, W. P. (1971) An Economic History of Colombia: 1856-1930. Cambridge, England: Cambridge Univ. Press.

OSPINA, T. (1915) "Conferencia dictada por Don Tulio Ospina, presidente de la Academia de Historia Antioqueño, en la sesión celebrada en Medellín por las academias de historia, jurisprudencia, y medicina, para conmemorar el contenário de la independencia de Antioquia." Boletín de Historia y Antigüedades (Bogotá) 9 (April): 905-918.

OSPINA RODRIGUEZ, M. (1905) "Los Israelitas y los Antioqueños." Boletín de Historia y Antigüedades (Bogotá) 3 (December): 511-512.

OSPINA VASQUEZ, L. (1955) Industria y Protección en Colombia 1810-1930. Medellín: Editorial Santa Fe.

OTERO D'COSTA, E. (1924) "El Semitismo Antioqueño." Archivo Historial (Manizales) 34 (October): 252-262.

PARSONS, J. (1968) Antioqueño Colonization in Western Colombia. Berkeley: Univ. of California Press.

PAYNE, J. (1968) Patterns of Conflict in Colombia. New Haven: Yale Univ. Press.

PAYNE, S. G. (1975) Basque Nationalism. Reno: Univ. of Nevada Press.

POSADA, A. (1965) "Rasgos del pueblo Antioqueño." Vínculo Shell (Bogotá) 17: 5-8.

RESTREPO, A. J. (1924) "Quien es el Felipe de Gutiérrez Gonzales?" Archivo Historial 34 (October): 262-279.

RESTREPO, V. (1952) Estudio sobre las Minas de Oro y Plata de Colombia. Bogotá: Archivo de la Economía Nacional. Vol. 7.

RIVAS, R. (1933) La Familia Santamaría. Bogotá.

——— (1925) "El mensajero de la victoria." Repertórico Histórico (Medellín) 57 (July): 137-159.

ROBLEDO, E. (1922) "El Semistismo Antioqueño." Colombia, Revista Semanal (Medellín) (July 22): 565-570.

SAFFORD, F. (1974) "Bases of political alignment in early republican Spanish America," pp. 70-111 in R. Graham and P. Smith (eds.) New Approaches to Latin American History. Austin: Univ. of Texas Press.

——— (1965a) "Foreign and national enterprise in nineteenth-century Colombia." Business History Rev. 39: 503-526.

——— (1965b) "Commerce and enterprise in central Colombia, 1821-1870." Ph.D. dissertation, Columbia University.

TWINAM, A. (1979) "Enterprise and elites in eighteenth-century Medellín." Hispanic Amer. Historical Rev. 57 (August): 444-479.

——— (1976) "Miners, merchants, and farmers: the roots of entrepreneurship in Antioquia, 1763-1810." Ph.D. dissertation, Yale University.

——— (1973) Antioqueño entrepreneurship: the myth and the reality," pp. 184-207 in Proceedings from S.U.L.A. Latin American Studies Conference. Vol 2. Buffalo: Council on International Studies, State University of New York at Buffalo.

WEST, R. C. (1952) Colonial Placer Mining in Colombia. Baton Rouge: Louisiana State Univ. Press.

WIBEL, J. F. (1975) "The evolution of a regional empire and Peruvian nation: Arequipa: 1780-1845." Ph.D. dissertation, Stanford University.

ZULETA, E. (1929) Papeles Viejos y Nuevos. Caracas: Vargas.

Ann Twinam, Assistant Professor of History at the University of Cincinnati and author of several articles on Antioquia, is presently a Fulbright Research Fellow in Medellín, Colombia, where she is continuing her research on Antioqueño economic development during independence and the early republic.

REVIEW ESSAY

GERMAN-LATIN AMERICAN RELATIONS
The First Half of the Twentieth Century

Baecker, T. DIE DEUTSCHE MEXIKOPOLITIK 1913-1914. Berlin: Coloquium Verlag, 1971.

Brunn, G. DEUTSCHLAND UND BRASILIEN (1889-1914). Cologne: Boehlau Verlag, 1971.

Ebel, A. DAS DRITTE REICH UND ARGENTINIEN. Cologne: Boehlau Verlag, 1971.

Schaefer, J. DEUTSCHE MILITAERHILFE AN SUEDAMERIKA. Dusseldorf: Bertelsmann Universitaetsverlag, 1974.

Volland, K. DAS DRITTE REICH UND MEXIKO. Frankfurt: Peter Lang; Bern: Herbert Lang, 1976.

Throughout the twentieth century, the relations of Germany with Latin America have been dominated by economic considerations. This is true of exports, such as weapons with their concomitant military training programs, and the importation of oil and foods essential to the survival of Germany's industrial society. Matters of ideology and power politics also emerged from time to time. Clashes over economic interests as well as political and social convictions or fears led to occasional rivalries between Germany on the one hand, and France or the United States on the other. These conflicts occurred notably in Argentina and Brazil, which were of key importance in German-Latin American exchanges, and in Mexico and Chile, both of which maintained somewhat less important connections with Germany.

Shortly before the outbreak of World War I, Germany was Latin America's third most important trade partner after Great Britain and

Journal of Interamerican Studies and World Affairs, Vol. 22 No. 1, February 1980 109-117

the United States. The greater part of German overseas investments flowed into the Latin American region. Impressive numbers of relatively unassimilated German immigrants resided in the temperate zones of South America. Brunn (1971: ix-xi) suggests the perspective of an "informal" German industrial and commercial imperialism that exploited such German institutions in Latin America as churches, chambers of commerce, schools, religious synods, investments—especially in railroad construction, German business management, telegraph and maritime services, as well as credit facilities. On the other hand, Ebel (1971: 2) states that the German Second Empire tended to ignore Latin America, with the possible exception of Mexico.

Actually, it was Brazil that reflected the most comprehensive variety of German-Latin American connections up to 1918, if not beyond. One-third of Germany's South American trade involved this nation, which provided Germany with unique tropical products. Sizable German investments also supported Brazilian commercial and plantation enterprise. The likely consumer preferences of approximately 300,000 German-speaking inhabitants of southern Brazil seemed to suggest an unusually great potential for the development of ever more voluminous German exports. But the splintering of German investments in Brazil and their absence in such key projects as railroad building or state-sponsored economic development enterprises suggested long-range limitations upon German economic activities. So did other foreign competition, especially that of the United States. These conditions evoked new attitudes on the part of the German government during the early years of the twentieth century (Brunn, 1971: 67).

The German chancellor, for instance, reacted sharply against the ridiculing of Brazilian national ambitions and the hostile criticism of American foreign policy toward Brazil by his minister in Rio de Janeiro. The diplomat was lectured bluntly that the more or less apt caricature of foreign environments was worthless. German representatives were to accomplish constructive work beyond the managing of routine business. They should become intimately acquainted with Brazilian conditions by traveling into the interior of the country and by cultivating personal relationships with local officials. German standards of behavior should be respected, but distinctive native customs and attitudes were to be judged with an open mind and an alertness toward furthering German economic and political interests. Specifically, exports were to be encouraged not by forcing German tastes upon Brazilian customers but by allowing oneself to be guided by Brazilian preferences. It is noteworthy that this respect for Brazil in leading German political circles as well as among outstanding industrial, shipping, and commercial entrepreneurs such as Krupp and Ballin, was reciprocated by the Brazilian elite from the presidents on down.

Yet the French were jealous because German exports were beginning to surpass their own, despite the fact that French investments remained sizable. In line with analogous contemporary developments in Argentina, the French were being shouldered out by the Germans in arms sales. Still, the French could console themelves by noting that they had helped to frustrate a German military training program in Brazil, as the Americans had in Mexico, and also by observing that they had surpassed the Germans in efforts to sell weapons to Mexico and Peru, and by recognizing the fact that their other great competitors in Brazil, the British, were being outdistanced not only by the Americans but by the Germans as well.

Undeniably, however, Germany was an excellent customer in the purchase of such important Brazilian staples as coffee, hides, tobacco, and cacao. In the period before World War I, besides weapons, the Germans in return delivered iron, steel, machines, electric goods, sophisticated machine products, leather, cement, paper, stockings, and dyes, to mention the more important products. At least some of these would also find a ready market in other major Latin American nations.

As in the development of other important Latin American markets, the Germans only occasionally succeeded in selling to Brazil by relying upon political influence or the preferences of German immigrants. Instead, they prevailed because of their growing industrial efficiency, well-trained business representatives, and price and credit competitiveness, as well as a noteworthy ability to cater to the unique desires of various customers (Brunn, 1971: 241-242). More precisely, well-trained German business representatives with fluent Portuguese cultivated personal contacts with customers on an extensive basis, a policy of importance not only in Brazil but also in Latin America as a whole. Brazilian clients were not restricted to participation only through letters or telephone exchanges but also obtained strictly personal service that ranged from energetic helpfulness while arranging purchases to eager provision of customer conveniences like German credit facilities and fast dependable German transportation.

Official German support of exports to Latin America was furnished primarily to large industrial enterprises, notably the firm of Krupp for arms sales, while the efforts of other German weapons firms were slighted by the government. In view of their tensions with neighboring states or the menace of domestic insurrection, two rival nations, Chile and Argentina, were in the forefront of Latin American governments being supplied with Krupp cannons even before 1900. As a matter of fact, Krupp dominated the entire Latin American market, but after 1900 was severely challenged by other German and French competition. In the meantime, in Argentina as well as in Chile, a relatively small number of influential German military advisors had emerged to play a significant role in safeguarding the interests of the German armaments industry, especially those of Krupp.

Events surrounding competition between Krupp and the giant French weapons firm of Schneider Creusot for cannon sales to Argentina during the first decade of the twentieth century are instructive as to the nature and ramifications of the arms trade. Since Schneider had recently succeeded in selling its cannons to Mexico, Peru, and Bolivia, Krupp was determined not to lose the Argentine market, still one of the best in all of Latin America. Involved were not only concrete immediate losses but also vague fears, held by both Krupp and German military advisors in Argentina, that Schneider's success would set off a chain reaction in all of Latin America that would benefit not only French weapon sales but also French military training systems.

The German minister in Buenos Aires was a friend of the Krupp family and one of the wealthiest German diplomats. He was popular among Argentine official circles and created much goodwill in high Argentine society with lavish banquets and parties. The Argentine foreign ministry in particular provided the German diplomat with much useful information. Furthermore, Krupp's permanent representative in Argentina, a friend of Friedrich Krupp, was a prominent banker who was respected by Argentina's top political leadership. His services, however, were supplemented by an intriguing, shadowy Krupp special representative, a German artillery officer who had recently played a prominent part in a ruthlessly successful sales competition with Schneider Creusot in Brazil. Soon Krupp and its sympathizers were challenged not only by a similarly arrayed opposing coalition, but also by all of those who wanted to destroy the increasingly effective and influential German military training system in Argentina. Due to motives of both idealistic integrity and political jealousy, Krupp's permanent representative emerged through press statements and political maneuvering as such an embarrassingly bitter opponent of extensive Argentine arms expenditures that Krupp and its German and

Argentinian allies forced him to sever his long-standing connections with the arms firm. In the meantime, the French government unsuccessfully pressured French financiers to deprive Argentina of important French credit facilities if Schneider Creusot were frustrated in its sales efforts. Eventually, the Krupp sympathizers arranged a well publicized demonstration in behalf of the German military training program (Schaefer, 1974: 139-151).

These events helped pave the way not only for a mayor Krupp cannon sale to Argentina, which was of questionable competitive merit, but also for other weapon and military equipment sales to Chile as well. Overall, they suggested what was at stake in the Latin American arms trade. By the turn of the twentieth century, Latin American states had become ever more imbued with a sense of nationalistic mission, the consequences of which were military reorganizations and the purchases of modern foreign military equipment. These endeavors, in turn, encouraged the meddling by rival foreign industrial interests in the internal affairs of Latin American nations by such ruthless means as bribery and planted press articles. This trend obviously did not advance the cause of Latin American independence. Worse, highly industrialized countries, including Germany, encouraged dangerous and oppressively expensive arms races by dangling the news of a recent arms purchase by one Latin American state before the leadership of neighboring nations and by providing credit facilities, a service which constituted an additional financial burden upon Latin Americans (Schaefer, 1974: 29). Yet, intriguingly, as noted, an Argentine representative of a German arms firm eventually combated this type of enterprise with great vehemence. And, against the desire of their governments, profit-hungry French financiers were capable of providing loans that aided Argentina in the purchase of German weapons.

Ebel (1971: xiii) concentrates upon the overall significance of German-Argentine economic relations. He notes that, due to the impact of World War I, virtually no further German arms deliveries were arranged until just prior to the outbreak of World War II. German military advisers became somewhat less active and influential, although the professional bonds between the officer corps of the two nations remained strong, and Germany and Argentina enjoyed a fundamental and traditional friendship. This was due first of all to the fact that Argentina was Germany's most important trading partner in Latin America. Argentine staples, such as beef, were exchanged for German industrial products. Second, Argentina preserved her neutrality during

World War I in a rather typical defiance of American entreaties, a foreign policy that she repeated during World War II until at least 1944. Even during the days of Hitler, Argentina thus remained reluctant to endanger her "good" relations with Europe, unconvinced that the Western Hemisphere was seriously menaced by powerful and aggressive totalitarian powers (Ebel, 1971: 430). But as Ebel suggests, the matter of supposedly endemic Argentine goodwill toward all of Europe deserves some special scrutiny, especially in regard to tense Anglo-Argentinian relations. The extent to which Argentine public opinion was unreceptive to totalitarian indoctrination is presented most compellingly by Ebel. As a matter of fact, the public became alarmed over the much-heralded machinations of the fascist Integralistas in Brazil, Argentina's traditional rival for regional hegemony. Within Argentina, energetic measures were taken until 1939 against the plots of a relatively small group of Nazi sympathizers. The political influence of Nazi Germany upon Argentine official policy remained minimal until the outbreak of World War II. Even basic German bilateral or barter trade policies, countering American policies of freer trade, were not primarily aimed at Argentina, or at Latin American in general.

A mixture of questions of ideology, international intercourse, and trade emerged in the relationship between Germany and Mexico, especially after the outbreak of the Mexican Revolution. Before this epochal event, German trade, banking, and shipping activities were important to both nations, as were some German investments. However, the Germans typically failed to control to any noteworthy degree such key economic sectors as the oil or railroad industries. The French, furthermore, had bested them in efforts to arrange large-scale cannon scales. And the United States had blocked a scheme to train the Mexican army along German lines. Baecker, a history-oriented political scientist, discussed German perspectives of and reactions to the Mexican revolution, suggesting comparisons with Volland's survey of Mexico's relations with the Nazi regime.

In both instances, for example, the Germans were forced to cope with the United States. This reflected the historic fact that Mexico was caught between various European and American drives for ascendancy in Latin America. Illustrative of the distinct approaches of Germany and the United States was their reaction in 1913-1914 to the regime of General Huerta, a ruthless dictator and usurper who intended to stifle several revolutionary movements that had erupted since 1910. As in South America, Germany concentrated largely upon the advancement and protection of economic interests. Insofar as ideology mattered at all, authoritarianism, discipline, and order were admired, preferably accompanied by the incorporation of military ideals. General Huerta, therefore, aroused some official German sympathy. A majority of the German people, like their government, were also generally hostile to revolutionary or even socialist movements. These predilections contributed to an overestimation of the strength of the Huerta regime, which neatly safeguarded foreign economic interests, and an underestimation of the popularity of Mexican revolutionary causes, including some socialist enthusiasm.

The very different dogmas of a domineering President Wilson, who was inaugurated in 1913, likewise hindered the shaping of a realistic and knowledgeable American policy toward Mexico. He visualized the aspirations of the Mexican people in terms of political democracy and constitutional government. Imbued with moral righteousness and a sense of national mission, which was quite acceptable in his own country, Wilson believed simplistically that his aims could be accomplished by the single act of removing Huerta from power. Thus, by refusing to entertain other considerations, he, too, like the Germans, disdained crucially important revolutionary factions. During the spring of 1914, Wilson intervened militarily after his and America's motivations had already been questioned repeatedly in German official and journalistic circles. Still, the Germans confined themselves to a narrow official policy of protecting their economic interests and the safety of their nationals (Baecker, 1971: 5, 18-51). Toward these ends, they were determined to help end the revolutionary turmoil by supporting, in collaboration with the British and French, the mediation efforts of Argentina, Brazil, and Chile which finally contributed to the downfall of Huerta only weeks before the outbreak of World War I.

For his part, Volland (1976: 19-27) explains why, temporary ideological misunderstandings notwithstanding, Mexico and Germany prided themselves on their excellent understandng until the mid-1930s. There existed between them little mutual fear and much mutual admiration. Unlike the United States and France, Germany never held annexationist designs upon Mexico. Due to a traditional policy of balancing off menacing states, especially the United States, Mexican presidents tended to be pro-German in their politics. However, beyond being a late participant in global imperialism, Germany was in no geographic or other position to challenge the political and economic preeminence of the United States and Great Britain in Mexico. Therefore Germany had to confine itself to a significant complementary trade activity in which, for instance, German machinery, iron goods, dyes, and drugs were exchanged for Mexican oil and other mineral products. Furthermore, it is noteworthy that the Mexicans were quite receptive to German ideas of economic and financial management. Germans and Mexicans also shared a rather lasting fascination with Mexican ethnography and archaeology. Finally, Mexicans admired German science as well as German art and literature.

But Hitler's reliance upon brute force in international affairs alienated Mexicans increasingly. By contrast, Mexico's statesmen typically championed international law and were fond of formulating international doctrines. By the mid-1930s President Cárdenas even showed a great readiness to respond emphatically to great global issues. Still, the Latin American continent did not loom large in Hitler's mind, and he disdained its people because of his racial prejudices.

Nonetheless, a Mexican-German political confrontation arose in 1936 over leftist Mexico's outrage against Germany's pro-fascist military intervention in the Spanish Civil War. Mexico and the Soviet Union became the only countries to support officially the legitimate and anti-fascist Spanish Republican Government. Weapon supplies to Spain were speedily arranged by Mexico from domestic, European, and American quarters. Cárdenas also initiated an international campaign to support the Spanish government materially and morally.

By 1938, however, Mexico's idealism lay in sharp contrast to its far-reaching trade connections with Germany, especially in respect to oil. The most consequential event in Mexican history since the Mexican Revolution occurred in 1938 when Mexico nationalized American, British, and Dutch oil concessions. Soon, an effective international boycott of Mexico oil, encouraged by the expropriated companies, menaced Mexico's national survival. The loss of large oil revenues threatened Mexico's ambitious economic development program, entailed the prospect of mass unemployment, and strongly suggested the growth of large government deficits. These and other possible woes posed the likelihood of great political unrest, if not the overturn of the constitutional government (Volland, 1976: 119). Sizable oil deliveries that were made to Germany to forestall these dangers were useful to the Nazis and their allies not only in the defeat of the Spanish Republicans, but also in large-scale World War II offensives during 1940 (Volland, 1976: 199).

However, early during World War II, Allied pressure and pressure from a still neutral United States further thwarted Mexican oil sales to Germany. In 1941, at last, the United States concluded an oil agreement with Mexico and thus became Mexico's virtually sole oil customer. And late in May 1942 there occurred a tragic, if not fitting, twist of irony when Mexico declared war against Germany after German submarines had sunk Mexican oil tankers. Mexico's most vital contribution to the defeat of Germany in 1945 lay in supplying oil and other minerals to the Allied war effort.

It is tempting to conclude from the reading of these five superb scholarly monographs that the recent evolution of Latin American-German relations reflected economic determinism. History suggests that ideology and a sense of national mission were overcome by the profit motive again and again.

It is even more tempting to pose innumerable questions in the hope that other interested parties might wish to investigate the subject matter further. To address sample inquiries: Did German military influence encourage or strengthen militaristic tyranny in Latin America? Or did various liberal and progressive Latin American leaderships succeed when they invited "apolitical" German military professionals to safeguard their fragile nation states against domestic violence and opportunistic lawlessness or against foreign invasion? To what extent did Latin American-German cultural differences result in an attraction of opposites or in mutual alienation? How successfully did Latin Americans rely upon Germans in efforts to combat the sometimes great pressures that came from the United States, Great Britain, or France?

—*Warren Schiff*

Warren Schiff, Professor of History at the College of the Holy Cross in Worcester, Massachusetts, is primarily concerned with a comparative study of German relations with Argentina and Mexico during the first half of the twentieth century. Among his articles and book reviews, his most recent publication is an essay, "The Influence of the German Armed Forces and War Industry on Argentina, 1880-1914," which appeared in Loveman and Davies's 1978 book, The Politics of Antipolitics: The Military in Latin America.

BOOKS RECEIVED

GENERAL AND REGIONAL LATIN AMERICA

Brotherston, Gordon. THE EMERGENCE OF THE LATIN AMERICAN NOVEL. New York: Cambridge University Press, 1979. Notes, select bibliography, index. viii, 164 pp. Paper.

California State University. BLACK LATIN AMERICAS: A BIBLIOGRAPHY. Latin America Bibliography Series 5. Los Angeles: Latin American Studies Center, California State University, 1977. vii, 73 pp. Paper.

CENDES e ILDIS. FOMENTO INDUSTRIAL EN AMERICA LATINA. Una selección de algunos ensayos presentados en el Seminario Internacional sobre "El Ecuador y las Políticas de Fomento Industrial." Bogotá: ILDIS and Ediciones Internacionales, 1977. 205 pp. Paper.

Gooch, Herbert E., III. THE MILITARY AND POLITICS IN LATIN AMERICA. Latin American Bibliography Series 7. Los Angeles: Latin American Studies Center, California State University, 1977. iv, 76 pp. Paper.

Grow, Michael. SCHOLAR'S GUIDE TO WASHINGTON, D.C. FOR LATIN AMERICAN AND CARIBBEAN STUDIES. Washington, DC: Latin American Program of the Woodrow Wilson International Center for Scholars, Smithsonian Institution Press, 1979. 346 pp. Paper.

Hill, Eduardo and Luciano Tomassini, eds. AMERICA LATINA Y EL NUEVO ORDEN ECONOMICO INTERNACIONAL. Santiago, Chile: Corporación de Promoción Universitaria (CPU), 1979. Indice. xi, 306 pp. Paper.

Inter-American Development Bank. ECONOMIC AND SOCIAL PROGRESS IN LATIN AMERICA. 1978 Report. Washington, DC: IDB, 1979. Statistical appendix. 473 pp. Paper.

Lowenthal, Abraham F. and Albert Fishlow. LATIN AMERICA'S EMERGENCE: TOWARD A U.S. RESPONSE. Foreign Policy Association Headline Series 243. New York: Foreign Policy Association, 1979. 80 pp. Paper.

Meehan, Eugene J. IN PARTNERSHIP WITH PEOPLE: AN ALTERNATIVE DEVELOPMENT STRATEGY. Rosslyn, VA: Inter-American Foundation, 1978. 178 pp. paper.

Ozzlak, Oscar. FORMACION HISTORICA DEL ESTADO EN AMERICA LATINA: ELEMENTOS TEORICO-METOLOGICOS PARA SU ESTUDIO. Vol. 1, No. 3, Estudios Cedes. Buenos Aires: CEDES, 1978. 46 pp. Paper.

Romano, Ruggiero and Marcello Carmagnani. NOVA AMERICANA. No. 1. Torino, Italy: Giulio Einaudi Editore, 1978. 380 pp. Paper. This is the first issue of an annual book-length series of significant and well-documented articles with each volume organized around a specific theme. The stated purpose of the series, to improve the understanding of Latin America toward historical experience, is well met in the initial volume on regional economy. The articles appear in the language of the contributor.

ARGENTINA

Brown, Jonathan C. A SOCIOECONOMIC HISTORY OF ARGENTINA, 1776-1806. Cambridge Latin American Series 35. New York: Cambridge University Press, 1979. List of tables and figures, appendices, notes, selected bibliography, index. xiv, 307 pp. $24.95.

Jelin, Elizabeth. LA MUJER Y EL MERCADO DE TRABAJO URBANO. Buenos Aires: CEDES, 1979. Notas finales, referencias bibliográficas. 45 pp. Paper.

Roldan, I. M. SINDICATOS Y PROTESTA SOCIAL EN LA ARGENTINA, 1969-1974. UN ESTUDIO DE CASO: EL SINDICATO DE LUZ Y FUERZA DE CORDOBA. Incidentele Publicaties 11. Amsterdam: CEDLA, 1979. Apéndices, bibliografía, resumen. xxxi, 484 pp. Paper.

Sourrouille, Juan V. LA PRESENCIA Y EL COMPORTAMIENTO DE LAS EMPRESAS EXTRANJERAS EN EL SECTOR INDUSTRIAL ARGENTINO. Vol. 1, No. 2. Buenos Aires: CEDES, 1978. Estudios Cedes. 76 pp. Paper.

Zinn, Ricardo. ARGENTINA: A NATION AT THE CROSSROADS OF MYTH AND REALITY. New York: Robert Speller and Sons, 1979. Appendices, bibliography, xi, 211 pp. $15.00 cloth, $5.95 paper.

BRAZIL

Campos, Renato Carniero. IDEOLOGIA DOS POETAS POPULARES DO NORDESTE. Serie Estudos e Pesquisas 5. Recife: Instituto Joaquim Nabuco de Pesquisas Sociais, 1977. Bibliografia. 76 pp. Paper.

Ferraz, Eneas. ADOLESCENCIA TROPICAL. Vol. 8. São Paulo: Academia Paulista de Letras, 1978. 147 pp. Paper.

Novaes, Fernando C. ORNITOLOGIA DO TERRITORIO DO AMAPA II. Belém: Museu Paraense Emílio Goeldi, 1978. Bibliografia citada. 75 pp. Paper.

Pang, Eul-Soo. BAHIA IN THE FIRST BRAZILIAN REPUBLIC: CORONELISMO AND OLIGARCHIES, 1889-1934. Latin American Monographs, Second Series 23. Gainesville: Center for Latin American Studies, University of Florida, 1979. Tables, appendices, glossary, bibliography, index, maps, picture section. xvi, 256 pp. $14.75.

Parker, Phyllis R. BRAZIL AND THE QUIET INTERVENTION, 1964. Texas Pan American Series. University of Texas Press, 1979. Notes, list of sources, index, xiv, 147 pp. $9.95.

Schwartz, Stuart B., ed. A GOVERNOR AND HIS IMAGE IN BAROQUE BRAZIL: THE FUNEREAL EULOGY OF ALFONSO FUTADO DE CASTRO DO RIO DE MENDONCA by Juan Lopes Sierra. Minneapolis: University of Minnesota Press, 1979. Notes, index, appendices. x, 216 pp. $15.00.

Simões, Mario F. and Fernanda Araujo-Costa. AREAS DE AMAZONIA LEGAL BRASILEIRA PARA PESQUISA E CADASTRO DE SITIOS ARQUEOLOGICOS. Belém: Museu Paraense Emílio Goeldi, 1978. Bibliografia citada. 160 pp.

CARIBBEAN REGION

Blasier, Cole and Carmelo Mesa-Lago, eds. CUBA IN THE WORLD. Pitt Latin American Series. Pittsburgh, PA: University of Pittsburgh Press, 1979. Bibliographical notes, index. vii, 343 pp. $21.95 cloth, $5.95 paper.

Crahan, Margaret E. and Franklin W. Knight (eds.) AFRICA AND THE CARIBBEAN: THE LEGACIES OF A LINK. Baltimore: Johns Hopkins University Press, 1979. Selected bibliography, bits on contributors. xii, 159 pp. $28.50 cloth, $8.95 paper.

Cross, Malcolm. URBANIZATION AND URBAN GROWTH IN THE CARIBBEAN: AN ESSAY ON SOCIAL CHANGE IN DEPENDENT SOCIETIES. New York: Cambridge University Press, 1979. Map, notes, references index. xii, 174 pp. $19.95 cloth, $5.95 paper.

Higman, B. W. SLAVE POPULATION AND ECONOMY IN JAMAICA, 1807-1834. New York: Cambridge University Press, 1979. Conventions, abbreviations and symbols, appendices, noters, bibliography, index. viii, 327 pp. $9.95 paper.

Ince, Basil A., ed. CONTEMPORARY INTERNATIONAL RELATIONS OF THE CARIBBEAN. Trinidad/Tobago: Institute of International Relations, British West Indies, 1979. Index. iv, 367 pp. Paper.

Lent, John A. THIRD WORLD MASS MEDIA AND THEIR SEARCH FOR MODERNITY: THE CASE OF COMMONWEALTH CARIBBEAN, 1717-1976. Lewisburg, PA: Bucknell University Press, 1977. List of tables, appendices, bibliography. 405 pp. $22.50.

Vega B., Wenceslao. HISTORIA DEL DERECHO COLONIAL DOMINICANO. Colección ensayo 1. Santo Domingo, RD: Editoria Taller, 1979. Apéndice, bibliografía, índice, analítico. 165 pp. Paper.

CENTRAL AMERICA

Durham, William H. SCARCITY AND SURVIVAL IN CENTRAL AMERICA: ECOLOGICAL ORIGINS OF THE SOCCER WAR. Stanford, CA: Stanford University Press, 1979. Lists of tables and figures, appendices, bibliography, index. xvii, 209 pp. $14.50.

Falla, Ricardo. QUICHE REBELDE: ESTUDIO DE UN MOVIMIENTO DE CONVERSION RELIGIOSA, REBELDE A LAS CREENCIAS TRADICIONALES, EN SAN ANTONIO ILOTENANGO, QUICHE (1948-1970) Collección "Realidad Nuestra" Vol. 7. Guatemala: Editorial Universitaria de Guatemala, Universidad de San Carlos de Guatemala, 1978. 574 pp. Paper.

González Quezada, Carlos. ANALISIS POLITICO GUATEMALA 1978 Y SUS IMPLICACIONES PARA EL 79. Ciencia y Política II. Guatemala: Universidad Rafael Landivar, Instituto de Ciencias Políticas y Sociales, 1979. 67 pp. Paper.

Grieb, Kenneth J. GUATEMALAN CAUDILLO: THE REGIME OF JORGE UBICO, GUATEMALA: 1931 TO 1944. Athens, OH: Ohio University Press, 1979. List of abbreviations, tables, epilogue, notes, bibliography. xvii, 384 pp. $16.00.

OAS. REPORT ON THE SITUATION OF HUMAN RIGHTS IN EL SALVADOR. Washington, DC: General Secretariat, OAS, CIDH. 188 pp. Paper.

Sherman, William L. FORCED NATIVE LABOR IN SIXTEENTH CENTURY CENTRAL AMERICA. Lincoln: University of Nebraska Press, 1979. Appendices, notes, bibliography, index. xvi, 496 pp. $18.50.

CHILE

Claro Valdes, Samuel. OYENDO A CHILE. With cassette. Santiago; Editorial Andés Bello, 1979. Reflexión final, bibliografía, índice de nombres y materias y de ilustraciones. 139 pp. Paper.

Dirección de Presupuestos. SOMOS REALMENTE INDEPENDIENTES GRACIAS AL ESFUERZO DE TODOS LOS CHILENOS. Documento de Política Económica. Santiago de Chile: Ministerio de Hacienda, 1978. Includes 52 policy statements on Chilean economic conditions, all but 3 by the Ministers of Hacienda and Economia, arranged chronologically from September 28, 1973 to May 24, 1978. 396 pp. Paper.

Oppenheimer, Robert, compiler. CHILE. Latin America Bibliography Series 6. Los Angeles: Latin American Studies Center, California State University, 1979. vi, 91 pp. Paper.

COLOMBIA

Bejarano, Jesús Antonio, compilador. EL SIGLO XIX EN COLOMBIA VISTO POR HISTORIADORES NORTEAMERICANOS. Bogotá: Editorial La Carreta, 1979. 389 pp. Paper.

Bergquist, Charles W. COFFEE AND CONFLICT IN COLOMBIA, 1886-1910. Durham, NC: Duke University Press, 1978. List of figures, maps, and tables, bibliography of sources cited, index. x, 277 pp. $16.95.

Parsons, James. LA COLONIZACION ANTIQUENA EN EL OCCIDENTE DE COLOMBIA. Bogotá: Carlos Valencia Editores, 1979. Mapas, bibliografía, fotos. 241 pp. Paper.

Selowsky, Marcelo. WHO BENEFITS FROM GOVERNMENT EXPENDITURE? A CASE STUDY OF COLOMBIA. New York: Oxford University Press, 1979. Statistical appendix, references, index, figures, tables. xv, 186 pp. $12.50 cloth, $4.95 paper.

MEXICO

Coerver, don M. THE PORFIRIAN INTERREGUNUM: THE PRESIDENCY OF MANUEL GONZALEZ OF MEXICO, 1880-1884. Fort Worth, TX: Texas Christian University Press, 1979. Bibliography, index. iv, 322 pp. Paper.

De Marquez, Viviane B., compilador. DINAMICA DE LA EMPRESA MEXICANA: PERSPECTIVAS POLITICAS, ECONOMICAS Y SOCIALES. México, D.F. El Colegio de México, Centro de Estudios Sociológicos, 1979. viii, 442 pp. Paper.

El Colegio de México. INDOCUMENTADOS: MITOS Y REALIDADES. México, D.F.: El Colegio de México, Centro de Estudios Internacionales, 1979. viii, 238 pp. Paper.

El Colegio de México, LAS PERSPECTIVAS DEL PETROLEO MEXICANO. México, D.F.: El Colegio de México, Centro de Estudios Internacionales, 1979. Apéndice estadístico. x, 403 pp. Paper.

El Colegio de México. PRIMER ENCUENTRO HISPANOMEXICANO DE CIENTIFICOS SOCIALES. Jornadas 91. México, D.F.: El Colegio de México, 1979. v, 86 pp. Paper.

Gobierno del Estado de Nuevo Leon Oficialia Mayor. Dirección del Registro Civil. INDICE GENERAL DEL PERIODICO OFICIAL NUEVO LEON, 1931-1950. Monterrey, N.L.: México, 1979. 582 pp. Paper.

Kiser, George C. and Martha Woody Kiser, eds. MEXICAN WORKERS IN THE UNITED STATES: HISTORICAL AND POLITICAL PERSPECTIVES. Albuquerque: University of New Mexico Press, 1979. Selected bibliography, index. xi, 295 pp. $7.50 paper.

Perry, Laurens Ballard. JUAREZ AND DIAZ: MACHINE POLITICS IN MEXICO. De Kalb, IL: Northern Illinois University Press, 1978. Appendices, bibliography, index, list of maps, abbreviations of archival sources. xx, 467 pp. $25.00.

Rangel Guerra, Alfonso. SYSTEM OF HIGHER EDUCATION: MEXICO. New York: International Council for Educational Development. Appendix, bibliography, list of country directors. xii, 84 pp.

Schmidt, Henry C. THE ROOTS OF *LO MEXICANO:* SELF AND SOCIETY IN MEXICAN THOUGHT, 1900-1934. College Station, TX: Texas A & M University Press, 1978. Postscript, bibliography, index. xiii, 195 pp.

Van Oss, A. C. INVENTORY OF 861 MONUMENTS OF MEXICAN COLONIAL ARCHITECTURE. Incidentele Publicaties 12. Amsterdam: CEDLA, 1979. Geographical distribution of the monuments, chronology of construction. 175 pp. Paper.

Vásquez, Josefina Zoraída. MEXICANOS Y NORTEAMERICANOS ANTE LA GUERRA DEL 47. México, D.F.: Ediciones Ateneo, S.A., 1977. 284 pp. Paper.

PERU

Ballón Echegaray, Eduardo, César Pezo del Piño and Luís Peirano Falconi. LA CONDICION DEL MAESTRO EN EL PERU. Praxis 14. Lima: DESCO, 1979. 173 pp. Paper.

Calderón Cockburn, Julio and Luis Olivera Cárdenas. MANUAL DEL POBLADOR DE PUEBLOS JOVENES. Lima: DESCO, 1979. Anexos, bibliografía. 143 pp. Paper.

Chavarría, Jesús. JOSE CARLOS MARIATEGUI AND THE RISE OF MODERN PERU, 1890-1930. Albuquerque: University of New Mexico Press, 1979. Notes, bibliographical essay, index. xi, 247 pp. $14.95.

Cotler, Julio. CLASES, ESTADO Y NACION EN EL PERU. Peru Problema 17; Lima: Instituto de Estudios Peruanos, 1978. Bibliografia. 407 pp. Paper.

Flores-Galindo, Alberto. AREQUIPA Y EL SUR ANDINO: ENSAYO DE HISTORIA REGIONAL (SIGLOS XVIII-XX). Lima: Editorial Horizonte, 1977. Bibliografía citada, nota sobre bibliografía y fuentes. 194 pp. Paper.

Himelblau, Jack. ALEJANDRO O. DUESTUA: PHILOSOPHY IN DEFENSE OF MAN. Gainesville: University of Florida Press, 1979. Chronology, bibliography. xiii, 119 pp. $11.00.

Pease Garcia, Henry. LOS CAMINOS DEL PODER: TRES AÑOS DE CRISIS EN LA ESCENA POLITICA. Lima: Desco, 1979. 363 pp. Paper.

——— and Alfredo Filomeno. PERU 1977: CRONOLOGICA POLITICA, Tomo VI. Lima: DESCO, Area de Estudios Políticos, 1979. Indices temáticos. xiv, 2923 pp. Paper.

Pillado M., Armando. EL CAPITAL HACIA LA CRISIS: PERU 1965-1978. Lima: DESCO, 1979. Glosario de terminos y conceptos utiles, anexos estadísticos. 96 pp. Paper.

Sánchez León, Abelardo, et al. TUGURIZACION EN LIMA METROPOLITANA. Lima: DESCO, 1979. Anexos. 190 pp. Paper.

URUGUAY

Kaufman, Edy. URUGUAY IN TRANSITION: FROM CIVILIAN TO MILITARY RULE. New Brunswick, NJ: Transaction Books, 1979. List of illustrations, appendix, bibliography, index, xv, 126 pp. $9.95.

VENEZUELA

Alborñoz, Orlando. TEORIA Y PRAXIS DE LA EDUCACION SUPERIOR VENEZOLANA. Caracas: Universidad Central de Venezuela, Facultad de Humanidades y Educación, 1979. Notas. 172 pp. Paper.

Baloyra, Enrique A. and John D. Martz. POLITICAL ATTITUDES IN VENEZUELA: SOCIETAL CLEAVAGES AND POLITICAL OPINION. Texas Pan American Series. Austin: University of Texas Press, 1979. Appendices, notes, subject and author index, list of illustrations. xix, 300 pp. $19.95.

Margolies, Luise, ed. THE VENEZUELAN PEASANT IN COUNTRY AND CITY. Série: Antropología Social 1. Caracas: EDIVA (Ediciones Venezolanas de Antropología). 126 pp. Paper.

MISCELLANEOUS

Amengual S., Ataliva y Jaime Lavados M., editores. EL ROL DE LA CIENCIA EN EL DESARROLLO. Santiago: CPU, 1978. 279 pp. Paper.

Blaney, Harry Clay, III. GLOBAL CHALLENGES: A WORLD AT RISK. New York: New Viewpoints, 1979. Notes, index. xiv, 270 pp. $12.95 cloth, $6.95 paper.

Cook, Sherburne F. and Woodrow Borah. ESSAYS IN POPULATION HISTORY: MEXICO AND CALIFORNIA. Vol. 3. Berkeley: University of California Press, 1979. Index, list of tables and maps. xi, 333 pp.

Eckhardt, Caroline D. INTERDISCIPLINARY PROGRAMS AND ADMINISTRATIVE STRUCTURES: PROBLEMS AND PROSPECTS FOR THE 1980's. University Park, PA: Pennsylvania State University, 1979. References, appendices. ix, 61 pp. Paper.

Edel, Silbur. THE STATE DEPARTMENT, THE PUBLIC, AND THE UNITED NATIONS. New York: Vantage Press, 1979. Glossary of citation abbreviations, appendices, bibliography, index. 339 pp. $12.50.

Fascell, Dante B., ed. INTERNATIONAL NEWS: FREEDOM UNDER ATTACK. Beverly Hills, CA: Sage Publications, 1979. 317 pp. $15.00.

Nuscheler, Franz. STRATEGIEWANDEL DER AMERIKANISCHEN ENTWICKLUNGSPOLITIK. Diskussionsbeitrage 18. Munich: Weltforum Verlag, 1979. 156 pp. DM 26 paper.

OAS. HANDBOOK OF EXISTING RULES PERTAINING TO HUMAN RIGHTS. Washington, DC: OAS, 1979. Appendices. iv, 75 pp. Paper.

O'Connor, Raymond G. WAR, DIPLOMACY, AND HISTORY: PAPERS AND REVIEWS. Washington, DC: University Press of America, 1979. viii, 295 pp. $11.00 paper.

OECD. GEOGRAPHICAL DISTRIBUTION OF FINANCIAL FLOWS TO DEVELOPING COUNTRIES: DATA ON DISBURSEMENTS, 1971 TO 1977. Paris: OECD, 1978. Summary tables, annex. xv, 285 pp. Paper.

Rothrock, George A. THE HUGUENOTS: A BIOGRAPHY OF A MINORITY. Chicago: Nelson-Hall, 1979. Bibliographical essay, index. xxv, 201 pp. $16.95.

Smith, Joseph. ILLUSIONS OF CONFLICT: ANGLO-AMERICAN DIPLOMACY TOWARD LATIN AMERICA, 1865-1896. Pitt Latin American Series. Pittsburgh, PA: University of Pittsburgh Press, 1979. Notes, note on sources, index. xv, 276 pp.

Wilson, Joe F. THE UNITED STATES, CHILE AND PERU IN THE TACNA AND ARICA PLEBISCITE. Washington, DC: University Press of America, 1979. Footnotes section, bibliography, maps, drawings. xii, 312 pp. $10.75 paper.

Winks, Robin W. THE RELEVANCE OF CANADIAN HISTORY: U.S. AND IMPERIAL PERSPECTIVES. The 1977 Joanne Goodman Lectures. Toronto: Macmillan Company of Canada, 1979. References. xv, 99 pp. $6.95.

Woods, Randall Bennett. THE ROOSEVELT FOREIGN POLICY ESTABLISHMENT AND THE "GOOD NEIGHBORS": THE UNITED STATES AND ARGENTINA, 1941-1945. Lawrence, KS: Regents Press of Kansas, 1979. Notes, bibliographic essay, index. xiii, 277 pp. $18.00.

Publisher's Note: The following information is printed in accordance with U.S. postal regulations: Statement of Ownership, Management and Circulation (required by 39 U.S.C. 3685). 1. Title of Publication: JOURNAL OF INTERAMERICAN STUDIES AND WORLD AFFAIRS. 1A. Publication No.: 0022-1937. 2. Date of Filing: October 31, 1979. 3. Frequency of Issue: Quarterly. 3A. No. of Issues Published Annually: 4 (four). 3B. Annual Subscription Price: institutions, $32.00; individuals, $16.50. 4. Location of Known Office of Publication: 275 South Beverly Drive, Beverly Hills (Los Angeles), California 90212. 5. Location of the Headquarters or General Business Offices of the Publishers: 275 South Beverly Drive, Beverly Hills (Los Angeles), California 90212. 6. Names and Complete Addresses of Publisher, Editor, and Managing Editor: Publisher: Sara Miller McCune, 1102 South Oakhurst Drive, Los Angeles, California 90035; Editor: John P. Harrison, University of Miami, Box 24-8134, Coral Gables, FL 33124; Managing Editor: None. 7. Owner (If owned by a corporation, its name and address must be stated and also immediately thereunder the names and addresses of stockholders owning or holding 1% or more of total amount of stock. If not owned by a corporation, the names and addresses of the individual owners must be given. If owned by a partnership or other unincorporated firm, its name and address, as well as that of each individual must be given.): Sage Publications, Inc., 275 South Beverly Drive, Beverly Hills, California 90212; Sara Miller McCune, 1102 South Oakhurst Drive, Los Angeles, California 90035; Marvin Sirot, Mohawk Lane, Greenwich, Connecticut 06830; Gustave Sirot, Wingate Road, Guilford, Connecticut 06340; John B. Hurford, 220 East 63rd Street, New York, New York 10021; Albert L. Zesiger, 1125 Fifth Avenue, New York, New York 10028; Judith C. Zesiger, 1125 Fifth Avenue, New York, New York 10028. 8. Known Bondholders, Mortgagees, and Other Security Holders Owning or Holding 1% or More of Total Amount of Bonds, Mortgages or Other Securities: None. 9. For Completion by Nonprofit Organizations Authorized to Mail at Special Rates (Section 132.122, PSM): Not Applicable.

10. Extent and Nature of Circulation	Av. No. Copies Each Issue During Preceding 12 Months	Actual No. of Copies of Single Issue Published Nearest to Filing Date
A. Total no. copies printed (net press run)	1677	1836
B. Paid circulation:		
1. Sales through dealers and carriers, street vendors and counter sales	186	157
2. Mail subscriptions	1211	1280
C. Total paid circulation (sum of 10B1 and 10B2)	1397	1437
D. Free distribution by mail, carrier or other means: samples, complimentary, and other free copies	45	48
E. Total distribution (sum of C & D)	1442	1485
F. Copies not distributed:		
1. Office use, left-over, unaccounted, spoiled after printing	235	351
2. Returns from news agents	______	______
G. Total (sum of E, F1 and 2—should equal net press run shown in A)	1677	1836

11. I certify that the statements made by me above are correct and complete. (Signed) Gary Polinsky, General Manager. 12. 39 U.S.C. 3626 provides in pertinent part: "No person who would have been entitled to mail matter under former section 4359 of this title shall mail such matter at the rates provided under this subsection unless he files annually with the Postal Service a written request for permission to mail matter at such rates." In accordance with the provisions of this statute, I hereby request permission to mail the publication named in item 1 at the reduced postage rates presently authorized by 39 U.S.C. 3626. (Signed) Gary Polinsky, General Manager.

Vol. 22 No. 2
May 1980

JOURNAL OF INTERAMERICAN STUDIES

and WORLD AFFAIRS

A Publication of the Center for Advanced International Studies,
The University of Miami

SAGE PUBLICATIONS

Journal of INTERAMERICAN STUDIES
and WORLD AFFAIRS

The editors and publisher wish to acknowledge with gratitude the assistance and encouragement of the Center for Advanced International Studies, University of Miami, in providing ancillary services and support for this journal.

Journal of
INTERAMERICAN
STUDIES
and WORLD AFFAIRS

Vol. 22
No. 2
May
1980

CONTENTS

The Argentine Economy, 1976-1979
ALDO FERRER 131

Mexico's Recent Science and Technology Planning: An Outsider Economist's Critique
DILMUS D. JAMES 163

A Guatemalan Nightmare: Levels of Political Violence, 1966-1972
JOHN A. BOOTH 195

REVIEW ESSAYS

German Colonies in South America: A New Germany in the Cono Sur?
HANS WERNER TOBLER
PETER WALDMANN
(translated by Ronald C. Newton) 227

The United States and the Dominican Republic: Intervention, Dependency, and Tyrannicide
HOWARD J. WIARDA 247

BOOKS RECEIVED 261

SAGE PUBLICATIONS / *Beverly Hills* *London*

Policy: The **JOURNAL OF INTERAMERICAN STUDIES AND WORLD AFFAIRS** reflects the interests of the scholarly community and interested public concerned with the social, economic, political, and cultural aspects of life in Latin America (including the Caribbean), particularly in those instances where the subject is of concern to more than one of the traditional disciplines. As these concerns change, so will the content of the journal.

Articles which have special relevance for interrelationships between American nations and of those nations with the rest of the world will be given special consideration. An effort will be made to include occasional articles that state an unusual or even discordant position on a subject of broad interest to be supplemented by critical comments of authorities representing differing positions on the topic. The editors continue to welcome articles by scholars from all parts of the world.

Manuscripts should be submitted in duplicate to: Editor, **JOURNAL OF INTERAMERICAN STUDIES AND WORLD AFFAIRS,** Box 24-8134, University of Miami, Coral Gables, Florida 33124. Manuscripts should be typewritten, double-spaced, with footnotes, references, tables, and charts on separate pages, and should follow the current journal style. A brief biographical paragraph describing each author's current affiliation, research interests, and recent publications should accompany the manuscript.

Correspondence regarding book reviews should be sent directly to: Book Review Editor, **JOURNAL OF INTERAMERICAN STUDIES AND WORLD AFFAIRS,** Box 24-8134, University of Miami, Coral Gables, Florida 33124.

JOURNAL OF INTERAMERICAN STUDIES AND WORLD AFFAIRS is published four times annually—in February, May, August, and November.

Subscriptions: Regular institutional rate $32.00 per year. Individuals may subscribe at a one-year rate of $16.50. Add $1.00 for subscriptions outside the United States. Orders from the U.K., Europe, the Middle East, and Africa should be sent to the London office (address below). Noninstitutional orders **must** be paid by personal check.

Second class postage paid at Beverly Hills, California. ISSN 0022-1937

This journal is abstracted or indexed in **Historical Abstracts, Human Resources Abstracts, Sage Urban Studies Abstracts, International Political Science Abstracts, Public Affairs Information Service, Current Contents, Social Sciences Citation Index, Social Sciences Index, ABC POL SCI,** and **United States Political Science Documents.**

Back Issues: Information about availability and prices of back issues may be obtained from the publisher's order department (address below). Write to London office for sterling prices.

Inquiries: Address all correspondence and permissions requests to SAGE PUBLICATIONS, Inc., 275 South Beverly Drive, Beverly Hills, California 90212. Inquiries and subscriptions from the U.K., Europe, the Middle East, and Africa should be sent to SAGE PUBLICATIONS Ltd, 28 Banner Street, London EC1Y 8QE, England. Other orders should be sent to the Beverly Hills office.

Advertising: Current rates and specifications may be obtained by writing to the Advertising Manager at the Beverly Hills office (address above).

Claims: Claims for undelivered copies must be made no later than three months following month of publication. The publisher will supply missing copies when losses have been sustained in transit and when the reserve stock will permit.

Change of Address: Six weeks' advance notice must be given when notifying of change of address. Please send old address label along with the new address to insure proper identification. Please specify name of journal. Send change of address to: Journal name, c/o 275 South Beverly Drive, Beverly Hills, CA 90212.

ALDO FERRER
Centro de Estudios de Coyuntura
Instituto de Desarrollo Económico y Social

THE ARGENTINE ECONOMY, 1976-1979

This article presents an overall view of the performance of the Argentine economy under the policies inaugurated in April 1976. Section I describes the conditions prevailing at the beginning of 1976, the main goals and arguments of the new economic authorities. Section II explores the implementation of the economic program and how the government insisted on its basic goals under rapidly changing conditions. Finally, Section III summarizes the author's views on the consequences of the present economic program and provides suggestions on an alternative development strategy. A brief Statistical Appendix with basic data on the Argentine economy and relevant economic variables of the period under analysis is also included.

I. The Goals and the Context of the April 1976 Economic Program

On April 2, 1976, the new regime established after the fall of the last Peronist government launched its "program for recovery,

---

AUTHOR'S NOTE: The author appreciates the very useful comments on a preliminary version of this article from Mario Brodershon, Juan Sourrouille, Jaime Baintrub, Michael Sweet, and Peter Alhadeff, and the insights on the functioning of the labor market of Alvaro Orsatti. He has also benefitted from the debates at the seminars of the Centro de Estudios de Coyuntura del Instituto de Desarrollo Económico y Social of Buenos Aires.

Journal of Interamerican Studies and World Affairs, Vol. 22 No. 2, May 1980 131-162

reorganization and expansion of the Argentine economy." The immediate goals were to halt inflation, to eliminate the huge fiscal deficit, and to prevent default on the international financial obligations of the country. To meet these goals, the new development strategy adopted was designed to accelerate economic growth and to make the Argentine economy more competitive in the framework of the international market.

The new authorities had good reasons to aim for the elimination of the chaos prevailing in early 1976 and to redress the mistakes of previous economic strategies. In the first quarter of 1976, inflation was running at 1000% on an annual basis, monetary and fiscal conditions were truly in a mess, the balance of payments was in deficit, and production and employment levels were in a decline. The long-term record of the Argentine economy was not satisfactory either. Between 1945 and 1974, the GNP grew by 3.5% per annum, much below the 6% for the rest of Latin America and the 4.5% for the industrialized countries. The relative weight of the Argentine economy declined rapidly. In 1945, Argentina generated 25% of Latin America's GNP; by 1974 the proportion fell to 15%. In 1945 Argentina's GNP was 27% larger than Brazil's. By 1974 the size of the Brazilian economy was almost twice that of the Argentine (CEPAL, 1978: Table I, 14-19). The slow economic development discouraged inmigration and, given the low birth rate, total population increased at the annual rate of 1.5%. This was clearly insufficient for a country the size of Argentina, with a population density of 8.5 inhabitants per square kilometer and 15 inhabitants per square kilometer of arable land. Besides, in those thirty years, regional imbalances in the allocation of population and economic activity were increased. By 1974, 36% of the population and around two-thirds of manufacturing production was concentrated in the Buenos Aires metropolitan area.

This was clearly not a satisfactory record for a country with such resource endowment. The national territory (even excluding the Antarctic region) is the eighth largest in the world, stretches from north to south along 3700 kilometers, and encompasses practically all kinds of climates, from the subtropical northern region to the cold Patagonian area. The Pampas is one of the largest and most fertile natural prairies in the world. The country has large forestry, fishing, mining, oil, and hydroelectric resources. Over 95% of the population is literate, and cultural levels are considerable. There are no racial or religious cleavages that divide Argentine society. Income and wealth distribution might be inequitable, but much less so than in most other developing countries.

In April 1976 there were indeed very good reasons to introduce drastic changes in prevailing economic conditions and to remove the long-standing obstacles to the development of the Argentine economy.

What has been said in the previous paragraphs is not sufficient to describe the initial scenario of the current economic program. Attention should be paid to two additional points: first, the origin of the chaotic situation of early 1976; second, development trends from the 1960s to the early 1970s. Let us look briefly into these two subjects.

The economic and financial chaos was directly connected to an anarchic political situation. The Peronist government progressively became unable to maintain order and internal security and to control the most important economic variables. Public finance crumbled under the stampede of public expenditure and the collapse of the tax revenues system. Money supply increased rapidly, but the monetary and financial system fell apart due to the flight of money holdings. Price adjustments and wage claims became unmanageable. The balance of payments deficit was partly explained by deterioration in the terms of trade, the reduction in grain export surpluses, and new restrictions on imports of Argentine beef into the EEC market. But the sharp overvaluation of the peso and the huge differential between the official and black market rates stimulated exports underpricing, imports overpricing, smuggling, and capital flight. From the middle of 1975 onwards, the government became clearly unable to control the situation, and the political system could not find proper answers within the rules of a constitutional regime. The productive capacity of the country was intact. But hyperinflation, plus a huge public deficit and the critical balance of payments situation, clamored for immediate remedies that the prevailing political system was unable to provide.

The change of government on March 23, 1976, put an end, in 24 hours, to the basic cause of this malaise: the power *vacuum*. The new economic authorities were then in a position to reestablish order. This made it possible to reestablish labor discipline, eliminate inflationary expectations prevailing under the previous chaos, increase tax receipts and public utilities prices while at the same time controlling public expenditure, establish real positive interest rates and control monetary supply, adjust the exchange rate, and handle the balance of payments adjustment.

The second point refers to the development record in the 1960s up to the early 1970s. It was mentioned that during a thirty-year period after the World War II, the rate of growth was extremely low—3.5%—but the situation improved at the beginning of the 1960s. From 1960 to 1974 the growth rate increased to 4.4% per annum. It goes beyond the limits of this article to provide an explanation for this acceleration of economic development, but at least two main reasons should be mentioned: the increase in agricultural production and the expansion of exports of manufactures.

From 1945 to 1960 the agricultural product increased 17%. Between 1960 and 1975 it grew by 36%. The improvement in real prices, new technologies, mechanization, new crops such as sorgum and soya, and other factors helped to promote agricultural production. This is the main reason that the physical volume of exports grew by 5% between 1945 and 1960, while it grew by 30% between 1955 and 1975.

On the industrial front, many Argentine firms and foreign subsidiaries increased their sales abroad. By the early 1970s, Argentina was one of the principal exporters of manufactures among the newly industrializing countries (NICs). In several cases, exports came to represent a substantial proportion of total production, and many firms established foreign trade departments for the systematic promotion of exports. Argentina became one of the largest exporters of manufactures within LAFTA. Goods exported included turn key plants for food and beverages manufacturing, machine tools, automotive spare parts and vehicles, office and communications equipment, chemicals, and other goods from the so-called basic industries. Several transnational subsidiaries (such as Olivetti, IBM, vehicle and tractor manufacturers) and many Argentine firms gained a firm hold in international markets. In 1965 exports of durable consumer goods and capital goods amounted to $25 million. By 1974 the figure increased to $347 million. From a modest less than 2% participation in total export in 1965, those goods represented close to 10% by 1974.

From the late 1950s and early 1960s, Argentina, as did the other large Latin American countries, became more export-conscious. The creation of LAFTA and the Andean Group is a result of this trend. The issue became hotly debated in Argentina (Ferrer, 1968), and exports of manufactures were supported in multiple ways: through export credits and insurance, prefinancing, subsidies, and so on. These policies bore fruit and gradually several branches of the domestic industry became closely connected to the international market. It is true that in the early 1970s the proportion of exports to manufacturing product was still low, but progress was being made and it was not negligible. By 1974, almost one-third of the total exports were rather sophisticated manufactures.

The increase in manufactured exports, together with the export of larger surpluses of agricultural commodities, helped to raise the exchange earning capacity of the country and afforded a higher growth rate. This factor helps to explain the acceleration of economic development after the early 1960s despite the fact that political instability still prevailed. Between 1960 and 1976, Argentina had 10 presidents and 22 ministers of economy.

Briefly, despite the unsatisfactory development record of the previous thirty years, Argentina still ranks among the most developed middle-income economies of the world and as the most advanced Latin American country. With a population of 27 million and an income per capita close to $2700, the domestic market is not negligible and a savings ratio of over 20% of the GNP affords one of the highest investment potentials among developing countries. Only 15% of the labor force is employed in the primary sector; manufacturing and the services generate the largest proportion of the GNP. Although an import coefficient below 10% of the GNP is clearly low, it reveals, at the same time, a considerable degree of diversification and sophistication of the economic structure. With all their faults, import substitution and industrialization increased the technical level of the labor force and managerial cadres. The oil crises and the sharp increase of food prices in the early 1970s helped to reveal the economic potential of an economy close to self-sufficiency in oil supplies and with a large surplus in food and other staple commodities.

The new economic authorities made a frontal attack on the chaotic conditions prevailing at the beginning of 1976 and somehow implied that those conditions were the inevitable result of mischievous long-term economic policies. Accordingly, they decided to abandon the long-established import substitution development strategy and to allocate domestic resources along the comparative advantages of the Argentine economy. The following is a brief summary of the main goals and arguments of the government's economic strategists.

The domestic market is too small to sustain a diversified industrial structure, and development within closed boundaries has produced highly inefficient manufacturing activities. Thus, to redress the mistakes of the past, the economy should be open to international competition. At the same time the public sector should interfere less, and the market mechanism should be allowed to play its essential role as resource allocator and income distributor.

Industrialization has proceeded on the basis of two subsidies: high import duties and negative interest rates. The first one fostered oligopolistic structures and high costs; the second, an irrational allocation of capital. Both should be eliminated. Accordingly, drastic changes in the relative domestic prices should be introduced. Throughout the process of import substitution of the previous fifty years, the set of domestic prices has moved away from the relative prices prevailing in the international market. This means, in short, that domestic industrial prices are above those of the agricultural sector. In comparison with international standards, by 1976, industrial domestic prices were on the average around 40% above those for staple agricultural commodities. This average figure encompassed wide differences of effective protection on a product-by-product basis ranging, for example, from a negative protection for tractors to a positive 400% for motorcycles. Thus, it is necessary to depress manufacturing prices vis-à-vis primary sector ones and to eliminate price differentials within the industrial sector. This change in domestic relative prices should help to reallocate resources to the primary sector and, within manufacturing, to those activities able to compete internationally in the domestic as well as the world markets.

Real prices of fuel and public utilities should increase to eliminate the operating deficits of public concerns and to generate public savings. The handling of the public sector includes the increase in the tax burden, the reduction of expenditure, and the privatizing of all those state enterprises that are not essential for security, public welfare, or other basic reasons.

Workers' participation in national income should fall in order to increase profits and investment and to help fight inflation. Wages in Argentina in early 1976 were too high, given the country's income per capita. A fall in real wages would help to sustain employment, despite the reduction in domestic consumption and the recessionary effects of fiscal and monetary policies.

The rate of interest should increase and be positive in real terms to promote savings and insure a rational allocation of capital. The monetary authorities should regain control of the expansion of monetary and financial assets and the domestic money market should be locked into the world financial centers through the rate of interest and free capital movement. Finally, the rate of exchange should be adequate to promote exports and insure a smooth adjustment of the balance of payments accounts.

Price stability and growth should logically follow from this set of policies. The fall in unit labor costs, the increase in productivity due to a rational allocation of resources, the balanced budget, and the regulation of money creation should insure price stability. In turn, this would stimulate private domestic and foreign investment and increase the rate of growth. Accordingly, the economy would soon recover from the late 1975/early 1976 recession, and the future long-term annual GNP rate of growth would exceed 5%.

Such were the arguments and the expectations of the government's strategists in April 1976. But there was something else: Those ambitious targets were to be achieved without causing a large unemployment of the labor force. As will be seen, this was to become a serious obstacle to the stabilization and resource reallocation targets set by the new government. Now let us look what happened in the real world.

II. Implementation of the Program

From its inception, the economic policy aimed to achieve its basic goals of changing relative prices and reallocating resources while simultaneously trying to sustain employment and achieve price stability. From April 1976 to October 1979 the economy's behavior differed wildly from the basic targets and the price stabilization goal. To overcome those realities, economic policy has gone through different short-term strategies.[1] From this point of view, five main stages in the implementation of the economic program can be identified. In each of them, the economic authorities adhered to their basic goals under rapidly changing conditions. We shall go briefly through these five stages.

First Stage (April 1976-February 1977). The first task of the new government was to put an end to the chaotic conditions existing in early 1976. To this end, as well as to pursue the basic goals of the new economic policy, large price increases were approved for the forthcoming spring crops, export taxes on agricultural staples were reduced, and the effective exchange rate for primary exports was raised. At the same time, industrial prices that had been subjected to control were freed. Nominal wages were adjusted by decree below the cost of living increases, and all labor union activities were forbidden or strictly controlled. Taxes and public utilities prices were raised, and the real wages of public sector agents were sharply adjusted downwards. The rate of interest on time deposits was raised, and import duties were reduced across the board. On the balance of payments front, the effective exchange rate for exports and imports was raised, and differentials were reduced by lowering export taxes and subsidies. Negotiations were opened to reschedule the public sector foreign debt, a stand-by agreement with the IMF was signed, and new loans were negotiated to replenish the international reserves. Except for the inflation rate and relative prices in the last months of this stage, results were in accordance with those expected by the new government. Real prices for agriculture rose and those for manufacturing moved in the opposite direction. In 1976 the import volume fell from that of 1975 by 22%, and due to depressed conditions of domestic demand and the peso devaluation, the imports/GNP coefficient fell to 8%. Real wages declined and workers' participation in national income fell from 47% to 30% between 1975 and 1976.

The Treasury situation improved due to an increase in taxes and the prices of public utilities, while real income of public agents declined by 40%. The monetary situation improved, real interest rates became positive, and the flight of money was stopped.[2] The current account of the balance of payments moved into surplus, and this factor, together with an inflow of short-term capital, produced a substantial increase in foreign reserves.

Consumption and investment declined and so did the GNP. Manufacturing and construction fell sharply, but a very good harvest allowed for a 41% increase in export volume. Curiously enough, the unemployment rate declined.

Inflation declined rapidly from a 45.7% monthly rate in the first quarter of 1976 to an average of 6.3% for the last one. Yet in January 1977 the rate jumped again to 13.8%. After the sharp fall in real wages in the second quarter and the drastic improvement in real agricultural prices in the second half of the year, further downward pressures in manufacturing real prices and wages became more difficult to implement. However, the jump in the inflation rate and unexpected resistance to the resources reallocation targets provoked second thoughts among the government strategists and launched the second stage.

Second Stage (February-August 1977). In February, the government decided to enforce the desired changes in relative prices, reactivate the economy, stop the inflationary burst, and move ahead in its balanced budget and foreign payments surplus targets. To this end it appealed to an unorthodox instrument: price controls on manufactured goods—the so-called "tregua" (truce). Prices for 700 leading industrial firms were frozen for 120 days starting on March 9. The budget deficit was further reduced by additional increases of the tax burden, new reductions in current expenditures and, again, higher fuel and public utilities real prices. Interest rates were lowered to reactivate demand. Treasury bills were placed at rates below the market, forcing the Treasury to get additional finance from the Central Bank. In addition, the large surplus in current accounts and the increase in foreign reserves produced further increases in the monetary base. The peso rate of exchange kept pace with domestic price increases less international inflation, primary exports were stimulated by goods prices, and manufactured ones by a depressed domestic demand and the price freeze for the largest firms. Since Novem-ber, 1976, there was a single exchange rate, and exports taxes and import subsidies were further reduced. Restrictions on foreign payments were largely eliminated.

During this stage in July 1977, the *reform* of the financial and monetary system came into effect. The previous centralization of deposits in the Central Bank was abandoned, interest rates were freed and Treasury bills were placed at the market rates through public tenders instead of fixing the market *floor* as had been done previously.

As expected, the budget deficit was once again reduced, Central Bank credit to the Treasury expanded the monetary base, the balance of payments on current accounts showed a large surplus and production levels increased. Prerecession levels of 1975 were slightly surpassed by mid-1977. The recovery was led by exports (that increased by 50%), fixed investment and, once again, negative interest rates that stimulated inventories build-up. In March, prices increased by 3.9%, but during the rest of the "tregua" period the increases moved between 5.7% and 6.6%. Real prices moved again in favor of agriculture. When the "tregua" ended, the so-called One Hundred Twenty-First Day, inflation burst again: Prices increased by 12.6% in August. Between the first and second quarters of 1977 real wages increased by 15%. The unemployment rate fell from 4.1% in October 1976 to 3.3% in July 1977.

The resistance of the economic system to accept the drastic manipulation of relative prices and income distribution induced the government to change, once again, its short-term strategy.

Third stage (September-December 1977). After the inflation burst of August 1977, the government introduced a drastic change in its short-term policy. Its duration was short, but its effects were to last well into 1978. It was decided to cool the economy and discourage further readjustment in industrial real prices and real wages through a sharp reduction of domestic demand. Indexation of public utilities prices and of the rate of exchange were expected to further the official budget and balance of payments targets. It was also intended to strengthen the control of the monetary supply through a reduction in budget deficit financing by the Central Bank, restrictions to hot foreign capital inflows, and the manipulation of the banking system cash reserve requirements.

While private credit demand was expanding rapidly, real rates of interest changed dramatically. In June they were 8% negative, in December 36% positive.

As expected, the contractive fiscal and monetary policy rapidly reversed the expansion of economic activity. Unemployment rates grew from 2.2% in October 1977 to 3.9% in April 1978. Nevertheless, it was only slightly above the 1974 rate. This apparent paradox will be explained later on.

Large amounts of hot capital were attracted by positive real interest rates of over 30%. Inflation was not abated and industrial real prices kept moving against government expectations. To face the contraction of domestic demand, the manufacturing sector kept adjusting prices up instead of down. Naturally, this made the recession deeper. Real wages fell again. In the first quarter of 1978 they were 8% below the already depressed levels of the second quarter of 1976, when the present economic policy was launched, and almost 50% below 1974.

The third stage ended with the year 1977. After twenty months of the new economic policy, international reserves amounted to $2630 million, the budget deficit / GNP coefficient was reduced to 3.3%, and inflation to 147%. But inflationary pressures were not abating, the economy was once again geared toward recession, and the resource reallocation target was still far away. The Argentine economy still remained to a large extent a self-sufficient one.

Fourth stage (1978). The unsatisfactory results of the previous strategies provoked new changes in the implementation of the economic program. Government strategists apparently thought that failures were due to a still insufficient control of monetary supply and the financing of the public sector deficit. On the other hand, something had to be done to reverse the sharp fall in production levels. Indexation of the rate of exchange and utilities prices was also deemed to self-perpetuate inflation. In this stage, changes in relative prices and resource reallocation seem to have lost priority.

Accordingly, fiscal deficit was further reduced to 2.1% of the GNP. This helped practically to eliminate Central Bank financing of the budget deficit. The large inflow of short-term capital, together with a substantial current account surplus, induced further restrictive measures on foreign borrowing. Monetary authorities thus strengthened their capacity to control the monetary base. In the first semester of 1978, expansion of the monetary base relied heavily on the foreign sector. In the second semester, the rapid reduction in cash reserve requirements increased the credit multiplier and the secondary creation of private monetary assets. Monetary policy stopped being restrictive toward the end of 1977. Interest rates rapidly declined, and in March they were 9% negative in real terms.

The most important change introduced in the balance of payments front refers to the exchange rate. Progressively, particularly after May, the exchange rate adjustment began to lay behind the domestic price increase adjusted by international inflation. Devaluation of the peso was 30% less than domestic price increases in 1978. In the final quarter of 1978 there was a substantial capital flight because of prospective conflicts in the Austral region, but due to a substantial current account surplus, international reserves increased by $2000 million.

The consequences of the third-stage restrictive monetary policy lasted well into the fourth stage. GNP fell by 4.2% in 1978 over 1977. In 1978 manufacturing GNP was 11% below 1974 levels. Unemployment rates remained low during all of 1978, and in October they were 1.8, the lowest recorded—even lower than in the boom year of 1974. Real wages declined by 9% between the second quarters of 1977 and 1978.

One important consequence of the peso revaluation was the increasing gap between real interest rates in pesos and foreign currencies. While the former remained negative all through 1978, the latter were 20% positive toward the end of 1978. Nevertheless, the uncertain international situation discouraged a large inflow of foreign capital during this period.

Toward the end of 1978 several basic goals of the economic program were farther away than ever. The inflation rate did not decline in 1978, relative prices and resource allocation remained unmanageable, and production levels declined for the second time in three years and were almost 20% below the long-term growth rate. Contrary to official expectations, the control and sophistication of fiscal and monetary policy did not lead to growth with a reasonable price stability. Toward the end of 1978, negative real interest rates and the real wages increase induced a reactivation of economic activity that was to accelerate during 1979. But the time had come for a new short-term strategy.

Fifth stage (1979). Close to the end of 1978 and early in 1979, the government strategists decided to insist on the government's *structural* target: reallocation of resources along comparative advantages. After several across-the-board reductions of import duties, it was decided to bring them down to a maximum of 40% through a five-year period, 1979-1984. In January, they decided to do something else: to pass temporary 180-day ad hoc reductions to discipline those industrial branches that did not fall into line with the price stabilization targets. In April, duties for capital goods foreseen for 1984 were anticipated to 1979, creating, in fact, a negative protection for several branches of this industrial sector. Lowering of import duties and overvaluation of the peso thus became basic instruments to change relative prices, reallocate resources, and fight inflation.

In the price stabilization front the government insisted on its fourth-stage strategy: to abandon indexation fuel and public utilities prices, and the rate of exchange. This time the scheme was more sophisticated. "Pautas" (guidelines) were adopted for the next 12 months on the assumption that price increases would be half the size of the previous year. Basic wages were to be adjusted to keep them stable in real terms.

Management of monetary policy was adjusted to the new conditions created by the substantial reduction of the Central Bank credit to the Treasury and a larger secondary credit creation through the lower cash reserves requirements on bank deposits. Further expansion of the monetary base thus laid on the increase of international reserves. To this end, foreign funds inflows were again promoted. Real interest rates in pesos were 15% negative in June, and in dollars positive by 30% due to the continued peso overvaluation.

A permissive monetary policy was essential to sustain the undergoing economic recovery that the government did not want to frustrate again as in August 1977. The economic strategists were confident that their scheme was going to decelerate inflation, reallocate resources, and keep a healthy economic recovery. At the end of 1978, production increased rapidly. Negative interest rates and higher real wages expanded consumption and investment expenditures. Exports played a negligible role in this process.

Prices increased at a faster rate: in the first nine months of 1979, by 113%, against 92% in the same period of 1978. The accelera-tion of inflation was due mainly to a sharp increase in cattle and beef prices. Due to this factor, real agricultural prices increased again toward mid-1979.

The lag in public utilities prices and the rate of exchange were creating additional problems. Accordingly, public investment has been reduced to accommodate to the new situation, and it was recently decided that utilities prices should be adjusted above the "pautas."

To avoid a flight of capital, domestic interest rates should remain above those paid in international financial markets. On the other hand, domestic real interest rates should remain negative to sustain economic recovery. Nominal interest rates should then be below domestic inflation and at the same time should provide a substantial positive interest rate in foreign currencies. Therefore, peso devaluation should continue behind domestic price increases and interest rates. The government's economic strategists expect the domestic inflation rate to converge with the devaluation rate plus international inflation. The implicit assumption is that domestically traded goods and services move in the same direction as internationally traded goods; if prices of the former increase more than the latter, domestic production would be substituted by imports. This is rather high ideal for the real world to achieve.

As expected, the domestic money market became closely integrated to the international financial centers. But at the same time, the Central Bank lost control of the monetary supply. Open market operations to regulate the stock of private monetary assets would affect interest rates, and this, in turn, would provoke foreign funds flows that would upset the monetary policy targets.

TABLE 1
National Accounts

	1974	1975	1976	1977	1978	1979
GROSS NATIONAL PRODUCT						
Total (In 1979 US$ Millions)						
Potential	66,100	69,000	72,040	75,200	78,500	82,000
Real	66,100	65,000	63,100	66,100	62,900	68,000
Per Capita						
Potential	2,640	2,718	2,800	2,890	2,980	3,070
Real	2,640	2,560	2,453	2,540	2,380	2,520
BASIC RATIOS[1, 2]						
Consumption/GNP	79.6	82.6	77.9	72.1	72.6	
Investment/GNP	21.6	20.4	20.0	23.1	21.6	
Exports/GNP	8.3	7.0	10.2	14.6	15.9	
Imports/GNP	9.5	10.0	8.0	9.8	9.6	
Salaried Workers Income/GNP	52.2	47.2	29.8	32.5	34.3	
MACRO INDICATORS[1, 2]						
Industrial Production (1974 = 100)	100	97.2	92.8	96.7	89.1	
Agriculture Production (1974 = 100)	100	98.1	104.1	108.3	109.5	
Unemployment Rate	3.4	3.7	4.5	2.9	2.8	
Terms of Trade (1970 = 100)	111.0	71.9	71.7	68.2	68.7	

SOURCES:
1. FIDE, 1979.
2. FIEL, various issues; INDEC, 1976-1979; CEC-IDES, 1979.

In the second semester of 1979, balance of payments estimates anticipate a deficit of $400 million because of a sharp increase in imports, a modest growth of exports, and a substantial increase in tourist expenditures overseas.

It seems curious, but, after almost four years and five short-term strategies, economic policy is going full circle to hyperinflation and foreign payments imbalances.

The overall record (1976-1979). Despite the strong recovery of economic activity in 1979, GNP this year will be 17% below the potential GNP that would have been achieved if the economy had only maintained its 1960-1974 growth rate. The accumulated gap between real and potential GNP for 1976-1979 amounts to $48 billion. Income per capita in 1979 will be 5% less than in 1974. The 1976-1979 period is the worst four-year period since the early 1930s. Besides, the inflation rate is six times larger than the average for 1945-1974.

TABLE 2
Prices and Wages[1]

PRICES AND WAGES	1976	1977	1978	1979
WHOLESALE PRICES	386.3	147.1	142.1	170.8
First Quarter	45.7	12.0	9.0	9.7
Second Quarter	13.0	6.7	8.3	9.4
Third Quarter	8.3	9.3	6.1	10.0
Fourth Quarter	6.3	9.3	8.7	
RELATIVE PRICES				
Agriculture/Industry (1960 = 100)	93.4	99.7	93.3	
First Quarter	74.7	94.5	88.0	89.7
Second Quarter	76.3	98.6	86.3	95.6
Third Quarter	97.5	94.5	95.9	101.0
Fourth Quarter	98.6	89.6	94.5	
Imports/Industry (1975 = 100)	139	127	87	
REAL WAGES[2] (1970 = 100)	71	73	71	75
First Quarter	93	68	66	70
Second Quarter	72	78	71	80
Third Quarter	69	69	67	
Fourth Quarter	71	76	79	

SOURCES:
1. INDEC: Precios mayoristas. Monthly rates for each quarter. Relative agriculture/industry prices refer to national agriculture and nonagriculture of the wholesale prices index. Relative imports/industry prices refer to imported goods and national nonagriculture of the same index.
2. CEC-IDES, 1978, 1979; Ministerio de Economía, 1979.

Real wages in 1979 are 25% below 1970 and 40% below 1974. Salaried workers' participation in national income declined from 47% in 1975 to 34% in 1979, while the investment/GNP coefficient grew only by 1.2 points. The accumulated balance of payments surplus represents 2.5% of the GNP. Thus, the fall of 13 points in workers' participation in the national income has only produced a 3.7-point increase in international reserves and fixed investment. Conspicuous consumption by high income groups seems to have increased substantially, particularly in imported goods and other overseas expenditures.

TABLE 3

Balance of Payments and Exchange Rate[1]

	1975	1976	1977	1978	1979
BALANCE OF PAYMENTS (In Millions Current U.S.Dollars)					
Current Account	-1.286	650	1.287	2.078	- 157
Exports	2.961	3.916	5.660	6.350	7.600
Imports	-3.947	-3.033	-4.100	-3.950	-5.360
Services	- 300	- 233	- 273	- 322	-2.397
Capital Movements	495	542	939	80	4.132
Noncompensatory	191	- 516	1.276	1.287	
Compensatory	304	1.058	337	1.367	
Reserves	- 791	1.192	2.226	1.998	3.975
RATE OF EXCHANGE AND WHOLESALE PRICES[2] (1976 = 100)					
Rate of Exchange (a)		100	217	361	525
Wholesale Prices (b)		100	247	597	1.265
Ratio a/b		100	88	60	42

SOURCES:
1. Estimate for 1979 (Banco Central, 1976, 1978).
2. Data for December of each year and for September in 1979.

The wage-earning labor force seems to have declined approximately by 10% between 1974 and 1978. The increase of self-employed persons reduced the salaried labor force by approximately 300,000 persons. People discouraged by low wages have moved to services, repairing, and several other self-employed jobs. On the other hand, the withdrawal of women, youngsters, and aged people from the lowest paid jobs seems to have produced a further reduction of 150,000 salaried workers. Argentina has traditionally been a net immigration country—its immigrants mostly from neighboring countries—from the 1950s onwards. Although there are no official figures since the middle of 1975, it seems that in the 1976-1979 period there has been a net emigration of from 500,000 to 800,000 Argentines and nationals of neighboring countries. Of this number, around 50% can be considered persons of working age. Adding up these figures, it might be estimated that the Argentine salaried labor force in 1979 is around 750,000 persons less than could have been expected.

Several aggregates of the public sector show considerable improvement over the 1973-1975 record and are comparable to the situation prevailing before the last Peronist government. Employment in the national, provincial, and municipal administrations and in public enterprises declined from 1,760,000 to 1,530,000 persons between the end of 1975 and 1978. The Treasury deficit amounts to around 2% of the GNP and is mostly financed in the domestic and foreign capital markets, not by the Central Bank. Public investment represents, again, around 30% of total expenditure, with public savings finance around 50% of public investment. The tax burden and social security charges in 1979 will be over 23% of the GNP, 6 points above the 1975 figure. The size of the public sector has not changed significantly. The public expenditure/GNP coefficient in 1979 is around 40%, 2 points below 1975 but close to 8 points above the 1970 figure.

The management of monetary policy contributed to overcome the chaotic situation of early 1976. Nevertheless, the "monetization" of the economy is still much below previous levels. In 1979 the private monetary assets/GNP coefficient is 18%, against 27% in the early 1970s. The financial system expanded and became more sophisticated. Operations of banks and other financial agents have increased around four-fold in real terms between March 1976 and mid-1979. Profits of the financial system have climbed even more due to larger profit margins. Rates of interest are largely established by the market, but the market reflects the impact of the economic policy on production levels, income distribution, the rate of exchange, and other crucial variables. Much of the discussion in official circles and beyond on the problems of the Argentine economy centers mainly, nowadays, around the behavior of the monetary aggregates and policies.

The overvaluation of the peso is moving relative prices against internationally traded goods. Given the low imports/GNP coefficient, such a policy is having a perverse effect on the original resource reallocation targets. Relative prices have moved erratically and frequently against the official targets. In particular, public utilities real prices in the last eighteen months have declined sharply. The lowering of import duties has lost a sense of direction as far as resources reallocation targets are concerned. In several instances manipulation of import duties seems to have followed ad hoc criteria not related to the efficiency or competitive ability of firms. Bankruptcies have increased in the industrial sector, even among firms that were competitive and very active in the international markets. The contraction of the domestic market and overvaluation of the peso have put many firms out of business, and many others are sustained only by special support programs of their principal creditors (the so-called "bank clubs"). Foreign private investment remains at low levels. The shrinkage of the domestic market and overvaluation of the peso are not attractive for foreign direct private investment. Research and development expenditures among private firms seem to have declined abruptly, and many firms have closed or scaled down their export departments. Nothing new and significant seems to be happening in research and development connected with agriculture or in the acceleration of the long-term improvement trend in rural productivity. As a whole, there seems to be a considerable loss of productivity in Argentine economy measured by GNP levels, employment of available resources, and disorganization of the preexisting economic structure. It does not seem that this is an adjustment cost of a new development path for the Argentine economy, more efficient and expansive than the old one.

On the balance of payments front, there is a remarkable increase in foreign reserves but a weaker basic balance of payments position. It is interesting to observe that in 1976, balance of payments difficulties were largely exaggerated. In fact, the situation was beginning to improve before the end of March 1976 due to the devaluation of the second half of 1975. The Argentine payments problem was not then unique. In the aftermath of the oil prices increases and the 1974-1975 world economic recession, many industrial and developing countries faced acute payments imbalances. On the other hand, Argentina has an impeccable record as a debtor since the end of the nineteenth century, and its considerable potential strengthens its credit worthiness. I insist on this point because it has been traditional of orthodox economic thinking in Argentina to exaggerate international payments problems to promote policies that go much beyond the necessary adjustment process.

III. Some Basic Policy Issues

An overall view of the program implementation. It was seen in Section II that the economic program has been subject to frequent changes when the rate of inflation, relative prices or production levels fell out of line with the official targets. Nevertheless, in the framework of rapidly changing economic conditions, the regime remained faithful to the basic goals of the April 1976 economic program. There are not, in fact, five different policies within one government but a single policy with several short-term strategies dictated by the course of events.

During the 1976-1979 period, the government kept insisting on the modification of relative prices and the reallocation of resources conforming with the comparative, or natural, advantages of the Argentine economy. Real agricultural prices were to be improved in stage one by high support prices, in stage two by the "tregua," in stage three by monetary shock therapy, and stages four and five by rapidly diminishing import duties.

The antiindustrial bias of the present policy is apparent in such assumptions as the small size of the domestic market and the permanent attack on import substitution. Above all, the record of the 1976-1979 period—the increasing number of bankruptcies among industrial firms, the dismantling of research and development and export departments, the migration of skilled labor and even of managers and firm owners, the reduction of the domestic market, the stalemate of investment, and the fall in the manufacturing GNP—indicates that 1979 will still be below the 1974 levels. In particular, the fall in manufactured exports reveals that Argentina is losing foreign markets won on the basis of dynamic comparative advantages founded on its previous industrial development and its management and skilled labor endowment. The difficulties of the industrial sector under the present economic policy affect all kinds of firms, large and small, national and foreign. General Motors has closed operations in Argentina, and a large European car manufacturer that has been suffering bid losses in the last few years has moved the headquarters of its South American operations from Argentina to Brazil. Many large traditional Argentine firms in multiple manufacturing branches are also suffering big losses, for instance, in the textile sector. Small- and medium-size firms, with a weaker ability to benefit from the lower interest rates of foreign financing, have suffered most. The firms that showed greater ability to overcome the prevailing trends are those that have reduced their operations scales more rapidly and have become importers rather than producers. The two most dynamic industrial branches in a modern economy, capital goods and electronics, are being rapidly dismantled or scaled down. The government strategists argue that it is the necessary adjustment cost for a more efficient industrial sector. Beyond intentions, the fact remains that Argentine industry is facing its gravest crisis since the end of the World War II.

Another basic goal of the economic program, reduction of real wages and regressive income distribution, was successfully achieved in the first stage. As will be seen later on, the labor market behavior precluded further substantial losses in real wages, except in the sharp recession of late 1977 and early 1978. Wage earner participation in national income has declined, and salary differentials among different categories of workers and productive sectors have increased. In certain areas—for example, the financial sector—real wages have increased substantially. Managers and skilled personnel in several branches have larger real incomes. This corresponds to the government policy to differentiate income levels in response to differential productivity increases. The ability of firms to pay higher wages does not always correspond to a real increase in productivity but rather to changes in relative prices and the resource reallocation implicit in the regressive income distribution. The regime remains firm in its belief that lower wages produce higher savings and investments. Public officials frequently complain that they cannot move further along this road because of political restrictions—namely the need to maintain full employment.

Another basic feature of the April 1976 program is its firm belief in the ability of monetary policy to influence resource allocation and control inflation. In all five stages, great efforts were displayed in the development of the monetary and financial markets, the regulation of monetary expansion, and the development of sophisticated tools to achieve the desired goals. The government strategists have not been discouraged by the meager result of their efforts. Instead, they have repeatedly expressed their perplexity with regard to the downward inflexibility of the inflation rate despite the success in controlling the Treasury deficit and regulating the increase in monetary assets. It has been frequently argued that the fault lies in the inability, or resistance, of economic agents to respond as they should when faced with a set of soundly based economic policies. The blame is to be put on the real world, not on the policy makers.

Finally, the government has been firm in its bias against state intervention in the economy, although the public expenditure/GNP coefficient remains unchanged. Many firms previously in the government sphere have been sold, and so-called "peripheral" activities within public utilities transferred, to the private sector. On the other hand, the largest remaining private electricity utility has recently been nationalized. The amount of this purchase largely exceeds the privatization of firms and activities previously under government control. Except for the second stage "tregua," price control was abandoned, although salaries remained under firm control. Only recently, private firms were authorized to negotiate salaries with their employees freely. Government strategists are firmly convinced of the structural or inherent inefficiency of the government and of state controls. Somehow, it becomes a self-fulfilling prophecy when government agencies and enterprises are managed with this type of approach.

There can be agreement that the proper functioning of a mixed economy requires clear rules of the game for the private and public sectors and the restriction of state intervention to what is essential to achieve desired economic and social goals. However, in the framework of the April 1976 program, the antistate bias becomes an essential instrument of the overall antiindustrial strategy and of the international accommodation of the Argentine economy along its static comparative advantages. Industrialization of a developing country requires the utilization of public expenditure to promote technological and industrial domestic development, and a very active public support for exports of manufactures, development of basic industries, technological development, labor training, and negotiation with foreign firms, financial circles, capital goods, and technology suppliers. This is so in all rapidly industrializing countries, whatever the specific development model: Brazil and South Korea, Mexico and Taiwan, Yugoslavia and Spain. In the present Argentine experience the antistate bias forms part of the overall goals of the economic program.

The present Argentine experience throws new light on two basic problems of the country's economic development. The first problem refers to the nonviability of an economic strategy based on specialization along the natural resources endowment, income concentration, and a noninterfering public sector. The second problem refers to the incapacity of orthodox economic policy to achieve price stabilization and resource reallocation under full employment conditions. Let us look briefly into these two subjects.

Nonviability of the program's development strategy. Argentina is too big for the present economic strategy. It is impossible to give up an industrialization process that began in the 1930s and reestablish a preindustrial productive structure without creating the problems that Argentina is facing today. If economic resources are allocated in accordance with the relative prices prevailing in the international markets and a rate of exchange sufficient only to export agricultural products, a large section of domestic industry would disappear—perhaps at least 50% of it (Ferrer, 1979). Taking into account only the direct effects, that would imply an income fall of 15%, unemployment of over one million workers, and scrapping a huge amount of fixed capital. It is not possible to frame a country of Argentina's dimensions in a preindustrial economic system. Besides, the "new" economic structure presumably would be unable to expand income and employment in the long run. An economy that employs no more than 15% of its labor force in agriculture cannot build up a viable economic system based mainly on the expansion of primary exports. We have known that since the 1930s. Proposals for industrial redeployment and continued specialization by developing countries in primary production, emerging from some quarters of the developed world, are not sustained by the course of events.[3] While unemployment remains a basic problem in industrial countries and, what is more important, income elasticities remain what they are, it does not seem that the old center-periphery model could offer a viable growth alternative for developing countries, certainly not for a country of Argentina's dimension.

The author is among those who have been insisting during the last fifteen or twenty years on the need for Argentina to open up toward the international economy, and on the limits of a development process confined to the limits of the domestic market. The question is not whether foreign trade/GNP coefficients should increase, but how that is to be achieved. There is not room in this article to recall the debate that has gone on about this subject since the end of the 1950s. I will only insist on the point that Argentine economic development demands an integrated economic structure with full development of agriculture and basic and technological complex industries. In this context, specialization within the world markets should largely proceed on a product by product basis—that is, the so-called intraindustrial specialization which prevails in trade among developed economies. It is important to note that up to 1975 much had been achieved along this road, as was recounted in previous paragraphs.

From this point of view, income concentration and the pruning of the public sector's role in economic development, promoted by the present program, become basic obstacles to the growth process. Given the income and savings levels prevailing in

Argentina, capital accumulation can proceed at appropriate rates simultaneously with a permanent improvement in the standard of living. In fact, as has been recalled, income concentration lessens incentives for investment and growth. Profits largely depend on the utilization of productive capacity and the expansion of domestic demand. It is traditional in Argentine economic experience that orthodox policies discourage savings and private investment. Concerning the public sector, the scale-down of public intervention in the functioning of the market mechanisms and in the utilization of available resources does not preclude a very strong support of the development process. In fact, orthodox policies end by being strongly interventionist and inefficient.

A short comment should be made on the Argentine case within the framework of the new industrializing countries (NICs). Let us look, for example, at the case of South Korea, where recent fast industrialization, rapid growth, and export expansion have proceeded on the basis of a previously preindustrial and mostly agricultural economy. In this case, resource allocation along comparative advantages was, from the start, the big push of economic development. Thus, manufacturing was from the very beginning closely connected with the international markets in the framework of a very active state intervention, a markedly nationalistic policy, and progressive income distribution. Let us recall that over 80% of Korea's exports originate in national firms and that the expansion of Korean construction firms in foreign markets has met with strong government support. From an industrialization based on exports, the Korean economy is moving toward a more internally integrated economic structure, and specialization is assuming a more intraindustrial, product-by-product, orientation.

The connection of manufacturing with the world markets has to be different for countries—such as Argentina, Brazil, and Mexico—that have established a substantial and integrated industrial sector based on import substitution for the domestic markets. In these cases, the existing economic structure should be the foundation for a more aggressive export policy and stronger ties with the world markets. Of course, it can be argued how rapidly and by what means, this process should proceed. Nevertheless, closer connection with the world markets should not imply the destruction of large sections of domestic industry. After all, the past cannot be buried. It is curious that those who insist that mistakes of the recent past should not be repeated propose the repetition of mistakes of the distant past. What the Argentine economy is today, with all its virtues and defects, should be the foundation of a more efficient and expansive system. In a final analysis, the consequences of the present economic program can be explained as being based on ideological and political considerations rather than on the real needs of the Argentine society in the present world context.

It has been permanently emphasized by the government economic strategists that the present policy has solid support in foreign financial and private sector groups. This has not materialized, however from a larger flow of foreign long-term private direct investment. Naturally, incentives for foreign as well as domestic private investment depend on the same basic conditions: an expanding domestic market, real incentives to export, and the conviction that a particular economic strategy will endure over time. None of these conditions exist today. In fact, only sound nationalistic and expansive economic policies can set real bases for larger foreign investment and closer connections with the rest of the world.

The program goals under full employment. Argentine experience shows that abrupt changes of prevailing income distribution patterns have always provoked higher inflation rates. Real wages, agricultural prices, and industrial profits, always tend to regain lost positions whenever economic trends move against any one of them. Thus, drastic changes generate repressed inflationary pressures in the product and factor prices that lay behind the inflation rate. In Section II several hints were provided on the working of these mechanisms under the April 1976 economic program.

A second point refers to the fact that to achieve resource reallocation rapidly along comparative advantages, domestic production of the "noncompetitive" or "inefficient" industrial sectors should be replaced by imports. In other words, to match domestic relative prices to those prevailing in international markets, it is necessary to change supply sources and increase the imports/GHP coefficient. At the same time, the scale-down of the public sector weight requires a rapid and drastic reduction of personnel employed in state activities. On the other hand, domestic real interest rates should be continuously positive to channel resources to activities benefitted by relative price changes adjust to new demand patterns, and to charge "noncompetitive" activities unbearable financial costs.

Under the present strategy, changes in relative prices and resource reallocation with lower inflation depend on three basic conditions: the swift rise of the imports/GNP coefficient, a drastic reduction of employment in the public sector, and permanently positive real interest rates. If these do not exist, "inefficient" and "noncompetitive" sectors will survive and fight back to reestablish the previous income distribution patterns, while resources will not be allocated along comparative advantages.

The April 1976 program could not fulfill any of those three conditions. For political or other reasons, with the sole exception of stage three, full employment remained, all along, a restriction that the program strategists complied with. Thus, the import/GNP coefficient remained unchanged up to the middle of 1979, employment in the public sector declined slightly, and real interest rates remained negative for most of the 1976-1979 period. The consequences were persistent high inflation rates and the collapse of the resources reallocation goals. In this framework, the continuous search for the desired relative prices changes produced stronger inflationary pressures. That is clear in all five stages described in Section II.

Two other points should be noticed in this context. The first one refers to what might be called *expectations of well being*.

Argentine society, and probably all open and pluralistic societies, got used to an increase in well-being connected with the rate of economic growth. It might be assumed that the gap between potential and real per capita income increases the income distribution dispute. If this is so, frustration of well-being expectations tends to increase the inflation rate.

The second point refers to the behavior of the labor market. Government strategists plainly stated from the very beginning that the adjustment process should proceed by lowering real wages, not by increasing unemployment. However, the fall in real wages has produced deep changes in the labor market that create labor shortages and wages pressures when demand increases, as has happened since late 1978. It was mentioned before how through different ways (migration, transfer to self-employed jobs, retirement of women, youngsters, and aged people), the salaried labor force has declined. Only high open unemployment can keep wages permanently in the desired depressed levels. The wages policy contributed to the maintenance of real wages well below the 1974, and even the 1970, levels. Nevertheless, given the above-mentioned behavior of the labor market, real wages tend to increase post-1976 unit labor costs and push prices up. In certain areas there is a true shortage of personnel and active competition among firms to hire scarce personnel.

The permanent shift of short-term policies within the April 1976 economic program and the five stages described above can be explained by the frustration of the program strategists. They tried to accommodate to changing economic conditions and pursue their main goals. The full employment restriction forbade the implementation of the basic tools of an orthodox economic policy. Nevertheless, they did not resign their basic goals of resource allocation and income distribution, hoping, perhaps, that in the long run, despite continuous high inflation rates, success would crown their efforts. One of the victims of this process has been monetary policy, unable to play its useful role to control inflation and promote economic growth.

The alternatives of an orthodox economic policy are rather unpleasant. If the imports/GNP coefficient is increased, monetary supply is reduced, a large proportion of public personnel is fired, then inflation might be reduced and resources would be reallocated. But the costs of such a policy are high unemployment, a drastic fall in production levels, and prolonged stagnation. If orthodox policy tries to sustain employment, it gives birth to a remarkable stagflation engine. Although I have restricted this analysis to contemporary Argentine experience, I would add that while the second orthodox approach corresponds to the Argentine case, the first corresponds to Chile's.

Economic policy and the political system. Probably the gravest drama of Argentina in the last fifty years has been its failure to implement an economic policy compatible with a democratic political system. Populist policies have ended in chaotic or unmanageable situations. Orthodox policies have ended in the aggravation of basic economic conditions and deep social resentment. It is not accidental that all orthodox economic policies in contemporary Argentina have always been based in de facto political regimes. It seems that they can not be implemented otherwise. Other strategies, neither populist nor orthodox, including policies carried out while I was Minister of Economy and Labor between 1970 and 1971, lacked sufficient political support to last and prove their viability.

On the threshold of the 1980s, Argentina is once again faced with the need to implement an economic policy capable of promoting economic growth, price stability, and long-term balance of payments equilibrium. At the same time, this should be compatible with a democratic and open political system. The goal of a developed and free society is not impossible in a country with such a huge economic potential.

APPENDIX: BASIC DATA ON ARGENTINA[4]

Continental Area: 2,776,889 km
Arable land: 1,700,000 km

Population (1979): 26,800,000
Growth Rate (1960-1979): 1.3%
Adult Literacy Rate (1970): 93%

NOTES

1. Various analysts have emphasized the existence of several stages within the present economic program. See, in particular, Brodersohn (1979). What follows draws on this "stages" approach and on my assumption that the economic program pursues unrelentingly the same basic goals (Ferrer, 1979).

2. Due to the spread between passive and active interest rates on several occasions during the 1976-1979 period, active interest rates were positive in real terms, while passive remained negative.

3. For the author's views on prevailing trends in the world markets, see Ferrer (1978).

4. Statistics are from FIDE (1979).

REFERENCES

Banco Central (1976, 1978) Memorias Anuales. Buenos Aires: Banco Central.

BRODERSOHN, M. (1979) "La apertura externa y la estrategia antinflacionaria." Colegio de Graduados de Ciencias Económicas, Buenos Aires, Junio 5. (mimeo)

CEC-IDES [Centro de Estudios de Coyuntura del Instituto de Desarrollo Económico y Social de Buenos Aires] (1979), "Política salarial." Draft report, Agosto.

——— (1978, 1979) Data for Seminars. Buenos Aires: CEC-IDES.

CEPAL [Comisión Económica para América Latina] (1978) Series históricas del crecimiento de América Latina. Santiago: CEPAL.

FERRER, A. (1979) "El retorno del liberalismo: reflexiones sobre la política económica vigente en la Argentina." Desarrollo Económico 18 (January-March).

——— (1978) "Latin America and the world economy: some observations on external indebtedness and the international monetary system." J. of Interamerican Studies and World Affairs 20 (August): 321-339.

——— (1968) "Hacia un sistema industrial integrado y abierto." El Cronista Comercial (December).

FIDE [Fundación de Investigaciones de Desarrollo Económico] (1979) "Coyuntura y desarrollo." Anexo Estadístico 3 (Julio).

FIEL [Fundación de Investigaciones Económicas Latinoamericanas] Indicadores de coyuntura. (various issues)

INDEC [Instituto Nacional de Estadística y Censo] (1976, 1977, 1978, 1979) Periodical surveys on unemployment from 1976-1979.

Ministerio de Económica (1979) "Encuesta oficial sobre salarios." Ministerio de Economía, Buenos Aires, September.

Aldo Ferrer, a former Minister of Economy and Labor of Argentina, is Director of the Centro de Estudios de Coyuntura at the Instituto de Desarrollo Económico y Social, Buenos Aires. A graduate of the University of Buenos Aires, he is also former Executive Secretary of the Latin American Social Sciences Council, author of The Argentine Economy *(University of California Press, 1967),* Tecnología y Política Económica en América Latina *(Paídos, Buenos Aires, 1975), and* Crisis y Alternativas de la Política Económica Argentina *(Fonda de Cultura Económica, Buenos Aires, 1977).*

DILMUS D. JAMES
University of Texas at El Paso

MEXICO'S RECENT SCIENCE AND TECHNOLOGY PLANNING
An Outsider Economist's Critique

I. Introduction

There are a number of reasons why Mexico attracts students of economic development. Boasting an impressive rate of economic growth that has been sustained for four decades, yet plagued with discouraging and mounting problems of surplus labor and maldistribution of income, Mexico is one of the prime cases that has sparked the discussion over the distinctions between "economic growth" and "economic development." Furthermore, Mexico affords a classic test of the validity of some dependency writers' claim that periphery countries' subjugation to external control varies directly with the length and intensity of contact with center nations (Frank, 1972: 10). The sudden revelation of Mexico's potential as an energy supplier, the growing concern with the magnitude and consequences of illegal Mexican migration to the United States, and the increasing recognition of the uniqueness and importance of the Mexico-U.S. border economy add further appeal for economists, political scientists, and sociologists. Mexico's accelerating science and technology program adds another alluring area for scholarly effort. Expendi-

---

AUTHOR'S NOTE: The author wishes to thank James H. Street and Miguel S. Wionczek for helpful comments of earlier drafts of this article. Grateful acknowledgement is also made to the University Research Institute, University of Texas at El Paso, for financial assistance.

Journal of Interamerican Studies and World Affairs, Vol. 22 No. 2, May 1980 163-193

tures on research and development (R&D) increased from 770.4 million pesos in 1968 to 1.4 billion pesos in 1973, a rise of 80.6% (CONACYT, 1976: 14). The figure rose to 9.5 billion pesos in 1978 and is schedules to reach 19 billion pesos in 1982, an impressive rate of growth, even after taking into account rapid inflation (CONACYT, 1978: 41). R&D accounted for .22% of Mexico's Gross Domestic Product in 1973, in contrast to the planned 1.0% in 1982 (CONACYT, 1976: 14, 1978: 41). The annual budget of the primary national science and technology agency, Consejo Nacional de Ciencia y Technología (CONACYT), created in 1971, grew from 43 million pesos in that year to 901 million pesos in 1978.

Along with these figures of actual past and prospective future expenditures, two CONACYT documents symbolize Mexico's determination to gain control over her own scientific and technological affairs. In July 1974 a presidential mandate directed CONACYT to prepare a national plan for science and technology. Building on earlier works dating back to *Política Nacional y Programas en Ciencia y Technología,* produced by CONACYT's predecessor, Instituto Nacional de Investigacíon Científica, there emerged in November 1976 the *National Indicative Plan for Science and Technology (Plan,* hereafter). By any standards it is a remarkable document. Approximately 300 public officials, scientists, technicians, and users of technology contributed to the final product. The wide-ranging work deals with the role of science and technology in the general scheme of Mexican development; elaborates goals, priorities, and planning instruments for science and technology policy through 1982; examines in detail the scientific/technological infrastructure, individual fields of scientific study, economic sectors, renewable resources and natural phenomena; and summarizes technological policy instruments such as legislation, government legislation, and financial measures.

The more recent document, *National Program for Science and Technology, 1978-1982 (Program,* hereafter), appearing in October 1978, is essentially the response of the new President López

Portillo's regime to the older *Plan* formulated under the Presidency of Echeverriá. The history of Mexico's earlier scientific evolution is amplified; recent developments in science and technology are identified; the responsibilities, human resources, and budget of governmental agencies, especially CONACYT, are discussed; priorities for specific areas are reidentified, presumably with the approval of the new administration; and the macropolitical coordination for the program is described.

Although the *Program* is highly informative and to a limited extent complements the earlier *Plan,* the 1976 document is more likely to be of interest to the student of science and technology policy of Third World nations. The *Plan*'s comprehensive coverage, candid self-evaluations and self-criticisms, and explicit statement of value judgments are rare for a public document issued anywhere in the world. Given the wide participation in its formulation, the *Plan* represents a consensus of a large segment of one of the most technologically advanced Third World nations. These attributes provide an unusual opportunity for appraising the "state of the art" in science and technology planning of developing areas. My intent is to use primarily the *Plan,* and to a lesser extent the more recent *Program,* as a departure for critically examining Mexico's science and technology planning. Although the primary thrust is toward Mexico, interviews conducted in Colombia, Peru, and Argentina during the summer of 1978 lead me to feel that the arguments contained herein apply to much of Latin America as well.

Five issues are addressed in the following five sections of the article. First, although science and technology policy cannot bear the entire burden of solving the most dire and recalcitrant socioeconomic problems of Mexico, it should be a vital part of the policy mix. This will require a conscious, deliberate, and determined channeling of research and development activities. Second, there are sizable potential gains that can be reaped by reducing the dispersion of research effort and achieving the necessary critical mass for more projects. Some reorganization of incentives coupled with political direction is required. Third, there is a danger in overestimating the state of dependency on external forces and thereby devoting too little attention to high payoff actions that are subject to internal control. Fourth, political policy formulation at the macro level should be tempered by healthy doses of market forces, outside objective appraisals, and technocratic participation in the decision-making process by scientists and technicians. And fifth, the failure of the more recent *Program* to live up to the *Plan* implies an abiding dearth of political and social internalization of the potential place of science in Mexican development. The final section consists of a summary and conclusions.

II. Surplus Labor, Income Distribution, and Science and Technology Policy

Of the various socioeconomic difficulties confronting Mexico, two are salient: the inability to provide productive employment opportunities for a substantial proportion of the labor force and the failure of the bulk of the population to share fully in the benefits of economic growth. A review of the available studies on unemployment and underemployment in Mexico leads to the following conclusions: (1) Approximately one-fourth of the labor force is "unemployed equivalent"; (2) when estimates include those either too discouraged to enter the labor force or those who drop out of the labor force because of the dearth of job openings, it appears that approximately one-third of the potential labor supply is "unemployed equivalent"; and (3) about one-half of the population is in one way or another severely affected by the lack of productive employment opportunities. Furthermore, until recently the backlog of surplus labor was growing by more than one-half million per year. In a previous study of the situation by John S. Evans and the present writer, we concluded that even assuming continued economic growth, sociopolitical stability and a concerted effort by the Mexican government to deal with the problem, surplus labor will continue to persist well into the next century.[1]

As for distribution of income, from 1950 to 1969 the proportion of income going to the lower 70% of the population shrank! Mexico has a distribution of income more skewed in favor of upper income groups than India! In addition, the impact on income distribution of rapid inflation since 1973, the Green Revolution in agriculture, and a big push in higher education beginning in the Echeverría administration suggests, if anything, a further reduction in the share of income going to the lower half of the population.[2]

By no means are these grave conditions ignored in the *Plan,* but the role of science and technology as one component in a remedial policy is not delineated. Indeed, there are indications that the connection between technology and employment are not fully understood or appreciated. Two minor items can be adduced first. The *Plan* (CONACYT, 1976: 14) cites a lower Mexican productivity per man-hour in producing paper pulp, compared to international man-hour productivity, as evidence that Mexico lags behind in the pulp and paper industry. But as Louis Wells, Jr. (1975) has convincingly shown, use of such "engineering criteria" can be extremely misleading in a labor-abundant, capital-scarce economy. As I have shown elsewhere (James, 1973), earlier vintage, smaller scale, and more labor-intensive technology, embodied in secondhand capital equipment, can be highly efficient in the Mexican paper industry. Also, even when the core equipment is associated with a more or less fixed number of operators, a larger number of ancillary workers occupied by material handling, storage, plant and grounds maintenance, equipment maintenance, and so on is compatible with efficiency in a low-wage country. Nor should mini-scale plants producing kraft paper based on mechanical-chemical processes be automatically ruled out when ecological costs of large plants are taken into account, transportation costs are high, and decentralized rural communities have a need for the product (Suri, 1975).

Labor productivity, then, is no unambiguous measure of efficiency when the social opportunity cost of labor is very low and that for capital is high.

A similar engineering criterion may be operative when recommending a continuation of support going to "massive centralized technologies for housing construction operated by specialized groups" (CONACYT, 1976: 35). Why? W. Paul Strassman (1979) after investigating the "disciplined and integrated application of mass production technology to construction and manufacture of large building components," found such "industrialized systems building" a failure virtually everywhere in Latin America except Puerto Rico, and even here he found individual cases of failure. Strassmann contrasts this approach to a series of construction innovations that are extensions of, or complements to, existing traditional building methods. These less spectacular innovations often cut costs substantially, use less capital, employ more labor, and utilize a higher proportion of locally available materials.

But these are quibbles over a couple of lapses. Far more disconcerting is the statement that "it must be realized that unemployment in Mexico is not fundamentally a technological problem, nor will the basic remedy be found in the use of labor-intensive technologies" (CONACYT, 1976: 35).[3] There is much truth to this view. An entire constellation of policies will be necessary—including the reduction of distortions in the price of labor and capital—encouraging multiple shift work, changing the way in which labor benefits are financed, expanding educational opportunities and broadening the base of those with access to it, continuing family planning, supporting small- and medium-sized enterprises, promoting peasant agriculture, changing the amount and composition of residential housing construction, undertaking labor-intensive public works, altering attitudes of entrepreneurs and labor leaders, and promoting exports.[4] The point is, however, that science and technology policy should become a vital contributor to any eventual solution or accommodation of these major socioeconomic problems. The magnitude, severity, and persistence of these socioeconomic difficulties should explicitly influence the character of scientific and technological knowledge imported and assimilated or, alternatively, generated through domestic research and development.

For one thing, economic decisions made in the political arena interact with the state of technological capabilities. For example, if a slowdown in agricultural activity coincides with a balance of payments crisis, there is great temptation for the agricultural policy makers to look even more favorably on large agricultural units. If it becomes obvious that this is the policy stance, innovational activity will naturally concentrate on new techniques that promote economies of scale on extensive land units. A policy of concentrating on scale-neutral agricultural innovations to promote small, labor-intensive agricultural units that are usually more efficient per unit of land, becomes increasingly difficult to implement. Technological policies interact with economic policies and reinforce many of the same trends that have contributed to a labor surplus. Thus a conscious, deliberate guidance of science and technology policy is necessary to counteract the momentum.

A similar interaction of social, technical, and economic phenomena has been described earlier by Celso Furtado (1973) and more recently by Frances Stewart (1977). Product choices by producers, especially foreign firms accustomed to producing similar products for their home markets, are heavily influenced by the purchasing habits of upper income groups in developing countries. The choice of luxury and semi-luxury products encourages the selection of associated production techniques that tend to be relatively capital-intensive and large-scale. The cycle is closed when the capital-intensity further distorts income distribution through its detrimental impact on employment. We can add a political dimension as vested interests by those benefiting from the system kindle a conscious or subliminal desire to perpetuate the system. Policy suggestions for countering the cycle have included regulation of foreign investment and technology transfers, expanded trade among Third World countries, rationalization of factor prices, and an evolution toward a more egalitarian income distribution. Also, to address the point at hand, a richer variety of technologies suitable for use under the conditions of a lower wage-capital cost ratio, increased demand for basic products, and an expanding, reciprocal Third World trade would assuredly ease a difficult policy transition.

Pursuing the point further runs the risk of leading us into the bewildering terminology applied to technologies thought to fit more comfortably with conditions found in less developed countries. Candidates for the terminology title include "village level," "intermediate," "alternative," "radical," "soft," "capital-light," "labor-intensive," "ecology-sound," and "appropriate" technology, but for the moment it appears "appropriate technology" is the leading designation. In addition, there is an equally muddled variety of motivations for being attracted by the appropriate technology movement. Some are interested in improving efficiency of production in the traditional cost-benefit sense, others weigh ecological preservation or improvement heavily, while still others emphasize the "way of life" benefits from a decentralized socioeconomy made possible by small-scale technology, or the escape from work alienation allegedly caused by mammoth organizations and large-scale technology.

Even clinging to the narrowly viewed economic criteria, however, there is some room for cautious optimism. Particularly worthy of note are the hard-headed "does it work or not" case studies of the International Labour Office and the University of Sussex, which indicate that earlier vintage, labor-intensive, smaller scale techniques still is use are sometimes more efficient in a poor country setting than competing modern modes of production.[5] Furthermore, the feasibility for adopting such techniques widens considerably if the production process is divided into subprocesses or if consumers are willing to accept a slightly inferior product in exchange for a lower price (Stewart, 1974, 1975; Baron, 1975).

Uncovering vestigial appropriate technologies is one thing, but adopting such techniques would be a rear guard action at best if there were no prospects for the continual generation of and innovation on newly developed appropriate technologies. Here again, there is some allowance for muted optimism in the view of the progress reported by the Technology Consultancy Centre of the University of Kumasi, Ghana (Powell, 1976, 1977; Ntim and Powell, 1976), the Intermediate Technology Development Group of London; the Bandung Institute of Technology of Indonesia (Harahap and Alisyahbana, 1977); the Department of Chemical Engineering, National Autonomous University of Mexico (Giral Barnes, 1974); the International Rice Research Institute in Los Baños, the Philippines (Khan, 1974, 1976); and appropriate technology "cells" operating in India (Behari, 1974; Roy, 1977). The appropriate technology movement, once considered a joke, is achieving a certain amount of respectability now that the World Bank Group, United Nations Industrial Development Organization, U.S. government, and the Brace Research Institute of Quebec are getting into the act.[6] Frances Stewart, a specialist well versed in the ultra-microeconomic aspects of comparing production techniques, has observed that when research and development have been undertaken on techniques suitable for appropriate technologies, results have exceeded original expectations (Stewart, 1977: 66).

Two actions by developing countries are minimal. First, a systematic scanning of available appropriate technologies should be a routine function of agencies involved with applied technology. Second, on a modest and exploratory basis, active research and development designed to improve existing appropriate techniques or discover new ones should be directed to appropriate technologies already indicating an adequate potential payoff. These areas include unconventional energy sources such as biogas, wind power, and solar collectors; construction techniques for residential housing and large-scale infrastructure; scaling down of industrial process equipment; developing appropriate agricultural equipment; production methods for light and medium sized industries; and the recycling of waste material.

I must emphasize that the *Plan* certainly does not neglect these issues. High levels of underemployment are mentioned throughout, the use of labor-intensive technology is recommended where possible, and the feasibility of labor-intensive construction of infrastructure is recognized, as are the potential benefits of techniques for decentralized housing. The plight of the poor is highlighted by noting that two-thirds of the Mexican population suffers to some degree from malnutrition. The report correctly laments the concentration of agricultural research on innovations applicable to rain-fed or irrigated lands and the dearth of effort on improving yields in arid regions (CONACYT, 1976: 35, 165, 112, 186). The *Program* also mentions such issues in Section E, on "Science and Technology Development."

Yet nowhere is there a recognition, much less a comprehensive analysis, of the proper weight of science and technology policy in wrestling with a level of fallow labor and a pattern of income distribution that is already intolerable and continues to drift in the wrong direction. There is no consensus that these problems are so grave that they demand a *deliberate, concerted,* and *organized* effort to shift the spectrum of scientific and technological research activities more in favor of economic sectors that are capable of generating productive employment opportunities and/or those that clearly benefit the lot of the bulk of the population. Note the expression "shift the spectrum" in the previous sentence. No plea is being made to curtail completely the acquisition of "high" technology or technologies associated with the heavy industrial and processing sectors. Rather, it is an argument for a *relative* shift of resources allocated to alternative areas of research. If this advice is valid for the Mexican situation, I should think the arguments also apply to much of Latin America as a whole, which suffers from a disturbing amount of underutilized human capital and from what most of us, I feel, would subjectively consider an unfair and inhumane distribution of income.[7]

III. Critical Minimum Thresholds

The literature on science and technology is replete with mentions of "critical minima" thresholds for research and development. The implication is that below some minimum combination of inputs, especially some number of able researchers, little useful is likely to result. It is impossible to say where such thresholds are encountered; any specification is a matter of intuition or "feel" on the part of knowledgeable persons. Undoubtedly, the relevant minima will differ according to individual abilities, quality of material inputs, supporting infrastructure, position on the pure to applied research spectrum, and exact nature of the undertaking.

Despite the empirical difficulties, C. Richard Bath and I have attempted to clarify the issue by conceptually distinguishing four levels of generalization (Bath and James, 1979): (a) a *micro*-minimum for an individual research team whose members closely interact, (b) a *meso*minimum for interdisciplinary projects which require contributions from several distinct disciplines, (c) a *macro*minimum beyond which the scientific and technological community can begin to have some concrete influence on the amount of resources devoted to research and supporting infrastructure, and (d) a *mega*minimum beyond which scientific and technological achievements begin to exercise noticeable influence on social institutions and cultural values.

The *Plan* not only recognizes the existence of critical minima but also provides some excellent data on the magnitude of effort per project. In 1974 64.4% of the research institutions employed 5 researchers or less, and only 3.5% employed more than 20 employees. Presumably, full-time equivalent researchers are even lower, since the total of 7582 researchers in sectors covered converts to 4723.6 full-time equivalents, a reduction of about one-third. In fact, per *project,* less than one full-time researcher is employed. For the 122 units involved in basic research, 57.4% employed 4 researchers or less, and 36.9% used only 1 or 2 researchers. In health and medical research, of 234 research units, 63.7% employed 4 or less (CONACYT, 1976: 15, 32, 104, 172; Table 4 [242]).

If we can take something like 10 working scientists and technicians as a rough rule of thumb for a microminimum,[8] clearly—barring a massive increase in resources channeled into scientific and technological research as a whole—the number of projects must be consolidated and/or reduced. The *Plan* explicitly states that "one of the most important immediate objectives must be the creation of scientific critical masses which could make substantial contributions to the advancement of knowledge in a *reduced number of areas*" (CONACYT, 1976: 32; emphasis supplied). Who will decide on the areas to be pushed? "Within the policy framework defined in the Plan, the *scientific community must decide* in which areas it is feasible to form critical masses and to concentrate basic research" (CONACYT, 1976: 32; emphasis supplied). Indeed, the scientific community should have an important input into the selection of projects. This is desirable for a variety of reasons, the most important one in this context being their superior ability to estimate those research projects closest to their minimum effort thresholds. However, narrowing the number of projects, while increasing the resources per surviving project, is bound to require a more complex set of controlling agents. Both the *Plan* and the *Program* do a magnificent job of spelling out research priorities in each economic and scientific subsector. Specific research suggestions are made, for example, for Food, Agriculture and Forestry, Fishing, Industry, and so on. There is, however, no existing mechanism to choose projects from *among* the sectors. It seems to me that in order to achieve critical masses in individual projects, the next important task of rationalizing the research and development effort is to find some satisfactory combination of market forces—decisions in the political arena and participation by the scientific and technical community—that will provide the incentive to reduce projects at the external margin and expand them at the internal margin. Some remarks in Sections IV and V below will be pertinent.

The critical minimum concept applies not only to individual projects; it also has a geographical and institutional dimension. Institutions located in the Federal District accounted for 81.7% of the national research budget in 1973 and employed 80.9% of the personnel. Five institutions, Secretaría de Agricultura y Ganadería, Instituto Mexicano del Petróleo, Instituto Nacional de Energía Nuclear, Petroleo Mexicanos, S.A., and the Universidad Nacional Autónoma de México, accounted for 44.8% of research and development expenditures in 1973 and employed 38.9% of the personnel (CONACYT, 1976: 15). Bringing provincial institutions up to minimal standards is justified on economic grounds due to the potential payoff after crossing minimal thresholds, as a supporting element to Mexico's attempts to decentralize her industrial base, and in the hope that provincial institutions will be closer to relevant domestic problems directly affecting human welfare and choose their research projects accordingly.

In summary, the *Plan* recognizes the need for a critical minimum effort on the one hand, and, on the other, Mexico's excessively dispersed resources among projects and excessive geographic and institutional concentration. What is lacking is some mechanism to decide on intersectoral priorities and concomitantly bring about a minimally adequate mass of personnel, equipment, and infrastructure per project, institution, and geographic region.[9]

IV. Technological Dependence

A theme permeating the *Plan* and, in fact, one rationale for producing the document, is Mexico's dependence on external sources for acquiring scientific and technological knowledge. Scientific and technological development in mature industrial countries. "has become an essential factor in their political, economic, and cultural dominance over less developed nations" (CONACYT, 1976: 1). The eventual goal of scientific and technological planning is "technological self-reliance," which implies "freedom of choice in the search, selection, negotiation, utilization, assimilation, adaptation, and generation of technology, that is to say, the development of the capability to establish independent relationships" (CONACYT, 1976: 33).

Technological dependency manifests itself in several ways. Mexico in 1970 spent $40 million on scientific and technological activities, less than $1 per person, while spending more than $250 million on royalties to pay for technological imports (Soberón and Poveda, 1973: 183-84). There is nothing, of course, intrinsically undesirable about the large proportion of imported knowledge. Complaints, however, center on monopolistic practices by sellers of technology in charging exhorbitant prices, often through price transfers with affiliated firms (Vaitsos, 1974); exercising control over the technology licensees with regard to exports, pricing, product specification, and so on. (Vaitsos, 1974; Germidis and Brochet, 1975); and abusing of the international patent system (Vaitsos, 1972; Vaerynen, 1978). Often the technology imported fits poorly with existing economic conditions or needs (Stewart, 1977; Berrios, 1978). The concentrated pattern of foreign direct investment in high technology industries in Mexico is a source of alarm (Newfarmer and Mueller, 1975). Concern has been voiced over the denationalization of the Mexican engineering industry through foreign purchase or association with existing national firms (Nadal, 1977). Mexican engineering firms are also said to be at a disadvantage in the face of competition from foreign firms that have been able to become more specialized (CONACYT, 1976: 85). Finally, developing countries suffer from an "internal brain drain," i.e., a tendency for scientists and technicians to shun research projects of obvious applicability to domestic problems in favor of those most prestigious in the international scientific community. In this connection, the *Plan* points out that around 70% of Mexican research articles are published in foreign journals and that "institutions consider that publishing in a foreign journal is almost twice as important as publishing domestically" (CONACYT, 1976: 65).

I have absolutely no doubt that all of the above conditions exist and are serious; yet, in my opinion, the general tenor of the *Plan* is unjustifiably pessimistic about the degree of external dominance over Mexico's scientific and technological program. First, the *Plan* itself has an excellent section detailing the provisions of the 1972 Law Governing the Registry for the Transfer of Technology and the Use and Exploitation of Patents and Trademarks. In essence, the law with embellishments and clarifications in a 1973 law regulating foreign investment, prohibits most of the objectionable restrictions that had been routinely imposed on licensee firms, and establishes the power to prohibit excessive charges for technology transfers. The Mexican Ministry of Industry and Commerce estimates that savings on payments for royalties, technical assistance, engineering services, and so on, due to regulatory actions of the National Registry for the Transfer of Technology, amounted to $5.6 billion pesos by July 1976. By March 31, 1976, approximately 30% of the resolved contract applications had been rejected on the first submission (CONACYT, 1976: 207, 208). In 1976, Mexico made major changes in her patent and trademark legislation designed to reduce or abolish some of the most troublesome problems in these areas. These legislative provisions, while no panacea, have at least provided a means of partially countering the disadvantageous market imperfections inherent in the international transfer of technology.

Second, the Mexican firm does not appear as far "out of it" in securing technology as the dependency literature and the *Plan* imply. In the late 1960s Loretta Fairchild (then Loretta Good) matched pairs of Monterrey industrial firms so that each pair consisted of a United States controlled firm and a Mexican national counterpart producing the same or similar product. Fairchild's original hypothesis was that Mexican firms suffered serious disadvantages in acquiring technology. After extensive interviews with officials of the firms, she could find no such evidence. Incredulous, she returned in the early 1970s and repeated the research, this time with stricter controls on the research design. The same conclusions were reached: the Mexican firms are competitive with foreign firms in obtaining technology even though, interestingly enough, the Mexican entrepreneurs *think* foreign firms outshine them in this regard (Fairchild, 1977). While true that Monterrey is considered more entrepreneurial than the rest of Mexico (Derossi, 1971), Fairchild's research indicates that the more vigorous Mexican firms are not doomed to technological subservience.

Third, Mexico is beginning to show some success with exporting technology which in itself indicates some autonomous progress for her technological endeavors. The 13-year-old Instituto Mexicano del Petróleo (IMP), for example, has not only developed chemical products saving about $3.3 million in imports per year—but is actively selling technological expertise abroad. Among IMP's technological export projects are: Jamaica—technology to the state firm Petrojam for engineering a refinery at Launa Point; Ecuador—training of technical personnel in the state petroleum corporation and a study of hydrocarbon distribution; Costa Rica—a feasibility study for a petrochemical complex; Brazil—a study of catalytic plants for Brazil's Petrobras; Colombia—a general transfer of technologies which IMP markets under the trademark "DeMex" for a plant being constructed in Barrancabermeja: United States—"DeMex" techniques for Universal Oil Products to design a refinery; and Saudi Arabia—a refinery design for a facility in Ryaden (Nelson, 1977; Burg, 1978). IMP has also signed a technical exchange pact with Technipetrol, an Italian firm, and is operating in Peru and Venezuela (Journal of Commerce, 1978). Hojalata y Lamina has sold technology for direct reduction in steel-making to Brazil, Iraq, Iran, Indonesia, and Zambia; a method for premolding concrete for use in construction has been transferred to Colombia and Venezuela by the Mexican firm conceiving the method, I.C. Construcciones; and Bufete Industrial has exported technology called the "Cusi" process for manufacturing paper from sugar cane wastes. From January 1973 to July 1975, exports of Mexican technology and supporting services were $137 million. One paper plant alone using the Cusi technology was sold for $200 million to Argentina in 1976 for operation in Tucumán province (Katz and Albin, 1977: 4). A subsidiary of Fomento de

Industria y Comercio is increasing exports of glass-making technology to Colombia, Brazil, Venezuela, Guatemala, United States, and England (American Chamber of Commerce of Mexico, 1978: 17). Mexicana de Technología has been created by CONACYT as a company promoting and commercializing Mexican technology. Feasibility studies, experimental development, marketing, patents, and consulting services are offered (CONACYT, 1978: 22).

Fourth, the Mexican government, if it chooses, can exercise significant influence over the direction of science and technology. In 1973 the federal government, decentralized agencies, and state-owned companies accounted for about 60% of Mexico's research and development budget, while institutions of higher learning funded largely from government sources account for another 22%. Thus, over four-fifths of research and development expenditures are under potential government influence (CONACYT, 1976: 14). Aside from direct administrative direction over government-financed research, Mexican purchasing policy of government agencies could encourage the use of national technology and consulting services when cost comparisons are favorable or reasonably close.[10] The *Plan* mentions these possibilities (CONACYT, 1976: 29), as does Banco Nacional de Comercio Exterior (1976: 18), which places particular emphasis on the potential for organizing small- and medium-sized industrial production through regularized state purchasing.

Finally, and perhaps most important, there are numerous inefficiencies mentioned in the *Plan* that are clearly not attributable to external forces. Until recently, scientific equipment and materials were subject to regular tariffs and customs procedures. The *Plan* speaks of unnecessary duplication of effort due to the absence of communication and coordination among research institutions. Only 10% of research projects are multi-institutional. There were virtually no interinstitutional agreements for equipment sharing and very little equipment-sharing within institutions. Bottlenecks in supporting technical staff divert scientists' time to routine administrative chores. Because of poor or nonexistent maintenance, 60% of equipment and materials "are not in usable condition." Lack of centralized purchases increases the price of equipment 2.5 times, the higher price going mainly to middlemen. Administrators of institutions often purchase according to their own criteria, with little or no input from the researchers themselves. Institutions, in almost every case, do not participate in planning and budgeting. Finally, there is a lack of rationalization and coordination in the system of awarding scholarships (CONACYT, 1976: 13, 23, 61, 89, 91, 104, 183).

No doubt, any country's science and technology program will harbor defects, but in the case of Mexico, they appear so severe and numerous that a major effort devoted to increasing efficiency of the existing system should receive top priority. Indeed, some steps have been taken. In 1976, CONACYT successfully argued for exempting scientific equipment and materials from import taxes and fees, and some steps are being taken by that agency to improve equipment maintenance (CONACYT, 1976: 90, 219; CONACYT, 1978: 52, 53). But obviously, much remains to be done.

The arguments contained in this section are not intended to deny the condition of dependency, but to shed some light on its severity. In my opinion, Mexico's potential autodetermination over her scientific and technological destiny is underrated by the *Plan* as well as much of the Latin American dependency literature.

V. The Market and Participatory Decisions

Left to itself, the scientific community, given the existing pattern of incentives, will not be able to reorder Mexico's research effort. Some guidance at the macropolitical level is needed to point out the general direction of the nation's science and technology endeavors. The *Program* delineates a number of institutional arrangements, consultancy groups, and agencies that should provide some overall guidance, and could perhaps contribute to a partial resolution of intersectoral priorities alluded to in a previous section of this article (CONACYT, 1978: 93-98).

In addition to coordination of institutional activities and budgetary matters, however, each institution and program should ordinarily be subject to the discipline of an objective, impersonal, outside appraisal. Normally, for applied research, the verdict should be handed down by the market. When externalities exist, and this would be true for some applied research and at the interface between applied and pure research, a cost-benefit analysis should be performed by an outside agency. In the case of pure research, some peer evaluation of its worthiness and promise, with at least some input from outside the performing institution, is warranted.

Focusing on the role of the market, a case can be made that government-funded research organizations charged with allocating X percentage of their resources at the applied end of the research spectrum, should, after a reasonable start-up period, be expected to generate roughly X percentage of its own funding. The reasons for supporting such a measure can begin by contending that parastatal agencies as they are normally operated are highly resistant to a process of "creative destruction," to borrow Joseph Schumpeter's term. Perpetuation of scarce resources tied up in poorly performing agencies is a cost too expensive to bear.[11]

Market incentives for institutions should also contribute to improving the match between the research being done and the pattern of demand for the results of scientific and technological investigation. Under present circumstances, most scientists choose their own projects, choices that are inordinately influenced by the appeal of international prestige with the result that much research performed is unrelated to domestic demand. This is true even for some applied research projects (CONACYT, 1976: 105, 17). In the absence of market incentives, there is every reason for institutions to perpetuate the pattern and bask in the glory of any internationally recognized achievement, however remote it may be from internal needs.

The market offers at least some buffering from political intervention. Scientific investigation requires continuous activity over an extended period of time. Compared to other Latin American countries, Mexico's problems in this context are mild, but an administrative shake-up associated with Mexico's presidential cycle is a disruptive force mentioned by the *Plan.* Presumably an institution performing well and contributing to its support would be less vulnerable to political intervention.[12]

In addition, market forces are the best means for encouraging creative adaptation, minor innovation, and individual inventiveness. Much innovation is never picked up in the aggregate research and development data. Conversations with Viviane B. de Márquez, a sociologist with El Colegio de México who has done work on innovation in the paper industry (1979), and Jorge Katz, who has investigated innovations in Argentina (e.g., Katz and Albin, 1977), have been instructive in this regard. Often the manager of a firm will initially report zero expenditures and effort on research and development, but closer questioning of the machine operators and engineers reveals all sorts of incremental improvements which, taken cumulatively, are important to cost reduction and product development. Similarly, the existence of critical minima for most organized research effort does not preclude contributions from independent inventors outside a formal research institution. Independent invention still remains important in developed countries (Jewkes et al., 1953) and, it would seem on a priori grounds, independent inventors could make valuable contributions to developing countries in areas such as appropriate technology, where ingenuity, time, and determination are more important inputs than capital. Despite serious departures from perfect competition, including free access to knowledge, market incentives remain one of the best instruments for expanding innovational activity and individual, informal research. One might also be justified in surmising that if careers as well as institutional life rested on some objective, outside assessment of performance, colleague incompetence, poor maintenance of equipment, and refusals by fellow researchers to share equipment would not be so widely countenanced. Finally, we can note that a program of government purchasing to encourage the development of local technological capability would operate through the impact of the market.

In addition to the market and outsider-performed cost-benefit studies, or peer assessment, there is a role for greater technocratic participation in decisions affecting science and technology policy directly, its supporting infrastructure, and its end use. Participatory decisions are justified on several scores. As John Kenneth Galbraith has reminded us, as the knowledge explosion causes the degree of complexity in any subsector of knowledge to be more and more beyond the ken of the decision makers, de facto power is either ceded to the technocracy or decisions become increasingly irrational.

Participatory decisions also are the best means of internalizing important cultural values that otherwise are externalized by a market system (Goulet, 1977) and, for that matter, very often by macropolitical decisions as well. From this standpoint there is every reason to encourage participatory interfaces with technology users. The cooperation of peasants in deciding technological options is suggested by the *Plan* (CONACYT, 1976: 35), and Allen Jedlicka (1977, 1979) has convincingly demonstrated that, in addition to being somewhat less disruptive to cultural values, it is a more efficient method of persuasion even if we use a narrowly defined economic set of criteria for judging the results. The same might be true of technocratic participation in budgetary decisions, equipment orders, project selection, and the like. This would seem to be an improvement over a situation in which each individual researchers have too much control over project selection, and all too little in matters affecting their financial, administrative, and material support. The *Plan* suggests such an arrangement (CONACYT, 1976: 46); the next task consists of experimenting with participatory arrangements and improving them as experience dictates.

VI. Lamentable Fate of the Plan

In some ways the *Program* can be considered a more businesslike implementation of the *Plan.* After all, national expenditures on science and technology are slated to rise substantially, approximately 2500 projects costing $260 million have been approved and $130 million are earmarked for 17,000 scholarships (Flores, 1979). Why, then, does an outsider, when comparing the *Plan* and *Program,* get the distinct impression that only in a very limited and superficial sense is the latter a true reflection and extension of the former?

For one thing, the *Program,* and evidently its implementation thus far, does little beyond the purely quantitative function of financing research projects and scholarships. The *Plan* insisted on a variety of crucial points, including: (1) Given conditions in a developing country, some form of indicative planning applied to science and technology is needed; (2) such planning should include a long-term dimension, and to be really effective must be coordinated with a more general scheme for socioeconomic development; (3) much, and perhaps the brunt, of the public sector support should focus on increasing and upgrading the supporting infrastructure for science and technology; (4) a national budget for science and technology should be formulated with participation by research, development, and supporting institutions; (5) the existing network of suppliers, supporters, and users of newly produced scientific and technological knowledge must be more fully integrated; and (6) efforts and expense directed toward increasing the social awareness of the potential of science and technology are warranted. While some of these issues are not entirely neglected in the *Program,* one is likely to sense that the fervor and general commitment to planning along these lines are no longer present.

These suspicions are corroborated by Eduardo Amadeo, formerly with the National Council on Science and Technology of Argentina. Speaking about the *Plan,* he asserts:

> in early 1977, all this enormous effort was disregarded by the new authorities of CONACYT, and the Plan rests only as an example of serious academic work [1979: 15].

Miguel S. Wionczek, one of the chief architects of the *Plan,* agrees that the dictates of the earlier document are being systematically ignored (1977, 1979a). It is significant that when presenting an updated version of his 1977 article at a conference during April 1978, Wionczek (1979b) had added a section entitled "The Demise of the Plan" in which he concludes:

> From the perspective of early 1978, about one-and-a-half years after the official release of the first Science and Technology Plan in Mexico, it seems clear that the plan is not going to be implemented during the present administration that started in 1976.

In the wake of such a path-breaking, penetrating, and impressive document as the *Plan,* how can we explain a return to the business-as-usual approach of financing projects and scholarships? Several immediate causes suggest themselves. The *Plan,* appearing at the transition period of the six-year Mexican presidency, was subject to the normal administrative shuffle, perhaps made more severe in this case by the general feeling that the Echeverría regime had been characterized by a super abundance of newly created institutions and interference by the public sector. Also, the appearance of the *Plan* coincided with the financial and economic discord, which rapidly translated into political and social unrest, that centered around the devaluations and floats of the Mexican peso during late 1976. In the most inviting circumstances, it is difficult enough to convince the political arena to concentrate on long-run payoffs; it is well-nigh impossible when all attention, energies, and resources are usurped by a serious short-term catastrophe demanding financial conservatism.

While these immediate difficulties were real, there may be even more basic conditions explaining the lack of acceptance of the *Plan.* Wionczek suggests that the unprecedented cooperation of the Mexican president and CONACYT's Council of Directors led to an overestimation of the political system's fundamental interest in science and technology planning (1979: 230). As Amadeo put it, in retrospect the political support for CON-

ACYT, seems to have been "more formal than real" (1979: 158). Closely related, it appears that the static inertia of entrenched bureaucratic interests, in the government and within the scientific and technological community itself, were similarly underestimated. Joseph Hodara (1978: 21), in his classification of Mexican scientific intellectuals, speaks of one type who is likely to view any attempts at public sector orientation of scientific activity as "constituting signs of a dangerous and suffocating bureaucratization." Indeed, the manner in which the projects were chosen under the current *Program,* allowing research entities to nominate their own and fitting them into nine broad categories of priorities (Flores, 1979), would seem a method calculated to do the least violence to entrenched vested interests of the existing pattern of power and privilege within the research establishment.

Finally, both Wionczek and Hodara point out that the 'socialization" of science and technology in Mexico is far from complete. According to Hodara, there is only a precarious internalization of the "scientific spirit" in Mexico wherein the "intrinsic value of science as an expression of human culture is taken for granted" (1978: 20).

VII. Summary

It is hoped that differences of opinion regarding emphasis and accentuation expressed and documented by an outsider economist may be of some value in suggesting either problems attracting too little attention or, in the case of dependency, too much. The contentions have been that first, science and technology planning should be directly made on an important component in any policy mix for ameliorating the dearth of productive employment opportunities and maldistribution of income. Second, an effective institutional arrangement must be found for achieving a greater concentration of effort on a smaller number of research projects, along with some more rational geographic dispersion. Third, there is a danger of becoming unjustifiably preoccupied with and overestimating the degree of restriction attributable to dependency on external sources for scientific and technological knowledge. Fourth, it is suggested that a combination of market forces, outside cost-benefit and peer assessment, and participatory decisions be added to the existing network of macropolitical and interagency controls that exist for influencing the allocation of resources to scientific and technological endeavors.

Finally, the intent of this article was decidedly not to detract from Mexico's science and technology policy. Amadeo (1978: 1445) once remarked that no voice had been raised to defend the *Plan* or point out its possibilities. Despite the criticisms elaborated above, in my opinion, the *Plan* remains a superb summation and critique of the state of science and technology in Mexico and is one of the most honest, forthright documents one is likely to encounter anywhere. Now that the dust has settled from the pressing financial crisis of late 1976, and as Mexican energy export earnings begin to come on stream, perhaps conditions more propitious for long-run endeavors will prevail, and at least some of the thrust and direction of the *Plan* can be salvaged.

NOTES

1. For citations on studies of Mexican employment and underemployment, see Evans and James (1979). Also, for corroborative evidence, see Gollás (1978: 74), who estimates the 1977 underemployed at 49.3% and unemployment at 6.0% of the economically active population. He does not attempt to convert this into an unemployment equivalent, however.

2. The results of four income distribution studies for Mexico in 1950, 1958, 1963, and 1969 can be found in Barkin (1975: 65). Note, however, that he perpetuated an old "typo" from the original study. The figure for the second decile, 1950, should be 3.4, not 2.4. Regarding Mexico and India, in 1969 for Mexico's lowest 40%, middle 40%, and highest 20% of the population, the income shares were 10.5%, 25.5%, and 64.0%. The corresponding figures for India in 1964 were 16.0%, 32.0%, and 52.0% (Ahluwalia, 1974: 8). For elaboration on the suspected income distributional effects of the Green Revolution, expanded higher education, and inflation, see Evans and James (1979).

3. This precise position was repeated in response to a question from the floor by a CONACYT official who was a fellow participant in a December 1978 symposium dealing with science and technology policy at the North American Economic Studies Association in Mexico City.

4. John Evans and I have elaborated elsewhere (1978) on a policy mix for ameliorating Mexico's employment problems.

5. See Bhalla (1975), Baron (1975), Cooper et al. (1975), Cooper and Kaplinsky with Turner (1975), and Stewart (1975, 1977: 208-238). The International Labour Office (1976) also provides a useful review of the activities of that agency.

6. See World Bank (1976) and several publications listed in UNIDO (1978). For Brace's involvement, see Lawland et al. (1974). The United States has recently established a National Center for Appropriate Technology.

7. The unemployment equivalent of the labor force in 1970 is estimated at 13.6% (Argentina), 32.2% (Brazil), 29.6% (Colombia), 22.8% (Chile), and 27.2% (Venezuela). See PREALC (1976: 38). For income distribution in 44 developing countries, including many Latin American nations, see Adelman and Morris (1971).

8. Harrison Brown (1973: 24) puts the "micro-minimum" in basic research within a single university at about ten competent scientists. E.A.G. Robinson (1973: 88) reports "it was found [in the United Kingdom] that research units of less than ten people were almost purely channels of communication and were not adding to knowledge."

9. Several other matters pertaining to economies of scale are discussed briefly in James (1979).

10. For a comprehensive treatment of state purchasing and technological policy in Latin America, see Aráoz (1977).

11. For a general outline of what we know and do not know about the economic behavior of parastatal organizations in Latin America, see Glade (1977).

12. James H. Street is putting together a more comprehensive treatment of political intervention and other suggestions for reducing its detrimental impact. For a preliminary report on his thinking, see Street (1979).

REFERENCES

ADELMAN, I. and C. T. MORRIS (1971) An Anatomy of Income Distribution Patterns in Developing Countries. Washington, DC: International Bank for Reconstruction and Development.

AHLUWALIA, M. S. (1974) "Income inequality: some dimensions of the problem," pp. 3-37 in H. Chenery et al., Redistribution with Growth. London: Oxford Univ. Press.

AMADEO, E. (1979) "National science and technology councils in Latin America: achievement and failures of the first ten years," pp. 149-166 in D. B. Thomas and M. S. Wionczek (eds.) Integration of Science and Technology with Development: Caribbean and Latin American Problems in the Context of the United Nations Conference on Science and Technology for Development. New York: Pergamon.

——— (1978) "Los consejos nacionales de ciencia y technología en América Latina: exitos y fracasos del primer decenio." Comercio Exterior 28 (December): 1439-1447.

American Chamber of Commerce of Mexico (1978) "Monterrey: growing with Mexico." Mexican Amer. Rev. (November): 3-51.

ARAOZ, A. (1977) "Compras estatales y desarrollo tecnológico." Comercio Exterior 27 (Junio): 654-670.

Banco Nacional de Comercio Exterior, S. A. [BNCE] (1976) Mexico 1976: Facts, Figures, Trends. Mexico, DF: Author.

BARKIN, D. (1975) "Mexico's albatross: The U.S. economy." Latin American Perspectives 2 (Spring): 64-80.

BARON, C. G. (1975) "Sugar processing in India," pp. 175-202 in A. S. Bhalla (ed.) Technology and Employment in Industry. Geneva: International Labour Office.

BATH, C. R. and D. D. JAMES (1979) "The extent of technological dependence in Latin America," pp. 11-28 in J. H. Street and D. D. James (eds.) Technological Progress in Latin America: Prospects for Overcoming Dependency. Boulder, CO: Westview.

BEHARI, B. (1974) "Genesis, organization and action programme of the 'appropriate technology' cell," pp. 168-172 in Choice and Adaptation of Technology in Developing Countries: An Overview of Major Policy Issues. Paris: Organization for Economic Cooperation and Development.

BERRIOS, R. (1978) "The commercialization of advanced-country technology and its inappropriateness for less developed countries." Institute of Social Studies, The Hague. (unpublished)

BHALLA, A. S. (1975) Technology and Employment in Industry. Geneva: International Labour Office.

BROWN, H. (1973) "The role of science and technology in development," pp. 4-31 in Esquenazi-Mayo et al. (eds.) The Scientific and Technological Gap in Latin America. Lincoln: Univ. of Nebraska Press.

BURG, A. (1978) "El instituto del petróleo exporta technología." Ciencia y Desarrollo (March/April): 27-32.

CONACYT [Consejo Nacional de Ciencia y Tecnología] (1978) Mexico's Program for Science and Technology, 1978-1982. Mexico, D.F.: Author.

——— (1976) National Indicative Plan for Science and Technology. Mexico, D.F.: Author.

COOPER, C. and R. KAPLINSKY with R. TURNER (1975) "Second-hand equipment in developing countries: jute processing machinery in Kenya," pp. 123-151 in A. S. Bhalla (ed.) Technology and Employment in Industry. Geneva: International Labour Office.

COOPER, C., R. KAPLINSKY, R. BELL, and W. SATYARAKWIT (1975) "Choice of techniques for can making in Kenya, Tanzania and Thailand," pp. 35-81 in A. S. Bhallo (ed.) Technology and Employment in Industry. Geneva: International Labour Office.

DE MARQUEZ, V. B. (1979) "Organization structure and innovativeness: a comparison between transnational and national firms in the pulp and paper manufacturing industry in Mexico," pp. 149-172 in J. H. Street and D. D. James (eds.) Technological Progress in Latin America: Prospects for Overcoming Dependency. Boulder, CO: Westview.

DEROSSI, F. (1971) The Mexican Entrepreneur. Paris: Organization for Economic Cooperation and Development.

EDWARDS, E. O. [ed.] (1974) Employment in Developing Nations. New York: Columbia Univ. Press.

ESQUENAZI-MAYO, R., K. N. SHAHANI, and S. B. TREVES [eds.] (1973) The Scientific and Technological Gap in Latin America. Lincoln: University of Nebraska Institute for International Studies.

EVANS, J. S. and D. D. JAMES (1979) "Conditions of employment and income distribution in Mexico as incentives for Mexican migration to the United States: prospects to the end of the century." Int. Migration Rev. 13 (Spring): 4-24.

——— (1978) "Increasing productive employment in Mexico," pp. 342-350 in Structural Factors in Mexican and Caribbean Basin Migration: Proceedings of a Brookings Institution/El Colegia de México Symposium. Washington, DC: Brookings.

FAIRCHILD, L. G. (1977) "Performance and technology of United States and national firms in Mexico." J. of Development Studies 14 (October): 14-34.

FLORES, E. (1979) "Mexico's program for science and technology, 1978 to 1982." Science 204: 1279-1282.

FRANK, A. G. (1972) "The development of underdevelopment," pp. 3-17 in J. D. Cockcroft et al., Dependence and Underdevelopment: Latin America's Political Economy. Garden City, NY: Doubleday.

FURTADO, C. (1973) "The Brazilian 'model' of development," pp. 297-306 in C. K. Wilber (ed.) The Political Economy of Development and Underdevelopment. New York: Random House.

GERMIDIS, D. and C. BROCHET (1975) "The price of technology transfer in the developing countries." Organization for Economic Cooperation and Development. Paris: (mimeo)

GIRAL BARNES, J. (1974) "Development of appropriate chemical technology: a programme in Mexico," pp. 182-186 in Choice and Adaptation of Technology in Developing Countries: An Overview of Major Policy Issues. Paris: Organization for Economic Cooperation and Development.

GLADE, W. P. (1977) "Implications of growth of the public sector for Latin America." Prepared for the Southwestern Economics Association, Dallas, March/April.

GOLLAS, M. (1978) "El desempelo en México: soluciones posibles." Ciencia y Desarrollo (May/June): 73-86.

GOULET, D. (1977) The Uncertain Promise: Value Conflicts in Technology Transfer. New York: International Documentation/North America.

HARAHAP, F. and I. ALISYAHBANA (1977) "Indigenous scientific and technological research in Indonesia: its problems and prospects." Prepared for the American Association for the Advancement of Science, Denver, February.

HODARA, J. (1978) "El intelectual científico mexicano: una tipología" Interciencia 3 (January/February): 20-22.

International Labour Office (1976) World Employment Programme: Research in Retrospect and Prospect. Geneva: Author.

JAMES, D. D. (1979) "The economic case for more indigenous science and technology research and development in LDCs," pp. 83-108 in J. H. Street and D. D. James (eds.) Technological Progress in Latin America: Prospects for Overcoming Dependency. Boulder: Westview.

——— (1973) "Used automated plants in less developed countries: a case study of a Mexican firm." Inter-American Econ. Affairs 27 (Summer): 31-46.

JEDLICKA, A. D. (1979) "The acquisition and use of technical knowledge by Mexican farmers of limited resources," pp. 121-128 in J. H. Street and D. D. James (eds.) Technological Progress in Latin America: Prospects for Overcoming Dependency. Boulder: Westview.

——— (1977) Organization for Rural Development: Risk Taking and Appropriate Technology. New York: Praeger.

JEQUIER, N. [ed.] (1976) Appropriate Technology: Problems and Promises. Paris: Organization for Economic Cooperation and Development.

JEWKES, J., D. SAWYERS, and R. STILLERMAN (1958) The Sources of Invention. New York: Macmillan.

Journal of Commerce (1978) "Mexico, Italy to swap oil technology." March 8.

KATZ, J. and E. ALBIN (1977) "De la indústria incipiente a la exportación de technología: la experiencia Argentina en la venta internacional de plantas industriales y obras de ingeniería." Monografía de Trabajo 14. Buenos Aires: Inter-American Development Bank/Economic Commission for Latin America.

KHAN, A. U. (1976) "Mechanization technology for tropical agriculture," pp. 213-230 in N. Jéquier (ed.) Appropriate Technology: Problems and Promises. Paris: Organization for Economic Cooperation and Development.

——— (1974) "Appropriate technologies: Do we transfer, adapt or develop?" pp. 223-233 in E. O. Edwards (ed.) Employment in Developing Nations. New York: Columbia Univ. Press.

LAWLAND, T. A., F. HVELPLUND, R. ALWARD, and J. VOSS (1974) "Brace Research Institute's handbook of appropriate technology," pp. 124-136 in N. Jéquier (ed.) Appropriate Technology: Problems and Promises. Paris: Organization for Economic Cooperation and Development.

McROBIE, G. (1976) "The mobilization of knowledge on low-cost technology: outline of a strategy," pp. 114-123 in N. Jéquier (ed.) Appropriate Technology: Problems and Promises. Paris: Organization for Economic Cooperation and Development.

NADAL, A. (1977) "Multinational corporations and transfer of technology: the case of Mexico," pp. 219-250, Volume I, in D. Germidis (ed.) Transfer of Technology by Multinational Corporations. Paris: Organization for Economic Cooperation and Development.

NELSON, P. (1977) "Pemex ambitious growth program held key to economic devel opment." J. of Commerce (July 25).

NEWFARMER, R. S. and W. F. MUELLER (1975) Multinational Corporations in Brazil and Mexico: Structural Sources of Economic and Noneconomic Power. Washington, DC: Government Printing Office.

NTIM, B. A. and J. W. POWELL (1976) "Appropriate technology in Ghana: the experience of Kumsai University's technology consultancy centre," pp. 276-285 in N. Jéquier (ed.) Appropriate Technology: Problems and Promises. Paris: Organization for Economic Cooperation and Development.

OECD [Organization for Economic Cooperation and Development] (1974) Choice and Adaptation of Technology in Developing Countries: An Overview of Major Policy Issues. Paris: Author.

POWELL, J. W. (1977) "An intermediate technology role for a university in the third world." Prepared for the American Association for the Advancement of Science, Denver, February.

——— (1976) Technology Consultancy Centre Annual Review 4, 1975-1976. Kumsai, Ghana: University of Science and Technology.

PREALC [Programa Regional para Empleo en América Latina y El Caribe] (1976) The Employment Problem in Latin America: Facts, Outlooks and Policies. Santiago: Author.

ROBINSON, E.A.G. (1973) "Discussion of the paper by Professor Grilisches," pp. 88-89 in B. R. Williams (ed.) Science and Technology in Economic Growth. New York: John Wiley.

ROY, A. K. (1977) "Development planning and technology: some alternatives for the Indian case." Prepared for the American Association for the Advancement of Science, Denver, February.

SOBERON, G. and A. POVEDA (1973) "Mexico's scientific and technological gap and the program of scientific development of the Universidad Autónoma de México," pp. 181-191 in Esquenazi-Mayo et al. (eds.) The Scientific and Technological Gap in Latin America. Lincoln: Univ. of Nebraska Press.

STEWART, F. (1977) Technology and Underdevelopment. Boulder: Westview.

——— (1975) "Manufacture of cement blocks in Kenya,"pp. 272-293 in A. S. Bhalla (ed.) Technology and Employment in Industry. Geneva: International Labour Office. (Reprinted with changes in Stewart [1977] Technology and Underdevelopment. Boulder: Westview.)

——— (1974) "Technology and employment in LDCs," pp. 83-132 in E. Edwards (ed.) Employment in Developing Nations.

STRASSMANN, W. P. (1979) "The development of alternative construction techniques in Latin America," pp. 247-257 in J. H. Street and D. D. James (eds.) Technological Progress in Latin America: Prospects for Overcoming Dependency. Boulder: Westview.

STREET, J. H. (1979) "Reducing political intervention in Latin American science and technology: some unorthodox proposals." Prepared for the American Association for the Advancement of Science, Houston, January.

——— and D. D. JAMES [eds.] (1979) Technological Progress in Latin America: Prospects for Overcoming Dependency. Boulder: Westview.

STREET, J. H. and D. D. JAMES (1978) "Closing the technology gap in Latin America." J. of Econ. Issues 12 (June): 477-496.

SURI, M. M. (1975) "Local capability and preparedness for appropriate technology." Geneva: International Labour Office. (mimeo)

THOMAS, D. B. and M. S. WIONCZEK [eds.] (1979) Integration of Science and Technology with Development: Caribbean and Latin American Problems in the Context of the United Nations Conference on Science and Technology for Development. New York: Pergamon.

UNIDO [United Nations Industrial Development Organization] (1978) Newsletter (August).

VAITSOS, C. V. (1974) Intercounty Income Distribution and Transnational Enterprises. Oxford: Clarendon Press.

——— (1972) "Patents revisited: their function in developing countries." J. of Development Studies 9 (October): 71-97.

VAEYRYNEN, R. (1978) "International patenting as a means of technological dominance." Int. Social Sci. J. 30, 2: 315-337.

WELLS, L. T., Jr. (1975) "Economic man and engineering man: choice of technology in a low-wage country," pp. 69-93 in C. Peter Timmer et al., The Choice of Technology in Developing Countries: Some Cautionary Tales. Cambridge, MA: Harvard University Center for International Affairs.

WILLIAMS, B. R. [ed.] (1973) Science and Technology in Economic Growth. New York: John Wiley.

WIONCZEK, M. S. (1979a) "¿Es viable una política de ciencia y technología en México?" (unpublished)

——— (1979b) "Science and technology planning problems in a large circum-Caribbean country (Mexico)," pp. 220-232 in D. Thomas and M. S. Wionczek (eds.) Integration of Science and Technology with Development: Caribbean and Latin American Problems in the Context of the United Nations Conference on Science and Technology for Development. New York: Pergamon.

——— (1977) "Science and technology planning in Mexico and its relevance to other developing countries." Interciencia 2 (November/December): 328-334.

World Bank (1976) Appropriate Technology in World Bank Activities. Washington, DC: Authors.

Dilmus D. James is Professor of Economics at the University of Texas at El Paso. His research interests include dependency theory, U.S.-Mexican economic interactions, and the economic aspects of science and technology policy in the Third World, and he has coauthored several articles on these subjects.

JOHN A. BOOTH
University of Texas at San Antonio

A GUATEMALAN NIGHTMARE
Levels of Political Violence, 1966-1972

Since the late sixties, Guatemalans have murdered each other at an astonishing rate.[1] This wave of politically related terrorism and assassinations began to grow rapidly in 1966 and has continued, fluctuating in intensity, to the present. In 1967, for instance, incidents of violence averaged 70 per month, causing some 30 monthly deaths; in 1971 the figures had risen 60%. This article describes the historical antecedents of this conflict, its development as right-wing terrorists sought to counterbalance leftist guerrilla insurgency and the subsequent evolution of violence. Seeking an explanation for why violence was greater in some areas than in others, the essay examines two structural theories which suggest that conflict may be most intense where the strength of contending political parties is most nearly equal and where socioeconomic change is greatest.

Political Violence in Guatemala

The remote origins of political violence in Guatemala lie in a tradition of repression of rural labor dating back to the colonial

---

AUTHOR'S NOTE: This is a revised version of a paper presented at a meeting of the Southwestern Conference of Latin American Studies in Huntsville, Texas, in April 1975. Karl M. Schmitt, Jerry L. Weaver, Alejandro Portes, and Lawrence S. Graham made very helpful observations on earlier versions of this article. I especially wish to thank David Scott Palmer for comments and for assistance in getting important new data, and John P. Harrison for his patience until the State Department finally made them available.

Journal of Interamerican Studies and World Affairs, Vol. 22 No. 2, May 1980 195-225

era. With the advent of the coffee industry in the last third of the nineteenth century, larger coffee producers and the government collaborated to maintain a debt slavery system that legitimized both official and private use of force to ensure an adequate supply of Indian workers. Under the dictatorship of Jorge Ubico, new vagrancy laws replaced debt slavery as the major labor control device, increasing central government control over the repressive system without significantly improving the lot of workers. In fact, government troops earlier put down several peasant disturbances, using considerable force, in the 1920s and 1930s. Thus, Guatemala moved toward mid-twentieth century with a well-entrenched pattern of public and private violence to ensure conformity of workers with the established politicoeconomic order (Jones, 1940: 150-153; Murphy, 1970: 438-441; Schmid, 1967: 65-66; Adams, 1970: 174-182).

The period beginning with Ubico's overthrow in 1944 brought dramatic changes in that order, leading ultimately to the contemporary political violence. Democratization under the administration of Juan José Arévalo (1944-1950) encouraged the rapid mobilization of campesinos and industrial workers, bringing both sectors previously unknown economic and political power. President Jacobo Arbenz (1950-1954) accelerated this process and opened policy-making to marxists. The resultant pressures for greatly redistributive policies struck hard at the local business and landed elites, at such U.S. interests as United Fruit, at the "containment" orientation of U.S. cold war foreign policy, and—by democratic example—at Guatemala's neighboring dictatorships. By 1954 conservative forces had rallied, with the support of the United States, Nicaragua, Honduras, and El Salvador, and Colonel Castillo Armas invaded while the acquiescent army permitted the "liberators" to oust Arbenz. Past episodes of political violence, as is typical (Gurr, 1970), seem to have served as a template for the 1954-1957 period. Among the techniques both government and others employed to dismantle the revolution's programs were torture, beatings, imprisonment, and murder of labor and *campesino* leaders

(Murphy, 1970: 469; Fondo de Cultura Popular, 1969: 13-15). Police terror continued after Miguel Ydígoras Fuentes succeeded Castillo in 1957. This, plus the growing corruption of the Ydígoras government, prompted an abortive coup attempt by a reformist army officers' group in 1960. Escaped remnants of the plotters formed the nucleus of the first of soon-to-be several leftist guerrilla groups. Military operations against the guerrillas proved ineffective, promoting rising dissatisfaction within military ranks which culminated in Colonel Enrique Peralta Azurdia's *golpe* in 1963. A rapid expansion of the counterinsurgency program ensued.

In 1965 the military decided to return power to civilians the following year. The dry prose of a recently declassified U.S. Department of State (DOS) report from Guatemala (DOS, 1965b) proved prescient: "[Reports indicate] that Guatemala's subversive groups may be planning to attempt to step up their activities (and reports from the [State] Department that Castro may . . . increase his support for subversives in . . . Guatemala). The political situation in Guatemala is somewhat uncertain . . . as political leaders and the government maneuver to prepare themselves for the promulgation of the new Constitution (scheduled for March 15) and the presidential elections which should follow within six months. Guerrilla and terrorist groups may well be tempted to increase their activities in an attempt to increase the uncertainty." Though the expected increase was delayed somewhat, it came soon enough and with awful consequences.

Guatemalan society had become increasingly split between bitterly opposed segments favoring either progressive reform or conservative reaction (Adams, 1970: 197). The 1966 election campaign, rather free and open, saw the liberal *Partido Revolucionario* provoke a great debate over public policy and elect Julio Cesar Méndez Montenegro president. This prompted frightened conservatives in the police and armed forces, as well as private citizens, to take matters in hand: The first of many right-wing "death squads" with bizarre names formed and commenced terror against targets vaguely associated with the left and with reform. (For this section see Adams, 1970; Fondo de Cultura Popular, 1969; Booth, 1979: 101-107; DOS, 1964, 1965a, 1965b).

With the beginning of this right-wing counterterror, violence on both sides quickly escalated to horrorific proportions. The dissident belligerents of the Fuerzas Armadas Revolucionarias (FAR) and the Movimiento Revolucionario del 13 de Noviembre (MR-13) operated without connections to the national political party framework and included both full-time guerrillas and irregular, part-time elements. Regular national security forces (army and police), peasant irregulars armed by the government in areas of insurgency, and right-wing terrorist groups permitted (and encouraged) by sympathetic regimes and their security forces made up the proregime combatants. Drastic, often indiscriminate actions by the police and proregime terrorists struck primarily at the regime's political opposition, although the victims often lacked ties to the combatant groups. In fact, the victims of such acts were frequently members of the general populace completely innocent of any political association or activity. The dissident terrorists usually attacked members of the police and armed forces. (This material is synthesized from the following sources: Aguilera Peralta, 1972; Adams, 1970; Bodenheimer, 1971; Booth, 1979; Crain, 1975; DOS, 1966, 1967a, 1967b, 1968a, 1968b, 1968c, 1972a, 1972b, 1972c; Diamond, 1968; Fuentes Mohr, 1971; Galeano, 1969; Gilly, 1965; Giniger, 1968; Howard, 1966; Johnson, 1973; Méndez Montenegro, 1967; Perea, 1971, 1972; New York Times, 1970; Petras, 1968; Portes, 1972; Fondo de Cultura Popular, 1969.)

Data compiled by the U.S. Embassy in Guatemala and recently declassified under the freedom of information procedure shed considerable light upon the levels and regional distribution of political violence from 1966 through 1972. Unfortunately the time series data remain incomplete as this article goes to press because of the Department of State's continued delays in releasing requested material. These data, based on press reports of violence, include "shootings, bombings, and deaths, all of which appear to be politically motivated" (DOS, 1972a) and reflect the reporting officers' best-informed effort to eliminate nonpolitical acts of violence. They are subject to similar limitations to the departmental level violence indices described below, but provide the best systematic, logitudinal evidence available about the conflict.

Figure 1 plots, by quarters except where specified, the national average monthly incidence of violent political acts for three periods: December 1966-July 1968; February 1969-February 1970; and July 1971-September 1972. Several trends stand out clearly. Political violence escalated rapidly, beginning in 1966 (before these reports were initiated by the Embassy), reached a plateau of approximately 68 political shootings, bombings, and assassinations per month in 1967, then dropped considerably to around 30 per month beginning in 1968. The 1968 decline corresponds to the government's successful 1968 Zacapa department anti-insurgency campaign which seriously curtailed the FAR's and MR-13's rural operations. Also influential were the government's military command changes and new policy "which very much restricts the activities of the GOG's [Government of Guatemala's] covert counter terror organizations" (DOS, 1968b). Violent incidents remained on this lower plane in 1969, with a monthly average of around 38 incidents. Rapid escalation of violence characterized 1970-1971, so that by the third quarter of 1971 incidents averaged 110 per month, producing an estimated 40 deaths.

General Carlos Arana Osorio's assumption of the presidency in 1970 led to several initiatives by the government to reduce terrorism. These included certain measures aimed directly at government security forces' own death squads: reorganization of the security forces, reform of the public order law, and efforts by military moderates to curtail proregime terror. As a result, violence declined steadily from July 1971 to July 1972 (Riding, 1971a; Aguilera Peralta, 1972; New York Times, 1971; DOS, 1970a, 1971). In late 1972 violence began to rise once again, due

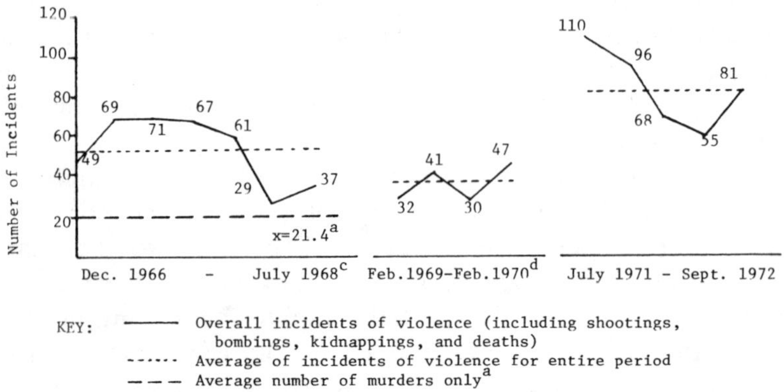

Figure1: Average Monthly Incidents of Violence, by Quarters: Guatemala

a. Source: Fonda de Cultura Popular (1969). See "Methods and Data" section. Average number of murders only.

b. Source: 1966-1968, DOS (1968a, 1968b); 1969-1970, DOS (1970b); 1971-1972, DOS (1972a, 1972b).

c. The last quarter unit is short one month (2 months total).

d. The last quarter unit is long one month (4 months total).

to proregime counterterror measures and excesses by the police (DOS, 1972a, 1972c; New York Times, 1972; Severo, 1972). Unfortunately, it is in September 1972 that our time series data end, reducing further efforts to track violence levels to educated guesses. The fraudulent outcome of the 1974 election produced another short period of unrest, which then subsided somewhat. Preliminary indications based on press reports for the 1977-1979 period suggest that the violence continues at very high levels. (For recent reports see Shoemaker, 1973; de Onis, 1970a, 1970b; Riding, 1971a, 1971b, 1973, 1974a, 1974b, 1974c, 1974d; New York Times, 1974a, 1974b, 1974c, 1974d, 1974e; Booth, 1979; Calderón Salazar, 1979; La Nación, 1979a, 1979b.)

Figure 2 displays the regional breakdown of violent incidents per month per 100,000 inhabitants. For the first three of the four periods graphed, the capital area led the nation in the

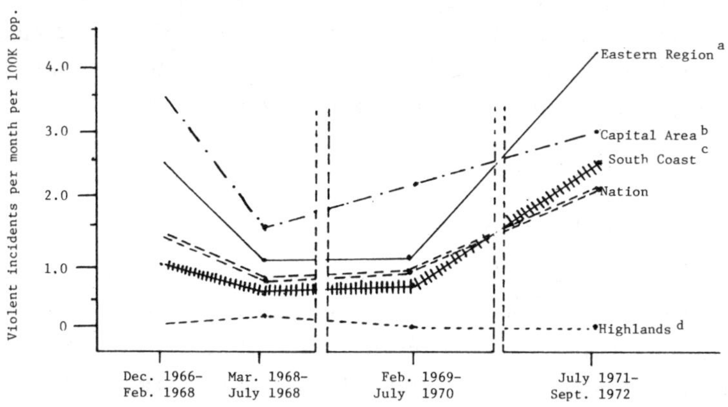

Figure 2: Violent Incidents per Month per 100,000 Population by Region: Guatemala
SOURCES: 1966-1968 (DOS, 1968a, 1968b); 1969-1970 (DOS, 1970b); 1971-1972 (DOS, 1972a, 1972c); for population data, see Adams (1970: 158).
a. Eastern region includes Jutiapa, Jalapa, El Progreso, Zacapa, Chiquimula, Izabel.
b. Capital area: Guatemala, Saquetepéquez.
c. South coast: San Marcos, Quetzaltenango, Retalhuleu, Suchitepéquez, Escuintla, Santa Rosa.
d. Highlands: Totonicapán, Chimaltenango, Huehuetenango, El Quiché, Baja Verapaz, Alta Verapaz, Sololá.

incidence of monthly violence, ranging between 1.7 and 3.0 violent incidents per month per 100,000 inhabitants. (See Figure 2 for the list of departments included in each region.) In 1972 the eastern region's slaughter outpaced the entire country, with 4.2 incidents per month per 100,000 inhabitants; that was an annual rate of over 50 politically violent acts—assassinations, bombings, kidnappings—for every 100,000 people. South coast departments paralleled the national average throughout the 6-year span. The Highlands have had very little political violence between 1966 and 1972 in comparison to the rest of the country.

But this brief history of the rise and fall of the violence tells us far too little about a very complex process. Conflict seared urban as well as rural and modern as well as traditional regions.

A broad spectrum of social strata contributed victims as well as killers. These problems suggest two important questions. What relationships exist between socioeconomic and political conditions and trends and the levels of conflict? Did any major changes in these relationships occur during the 1966-1971 period?

Structural Theories of Conflict

Explanations for widespread social violence[2] usually take one of two approaches: psychological theory or structural theory.[3] Psychological theories, generally based on the frustration-aggression model, often employ the concept of relative deprivation as the stimulus for aggressive and violent behavior (for example, Davies, 1962, 1969; Feierabend et al., 1969; Gurr, 1970; Himmelstrand, 1969). Theories which account for violence with collective structural characteristics generally suggest that stresses and strains in the objective conditions and behavior patterns within societies produce violence (e.g., Beals and Siegel, 1966; Archetti et al., 1970; Hobsbawm, 1959; Gjessing, 1967; Galtung, 1969). In general, one must test the psychological theories through individual-based data such as in-depth interviewing, surveys, and experimentation. One may test the structural theories, on the other hand, through participant observations of a collectivity (for example, Beals and Siegel, 1966) or by analysis of aggregate data on static or dynamic socioeconomic conditions and collective behavior (e.g., Rummel, 1967; Russet, 1964). Since the available information on Guatemala consists largely of aggregate data, I must confine the analysis to structural explanations.[4]

A first important structural theory holds that extensive or abrupt social change causes violence. Research has linked sociopolitical conflict in nations, regions, and communities to disruptions in traditional patterns of behavior and conflict resolution.[5] The rapid modification of economic structure—of patterns of exchange, employment relationships, values of goods and services, and so on—often realigns relationships among social institutions. Status positions shift, traditional sources of social control vary or disappear, new ones take their place. New sources of conflict arise, and institutions for the resolution of disputes weaken or vanish. As a result, clashes within a society become more frequent and more violent. The first hypothesis, then, predicts that the more intense and rapid the social change, the greater would have been the violence.

A second structural theory focuses on critical political phenomena. At the national and international levels, violence is most intense where the strength of contending parties is most nearly equal (Gurr, 1970: 234-350, ch. 8; Timasheff, 1965; Janos, 1964). Rationally speaking, when a group's size alone makes it dominant, the use of force wastes energy. Furthermore, in parity of strength situations, each group stands to gain the advantage simply by eliminating a few of the opposition. Both the intensity of political violence and the probability of internal war have been observed to vary positively with the ratio of opposition strength to regime strength until they are approximately equal and inversely beyond the point of equality. The second hypothesis is thus that where conflicting groups are approximately equal in strength, violence will have been more intense.

Methods and Data

The search for adequate explanations of conflictive behavior in Guatemala is made doubly difficult because it must deal with complex empirical phenomena and with complex theoretical attempts to account for them. Consequently, the analysis will employ the multivariate data manipulation techniques of factor analysis[6] and multiple regression to examine the social, economic, and political correlates of violence in Guatemala from 1966 to 1971. The power of factor analysis to explore the interrelationships among large numbers of variables (Rummel, 1970; Vincent, 1971) will permit both index construction and hypothesis testing. Although there are numerous case studies of national-level violence (Hobsbawm, 1959; Guzmán Campos et al., 1962; Weinert, 1966; Williamson, 1965; Booth, 1974; Himmelstrand, 1969), this analysis is relatively atypical in its use of aggregate data at the subnational level and in its use of factor analysis.

Unfortunately, a situation of terror such as that in Guatemala creates severe obstacles to research about its nature and causes. Systematically interviewing participants, victims, or officials, for example, is extremely difficult during or soon after the conflict because of fear and official hostility. Since a survey is impossible while the violence continues, alternative data about the conflict become necessary. Consequently, the level of violence is operationalized at the aggregate level as the per capita number of murders in each of Guatemala's 22 departments. These data come from separate summaries of Guatemalan daily newspaper reports: The first (Fondo de Cultura Popular, 1969: 50-175) covered a 23-month period from December 28, 1966 to November 27, 1968, and the second (Panorama, 1970, 1971) included 6 months in 1970 and 1971.[7] Note that the Department of State data reported earlier cannot serve here because they cannot be disaggregated to the departmental level. They do, however, provide a highly useful ancillary source of information. Upon comparison of the nationwide 1966-1968 and 1970-1971 political murder averages with overall violence (Department of State data) for 1966-1968 and an interpolated level for 1970-1971, the monthly assassination rate appears to behave in a stable and expectable ratio at a level below but parallel to overall violence. This provides an indirect confirmation of the validity of the measure.

The limitations of these data must be mentioned:

1. As newspaper accounts they may somewhat underestimate the level of killing in rural zones where reporting is less comprehensive and where low population density impedes the discovery of victims. However, since the police actively contributed to the murder level, public records are far less reliable.

Newspaper accounts thus provide the least biased source because the summaries compile data from several Guatemalan newspapers, thus spanning partisan interests. The reports simply record deaths without reference to editorial opinion or speculation about the group involved.

2. These indices count only verified corpses and therefore exclude surviving victims of kidnappings, arrests, and tortures—important manifestations of the terrorism. Nor do they include military actions, bombings, or other terrorist acts. The data reported earlier from State Department sources do include such wider phenomena.

3. It is not entirely possible to distinguish a department's political assassinations from its "normal" quota of nonpolitical killings. Two things mitigate this problem, however: First, the peculiar mutilation of bodies, means of killing, and messages accompanying political murder victims usually distinguishes them from others. Second, the extraordinarily high assassination level dwarfs other types of killings to the extent that per capita murders are a valid indicator of the relative level of violence in each department. Given these limitations with the dependent variable, the findings must be interpreted with caution. Claims for absolute accuracy are not made. I believe, however, that the data are sufficiently indicative of relative levels of violence among the departments that they can be of use for the exploration of the correlates of the levels of conflict. For instance, note by way of confirmation that the Department of State's data on all incidents of political violence (bombings, shootings, kidnappings, and assassinations) are consonant with the murder level index compiled here where they overlap. The 1966-1968 murder rate stands in a 1:2.6 ratio to overall incidents of violence for the same period from DOS sources. This ratio is reasonable, since only a portion of political incidents produced deaths.

Two demographic indices will reflect important aspects of the demand of the population upon land, agricultural output, and employment opportunity: (1) the percentage of increase in departmental population from 1950 to 1964 (Dirección General de Estadística, 1965: supplement); and (2) the net number of migrants into a department as a percentage of the native population in 1964.[8] The percentage of literate[9] and the number of hospital beds per 1000 inhabitants in 1962 (Dirección General de Estadística, 1965: 167) will provide rough indices of the standard of living.

The ethnic composition of Guatemala's population is clearly divided between Indians (estimated to be 43.4% in 1964) and Ladinos, or non-Indians. Because this dichotomy represents important linguistic and cultural differences within Guatemalan society, the percentage of the population that was Indian in 1964 is included for the analysis.[10]

Attention is directed to the agricultural economy in an attempt to focus on social change and its relationship to violence in rural areas. There is a close relationships between local agricultural systems and social norms/behavioral patterns (Adams, 1960; Smith, 1970: 277). Changes in local agricultural systems (the rationalization/capitalization of markets, the development of speculative agriculture, improved communications, changing land occupation patterns, crop changes, and so on) have profound effects upon local culture. Since 1944 several important developments in Guatemala have dramatically influenced rural agriculture (and presumably rural society). Cotton cultivation has developed rapidly in some regions (with substantial government encouragement) and then declined. A large amount of land has been confiscated and redistributed, parcelled out from public land, and colonized in recent decades. Furthermore, some of this land has been returned to its original owners after the 1954 "liberation" movement. In a dispute between growers and refiners, the sugar industry has experienced major intraindustry shifts in power over prices and production (Adams, 1970: 329-379, 394-407). Furthermore, the appearance of new zones of agricultural development, especially those of newly speculative cultivation, has stimulated significant rural migration. Substantial cultural changes have been attributed to these population shifts (Adams, 1970: 111-156; 1960: 244-245).

Five variables reflect these trends in agriculture. Though not dynamic indices in themselves, (1) cotton production in 1961-1962 and (2) per capita area in sugar production in 1961-1962 (Dirección General de Estadística, 1965: 50-60) do indicate the relative importance of industries with important changes going on. (3) The number of hectares of nonurban land redistributed per 1000 inhabitants from 1955 to 1963; (4) the number of beneficiaries of nonurban land redistributed per capita from 1955-1963; and (5) the net number of migrants into a department as a percentage of its native 1964 population (Adams, 1970: 137, 403) provide dynamic measures of rural change. Components factor analysis of these four items (see Table 1 for intercorrelations and factor loadings) extracted one factor with an eigenvalue greater than 1.0 explaining 69.9% of the variance. With such substantial evidence of scalability, the factor scores for each department on this factor will therefore provide an index of rural economic change. Other agricultural economic indices used are: (1) the mean departmental agricultural wage in 1963 (Adams, 1970: 388), which measures approximately the level of cash input into the departmental economies, and (2) the per capita coffee production in 1961-1962 (Dirección General de Estadística, 1965: 66), which roughly indicates the proportional distribution of income from Guatemala's principal export commodity and the mainstay of the economy—coffee.

Four variables indicate the level of urbanization of Guatemalan departments: (1) national government income from each department in 1961-1962, an index of the overall level of economic activity as reflected in revenue collections; (2) the redistribution of national revenue by department (national governmental departmental expenditure less departmental income), an index of governmental priorities for development stimulated through resource reallocation; (3) hospital beds per 1000 inhabitants in 1961-1962, indicating resource allocation to health care (Dirección General de Estadística, 1965: 113, 1967); and (4) the percentage of the nation's total manufacturing enterprises located in each department in 1966 (Adams, 1970: 1972), an

TABLE 1
Agricultural and Economic Variables

VARIABLES	CORRELATIONS 1	2	3	4	RURAL ECONOMIC CHANGE FACTOR LOADINGS
1. Cotton Production	-				.95
2. Sugar Area	.91	-			.87
3. Hectares Redistributed	.52	.59	-		.80
4. Beneficiaries Per Capita	.63	.62	.65	-	.76
5. Net Migration	.86	.42	.65	.30	.79
					% Variation 69.95
					Eigenvalue 3.497

index of industrialization. Components factoring (see Table 2) of the correlation matrix for these variables extracts one factor with an eigenvalue greater than 1.0, which accounts for 82.24% of the variation. Factor scores for each department on this factor indicate the level of urbanization and economic modernization (UEM).

The eleventh variable included in the matrix operationalizes a measure of the Guatemalan political party infrastructure related to the parity of opposing groups hypothesis. There is clear evidence of a left-right dimension in Guatemalan voting patterns for the period of interest here. The 1944-1954 revolution generated substantial political affect within the Guatemalan electorate. A series of relatively conservative regimes from 1954 to 1966 suppressed the tendency to support the Partido Revolucionario (PR), the party which since its founding in 1956 has identified itself with the 1944-1954 revolution. However, in the relatively free 1966 election, the PR revealed its strength by capturing 44% of the presidential vote, a plurality. Of the conservative parties, the moderately promilitarist Partido

TABLE 2
Urbanization and Economic Modernization Variables

VARIABLES	CORRELATIONS 1	2	3	4	URBANIZATION-ECONOMIC MODERNIZATION FACTOR LOADINGS
1. Government Income	–				.98
2. Revenue Redistribution	.89	–			.92
3. Hospital Beds/1000	.61	.49	–		.72
4. Percent Manufacture	.99	.91	.62	–	.98
					% Variation 82.24
					Eigenvalue 3.290

Institutional Democrático (PID) won 32% of the vote, and the strongly promilitarist Movimiento de Liberación Nacional (MLN)—the direct descendant of the Castillo Armas "liberation" movement—took only 24%. Students of the election concur that the split between the supporters of the PR and those of the MLN and PID represents a clear left-right or liberal-conservative dichotomy within the electorate (Adams, 1970: 205-114; Sloan, 1968: 65-165). Accordingly, I have constructed an index of left-right parity from the 1966 presidential election data so that the more equally the PR vote was balanced with the MLN-PID combined vote (Sloan, 1968: 150), the greater a department's score.

Results

Pearsonian correlations provide some interesting information about 1966-1968 per capita murders.[12] The 1966-1968 political killings level correlates most highly with the percentage of Indian population (–.58). supporting the finding of Figure 2 that violence tended to occur in predominantly Ladino zones. The 1966-1968 violence correlates with left-right parity at .40, further supporting the predicted relationship between equality of party strength and the intensity of conflict.

A common factor analysis of a correlation matrix (not reproduced here to save space), including 1966-1968 violence and the ten socioeconomic indices, extracts four factors with eigenvalues greater than 1.0, accounting for 97.7% of the common variation of the data (see Table 3). A varimax rotation of these four factors facilitates interpretation of their meaning. Factor I, with high loadings for hospital beds, agricultural wages, UEM, and literacy, represents a socioeconomic development dimension. Factor II isolates population increase, migration, and rural economic change. Factor IV singles out the coffee production variable. The first two factors obviously measure the most extreme aspects of social change, but none of the three correlates with violence.

Factor III reveals that cluster of variables with which the 1966-1968 level of violence covaries. The violence loads highly on the factor (.79), as do left-right parity (.64), percentage Indian (–.80), and literacy (.57). Factor III accounts for about 63% of the common variation in the 1966-1968 level of conflict, which is about 41% of its total variation. This factor, then, gives us a clear view of the ecological conditions related to conflict for the 1966-1968 period. Parity of support for the liberal and the conservative parties occurred in departments with a high proportion of Ladinos and a high literacy level. Conflict was most severe in these departments from 1966 to 1968. This finding supports the hypothesis that areas where the support of antagonistic political groups is more nearly equal will experience more intense violence. It also suggests that the south coast and east of Guatemala, the regions of greatest parity and predominant Ladino concentration, formed in 1966-1968 the violent end of a continuum, the less violent end of which was constituted by the conservative, Indian north and west.

TABLE 3
Varimax Rotated Common Factors for Violence, 1966-1968, and Ten Other Socioeconomic and Political Variables

VARIABLES	FACTORS				h^2 *
	I SOCIO-ECONOMIC DEVELOPMENT	II DEMOGRAPHIC PRESSURE-RURAL ECONOMIC CHANGE	III PARTY PARITY	IV COFFEE PRODUCTION	
Violence 1966-1968	-.08	.07	.79	-.15	.66
Population Increase	.34	.89	.26	-.10	.97
Left-Right Parity	.33	.19	.65	.42	.72
Hospital Beds Per 1000	.76	.17	.20	-.08	.65
Agricultural Wages	.82	.31	-.03	.27	.84
Coffee Production	-.01	.04	-.06	.92	.86
Percent Indian	-.22	-.17	-.80	.03	.71
Net Migration	.28	.93	.01	-.04	.95
Literacy	.64	.10	.57	.23	.81
UEM	.93	.03	.08	-.10	.88
REC	-.06	.85	.17	.27	.83
% of Variance	50.8	19.0	16.5	13.7	*Four Factors

The second step in the data manipulation repeats the process described above, substituting the 1970-1971 intensity of violence index. The intercorrelations of the 1970-1971 intensity of violence with other variables reveal some differences worthy of note. Violence in 1970-1971 correlates with left-right parity at .72, substantially higher than the level for 1966-1968, which was .40. The percentage Indian associates with 1970-1971 conflict is about the same level, –.51. The 1970-1971 correlation of conflict with population increase, .45, has risen from .22. The association of conflict with agricultural wages (.42) is much greater than for 1966-1968, up from .11. Rural economic change's correlation with conflict stayed about the same (.26), but the UEM variable's correlation has risen from .02 to .39. These findings, then, also support the parity-violence hypothesis, as did the findings for 1966-1968. It also appears that by 1970-1971 violence might have become more associated than previously with the socioeconomic variables in the urbanism variable cluster and the economic change/demographic pressure cluster.

A common factor analysis of the Pearsonian correlation matrix (not reproduced) of the 1970-1971 political killing rate plus the ten socioeconomic variables extracts four useful factors (eigenvalues greater than 1.0), accounting for some 95% of the common variation in the data (see Table 4). Varimax rotated Factor I is the socioeconomic development dimension, as before; Factor II, the rural socioeconomic change factor; and Factor IV isolates coffee-growing. The 1970-1971 conflict scale loads somewhat more heavily on Factor I (.26) than for 1966-1968, accounting for about 7% of the common variance of violence. Violence loads only marginally more upon Factor II (.18—3% of its common variance) than it did for 1966-1968.

Rotated Factor III again reveals the group of variables—left-right parity (.83) and percentage Indian (–.77)—with which violence correlated most strongly. Conflict in 1970-1971 loads on this factor at .74, amounting to about 56% of its common variation explained. (This is about 38% of the total variation in conflict.) Once again, equality of support of the left and right parties coincides with the highest levels of conflict, further buttressing the parity-violence hypothesis.

Clearly, then, parity of support between the political-ideological right and left contributed positively to the intensity of political conflict in Guatemala for the whole 1966-1971 period. Furthermore, it appears at this stage of the analysis that the liberal-conservative parity, as well as violence, tended to occur in departments where Ladinos are the preponderant majority.

For the period 1966-1968 there is little evidence to support the hypothesis that more violence would occur where social and economic change were the greatest. After approximately three

TABLE 4
Varimax Rotated Common Factors for Violence, 1970-1971, and Ten Other Socioeconomic and Political Variables

VARIABLES	FACTORS				h^2 *
	I SOCIO-ECONOMIC DEVELOPMENT	II DEMOGRAPHIC PRESSURE-RURAL ECONOMIC CHANGE	III PARTY PARITY	IV COFFEE PRODUCTION	
Violence 1970-1971	.26	.18	.74	.08	.66
Population Increase	.27	.86	.34	-.20	.97
Left-Right Parity	.22	.16	.83	.32	.87
Hospital Beds Per 1000	.76	.15	.27	-.11	.69
Agricultural Wages	.81	.33	.13	.27	.85
Coffee Production	-.04	.09	.06	.91	.84
Percent Indian	-.10	-.16	-.77	.16	.65
Net Migration	.28	.91	.08	-.10	.92
Literacy	.09	.53	.12	.22	.35
UEM	.90	.01	.18	-.10	.85
REC	-.06	.88	.14	.21	.83
% of Variance	53.1	19.7	15.2	12.0	*Four Factors

years, however, trends in the geographical distribution of conflict in Guatemala had very slightly increased the association between rural socioeconomic change phenomena (REC/demographic pressure) and violence. This suggests that, with time, social change might have been increasing its influence on violence, a possibility further explored below.

The third and final step in the analysis uses multiple regression to test a hypothetical model of the conditions related to conflict levels. This will let us examine certain unclear relationships from a different perspective and crosscheck the factor analytic findings. The results so far suggest the elements of the model.

First is the hypothesis that the intensity of violence (X_1) will be positively associated with the equality of support for the antagonistic political-ideological camps, or left-right parity (X_2). Second is the hypothesis that violence will be positively related to extensive socioeconomic change, REC(X_3). Furthermore, if socioeconomic change did increase levels of conflict between the two periods, the proportional importance of REC should be greater for 1970-1971 than 1966-1968. Third, the findings of the previous factor analyses suggest that ethnic composition of the populace may be an important conditioning variable for conflict. Conflict was low where Indians were most concentrated, probably due to their political conservatism and marginal political participation. The percentage Indian (X_4) is therefore expected to be negatively related to the level of violence. And fourth, some argue that the conflict became more intense in urban areas between 1966-1968 and 1970-1971, though the regional data in Figure 2 do not support this impression. Thus urbanism, UEM (X_5), may be expected to contribute more heavily to the 1970-1971 violence level than for 1966-1968.

Multiple regression results (Table 5) permit comparison of the beta coefficients (β) to determine the proportional contribution of each independent variable to the intensity of violence. The coefficient of multiple determination (R) for 1966-1968 violence is .61, explaining about 37% of the conflict's variance (Table 5). For 1970-1971, the multiple correlation increases to .76, 57% explained variance. The contribution of left-right parity to the explained level of violence apparently increases from less than 2% to about 34% for 1970-1971. However, this low beta weight for parity for 1966-1968 does not reflect real conditions but stems from the collinearity of that variable and percentage Indian ($r = -.59$). The zero-order correlation between parity and violence 1966-1968 (.40) reveals a more reasonable degree of association. However, the independent contribution of the parity between antagonistic groups to the 1970-1971 violence level had increased substantially. Once again we find the parity-violence hypothesis solidly supported.

TABLE 5
Beta Weights (B) for 1966-1968 and 1970-1971
Models of Violence

	VIOLENCE 1966-1968		VIOLENCE 1970-1971	
VARIABLES	B	% VARIANCE	B	% VARIANCE
Left-Right Parity (X_2)	.12	1.54	.58	33.76
REC (X_3)	.04	0.17	.09	0.72
Percent Indian (X_4)	-.54	29.16	-.10	0.98
UEM (X_5)	-.16	2.69	.20	4.00
	R=.61	R^2=.37	R=.76	R^2=.57

Rural economic change as measured here contributes little to the explained variation of violence either for 1966-1968 (0.2%) or for 1970-1971 (0.7%). The explained variation is so insignificant that one cannot interpret it as supporting the hypothesis that high socioeconomic change levels might be a cause of violence in Guatemala (see also Booth, 1979).

Though for 1966-1968 the percentage Indian in a department accounts for 29% of the variation in the level of conflict, for 1970-1971 this contribution drops to 1%. Although the relation for 1966-1968 supports the hypothesized model, departmental shifts in the intensity of violence by 1970-1971 had reduced the strength of the association. Specifically, two departments with a population more than 50% Indian, Quetzaltenango and San Marcos in the southeast, had major increases in violence. Both, however, include lowland areas of predominant Ladino concentration as well as highland Indian municipalities. Though department level data obscure this, the increase was most likely in the lowland areas. On the other hand, four departments less than 20% Indian—Escuintla, Zacapa, Izabal and El Progreso—showed marked decreases in conflict. In the latter three (eastern) departments, the decline most likely resulted from the counter-insurgency successes of the army after President Arana took office in July 1970. One must also recall that some of the change in β weight is also due to the collinearity between parity, percentage Indian, and violence. The regional data in Figure 2 reveal substantial stability for the Indian Highlands' low conflict levels.

While for 1966-1968 the association of UEM with violence is very low (2.7% of the total variance) and is negative, for 1970-1971 UEM's association is strengthened a little (to 4% explained variance) and becomes positive, as expected. Clearly, however, the change was small, not nearly as dramatic as journalistic observations have implied. In fact, guerrilla activity accounted for only a portion of the murders recorded, and the guerrillas had not completely abandoned rural operations. Further, the right-wing terrorists continued activity outside urban centers, so that overall violence was still very high in the less urban, less economically modernized departments during the 1970-1971 period. Figure 2 revals the eastern region to have experienced an exceptional relative increase in overall violence in 1971-1972, calling further into question the urbanizing pattern.

Discussion

The conservative reading of the factorial and multiple regression analyses warranted by the data and the exploratory nature of the enterprise indicate two major findings: First, the parity of support for left-of-center and right-of-center political parties in Guatemala contributes more than any other factor considered to the tragic levels of violent conflict in this beautiful but blighted country. Second, social change as measured did not contribute to the observed violence in a major way. A further, comparative exploration of these considerations will help clarify their significance and place them in perspective.

As for social change, despite social issues raised by the leftist insurgents, conflict has not really followed socioeconomic structural lines. The clearly defined rural economic change factor reveals but negligible correlation with levels of political murders for the 1976-1971 period. However, since a similar conflict of political origin, the Colombian violencia of 1948-1963, did eventually develop socioeconomic dimensions (Booth, 1979, 1974), comparison seems called for. While violence became more linked to socioeconomic change with time in Colombia, the shorter duration of conflict in Guatemala may have precluded the growth of such links. An while in Colombia the extensive mass involvement clearly accelerated and exacerbated rural socioeconomic change (Guzmán Campos et al., 1962; Hobsbawm, 1963), fewer economic and social ramifications have been observed in Guatemala. There may, however, be other yet unstudied dimensions of change which are related to conflict. The range of variables considered here is admittedly limited. Unfortunately, reliable statistics on Guatemalan social conditions are sparse, even at so high a level of aggregation as the department. (I found municipio-level data to be generally incomplete and far less reliable.) Thus, precluding the development of a better aggregate data base, the most promising technique for exploring the possible social origins of the conflict is probably field work in communities, which remains highly risky for the time being.

The finding that left-right parity contributes most strongly to violence in Guatamala also resembles Colombia's *violencia*, where equality of support for the antagonistic Liberal and Conservative parties was the major structural cause of violence (Booth, 1974, 1979). Clearly, then, the justaposition of opposing groups in equal numbers within an area provides a setting which may lead activists on either side to deal violently with one another. However, the ostensible similarity between the Guatemalan and Colombian cases should not obscure several important and illuminating differences.

First, the sociopolitical backgrounds of the conflicts differ. The Guatemalan electorate of the period was divided primarily among supporters of three relatively young parties (the oldest, the MLN, had been formed in 1954) within a rapidly changing party spectrum. Colombian Liberals and Conservatives, on the other hand, had hated each other for over a hundred years and had fought bitterly several times. The difference shows that extremely violent strife within a society can occur even in the absence of long-entrenched political antagonism.

Second, the Colombian violencia was largely a mass movement, while the Guatemalan terror occupied a far smaller proportion of the population, in spite of the observed links between party infrastructure and conflict. Vast numbers of partisan Colombian peasants took part in the killing (Guzmán Campos et al., 1962), while in Guatemala the belligerents have come mainly from conspiratorial groups not directly tied to the political parties. This apparent paradox raises the need to emphasize strongly that defining operationally the opposing camps by using electoral support for the parties does not imply that the political parties themselves were responsible for the murders that took place, nor that strong party identifiers make up the combatant groups, as in Colombia. But, then, why do the data reveal such a strong link between party support and violence levels? One must surmise that partisan support within a department provides the belligerents with negative reference points by defining target groups. Both insurgents and pro-regime forces attack the perceived supporters of their enemies. Thus, regardless of the parties' noncombatant status and the lack of important ties between major opposition parties and the revolutionary left, right-wing terrorists murder, kidnap, and torture activists of the PR and Christian Democratic Party, as well as other "leftists" such as students and labor leaders. The insurgents counterterrorize police officials, military personnel, and foreign military advisers in the parity areas where right-wing activity is most intense. Since neither side can easily engage the other in direct combat, terrorism is directed against a more easily identified "enemy."

A final question to consider in this comparative context is how conflict levels have changed. While in Colombia the violencia's prime cause was eliminated by the formation of the Frente Nacional by Conservative and Liberal elites, fighting in the countryside continued for years, taking on more of the nature of a class struggle. A determined counterinsurgency campaign reduced but never totally eliminated the number of guerrilla bands (Guzmán Campos, 1968; Hobsbawm, 1963; Booth, 1972: 68). The Guatemalan combatants, however, have reached no such accord. Countersinsurgency reduced the strength of the rural guerrillas in 1968, but violence rose again dramatically around 1970. Elite dissatisfaction with right-wing terrorism *within* the government (especially the army) has caused the level of conflict to fall more than once, but never to disappear. Indeed, elites appear to have recurred to violence periodically for their own purposes ever since 1970. So, while Colombian elites developed means to resolve that conflict *temporarily*, the Guatemalan elite has evidently only temporarily and sporadically even tried to suppress the violence. Thus, for example, the 1974 election was surprisingly tranquil, but when the opposition candidate General Rios Montt's solid popular majority was fraudulently overturned in favor of MLN candidate General Laugerud García, demonstrations by opposition supporters provoked an outbreak of right-wing terror in retaliation. Similarly, the resurgence of right-wing death squad activity in 1978 and 1979, documented by the International Jurists Commission and Amnesty International, corresponds to a change in the government's attitude as the administration of General Romeo Lucas García assumed power (La Nación, 1979a, 1979b).

Thus, it would seem that no real institutional solution for conflict has developed in Guatemala. Both the base and the targets for both sides remain—the underground left still seeking revolution, the underground right to seed sufficient terror to prevent even reform. Recognition and acceptance of a legitimate role for opposition by the governmental and military elite, plus effective control of conservative terrorists, stand out as necessary minimum steps toward reduction of violence. But prospects for such concessions seem minimal at the present, since conservative leaders seem unable to forego their addiction to the death squads. Perhaps the only chance lies in the rapid changes now occurring in Isthmian politics. One might suppose the combined effects of the Nicaraguan revolution, Salvadorean coup, and moderation by the Honduran regime could lead the Lucas government to seek reform in order to forestall even greater violence.

Evidently the major source of Guatemala's nightmare is surprisingly simple. Neither class conflict nor the nature of the ideological struggles have been considered with any detail, but what is startlingly clear is that conflict in Guatemala has been most intense where two hostile partisan poles claim roughly equal electoral support. This partisan geography has in turn defined targets and areas of operation for both anti- and proregime terrorists, the latter encouraged and tolerated but never completely controlled nor repudiated by national security elites. Eventual lasting peace will probably elude Guatemala until elites develop institutional solutions for this conflict. Unfortunately, the prospects for such change seem few at present, because nearly four progressively more violent decades may have caused irreparable rends in the Guatemalan social fabric. One wonders if Guatemala, as tragically as Colombia, Northern Ireland, or Lebanon, has not become a Humpty Dumpty society that no one can put back together again.

NOTES

1. Portes (1972: 47) has estimated that in the fall of 1971 at least five persons per day were being murdered for political reasons in Guatemala.

3. The most comprehensive review of violence-related literature may be found in Gurr (1970).

3. I suggest these categories at a broad, but, I hope, useful level of generalization, though they do not exhaust the entire range of approaches to violence. The violence literature has staggering proportions: international conflict, guerrilla warfare, and revolution are each massive topics. The basic literature to which I refer deals with the origins and nature of violent intrasocietal conflict.

4. As one might expect, the dichotomy between psychological and structural theorizing is not particularly neat in the real world: many works combine both elements. Thus, in the formulation of hypotheses I refer to structural aspects of what have been interpreted as psychological materials.

5. The Feierabends and Nesvold (1969, 1966) find that nations undergoing rapid social transition tend to be politically unstable. James C. Davies (1962, 1969) links prolonged periods of improvement in social and economic conditions, followed by short reversals, to revolution and rebellion. Mancur Olson, Jr. (1963) shows that rapid economic growth may significantly decrease the standard of living for lower income groups and thereby increase social discontent. Archetti et al. (1970) have linked peasant mobilization to shifts in agrarian economic patterns which reduce peasant autonomy over economic conditions. Beals and Siegel (1966) show that diffuse, complex external stress is likely to produce factional dispute within social systems. Booth (1974, 1979) has found that the persistence of violence in Colombia after 1958 was linked to the disruption of traditional agricultural systems.

6. Factor analysis (Rummel, 1970; Vincent, 1971) is employed in three ways: (1) index construction, scaling masses of interdependent data into more parsimonious indicators by means of factor scores (Rummel, 1970: 433-435); (2) "exploration" or "mapping" of an empirical domain (Rummel, 1970: 13); and (3) construction of a causal model relating large numbers of variables (Rummel, 1970).

7. The months included were July, August, September, and December 1970, and January and February 1971. Criteria for the inclusion of a datum in the tally of murders were: (1) the account of each death must have been credited to a journalistic source; (2) at least the department in which the victim was discovered must have been identifiable; and (3) since the press sources were all Guatemala city dailies, criterion 2 was waived in the case of victims listed with street addresses only, which were assumed to refer to the capital city. Population data are from Dirección General de Estadística y Censos (1965).

8. The source for these data is the 5% sample of the 1964 Census, cited in Adams (1970: 137).

9. This variable, from the 1964 Census 5% sample, was supplied by Jerry L. Weaver, to whom I extend my thanks.

10. From the 1964 Census 5% sample, cited in Adams (1970: 158).

11. The computational formula for the left-right parity index was: $x_i = 1 - |a_i - b_i|$, where a_i is the percentage of the vote for the PR in the ith department, and b_i the combined percentages of the votes for the MLN and the PID.

12. Since the data represent a universe rather than a sample, significance testing is not necessary. However, given the tentative nature of some of the data and the exploratory nature of the analysis, the significance level can serve as a rule of thumb for evaluating correlations. For an N of 22, a Pearson correlation should be about .40 to give us 95%

confidence that the measured association is not random. This conservative guide for evaluating the *substantive* significance of an association helps to assess the findings in a suitably sober manner.

REFERENCES

ADAMS, R. N. (1970) Crucifixion by Power. Austin: Univ. of Texas Press.

——— (1960) "Social change in Guatemala and U.S. policy," pp. 231-284 in R. N. Adams et al., Social Change in Latin America Today: Its Implications for United States Policy. New York: Vintage.

AGUILERA PERALTA, G. (1972) "El proceso del terror en Guatemala." Aportes 24 (April): 117-136.

ARCHETTI, E., E. FOSSUM, and P. O. REINTON (1970) "Agrarian structure and peasant autonomy." J. of Peace Research 3: 185-196.

BEALS, A. R. and B. J. SIEGEL (1966) Divisiveness and Social Conflict: An Anthropological Approach. Stanford: Stanford Univ. Press.

BODENHEIMER, S. (1971) "Inside a state of siege: legalized murder in Guatemala." Ramparts 9 (June): 50-52.

BOOTH, J. A. (1979) "Comparing political violence in Colombia and Guatemala," pp. 97-115 in M. A. Seligson and J. A. Booth (eds.) Political Participation in Latin America, Volume II: Politics and the Poor. New York: Holmes & Meier.

——— (1974) "Rural violence in Colombia: 1948-1963." Western Pol. Q. 27 (December): 657-679.

——— (1972) "La violencia rural en Colombia: 1948-1963." América Latina 15: 58-74.

CALDERON SALAZAR, J. (1979) "Asesinan impunemente a universitarios y dirigentes en Guatemala." Excelsior (August 11): 3A.

CRAIN, D. A. (1975) "Guatemalan revolutionaries and Havana's ideological offensive of 1966-1968." J. of Interamerican Studies 17 (May): 175-205.

DAVIES, J. C. (1969) "The J-curve of rising and declining satisfactions as a cause of some great revolutions and a contained rebellion," pp. 671-709 in H. D. Graham and T. R. Gurr (eds.) Violence in America: Historical and Comparative Perspectives. Washington, DC: National Commission on the Causes and Prevention of Violence.

——— (1962) "Toward a theory of revolution." Amer. Soc. Rev. 27 (February): 5-19.

DE ONIS, J. (1970a) "Guatemalan leader surprises some with promises of reform." New York Times (July 5): 12.

——— (1970b) "New Guatemalan chief: Carlos Arana Osorio." New York Times (July 3): 2.

DIAMOND, N. (1968) "Why they shoot Americans." Nation (February 5): 166-167.

Dirección General de Estadística (1965) Guatemala en Cifras: 1961-1962. Guatemala: Author.

DOS [U.S. Department of State] (1972a) "Internal security: monthly report of incidents, October 1972." American Embassy, Guatemala (AEG) to DOS, 8 November. (airgram A211)

——— (1972b) "Internal security: ten common criminals found knifed to death." AEG to DOS, 17 October. (telegram)

——— (1972c) "Internal security: monthly report of incidents, July 1972." AEG to DOS, 9 August. (airgram A153)

——— (1971) "Internal security: pres. (sic) addresses nation." AEG to DOS, 29 July. (telegram)

——— (1970a) "Reform of the law of public order." AEG to DOS, 4 December. (airgram A256)

——— (1970b) "Internal security: monthly report of incidents, February 1970." AEG to DOS, 20 March. (airgram A58)

——— (1968a) "Political (or quasi-political) violence." AEG to DOS, 17 August. (airgram A538)

——— (1968b) "Incidence of terrorism." AEG to DOS, 11 May. (airgram A409)

——— (1968c) "University students arrested—confess guerrilla activity." AEG to DOS, 9 March. (airgram A335)

——— (1967a) "Internal security sitrep January 10, 1967." AEG to DOS, 10 January. (telegram)

——— (1967b) "Internal security sitrep January 3." AEG to DOS, 3 January. (telegram)

——— (1966) "MLN and FAR communiques re presidential speech September 7." AEG to DOS, 17 September. (airgram A114)

——— (1965a) "Counter-insurgency activities: circuit riders." AEG to DOS, 23 October. (airgram A205)

——— (1965b) "Fifth monthly guerrilla report." AEG to DOS, 6 February. (airgram A358)

——— (1964) "Fourth monthly guerrilla report." AEG to DOS, 21 December. (airgram A284)

FEIERABEND, I. K. and R. L. FEIERABEND (1966) "Aggressive behaviors within polities: a cross-national study." J. of Conflict Resolution 10 (September): 249-271.

——— and B. A. NESVOLD (1969) "Social change and political violence," pp. 606-658 in H. D. Graham and T. R. Gurr (eds.) Violence in America: Historical and Comparative Perspectives. Washington, DC: National Commission on the Causes and Prevention of Violence.

Fondo de Cultura Popular (1969) La Violencia en Guatemala. México, D.F.: Author.

FUENTES MOHR, A. (1971) Secuestro y Prisión: Dos Caras de la Violencia en Guatemala. San José, C.R.: Editorial Universitaria Centroamericana.

GALEANO, E. (1969) Guatemala: Occupied Country. New York: Monthly Review.

GALTUNG, J. (1969) "Violence, peace and peace research." J. of Peace Research 3: 167-192.

GILLY, A. (1965) "The guerrilla movement in Guatemala." Monthly Rev. 17 (May): 9-40.

GINIGER, H. (1968) "Guatemala is a battleground." New York Times Magazine (June 16): 14-26.

GJESSING, G. (1967) "Ecology and peace research." J. of Peace Research 2: 125-139.

GURR, T. R. (1970) Why Men Rebel. Princeton, NJ: Princeton Univ. Press.

GUZMAN CAMPOS, G. (1968) La Violencia en Colombia: Parte Descriptiva. Cali: Ediciones Progreso.

——— O. FALS BORDA, and E. UMANA LUNA (1962) La Violencia en Colombia. Bogotá: Ediciones Tercer Mundo.
HIMMELSTRAND, U. (1969) "Tribalism, nationalism, rank-equilibration theory, and social structure." J. of Peace Research 2: 81-104.
HOBSBAWM, E. J. (1963) "The anatomy of violence." New Society (April 11): 16-18.
——— (1959) Social Bandits and Primitive Rebels. New York: Free Press.
HOWARD, A. (1966) "With the guerrillas in Guatemala." New York Times Magazine (June 26): 8.
JANOS, A. C. (1964) The Seizure of Power: A Study of Force and Popular Consent. Princeton, NJ: Center for International Studies.
JOHNSON, K. F. (1973) "On the Guatemalan political violence." Politics and Society 4 (fall): 55-82.
JONES, C. L. (1940) Guatemala: Past and Present. Minneapolis: Univ. of Minnesota Press.
MENDEZ MONTENEGRO, J. C. (1967) "Informe al honorable congreso de la república." Personal communication to Lic. Mario Fuentes Pieruccini, Presidente del Congreso (May 15).
MURPHY, B. (1970) "The stunted growth of campesino organizations," pp. 438-478 in R. N. Adams, Crucifixion by Power. Austin: Univ. of Texas Press.
La Nación [San José, Costa Rica] (1979a) "Lucas García pone en dude credibilidad de Amnistía Internacional." September 24: 35A.
——— (1979b) "Guatemala podría encontrarse en etapa prerevolucionaria." September 14: 39A.
New York Times (1974a) "Political activism in Guatemala is cause of death." May 12: IV, 5.
——— (1974b) "Laugerud is ruled Guatemala winner." March 13: 12.
——— (1974c) "Murder of leftist in Guatemala adds to political stress." March 12: 11.
——— (1974d) "Regime claiming Guatemala vote." March 8: 7.
——— (1974e) "Guatemalans vote, without turbulence, for new president." March 2: 3.
——— (1972) "Escalating terror." July 16: IV, 3.
——— (1971) "Guatemala gains in war on rebels." May 8: 5.
——— (1970) "President takes oath in Guatemala." July 2: 6.
OLSON, M., Jr. (1963) "Rapid growth as a destabilizing force." J. of Econ. History 23 (December): 529-552.
Panorama (1971) "Guatemala." January, February.
——— (1970) "Guatemala." July, August, September, December.
PERERA, V. (1972) "Guatemalan journal." Antioch Rev. 32 (spring/summer): 11-29.
——— (1971) "Guatemala: always *la violencia*." New York Times Magazine (June 13): 12.
PETRAS, J. (1968) "Revolution and guerrilla movements in Latin America: Venezuela, Guatemala, Colombia and Peru," pp. 329-369 in J. Petras and M. Zeitlin (eds.) Latin America: Reform or Revolution? New York: Fawcett.
PORTES, A. (1972) "Guatemala's right wing terror." Nation (January 10): 47-48.
RIDING, A. (1974a) "Bitter Guatemalan loser bows to dubious vote." New York Times (March 15): 4.
——— (1974b) "Guatemalan left threatens strike." New York Times (March 8): 7.
——— (1974c) "Opposition seems victor in Guatemala." New York Times (March 5): 14.

——— (1974d) "Army holds key to Guatemalan election." New York Times (March 2): 3.
——— (1973) "Guatemalan army holds on." Christian Science Monitor (July 21).
——— (1971a) "Guatemalan army moderates seek end to violence." New York Times (October 23): 6.
——— (1971b) "Guatemalan students begin strike as protest against violence and to press regime to lift state of siege." New York Times (October 10): 29.
RUMMEL, R. J. (1970) Applied Factor Analysis. Evanston, IL: Northwestern Univ. Press.
——— (1967) "Some attributes and behavioral patterns of nations." J. of Peace Research 2: 196-206.
RUSSETT, B. M. (1964) "Inequality and instability: the relations of land tenure to politics." World Politics 16 (April): 442-454.
SCHMID, L. (1967) "The role of migratory labor in the economic development of Guatemala." Ph.D. dissertation, University of Wisconsin, Madison.
SEVERO, R. (1972) "Guatemalans, three unquiet weeks after assassination, say land is peaceful." New York Times (July 18): 11.
SHOEMAKER, D. (1973) "Guatemala: an 'amazing' turnabout to stability." Miami Herald (April 5).
SLOAN, J. W. (1968) "The electoral game in Guatemala." Ph.D. dissertation, University of Texas, Austin.
SMITH, T. L. (1970) "Improvement of the systems of agriculture in Colombia," pp. 276-294 in T. L. Smith, Studies of Latin American Societies. Garden City, NY: Doubleday.
TIMASHEFF, N. S. (1965) War and Revolution. New York: Sheed & Ward.
VINCENT, J. E. (1971) Factor Analysis in International Relations. Gainesville, FL: Univ. of Florida Press.
WEINERT, R. S. (1966) "Violence in pre-modern societies: rural Colombia." Amer. Pol. Sci. Rev. 60 (June): 340-347.
WILLIAMSON, R. C. (1965) "Toward a theory of rural violence: the case of rural Colombia." Western Pol. Q. 18 (March): 35-44.

John A. Booth is Associate Professor of Political Science at the University of Texas at San Antonio, on leave for 1979-1980 as a Fulbright Lecturer at the Escuela de Relaciones Internacionales of the Universidad Nacional Autonoma of Costa Rica. Coeditor (with Mitchell Seligson) of Political Participation in Latin America, *Volumes I and II (Holmes and Meier, 1978, 1979), he is now writing* Democracy and Political Participation in Costa Rica *as well as a book on the Nicaraguan revolution (Westview, forthcoming).*

REVIEW ESSAY

GERMAN COLONIES IN SOUTH AMERICA
A New Germany in the Cono Sur?

Blancpain J. P. LES ALLEMAND AU CHILI (1816-1945). Koeln-Wien: Boehlau-Verlag, 1974.

Newton, R. C. GERMAN BUENOS AIRES, 1900-1933: SOCIAL CHANGE AND CULTURAL CRISIS. Austin: Texas University Press, 1977.

Roche, J. LA COLONISATION ALLEMANDE ET LE RIO GRANDE DO SUL. Paris: Institut des Hautes Etudes de l'Amérique Latine, 1959.

Young, G.F.W. GERMANS IN CHILE: IMMIGRATION AND COLONIZATION, 1849-1914. New York: Center for Migrations Studies, 1974.

Following Latin American independence, German trading firms—especially Hanseatic ones—were to be found alongside the British and French as the successors to the merchants of Iberia. These German trading houses laid a solid basis for a much-strengthened German economic expansion in Latin America, first under the kaiser and later in the 1930s, an expansion which the imperial regime and later that of the National Socialists sought to reinforce by political means. In retrospect,

---

EDITOR'S NOTE: This review essay was translated by Ronald C. Newton.

Journal of Interamerican Studies and World Affairs, Vol. 22 No. 2, May 1980 227-245

however, one is forced to conclude that when compared to that of England, France, or the United States, Germany's influence on newly independent Latin America was relatively limited.[1]

This generalization does not, of course, negate the fact that in certain areas Germany and the Germans were responsible for decisive developments. Especially obvious, for example, was the influence of the German armaments industry and of German training missions on the modernization of several Latin American armies at the beginning of the twentieth century. No less impressive was the decisive imprint left on certain regions, especially in the *Con Sur,* by the immigration of Germans (compared to that of Englishmen, Frenchmen, or Americans) since the early nineteenth century.

The German immigration will be examined in somewhat closer detail below; for the moment it should be emphasized that we are not speaking of the total German immigration into Latin America, but only their immigration into southern South America in the nineteenth and the first half of the twentieth centuries.[2] The lands of the *Cono Sur* were by far the most important destination of German emigrants, and German influence in this region has been studied thoroughly by scholars.

In the first section of this review, the monographs cited in the subtitle will be described and subjected to a critical evaluation. In the second part we shall, with the use of the empirical data at hand, attempt to extract some general conclusions concerning the meaning and consequences of German immigration into South America.

Part I

The numerically largest proportion of German immigrants into South America in the nineteenth century was received by southern Brazil. As a result of German colonization, regions such as Rio Grande do Sul, Santa Catarina, and Paraná underwent a thorough transformation; this transformation has been the subject of a highly impressive treatment, as comprehensive as it is scrupulously detailed: Jean Roche's study of Rio Grande do Sul.

Roche's work is a genuine pioneering study that has served as the point of departure for a number of other monographs on much more narrowly defined questions related to Germanic immigration into southern Brazil and the effects thereof. On the one hand, it is impressive for the multitude of its topics, which extend from politicoadministrative details of the colonization process, the social background of the immigrants, and their demographic evolution in Brazil, through detailed anthropological descriptions of the agricultural colonies, to the German contribution to the rapid growth of agriculture, artisanry, trade, and industry, and the complexity of political and social integration into the new homeland. The book's merit, however, relies equally on the fact that it is derived from a research project of many years' duration based on immense and extremely varied primary source material; it has thus, for many of the questions raised, provided solid research results for the first time.

A characteristic of German immigration into Rio Grande do Sul ever since the founding of the first colony at San Leopoldo in 1824 was the fact that it was guided and supervised by the Brazilian state. The objective of the Brazilian authorities was the agricultural occupation and colonization of the forested northen portion of the state, which first had to be made usable for row crops by an extensive clearing of the forest. This colonization was carried out virtually without reference to the latifundist stock-raising zone of the *campanha;* it conferred upon the closed Germanic settlements of a highly autarchic character in terms of both economy and culture. By the same token, the economic and social transformation of Rio Grande for which the Germans were responsible in the nineteenth and early twentieth centuries did not result from an interaction between newer Teuto-Brazilian and the older Luso-Brazilian economy and society, but primarily from the working out of the inner developmental logic of the German settlement area.

The economic basis of this colonization was family-operated agricultural units, in which as late as 1950 almost 90% of all German-Brazilians in Rio Grande do Sul were economically active. This agricultural zone continued to expand as a result of marked demographic growth in the German colonies as well as a rapidly declining yield per unit of land. The primitive agricultural techniques used by the colonists, basically those of slash-and-burn, led to a rapid exhaustion of the soil and made imperative the occupation of new potentially arable land and its preparation for cultivation. Being pioneer farmers rather than agrarian innovators, the German colonists or their descendants were periodically compelled to establish new settlements in still-virgin territory. Roche has documented this "secondary migration" intensively, and he has thereby shown, among other things, how through close family solidarity and a high endogamy rate, the Germanic character of the newly colonized areas was maintained intact.

As the German settlement of southern Brazil was, above all, a "self-colonization of German-Brazilian communities" (Willems, 1948/1949), the description of the inner development of these colonies takes on great importance. In numerous segments with an anthropological orientation, Roche describes in great detail housing and settlement forms, clothing, food, and customs of the settlers, the importance of their churches, their educational systems, periodical press, and clubs ("Vereine)." He also shows the growing social differentiation within the colonies themselves into, roughly, the merchants and the farmers—the latter heavily dependent economically upon the former.

Agriculture served as the basis and point of departure for the wholesale and retail trade organized by Germans. Village-type retail business in the colonies remained exclusively in the hands of German colonists; wholesale commerce, however, which developed primarily in Porto Alegre, was increasingly dominated by established German trading firms. The import trade, especially, owed its rise in the first place to its markedly "ethnic" basis: On the one hand, it was directed entirely toward a clientele in the German colonies; on the other, it derived its wares almost exclusively from producers in Germany. Germany itself was, as early as 1906, the most important single source of imports into Rio Grande do Sul.

Beginning in the late nineteenth century these trading houses also played a significant role in the industrialization of Rio Grande, which was carried out under the dominant influence of the Germans. Industrial entrepreneurs, however, were less often recruited from amongst the colonists and local artisans than from newly arrived Germans, whose personal and economic ties with Germany at first remained very close.[3]

In gross terms, the economic role of the Teuto-Brazilians in Rio Grande was highly significant: Although they made up little more than a fifth of the population, in 1950 they contributed more than a third of the agricultural and industrial production of the state. Nevertheless, this sort of economic success should not obscure the fact that the social, political, and cultural integration of the Germans into Brazilian society and the Brazilian political order was sluggish and rife with conflict.

During the nineteenth century there arose between the German colonization zone and its Brazilian surroundings hardly any relationships worthy of note in either the economic or the sociopolitical sphere. This isolation, taken together with the fact that the German colonies were being kept in the tutelage by the Brazilian authorities but were at the same time being neglected by them (as in the matter of schooling), had the effect of broadly preserving the German cultural tradition. Even toward the end of the nineteenth century, most Teuto-Brazilians in the agricultural colonies barely understood Portuguese.

In contrast to this, the Germans who settled in the cities—particularly the upper class, but also the lower—underwent a much more rapid assimilation into Brazilian society. German merchants and industrialists maintained active social interaction with the Luso-Brazilian elite: they formed, for example, 40% of the membership of the Porto Alegre Country Club, and were the pace setters in certain areas of social life. To an even greater extent, the Germanic proletariat became Brazilianized, for among them class solidarity appears increasingly to have driven out the ties of ethnicity (although Roche does not pursue this theme further). The pressure for integration had its smallest effects on the Teuto-Brazilian Protestant middle class, which even in the twentieth century revealed an unusual susceptibility to the claims of *Deutschtum* policy.

According to Roche, a kind of "agrarian democracy" centering on the small farmers arose in the agricultural colonies. Unfortunately, he does not penetrate its inner functioning; he does, however, make clear that this development—because of the segregated character of the German colonization zone within Rio Grande—had absolutely no impact on the political predominance of the riograndense oligarchy. Quite the reverse: The latter succeeded in enmeshing the Teuto-Brazilian colonists (who were, after all, themselves the products of pre- or pseudodemocratic political systems in Europe) in their traditional patrimonial politics, and thereby secured their support in exchange for some cultural-political concessions. What made the problem of the political integration of the Germans in Brazil particularly explosive was not their threat to the local monopolists of power, but rather the real or assumed ties of the Teuto-Brazilians to Germany. Crucial periods in this process were World War I and, above all, the 1930s, when the attempt on the part of National Socialist Germany to achieve a more energetic political mobilization of the German-Brazilians collided head-on with the increasingly nationalistic policies of the Vargas Regime.[4]

Of the movements of German immigrants into the Spanish-speaking lands of South America, that oriented toward Chile most closely resembles the Brazilian experience. This is as true for the forms of settlement as it is for the long-term evolution of the German-speaking communities, even though the German migration to Chile remained quantitatively far smaller than that to Brazil. On this point we have at hand two monographs produced quite independently of each other, although both appeared in the same year, 1974: the voluminous opus (altogether some 1150 pages) of J.-P. Blancpain, and George Young's much slimmer volume.

Blancpain's inquiry is divided into four "books." The first concerns itself with the prehistory of Southern Chile and conditions there before the immigration of the Germans and with the events leading to it. The final "book" contains an extremely comprehensive listing of the highly varied sources, published and unpublished, on which the study is based. In books two and three, the author describes in great detail the backgrounds and processes of German immigration and demonstrates the influence of the Germans on various sectors of Chilean society. Because of the remoteness of Chile from Europe and hence its relatively small attraction as a destination for emigrants, purposeful measures were called for on the part of the Chilean government to motivate a considerable number of Germans (estimates range between ten thousand and twenty thousand; exact statistics are not available) to emigrate to that country.

Within the German immigration, which began in the mid-nineteenth century and continued until World War I, three main groups can be identified, their identification being based on (temporal) waves of settlements and centers of settlement activity.

The first group was settled in the rural areas of the region of Valdivia and Osorno. As this group was composed in large part of artisans and business people, there soon set in a secondary migration to the nearby cities; these cities in turn, through the influx of qualified workers, thereupon experienced a considerable rise in activity. Newly arrived immigrants, most of them of middle-class origins and by no means impoverished, founded lines of artisan enterprise, some of which later, in a number of specialties—brewing, distilling, tanning—grew into full-fledged industries. They also gained control of the greater part of retail trade and of local large estates. Parallel to the emergence of this bourgeoisie of the middle-sized cities there occurred the founding of an agricultural settlement zone round about Lake Llanquihue, one which reveals many similarities to the agricultural colonization of southern Brazil. Here, too, is a case primarily of smallscale farmers who—partly under conditions of extreme privation—cleared a portion of the unpromising primeval forest of southern Chile. Their hallmarks were their tenacious hold on the middle-class property holdings they had acquired with such great effort, their conformity to the Protestant religion and its ethics, their exclusive intercourse among themselves and the corresponding isolation (at first forced, later voluntary) from the Chilean environment, and finally, their high rates of reproduction. Taken together, these factors made them into a swiftly expanding ethnic island in what had previously been an area occupied exclusively by Chileans.

In a third group, finally, are encompassed the diverse German immigrant contingents which were brought into the country by the Chilean government after 1880 in order to bring under its effective control the Chilean frontier area between Bío-Bío and Toltén, which had hitherto remained in the hands of the Mapuches. Concerned about the possibility of overpopulating the South with one single foreign nationality—the Germans—the Chilean government sought to obtain other Europeans as well as Germans for settlement of the newly won regions. According to Blancpain, the facts that here scattered settlements were the rule and that these settlers were of lower-class origins (most were recruited from among the big-city proletariat or landless East Elbian farm workers) explain why Germanic characteristics, including command of the German language, disappeared relatively rapidly from this third group.

The first two groups—the two which clung stubbornly to their Germanness—obviously engage the author's sympathies, even though he occasionally points out the questionable consequences of such a markedly ethnocentric position in such a different environment. He emphasizes the pioneer accomplishments of the early promoters and spokespersons of the German migration to Chile, and underlines their positive influence on the development of southern Chile. It becomes clear that Blancpain's forte lies in detail—in his knowledge, unexcelled in its thoroughness, of the situations and conditions of individual settlers, communities, events, and so on. He has, for example, traced out precisely the evolution of many immigrant families in Chile—from the mutual kinship relations created by marriage, through their business connections and successes, to their participation in voluntary associations and local politics. The care with which Blancpain reconstructs the circumstances of immigrant life creates for the reader a picture—as sharp as it is detailed—of the difficulties that confronted settlers, their economic behavior, the shape of their dwellings and settlements, their daily habits, customs, festivals, and assemblies—and thereby their mentality.

Against this must be set certain weaknesses of this method of conscientious and minute description. They become visible with respect to the presentation of wider relationships—e.g., in the third book, whose subject matter is the German influence on schooling, on missionary work in southern Chile, on the Chilean military system, and, in general, on the formal diplomatic relations between Chile and Germany in terms of foreign policy. Here also the knowledgeable analysis and preparation of the historical materials is engagingly done. Nevertheless, it is difficult, from the fund of information offered on the intentions and effects of individual persons, groups, and institutions, to move to more general conclusions concerning the significance of German behavioral and organizational models for Chilean development in the areas in question. It would be interesting to learn, for example, why the Germans were active in some sectors and not in others; or why the settlers did not attempt to gain influence in national politics. So far as the settlement colonies themselves are concerned, the question remains open: What were the basic causes of gradual social and economic differentiation? The question also rises: Were the relations between the individual families and groups really as harmonious and conducive to solidarity as the witnesses would have one believe? There are further questions. How did relations between Germans and Chileans develop in accordance with social class? In what concrete ways were the two parties mutually dependent? Which stereotyped views of the Chileans were dominant among Germans, and vice versa? Blancpain does indeed touch these points, but compared to the thorough description that he devotes, for example, to the ordering of the fields or the regional variations among the German school systems, they are given only quite marginal treatment.

In this respect, unfortunately, Young's study does not represent an amplification of Blancpain's work; rather, it is based on similar methodological premises, even though the emphases in the content are laid out somewhat differently. Thus, Young pays special attention to a calculation of the extent of German immigration (which in his opinion did not exceed 11,000 persons altogether) and pursues in some detail the origin of the concept of "national colony"—the concept with which Germans in the second half of the nineteenth century sought a rationalization and setting or goals for the disturbingly strong emigrant movement. With respect to the temporal variations in the waves of migration, in geographical concentrations, and in the processes of settlement in southern Chile, there are no notable deviations from Blancpain's far more thorough treatment. The most interesting chapter would seem to be the last, in which a number of general characteristics of the German colony in contrast to its Chilean surroundings are suggested. Here Young raises the question of the causes of the unbroken vitality of Chilean *Deutschtum* until well into the twentieth century. He proposes three answers: first, the relative geographical isolation of this region from the rest of Chile until the building of the railroad at the beginning of this century; second, the cultural superiority of the Germans to the indigenous Chilean population; and third—a factor, however, to which he assigns less weight—the continuing support which the German-speaking colonies received from influential German circles in Concepción, Valparaíso, and Santiago, not to mention that of the Empire itself. A survey of the imposing variety of institutions follows in which, on the one hand, the sociocultural autonomy of the Chilean Germans was manifested to the outside world, and which, on the other, explains the great inner cohesion of the settlement communities. Under this heading some athletic clubs, rifle clubs, bowling clubs, singing clubs, fire brigades, health insurance and burial funds, school-governing associations, religious congregations, and—not least—a periodical press. All these were supported by the dues, contributions, and assessments of members who belonged of their own free will. The different capacities of the members of different social classes to participate in the financing of these organizations is, according to Young, one of the reasons for the relatively swift secession of the lower class from the German cultural community and its absorption into the Chilean lower class. Further, the German elite raised little opposition to assimilation into Chilean society—through marriage, for example—so long as this step represented an augmentation of power and prestige. Protestants in general held more tenaciously to their Germanness than did Catholics. Hence, in view of all these criteria, the Protestant middle class turns out to be the hard core of the German colonies; it was they who defended with special stubbornness the German cultural tradition and the integrity of the German population itself. Regrettably, all these important insights and comments are thrown together in the final chapter in a partly sketchy way, while the remaining chapters, conscientiously documented, deal with the events and the intellectual life of the settlements, individual institutional measures taken by the Chilean authorities, the adventurous biographies of the initiators of the immigration (that of the most important of them, B. E. Philippi, alone takes up one-tenth of the text). Thus, one has no choice but to observe that, despite the appearance of two worthy monographs on the history of the Germans in Chile, there still remain important research desiderata, and we can only hope for further investigation into these themes.

A similar conclusion is appropriate for the third of the important South American immigrant countries for the Germans, Argentina, although it must be observed at once that here, in Newton's book on the Germans in Buenos Aires, pioneering work has been carried out too. In its point of departure this study is different from the two reviewed above: Here, less emphasis is placed on conditions of immigration itself, rather, the focus of the presentation is the evolution of the German colony within the Argentine metropolis during a particular historical period. Further, in the structure of the inquiry there are important differences from the two volumes on Chile. If in Blancpain the preservation of the German cultural community is in the foreground, here the processes of change receives emphasis; if the former holds high the solidarity and communal feeling of the Germans, the latter reviews the conflicts and tensions within the German colony; if in Blancpain's book the tenacious hold of the settlers onto traditional German values and virtues is held up for display, Newton presents, rather, the rapid adaptation of immigrants to the new homeland's criteria for material success; if, when all is said and done, Blancpain's book is the history of German success in Chile, Newton's book gives the failure and frustration among German immigrants in Buenos Aires a dominant position. Although these differences in emphasis reflect, in part, the different perspectives of the authors, surely they are also due, in greater part, to the very different subject matter under study. In the Chilean case, this is the rural and small-town settlements of the second half of the nineteenth century, while Newton is concerned with the question, much more complex in many ways, of the adaptation of German immigrant groups in a twentieth-century South American metropolis.

By way of introduction, Newton provides an excellent condensed overview of the development of the German colony in Buenos Aires up to World War I. Particularly stimulating are his comments concerning the changes within the German business community in the Argentine metropolis that took place as a result of the founding of the German Empire in 1871, and the rapid rise of German industry. If the older German merchant caste in Buenos Aires was distinguished by a markedly cosmopolitan outlook, after the 1870s the rapidly growing numbers of German businessmen aligned themselves economically as well as in terms of political ideology with Imperial Germany—a Germany which after 1900 underlined its economic presence in Buenos Aires with the founding of subsidiaries of German firms such as Mannesmann, Siemens, AEG, and so on. From this business elite, however, came hardly any impulse for the industrial development of the country; their activities, rather, remained limited to the traditional area of export trade and banking, as well as certain sectors of public service such as the provision of electrical power. Now as earlier, successful German businessmen invested their capital in *laftifundia.* This brought them profit and, even more important, prestige.

As is apparent already in this introductory chapter, throughout Newton's book, the importance of the domestic and international situation of the German Empire for the self-awareness and cohesion of German settlement groups in South America can hardly be overestimated. For example, the outbreak of war in 1914 led to a renewal of solidarity with the *Reich,* a position which in 1919, corresponding to the new state of affairs in Germany, resulted in serious conflicts between factions of the political right and left. The apparently parallel emergence of political positions and programs in both Germany and on the Rio de la Plata, however, should not obscure the fact that the conflicts on la Plata followed their own dynamics, one shaped by the problem of the survival of a German community in a foreign metropolis. It is to Newton's special credit that he has probed deeply into the process of social differentiation which, in the space of barely twenty-five years, transformed the highly egalitarian and homogeneously structured German *Gemeinschaft* into a social structure of hierarchical classes, a structure able to resist centrifugal forces only with the greatest difficulties. It became clear that the different social classes, notwithstanding their roots in a common cultural tradition, did not always manage to maintain their status in the society of Buenos Aires which was itself, at the time, in rapid transition. The small, extremely flexible, highly competent upper class of bankers, industrialists, and import-export entrepreneurs was able to increase its wealth before, during, and after the World War, and thereby also to improve its social position. At the same time, the wartime hostility in some quarters toward the Germans and the loss of prestige that accompanied the *Reich's* defeat had severe effects on other social classes. Using statistics on employment, average earnings, and cost of living, Newton shows that the German middle class, above all, came into tight straits in the 1920s. The employment crisis that confronted the business and professional people at that time was worsened again after the war by a renewed wave of German immigrants (also mainly of middle-class origins) into Argentina; the greater part of these, however, were after a time forced by lack of work to return to Germany. In a chapter entitled "The Immigrant Experience *im Affenland,"* the author creates out of autobiographical and literary materials a vivid picture of the painful experiences and successive stages of adaptation of the migrant after arrival from Germany. The material presented serves to confirm the experience noted in the other studies—namely, that members of the upper and lower classes, and Catholics generally, had less difficulty in becoming assimilated than did persons of the Protestant middle class. The status anxiety and frustration that resulted from widespread unemployment and the decline in collective prestige were, according to Newton, major reasons why the German middle class, especially the *lower* middle class, demonstrated a relatively high openness to National Socialism, and why the upper class, although for quite different reasons, displayed only weak resistance.

Despite occasional repetitions and weaknesses (as in the chapter on the German schools), Newton's very tightly written work carries out fully the promise made in the subtitle to analyze "social change and cultural crisis" among the Germans in Buenos Aires. It is to be hoped that further studies of the same high quality will be undertaken on the European immigration into Argentina, for this is an area of Argentine history in which, in relation to its importance for the country's present-day social structure, far too little research has been done.

Part II

From the survey of the literature just concluded, it is clear that the development of German settlement groups in Latin America depended upon a variety of factors. We should like, once again, to isolate a number of them which seem especially important in an attempt to elucidate them more thoroughly. Having done so, we will attempt to pull together a provisional synthesis covering the economic integration of German immigrants to Latin America, their cultural assimilation, and their medium- and long-term influence on the receiving nation.

The factors which weighed most heavily on the chances of the Germans in Latin America for adaptation and achievement can be placed in four groups: the social origins of the immigrants; the course of the migration itself, as well as the form and extent of the settlement; the then-effective as well as continuing influence of the mother country, Germany, on the colonies in South America; and finally, the changing economic, social, and political relationships in each of the receiver countries. The significance of the first two complexes of factors will not be examined in detail here. The monographs reviewed demonstrate clearly how important it was for the later evolution of the immigrants and the development of the colonies they founded—whether they were artisans and merchants or members of the urban proletariat; whether Catholic or Protestant; whether it was a movement of individuals or of half a closed village transplanted intact from Europe to South America. Just as clear is the characteristic long-term effect of the migration and settlement form; this could range from government-sponsored settlement policy in southern Brazil through privately sponsored agricultural colonizing ventures to the overwhelmingly individualistic migration to a metropolis like Buenos Aires.

A particularly interesting aspect, however, of German migration to South America is the influence of Germany on the South Americans of German origin. From the image of the "homeland" which the emigrants carried with them to South America, an afterimage continued to radiate whose strength should not be underestimated—an afterimage compounded of the assumptions, attitudes, rules of conduct, and values they had grown up with and which were built into their self-identity. All of the authors cited above discovered, in the colonies they studied, traces of a German cultural community (*Deutschtum*) which can only be described as remnants of traditions belonging to a bygone era. This traditional image of Germany was, however, increasingly overwhelmed after the late nineteenth century by the radiance of a new, politically and militarily strengthened, economically dynamic, Germany; these emanations penetrated the New World in diverse ways. This is especially true of the ambitiously rising industrial power of Germany, which steadily improved its economic position in international markets until World War I and which was even thereafter among the most important investors in Latin America.

In the wake of the penetration of certain sectors of the South American economy by German capital and merchandise, not only were the external trade relations between the *Cono Sur* countries and the German *Reich* strengthened, but these developments also opened supplemental entrepreneurial and occupational opportunties for the Germans already settled there—as, for example, employees in the branches of German firms—or allowed them to use their connections to seek export markets in Germany for local agricultural products. A strengthened influence and gain in prestige for the German colonies also resulted from efforts in other areas in which Germany was considered to set the standard for the world—first in military matters, of course, but also in certain branches of science and pedagogy. But on the other hand, the Germany colonies—because of Germany's international relations, such as its role in World War I, the defeat of 1918 and its sequels, or the Nazi agitation in South America—found themselves exposed not only to temporary economic boycotts and the like, but also, more importantly, to an ever-increasing pressure for political and cultural integration into the new homeland.

For the development of the German colonies, the economic, political, and social conditions in each receiving country, different to begin with and changing with time, were of the greatest importance. In general the chances for a rapid economic growth pattern were more favorable in the nineteenth century than after World War I. This is true not only for peasant settlers (keeping in mind the progressive shrinking of the area of good virgin land), but also for middle-class people of German origin.

The latter enjoyed, at first, a near monopoly in some occupations; later, however, they had to compete in these occupations not only with immigrants of other nationalities but also with the developing middle sectors of the country in question. In the case of Buenos Aires, Newton has shown nicely how this process began among the German artisans, who were not a match for their Spanish and Italian competition, and then overtook white-collar employees and professionals as well.

A further cause of occupational and economic difficulties with which some of the emigrants had to contend after 1900 lay in the sociopolitical evolution which Germany had undergone in the meantime. In line with their experience in the homeland, German employees and manual workers demanded decent working conditions. This included sickness, accident, unemployment, and income protections. These demands caused them to fall behind their native compeers, who were more accustomed to Latin America's conditions of early capitalism in the competition of the job market. As the German settlement areas increasingly lost their economic isolation, the room for maneuver in the struggle to maintain ethnic-cultural autonomy shrank, just as, amidst the rising nationalism of Latin America, toleration of immigrant groups which attempted to keep open the option of a second spiritual citizenship also shrank.

Against this background of conditioning factors, it is necessary to pose three basic questions if one wishes to strike a provisional balance for the growth and success of the German colonists in South America: (1) In the *Cono Sur* lands, what was the course of the economic integration of the German immigrants? (2) What was the extent of the social and cultural assimilation of the settlers? (3) What further far-reaching influences did the immigrants exert on the receptor societies, and how did they influence the latter's structures in the long term?

(1) The material success of the farmers, numerically the largest group of South American Germans, varied greatly. While in some measure the Germans of Southern Chile built up prosperous agricultural properties, the small holdings of southern Brazil—fragmented by demographic increase and testamentary practices—afforded the settlers only a modest standard of living. In southern Brazil it was the local businessmen, especially merchants and industrialists, who rose to prosperity; the German agricultural colonies were, of course, their original economic basis. Together with the internationally active big businessmen, bank-

ers, and managers of German branch concerns in the ports and metropolises of South America (Buenos Aires, for example), the German-speaking upper class of local origin formed the socioeconomic elite classes of the German colonies. These elite classes, especially after World War I, began to merge into their respective national bourgeoisies. On the other hand, we have little information on workers of German origin, particularly urban workers. This is due in part to the fact that they represented only a numerical minority among immigrants, and in part to the fact that in the German associations (*Vereine*), the focal point of the German-speaking colonies, they were scarcely represented. The extent to which they were successful in making the leap into the middle class that emigration promised remains an open question.

The most problematic economic outlook was that for the immigrants of middle-class origin. For the German immigration into Argentina in the interwar years, at least, we have Newton's demonstration that, in the face of a stagnant demand for technicians, teachers, administrators, and so on, more than half the immigrants were forced to return to Europe.

(2) The stubbornness with which most of the larger German colonies held for generations to the cultivation of the German language as well as German customs and institutions, has time and again impressed observers from the outside. Along with the already-mentioned geographical and social isolation (at times by choice, at times not) of numerous settlement communities, the explanation lies with the quantity of linked organizations, the *Vereine,* which served these immigrant groups as an essential support in that they satisfied basic social needs and also exercised a considerable conformist control over individual members. Despite this powerful force for cohesion, however, the bonds within numerous colonies began to loosen after World War I. Even though these symptoms of dissolution appeared more clearly in large cities like Buenos Aires than in more stable rural and small-town communities still dominated by ties of ethnicity, they reflected a general trend of development. This derived, in turn, from a growing differentiation within the colonies into socioeconomic classes with conflicting interests—a differentiation which increasingly undermined the requirement that common origin should be equivalent to group solidarity and cohesion. The upper class increasingly identified itself with the local oligarchy, while the German-speaking lower class felt itself closer to the native proletariat than to the German "colony" with its communal institutions—institutions in which the workers, because of their limited

financial resources, could scarcely participate. The core of the German colonies, therefore, and the principal support of their associations remained the (mainly Protestant) middle class—a social stratum which was nevertheless numerous and influential enough to manifest the survival capacity of *Deutschtum* in many towns and regions down to World War II.

(3) The fact that the immigrants concentrated a good portion of their energies on the preservation of their ethnic autonomy may be one reason that the influence of German settlement groups on the surrounding sociopolitical structures of the host country remained limited. One must mention, of course, that the sociopolitical abstention of the Germans had quite different, indeed contradictory, causes. In the "Baltic" (see Blancpain) situation of southern Chile, the Germans, as a new local elite, cultivated a splendid isolation vis-à-vis the Chilean population dependent upon them; in the rural colonies of southern Brazil, however, their tenacious grip on the German cultural tradition well into the twentieth century must be considered a defensive reaction against the Luso-Brazilian environment which they felt to be superior.

The most important long-term consequences were undoubtedly those that made up the German contribution to the economic development of the *Cono Sur*—in which, of course, were regions where the Germans were especially influential. First of all, agriculture in some regions experienced decisive innovations as a result of German immigration. Agrarian structures were thereby noticeably diversified, even though in southern Brazil and southern Chile the dominant agrarian form, the *latifundio,* was not to be driven out by small- and middle-sized German farming operations. As to the founding of German industries, especially in Brazil, the local concentration in German settlement centers was characteristic. Despite important individual accomplishments, however, it would be incorrect to single out the Germans as the real pacemakers of the industrialization of the *Cono Sur.*

Their strongest influence was on the foreign trade of South America. In 1939 Germany controlled no less than 10% of the total foreign investment in Latin America. Nevertheless, the German economic power never extended to the point that one could speak—as one could of Great Britain and later of the United States—of a German "informal empire" in South America.

Furthermore, the influences—some of them considerable but often only temporary—which the Germans exerted on the development of the

Latin American military establishment, educational systems, and science did not have profound effects. In summary, it can be said that they did not exert an autonomous political force at the national level; nor did they serve as style models in social respects, as did the British, or in cultural respects, as did the French.

—Hans Werner Tobler,
Peter Waldmann

NOTES

1. On German policy toward Latin America in the first decades of the twentieth century and its economic background, see also Katz's fine survey (1966).

2. Illi (1977) offers a useful bibliographical survey of German migration to Latin America in general. The article by Kellenbenz and Schneider (1976) is limited to quantitative aspects. Brief notes on archival resources and the state of research are to be found in the Kellenbenz/Schneider contribution of 1979. Shortly before completion of this essay, Froeschle's (1979) comprehensive work appeared. It contains articles on the role of the Germans in the various Latin American countries.

3. On the German contribution to the industrialization of southern Brazil, see also the thorough monographs by Kohlhepp (1968) and Delhaes-Guenther (1973).

4. This matter has been carefully studied in the well-researched dissertation by Harms-Baltzer (1970), which is based on the records of the former Foreign Ministry in Berlin.

5. A comprehensive study of the role of the Germans in Argentina, comparable to the works of Roche and Blancpain, remains to be written. In addition to the quite extensive article by Werner Hoffman in Froeschle's collective work, studies by Hugo Grothe (1932) and Wilhelm Luetge (1955), among others, give a good general overview.

REFERENCES

DELHAES-GUENTHER, D. VON (1973) Industrialisierung in Suedbrasilien—Die deutsche Einwanderung und die Anfaegne der Industrialisierung in Rio Grande do Sul. Koeln: Boehlau-Verlag.

FROESCHLE, H. [ed.] (1979) Die Deutschen in Lateinamerika. Shicksal und Leistung. Tuebingen und Basel: Erdmann Verlag.

GROTHE, H. (1932) Die Deutschen in Uebersee. Eine Skizze ihres Werdens, ihrer Verbreitung und kulturellen Arbeit. Berlin: Zentralverlag, GmbH.

HARMS-BALTZER, K. (1970) Die Nationalisierung der deutschen Einwanderer und ihrer Nachkommen in Brasilien als Problem der deutsch-brasilianischen Beziehungen 1930-1938. Berlin: Colloquium Verlag.

ILLI, M. (1977) Die deutsche Auswanderung nach Lateinamerika. Eine Literaturuebersicht. Lateinamerika Studien 2. Muenchen: W. Fink Verlag.

KATZ, F. (1966) "Einige Grundzuege der Politik des deutschen Imperialismus in Lateinamerika, 1898 bis 1941," pp. 9-69 in Humboldt Universitaet Berlin: Der deutsche Fascheismus in Lateinamerika, 1933-1943. Berlin: Humboldt-Universitaetsverlag.

KELLENBENZ, H. and J. SCHNEIDER (1976) "La emigración alemana á América Latina, 1821-1931," Jahrbuch fuer Geschichte von Staat, Wirtschaft und Gesell Schaft Lateinamerikas 13: 386-403.

———(1979) "La emigración alemana para América Latina, 1815-1929/31. Fuentes y estado de investigación," pp. 179-194 in H. Pietschmann (ed.) La emigración europea a la América Latina: fuentes y estado de investigación. Berlin: Colloquium Verlag.

KOHLHEPP, G. (1968) Industriegeographie des nordoestlichen Santa Catarina (Suedbrasilien)—Ein Beitrag zur Geographie eines deutschbrasilianischen Siedlungsgebietes. Heidelberg: Verlag des geographischen Instituts der Universitaet.

LUETGE, W. [ed.] et al. (1955) Geschichte des Deutschtums in Argentinien. Buenos Aires: Deutschen Klub en Buenos Aires.

WILLEMS, E. (1948/1949) "Zur sozialen Anpassung der Deutschen in Brasilien." Koelner Zeitschrift fuer Soziologie I: 316-323.

Hans Werner Tobler is Professor of History at the Swiss Federal Institute of Technology, Zurich, Switzerland. He is the author of several publications on contemporary European history and on twentieth-century Mexico. At present he is completing a study, Modernization and Revolution: Mexico, 1876-1940.

Peter Waldmann is Professor of Sociology at the University of Augsburg, Federal Republic of Germany. His major areas of research include sociology of law, organization, deviant behavior, and political sociology. He is the author of Der Peronismus 1943-1955, *editor of a reader on violence in Latin America, and has written numerous articles on violence and Argentine politics. At present he is preparing the publication of a* Political Dictionary of Latin America.

REVIEW ESSAY

THE UNITED STATES AND THE DOMINICAN REPUBLIC
Intervention, Dependency, and Tyrannicide

Gleijeses, Piero. THE DOMINICAN CRISIS: THE 1965 CONSTITUTIONALIST REVOLT AND THE AMERICAN INTERVENTION. Baltimore: Johns Hopkins University Press, 1978.

Diederich, Bernard. TRUJILLO: THE DEATH OF THE GOAT. Boston: Little, Brown, 1978.

On the evening of April 28, 1965, the United States troops were ordered into the Dominican Republic to thwart the democratic, Constitutionalist revolution apparently at that moment on the verge of succeeding. The success of the revolution would have meant the overthrow of the corrupt and oppressive military-oligarchic regime then in power and the restoration of a social-democratic and reformist government led by Juan Bosch and his Dominican Revolutionary Party (PRD), who had been ousted from power in a military coup staged nineteen months earlier. The American intervention frustrated the movement to restore democratic-constitutionalist rule.

On that same evening, Everett Dirksen and Jerry Ford, then minority leaders of the Senate and House, respectively, were attending a black-tie reception. A message arrived summoning them to the White House. There, still in their formal attire, they found Lyndon Johnson, clad in pajamas and with a drink in his hand. "I want you to know," he told the assembled stars of the "Ev and Jerry Show," "that I have just taken an action that will prove that Democratic presidents can deal with Communists as strongly as Republicans." Without further explanation,

Journal of Interamerican Studies and World Affairs, Vol. 22 No. 2, May 1980 247-260

the president turned, went into the bathroom and on to bed; meanwhile, the massive buildup of 23,000 troops to occupy the Dominican Republic and prevent its revolution from succeeding was already underway.[1]

The Dominican revolution and the American intervention were among those critically important turning points in history that have not yet received the attention they deserve. The revolt and the American response to it constituted one of the major foreign policy crises of our time, yet these events are now only dimly remembered and they remain obscured by myths and inaccuracies. Probably the reason the intervention in Santo Domingo has not been adequately studied is that it was quickly overshadowed by the even larger American intervention in Southeast Asia. But one can easily make the case that it was the Dominican intervention that first led to the "credibility gap" between what the United States government says it does abroad and what it actually does, prompted the disillusionment of informed opinion molders (the press, intellectuals) in this country with American foreign policy, initiated the poisoning of our political relations, and precipitated the ruin of Lyndon Johnson.[2] One might even go so far as to say, with only slight exaggeration, that if one were looking for a single day that one could identify as the day the United States *lost* the Cold War in Latin America and throughout the Third World, and from which point on the "American model"—politically, socially, culturally, developmentally—would no long serve as *the* model to which Third World nations aspire, that day would be April 28, 1965, the day of the American intervention in Santo Domingo.[3]

The previous literature on the Dominican revolution and the United States' intervention has left some important lacunae. Theodore Draper (1968), for example, wields a terribly sharp critical scalpel which he has honed devastatingly on the American policy actions. But while Draper is adept at sticking the knife in and twisting the cutting edges to maximum advantage, his analysis is informed neither by an inside view of how American foreign policy functions nor by much first-hand knowledge of the domestic Dominican situation. Jerome Slater's book (1970) on the intervention is excellent, but it is written almost exclusively from an American foreign policy perspective and he makes no claims to special expertise in Dominican internal politics. And even though he was in the country at the time of the revolution, Abraham Lowenthal's doctoral thesis (1971) is similarly framed in terms of American perspectives and the United States foreign policy-making process.

The books that present a Dominican and more sympathetic perspective of the revolution are unsatisfactory. José Moreno's account (1970), while motivated by sympathy and the best of intentions, is incomplete and especially weak on the political aspects of the revolution. My own research (Wiarda, 1969, 1975) concentrated on the period leading up to the revolution and not the revolution itself; indeed, I had left Santo Domingo with a first draft of my dissertation under my arm about two months before the revolution exploded.

Fortunately the gap in our knowledge, the one that concentrated on *Dominican* plans, perspectives, politics, and aspirations, has now been filled by Piero Gleijeses. Gleijeses has, additionally, the enormous advantage of not being an American by birth and is therefore without the same biases that most American scholars carry with them to their political analyses. In addition, he approaches the Dominican revolution and understand its goals sympathetically, without the condescension, selfrighteousness, patronizing perspective, and sense of superiority that U.S. observers so frequently exhibit.

While Gleijeses also has his prejudices, this is a serious, scholarly book. It is the longest, most thorough, most detailed analysis of the revolution—particularly from the Dominican side—yet attempted. It is based on both the already-available record and a wealth of heretofore unavailable documents that Gleijeses has acquired. In addition, he has interviewed, often several times and in great detail, virtually all the major Dominican protagonists.

While Gleijeses is sympathetic to the revolution and a man of the left, most particularly partial to the Dominican Republic's *Fidelista*-inspired fourteenth of June Movement, he does not allow that to interfere in crucial ways with his assessments. Because of this sympathy, Gleijeses devotes as much space in his book to the PSP (the Dominican Communist Party), MPD (a small, confused Marxist-Leninist group), and the *Catorce de Junio* as he does to the far larger and more important PRD, which launched and helped lead the revolution. This bias is also reflected in the disproportionate number of interviews the author held with members of the far left, as compared with the number for the moderately left PRD.

But this bias has not prevented Gleijeses from strongly criticizing the leftist groups or from using evidence garnered from them to depict just how weak, disorganized, and ineffective they were. Indeed, that is one of the major conclusions of the Gleijeses book. He shows clearly that the far left (Communists and Fidelistas) was an insignificant force in the planning of the revolution and that, contrary to the official American argument, it *never* had any possibility of seizing control of the revolution. The principal justification for the intervention (although others, such as "saving American lives," "preventing bloodshed," and so on, were invented), which was to prevent a potential "Castro- Communist" take-over, has been shown to have no legitimacy whatsoever.

There are numerous strengths in the Gleijeses book. One is the detailed historical perspective the author brings to his analysis, showing the rising tide of U.S. influence in the Dominican Republic from the nineteenth century on, which made the country a political and economic dependency of the United States. The intervention of 1965 was thus not a sudden aberration but only another, particularly heavy-handed, instance in a long history of American manipulation. The book helps show how the distinction between intervention and nonintervention is virtually meaningless in the Dominican case, since U.S. involvement there has been continuous, in one form or another, for over a century.

Gleijeses also shows, contrary to the "liberal" interpretations of Draper, Lowenthal, and Slater, that the intervention cannot be explained simply as a "mistake" or as a series of "errors" caused by an uninformed ambassador, faulty intelligence, or the presence of a non-Kennedy in the White House. Rather, the intervention flowed directly from the historic dependency relationship the United States had established vis-à-vis the Dominican Republic and from the conservative, antirevolutionary, status quo-oriented nation (but of course one permiting certain "acceptable" changes within the established structures) we had become. Gleijeses demonstrates that *right from the start,* on April 24, the first day of the revolt, the American position was anti-Bosch and anti-PRD. The "missed opportunities" for a compromise solution of which Lowenthal speaks were not "missed" at all but were never considered as serious alternatives to thwarting and/or crushing the revolt. Nor, *from the beginning,* were the American forces neutral in the conflict and concerned only with the establishment of a buffer zone and the prevention of further bloodshed. Rather, the Americans had ruled out immediately a Bosch- or PRD-dominated solution in favor of a more conservative military junta. Such a junta might have allowed some minimal presence for the PRD, but its chief purpose would have been to check the reformers and control the more "radical" elements. And from the moment they landed in Santo Domingo (at General Wessin's San Isidro air force base, the center of the antirevolutionary military), the American forces were deployed against the "Constitutionalists" and not as benignly neutral "peace keepers."

Further evidence not mentioned in Gleijeses' book helps bear out these conclusions. We know, for example, from the female students at the University of North Carolina at Greensboro, where Fort Bragg troops often went on weekends, that within hours of the outbreak of revolt in Santo Domingo on April 24 the men of the Eighty-Second Airborne were called back to the base and put on alert for whatever contingency might arise. And once the order to land in Santo Domingo had been issued on April 28, the troops were given hurried indoctrination in the transports en route that they were to assist the "loyalist" military against the "rebels" or "Constitutionalists," who were labeled "Communists" and "Castro-Communists."

Another strength of the Gleijeses book lies in its thorough analysis of the jockeying of the military factions and personalities in the months prior to the revolution. The revolution was not just a Bosch and PRD-led civilian revolution but also a military revolt in which several individuals and cliques were competing. While Gleijeses analyzes these rivalries well, he focuses almost exclusively on the political and ideological positions of the military officers. He does this, probably, to offset the Lowenthal argument that the Dominican officer corps is uniformly corrupt, venal, and self-serving, entirely devoid of any nobler or reformist political ideals. In actuality, interviews conducted in 1964 within the officer corps by this reviewer revealed both tendencies were present at the same time among military officers, and often within the same individual. Many of the junior officers who participated in the revolution ere fed up with the graft, brutality, and *trujillismo* of the older status quo-oriented officers; but these same interviews revealed that a number of them used ideological arguments to cover more self-serving motives—i.e., the desire to get rid of the senior officers so that the junior officers could have access to the same perquisites, economic opportunities, power, and status from which the seniors had excluded them. Both sets of motives were present in the officers that led the revolution, and any explanation—Gleijeses' or Lowenthal's—that concentrates on the one to the exclusion of the other is incomplete and misleading.

Gleijeses has done his research thoroughly, and his contribution is a major and original one. Nevertheless, a number of important but so far unexamined research frontiers remain, really at this stage only hypotheses, toward which future research efforts might be directed.

The first has to do with the connection between U.S. domestic politics and the American intervention in Santo Domingo. Foreign policy is never entirely encompassed in a series of all-inclusive options which policy makers weigh and rationally choose among; rather, foreign policy decisions are inexorably linked to domestic political concerns. As the story with which we began this discussion indicates, domestic U.S. politics were certainly high on President Johnson's list of reasons for intervening; and we know from various sources that a "second Cuba" in the Caribbean has been the one consistent complex that all American presidents from Kennedy on have had—chiefly because they fear no American president can be reelected who permits a "second Cuba" in "our lake."

Hence a "second Cuba" must be avoided at all costs, even if that means military intervention and proves enormously expensive in terms of the United States's stature abroad. But if this interpretation is correct—and certainly there is much in present American foreign policy to support the hypothesis of a growing tendency for foreign policy decisions to be based not on rational calculations of a *national* and *public* interest, but to placate partisan, domestic political interests—then the U.S. intervention in Santo Domingo would seem to have less to do with the internal Dominican situation and probably more to do with domestic U.S. political consideration and how the decision to intervene or, worse, to fail to act might be read domestically. To the "liberal," "radical," and "bureaucratic" approaches to foreign policy analysis, therefore, must also be added this connection with U.S. domestic politics. Such an interpretation would certainly conform to what we already know about the ethnocentrism and lack of concern or even interest in the rest of the world on the part of the American public and most American politicians and the latter's need to put short-term reelection considerations above longer-term foreign policy needs. Probably a good place to begin in pursuing this connection would be the Johnson papers in Texas and interviews, not with Johnson's foreign policy advisers (that has already been done) but with his *domestic* advisers and cronies.

A second unexplored terrain involves the connection between the Dominican intervention and Viet Nam and between Santo Domingo and the broader global context of U.S. policy. Santo Domingo and Viet Nam, Viet Nam and Santo Domingo, as Slater once put it, these are the two great foreign policy crises of the mid-1960s; yet no one has analyzed the relations between them. It would be interesting to see what the *Pentagon Papers* or other documents available have to say on this theme, or what the perspective with regard to the Dominican intervention was on the part of the key policy makers who had already decided on a stepped-up involvement in Viet Nam. Johnson himself has provided the connection between the Dominican action and Viet Nam by arguing that if we did not act in the first case, our credibility and threat to act in the second would not be taken seriously. The fact is that the planning and contingencies for the massive U.S. bombing and intervention in Viet Nam had been determined just about the time the Dominican crisis broke, yet we lack any systematic studies of the precise relations between these two so far apart but, one suspects, so closely linked interventions.

Even more broadly put, and thinking from a global perspective, it might be hypothesized that the Dominican intervention may well have had little to do with the events unfolding in Santo Domingo. Of course it did in an immediate and physical sense, and certainly for the many Dominicans (about 2000) killed in the revolution, and their friends, families, and political colleagues, the American intervention had some very real and tragic impacts. But thinking in terms of the global "chessboard" with which senior foreign policy makers view the world, it would appear that what the United States was trying to do in the spring of 1965 was to use the Dominican example to demonstrate to the Russians, once again, that, just as we do not interfere and stir up trouble in their sphere of influence (chiefly Eastern Europe), they had best not to do so in "ours" (the Caribbean and South America). Although it may not have been publicly or expressly articulated, President Johnson would probably have been thinking that he didn't want to face the possibility of having to go through another "missile crisis" like that in Cuba in 1962; or that if he acted forcefully in Santo Domingo, then the Soviets would perhaps put the brakes on the actions of the North Vietnamese in aiding the Viet Cong in the South. There is some mention of this linkage in Johnson's public statements, and in his private comments at the time of the Dominican intervention, he referred to the Russians as "wanting what is ours" and of the necessity to resist. There may be parallels, in short, with Chile in 1973, another intervention which may not have had all that much to do with Chile per se but, from Nixon's and Kissinger's global perspective, with the need to demonstrate still again that the Americas are our sphere of influence and the Russians (even if it happens to be domestic Socialists and Communists) had better not "mess" here, just as we will not interfere with their "internal housecleaning," as in Czechoslovakia in 1968.

A third area for future research has to do with the processes of Dominican politics and the precise nature of the revolution itself. This reviewer is not entirely convinced that Bosch and the PRD in 1965 really wanted a full-fledged revolution; moreover, they were surprised and woefully unprepared when it did occur and even more surprised when final success seemed about to befall them. This hypothesis, which may seem startling to some, may be more understandable to Latin Americanists, since it draws from the more general literature on Latin American politics and how the change process works, as well as from our own research experience in the Dominican Republic at the time. Specifically, it derives from Charles W. Anderson's notion (Anderson, 1964) that most political groups in Latin America that resort to violence and confrontational politics are not necessarily aiming at a revolutionary transformation that will topple or destroy the entire system, but only at demonstrating in a more limited way a "power capability" so that their voice will be legitimized and seriously listened to. It may be suggested that that is what the PRD was trying to do in 1965—acquire legitimacy and a power standing so that its presence in Dominican affairs would be recognized and its demands heard, but not stage a full-fledged revolution.

From 1964 to early 1965 the PRD was out of power, ignored and persecuted by the conservative civilian and military groups that held it. The PRD then began a long-term campaign to demonstrate its continued popular support and its power capability so that it would be granted renewed legitimacy and the right to bargain and be a participant in the system. That is why the PRD initially began to contact the younger officers in the Dominican armed forces: Having military allies is how one demonstrates a "power capability" in Santo Domingo. Another method of demonstrating its strength was the series of *agapes* the PRD organized in 1964 and early 1965. These receptions, to which prominent intellectuals, lawyers, journalists, engineers, and other professionals were invited, were impressively huge and lavish affairs, publicized widely, and designed to demonstrate to both the elite-dominated Triumvirate government and the U.S. Embassy how widespread the PRD's support was among informed Dominican professionals and opinion molders. As one of the few American scholars in the Dominican Republic at the time and known to be sympathetic to the policy goals of the PRD, this reviewer was also invited, doubtlessly because the PRD hoped to make an impression that might be reflected in some favorable writings about the party, and probably hoping too that the message of its growing strength among the professional "class" would be carried to the U.S. Embassy.

These are not the tactics of a party preparing for revolution but of one following the more limited—and familiar—strategy of demonstrating a power capability. In pursuing that strategy it may also be necessary to demonstrate armed might, but even that kind of demonstration falls short of and is not to be equated with revolution. One must bear in mind that within the PRD leadership, differences existed over strategy and the various factions sometimes pursued diverse paths. But the evidence we have indicates: (1) The PRD campaign in 1964-1965 was oriented toward demonstrating a power capability and gaining a legitimized voice for itself in national political affairs, not staging a full-fledged social revolution; (2) the use of violence was part of this strategy, but it was to be limited and structured violence short of revolution; (3) the PRD was not expecting the revolt to break out on April 24 and was ill-prepared when it occurred; (4) the PRD wanted to gain some recognition and concessions from Triumvirate leader Donald Reid Cabral, and was as surprised as the Americans when it actually toppled him; (5) the PRD was even more surprised two to three days later when it not only reached a stand off with General Wessin and the old-line military, but seemed poised on the verge of defeating them; and (6) the PRD was totally unprepared to fight a long guerilla struggle or engage in prolonged armed conflict as its "revolution" neared the point of succeeding.

The American intervention, coming precisely at this stage, made the whole point academic. What was to have been a quick and limited show of force by the PRD without bloodshed to reorganize and restructure the nation's balance of political forces, became instead a protracted and bloody civil war. The PRD was forced to defend the gains it had already won de facto not only against the local conservative elites but also against the American military, a struggle it had little heart to fight and could not possibly win. To the already long list of sins committed by the Americans in Santo Domingo, two more should therefore be added: first, that by our intervention in April 1965 we both prolonged and made far bloodier and destructive a Dominican conflict that would almost certainly have been resolved much more quickly and painlessly by the Dominicans themselves, employing typically Dominican compromises and solutions; and second, by our actions in Santo Domingo we demonstrated once more that we neither comprehend nor care to comprehend how the Latin American political process functions—a political process with its own rules and procedures, in which various groups employ a variety of techniques to demonstrate power capability and to make their voices heard, often using violence but violence short of complete revolution. There is much evidence that U.S. Latin America policy makers comprehend these processes no better now than they did in 1965.

Students of the Dominican revolution, hence, must be careful to separate the revolutionary rhetoric and rationalizations formulated *after* the fact by some of the revolution's leading participants, from the more limited goals the PRD leadership seemed to have up to April 24. In short, the Dominican "revolution" of 1965 did not really begin as a full-scale revolution but as a more limited movement with more limited goals. It became a genuine revolution almost by accident and in the course of events, both because of the actions of the Americans and because, as Merle Kling (1967) has elegantly argued, a cultural and political context such as that of the Dominican Republic in which political violence, however limited, is used and condoned as a means, can also produce highly diverse, violent, and often quite unexpected ends.

Journalist Bernard Diederich's book on the assassination of Trujillo provides much new information on that event, as well as establishing an interesting link to the revolution that followed four years later. It was in large part the conspirators' failure, once they had killed Trujillo, in their and the United States's plans to control the post-Trujillo transition, that led directly to the conflictual politics that followed and to the revolution and intervention of 1965.

Diederich, coauthor of *Papa Doc,* was in Haiti at the time of Trujillo's death and has a good sense of the violence and clan politics that often prevail in both countries of Hispaniola. His book is a riveting, almost Graham Greene-style account of these bloody and at the same time fantastic events. Diederich also unravels the complicated role of the United States—and the CIA—in propping up the hemisphere's longest-lived dictatorship in the twentieth century and then in undermining it and supplying the weapons to slay its leader.

The roots of the assassination plot, he says, were laid in the kidnapping and murder of Jesús de Galíndez, the Basque scholar and exile who had written a doctoral dissertation at Columbia critical of the Trujillo regime. Two pilots, one American and one Dominican, had been hired to fly Galíndez to the Dominican Republic and were then themselves murdered because they knew too much. It was the slain

Dominican's brother, Antonio de la Maza, who gathered the band of assassins to get revenge on Trujillo and inherit his wealth and mantle for themselves.

Diederich recreates the planning and the bumbling that went into the conspiracy, its progression from semi-idle patio conversation to serious plotting, the stalking of the target, and the acquisition of weapons (difficult because Trujillo monopolized all arms). In the process he shows the personalistic nature of Dominican politics, the political and *panelinha* (Leeds, 1964) system, the importance of family and clan feuds, revenge, and ambitions, as contrasted with more institutionalized party politics. He also shows (as does Gleijeses) the excessive importance of the U.S. Embassy in internal Dominical politics—and how both government and opposition are dependent upon it. Diederich traces the initial contacts of the conspirators with the CIA and shows how the promise of help from the Americans was eventually secured.

That help (according to Diederich limited to moral support and two M-1 rifles) encouraged the assassins to go ahead despite U.S. efforts at the last minute to abort the plot. But the conspirators were not professionals, and while they succeeded in killing Trujillo, they had no contingency plans to cover unexpected events, they miscalculated the Trujillo family's ability quickly to reassert control, and some of their own supporters proved contagiously weak-kneed. In the end, all but two of those involved in the conspiracy paid the ultimate price as the Trujillos sought their revenge.

Diederich has reported these events accurately and, so far as can be ascertained, with no particular axes to grind. But there are several major gaps in his analysis. For one, he does not know, as Gleijeses does for the 1965 intervention, how the Trujillo assassination was just another, albeit again especially dramatic, event in the continuous, almost constant—before and since—history of U.S. meddling in internal Dominican affairs. Second, he does not link the Trujillo assassination to the events in Cuba—specifically, to the Bay of Pigs invasion—occurring two months earlier and to which the Trujillo plot was intimately linked. Third, he does not place the group of conspirators plotting to assassinate Trujillo within the broader context of mounting Dominican opposition politics directed against the regime in the late 1950s and early 1960s.

The most serious lacuna, however, according to information this reviewer was given access to, is Diederich's ignoring the role apparently played in the conspiracy by the local American business community. This information indicates that the Dominican representatives of Alcoa, Esso, Texaco, Pan American Airlines, and perhaps others were all involved in or informed of the conspiracy. If the U.S. government involves local representatives of major corporations in its plotting, that must also be cleared with the corporate boards of directors in New York and elsewhere. Part of the reason the entire scenario failed—not only to kill Trujillo but also to seize control of the government—was that almost all the participants, Dominicans and Americans, were amateurs. Several drank too much and talked too much to wives, priests, and pastors, and their courage and staying power in the conspiracy could only be maintained with massive infusions of American money. At the end seemingly everyone in Santo Domingo knew about the plot—probably including *el jefe*. In any event, if one were looking for a prima facie example of collaboration between the CIA and some major American corporations, the Trujillo assassination would likely be a good case to follow up.

The story of the Trujillo assassination and the United States involvement in it used to shock and surprise students, but by now the shock value has been dissipated and perhaps we have become inured to such grisly tales of official murder. Or perhaps one can make the argument in Trujillo's case that tyrannicide is morally justified. Given the chief motive for the U.S. involvement, however—to get rid of Trujillo in a timely fashion so as to prevent in the Dominican Republic what had occurred in Cuba following Batista's downfall—the burden of proof would seem to rest on those who would argue that the American intervention (really a series of interventions) in the Dominican Republic in 1961 was any more justifiable than the intervention in 1965.

The Dominican Republic is one of those nations close to our shores where the United States's presence has been particularly heavy and almost continuous for over a hundred years. In Gleijeses's book and others now in preparation, the earlier period is receiving new and more detailed attention because it is clear that the American presence was no more happily neutral then than it was in the two episodes here under consideration. Moreover, this history of constant interventon has consistently served to bolster the status quo-oriented forces in the Dominican Republic and to work against the forces for change. One wonders how much has changed recently. While one may applaud the 1978 diplomatic intervention by the United States in Santo Domingo in the name of human rights and in securing an honest electoral count, one should also recognize that it is still intervention, and that by that act the Dominican government inaugurated has become, again, an American dependency. Antonio Guzmán is almost universally perceived in the Dominican Republic as Jimmy Carter's and Cyrus Vance's "boy." So long as they last and retain an interest in the Dominican Republic, he may last; but should they go or lose interest, Guzmán is almost certain to "go" as well. One wonders if there is any way for the Dominican Republic to retain viability as a nation and at the same time break out of the vicious circles of underdevelopment and dependency in which it is caught.

—*Howard J. Wiarda*

NOTES

1. This story is not in any of the books available on the revolution; it was told to the author by one of those present at the reception Dirksen and Ford attended, who heard it from Ford after he returned from the White House.

2. Symptomatic, perhaps, of this neglect of the Dominican intervention and its implications is Doris Kearns's biography and psychohistory of Lyndon B. Johnson (Kearns, 1976). Based on inside access and obviously preoccupied with the chain of events that drove Johnson from office, Kearns nevertheless entirely neglects the Dominican crisis.

3. This view is clearly at variance with the perspective, widespread in Washington, that the Dominican case is one of "successful" American intervention as compared with the "failure" of the Viet Nam intervention. In contrast to Viet Nam, in this view, the American intervention was carried out relatively quickly and "cleanly," our purposes (presumably, the prevention of the loss of American lives and of a successful "Castroite" or Communist take-over) were accomplished, and we withdrew within a reasonable time-frame rather than being bogged down, as in the Viet Nam imbroglio. This "success" story obviously does not take into account either the short- or long-term devastation wreaked by the intervention upon the Dominican Republic or its people, the number of *Dominican* lives lost, or the ruination inflicted upon the fragile Dominican economy, polity, or society and on the nation's course of development. Nor, if the arguments presented here have merit, does it adequately address the long-term damage done to the United States itself.

REFERENCES

ANDERSON, C. W. (1964) "Toward a theory of Latin American politics." Occasional Paper 2, Graduate Center for Latin American Studies, Vanderbilt University, Nashville, Tennessee.

DRAPER, T. (1968) The Dominican Revolt: A Case Study in American Policy. New York: Commentary Books.

KEARNS, D. (1976) Lyndon Johnson and the American Dream. New York: Harper & Row.

KLING, M. (1967) "Violence and politics in Latin America," pp. 119-132 in Paul Helmos The Sociological Review, Latin American Sociological Studies Monograph 11. Keele, England: Univ. of Keele.

LEEDS, A. (1964) "Brazilian careers and social structure: a case history and model." American Anthropologist 66: 1321-1347.

LOWENTHAL, A. (1971) The Dominican Intervention. Cambridge, MA: Harvard Univ. Press.

MORENO, J. (1970) Barrios in Arms: Revolution in Santo Domingo. Pittsburgh: Univ. Pittsburgh Press.

SLATER, J. (1970) Intervention and Negotiation: The United States and the Dominican Revolution. New York: Harper & Row.

WIARDA, H. J. (1975) Dictatorship, Development, and Disintegration: Politics and Social Change in the Dominican Republic. Ann Arbor, MI: Xerox University Microfilms.

——— (1969) The Dominican Republic: Nation in Transition. New York: Praeger.

Howard J. Wiarda is Professor of Political Science and Chairman of the Program of Latin American Studies at the University of Massachusetts. During 1978-1980 he is visiting Scholar at the Center for International Affairs at Harvard University. He is presently engaged in a project funded by the National Endowment for the Humanities involving state-society relations in Latin America and is the author of several books, the most recent of which is Latin American Politics and Development *(Houghton Mifflin, 1978), which he coauthored with Harvey F. Kline.*

BOOKS RECEIVED

GENERAL AND REGIONAL LATIN AMERICA

Collier, David, ed. THE NEW AUTHORITARIANISM IN LATIN AMERICA. Princeton, NJ: Princeton University Press, 1980. Glossary, bibliography, index. 456 pp. $25.00 cloth, $5.95 paper.

Fagen, Richard R., ed. CAPITALISM AND THE STATE IN U.S.-LATIN AMERICAN RELATIONS. Stanford, CA: Stanford University Press, 1979. Index. viii, 446 pp. $22.50 cloth, $6.95 paper.

ILDIS. LAS ORGANIZACIONES SINDICALES EN LOS PROCESOS DE DEMOCRATIZACION. 2 vols., Materiales de Trabajo 19 y 20. Quito: Fundación Friedrich Ebert Stiftung, Instituto Latinoamericano de Investigaciones Sociales, 1978. 199 pp. Paper.

Mesa-Lago, Carmelo, with the collaboration of Sandra E. Miller and Shirley A. Kregar. LATIN AMERICAN STUDIES IN EUROPE. Latin American Monograph and Document Series 1. Pittsburgh: Center for Latin American Studies, University of Pittsburgh, 1979. Lists of tables and abbreviations, country reports. vi, 190 pp. Paper.

M'Gonigle, R. Michael and Mark W. Zacher. POLLUTION, POLITICS, AND INTERNATIONAL LAW: TANKERS AT SEA. Berkeley: University of California Press, 1979. List of tables, maps, charts; glossary of acronyms, appendixes, index. xviii, 394 pp. $15.95.

Morris, Arthur. SOUTH AMERICA. New York: Harper & Row, 1980. List of plates, maps and diagrams, appendixes with conversion table, glossary of Portuguese and Spanish terms, bibliography, and index. xii, 271 pp. $26.50 cloth, $14.50 paper.

Rietti, Mario. MONEY AND BANKING IN LATIN AMERICA. Foreword by Antonio Ortiz Mena. New York: Praeger, 1979. List of tables and abbreviations, bibliography, statistical appendix. xviii, 295 pp.

Salcedo V., Danilo. VISIO Y PERSPECTIVAS DE LA EDUCACION SEXUAL EN AMERICA LATINA: RESULTADOS DE UNA INVESTIGACION. New York: Centro de Documentación y Publicaciones, IPPF/RHO, 1979. Anexos. 203 pp. Paper.

ARGENTINA

Balán, Jorge. URBANIZACION REGIONAL Y PRODUCCION AGRARIA EN ARGENTINA: UN ANALISIS COMPARATIVO. Vol. 2, No. 2. Buenos Aires: Estudios CEDES, 1979. 42 pp. Paper.

Cavarozzi, Marcelo. SINDICATOS Y POLITCA EN ARGENTINA: 1955-1958. Vol. 2, No. 1. Buenos Aires: Estudios CEDES, 1979. Referencias bibliográficas. 87 pp. Paper.

Moline de Berardoni, Enriqueta E. HISTORIA DE MARCOS PAZ: DESDE SUS ORIGENES HASTA LA CREACION DEL PARTIDO, 1636-1880. La Plata: Archivo Histórico de la Provincia de Buenos Aires, 1978. Indice de ilustraciones. 184 pp. Paper.

BOLIVIA

Nash, June. WE EAT THE MINES AND THE MINES EAT US: DEPENDENCY AND EXPLOITATION IN BOLIVIAN TIN MINES. New York: Columbia University Press, 1979. Appendix, references, index. xxi, 363 pp. $22.50.

BRAZIL

Instituto de Estudos Brasileiros, USP. REVISTA DO INSTITUTO DE ESTUDOS BRASILEIROS No. 20 (special issue devoted to work of Roger Bastide by French and Brazilian scholars). São Paulo: Instituto de Estudos Brasileiros, Universidade de São Paulo, 1978. 175 pp. Paper.

CENTRAL AMERICA

Durham, William H. SCARCITY AND SURVIVAL IN CENTRAL AMERICA: ECOLOGICAL ORIGINS OF THE SOCCER WAR. Stanford, CA: Stanford University Press, 1979. Lists of tables and figures, appendixes, bibliography, index. xvii, 209 pp.

COLOMBIA

ICFES. 1978 DIRECTORIO DE LA EDUCACION SUPERIOR EN COLOMBIA. Bogotá: División de Documentación e Información, ICFES (Instituto Colombiano para el Fomento de la Eucación Superior), 1978. Indice por carreras, índice de instituciones, glosario. vii, 224 pp. Paper.

MEXICO

Centro de Investigaciones Superiores del INAH. INMIGRANTES Y REFUGIADOS ESPANOLES EN MEXICO (SIGLO XX). México, D.F.: Centro de Investigaciones Superiories del INAH, Ediciones de La Casa Chata, 1979. Apendice, bibliografía. 369 pp. Paper.

Díaz, José and Román Rodríguez. EL MOVIMIENTO CRISTERO: SOCIEDAD Y CONFLICTO EN LOS ALTOS DE JALISCO (con un estudio introductorio de Andrés Fábregas). México, D.F.: CIS-INAH (Centro de Investigaciones Superiores del Instituto Nacional de Antropología e Historia), 1979. Apéndice, mapas, bibliografía. 242 pp. Paper.

Oswald, Ursula (coordinadora). MERCADO Y DEPENDENCIA. Producción agrícola comercial en el sur del estado de México y comercialización en el gran mercado capitalino de La Merced. México, D.F.: CIS-INAH, 1979. Anexo, bibliografía. 404 pp. Paper.

Villoro, Luis. LOS GRANDES MOMENTOS DEL INDIGENISMO EN MEXICO. México, D.F.: Centro de Investigaciones Superiores del INAH, Ediciones de La Casa Chata No. 9, 1979. Prólogo a la segunda edición (1ª edición, El Colegio de México, 1950), conclusion, obras citadas. 248 pp. Paper.

PERU

Alisky, Marvin. HISTORICAL DICTIONARY OF PERU. Latin American Historical Dictionaries No. 20. Metuchen, NJ: Scarecrow Press, 1979. Appendixes, bibliography. vi, 157 pp. $8.50.

Plaza J., Orlando presentación y selección de textos. ECONOMIA CAMPESINA. Lima, Perú: DESCO, 1979. 308 pp. Paper.

Zolezzi Chocano, Mario and Abelardo Sánchez León. MUNICIPALIDAD Y GOBIERNO LOCAL: EL D.L. 2250 EN EL TAPETE. Lima, Perú: DESCO, 1979. Anexos. 62 pp. Paper.

VENEZUELA

Pérez, Carlos Andrés. MANOS A LA OBRA: TEXTOS DE MENSAJES, DISCURSOS Y DECLARACIONES DEL PRESIDENTE DE LA REPUBLICA. Tomo III, Vol. 1: 17 de marzo 1976 a 14 de noviembre 1976, 499 pp.; Vol 2: 16 de noviembre 1976 a 11 de marzo 1977, 512 pp. Tomo IV, Vol. 1: 22 de marzo 1977 a 26 de setiembre 1977, 519 pp.; Vol. 2: 3 de octubre 1977 a 11 de marzo 1978, 491 pp. Caracas: Ediciones de la Presidencia de la República, 1979. Paper.

MISCELLANEOUS

Carr, Raymond and Juan Pablo Fusi. SPAIN: DICTATORSHIP TO DEMOCRACY. Winchester, MA: Allen & Unwin, 1979. Chronological table of events, glossary of political terms, notes, index. xxi, 282 pp. $23.95.

Foster, David William. STUDIES IN THE CONTEMPORARY SPANISH-AMERICAN SHORT STORY. Columbia: University of Missouri Press, 1979. Selected bibliography, index. vi, 126 pp. $15.50.

Frankel, Joseph. INTERNATIONAL RELATIONS IN A CHANGING WORLD. New York: Oxford University Press, 1979. Reading list, index. 218 pp. $14.50.

Goldsmith, John. VOYAGE IN THE BEAGLE. London: Chatto Windus, 1979. Prelude, list of illustrations, postscript, index. xviii, 196 pp. $15.50.

Vol. 22 No. 3
August 1980

JOURNAL OF INTERAMERICAN STUDIES

and WORLD AFFAIRS

A Publication of the Center for Advanced International Studies,
The University of Miami

SAGE PUBLICATIONS

Journal of INTERAMERICAN STUDIES and WORLD AFFAIRS

The editors and publisher wish to acknowledge with gratitude the assistance and encouragement of the Center for Advanced International Studies, University of Miami, in providing ancillary services and support for this journal.

Journal of
INTERAMERICAN
STUDIES
and WORLD AFFAIRS

Vol. 22
No. 3
August
1980

CONTENTS

Arms Production and National Security in Argentina
EDWARD S. MILENKY 267

The Regionalist Expression of Populism: Guayaquil and the CFP, 1948-1960
JOHN D. MARTZ 289

The Institutionalization of the Cuban State: A Political Perspective
MAX AZICRI 315

Operation Condor: Mexico's Antidrug Campaign Enters a New Era
RICHARD CRAIG 345

Why the Poor Remain Poor: The Experience of Bogotá Market Traders in the 1970s
CAROLINE O.N. MOSER 365

COMMENT

Leonardo Ruiz Pineda: Acción Democrática's Guerrillero for Liberty
STEVEN ELLNER 389

SAGE PUBLICATIONS / *Beverly Hills* *London*

Policy: The **JOURNAL OF INTERAMERICAN STUDIES AND WORLD AFFAIRS** reflects the interests of the scholarly community and interested public concerned with the social, economic, political, and cultural aspects of life in Latin America (including the Caribbean), particularly in those instances where the subject is of concern to more than one of the traditional disciplines. As these concerns change, so will the content of the journal.

Articles which have special relevance for interrelationships between American nations and of those nations with the rest of the world will be given special consideration. An effort will be made to include occasional articles that state an unusual or even discordant position on a subject of broad interest to be supplemented by critical comments of authorities representing differing positions on the topic. The editors continue to welcome articles by scholars from all parts of the world.

Manuscripts should be submitted in duplicate to: Editor, **JOURNAL OF INTERAMERICAN STUDIES AND WORLD AFFAIRS,** Box 24-8134, University of Miami, Coral Gables, Florida 33124. Manuscripts should be typewritten, double-spaced, with footnotes, references, tables, and charts on separate pages, and should follow the current journal style. A brief biographical paragraph describing each author's current affiliation, research interests, and recent publications should accompany the manuscript.

Correspondence regarding book reviews should be sent directly to: Book Review Editor, **JOURNAL OF INTERAMERICAN STUDIES AND WORLD AFFAIRS,** Box 24-8134, University of Miami, Coral Gables, Florida 33124.

JOURNAL OF INTERAMERICAN STUDIES AND WORLD AFFAIRS is published four times annually—in February, May, August, and November.

Subscriptions: Regular institutional rate $32.00 per year. Individuals may subscribe at a one-year rate of $16.50. Add $1.00 for subscriptions outside the United States. Orders from the U.K., Europe, the Middle East, and Africa should be sent to the London office (address below). Noninstitutional orders **must** be paid by personal check.

Second class postage paid at Beverly Hills, California. ISSN 0022-1937

This journal is abstracted or indexed in **Historical Abstracts, Human Resources Abstracts, Sage Urban Studies Abstracts, International Political Science Abstracts, Public Affairs Information Service, Current Contents, Social Sciences Citation Index, Social Sciences Index, ABC POL SCI,** and **United States Political Science Documents.**

Back Issues: Information about availability and prices of back issues may be obtained from the publisher's order department (address below). Write to London office for sterling prices.

Inquiries: Address all correspondence and permissions requests to SAGE PUBLICATIONS, Inc., 275 South Beverly Drive, Beverly Hills, California 90212. Inquiries and subscriptions from the U.K., Europe, the Middle East, and Africa should be sent to SAGE PUBLICATIONS Ltd, 28 Banner Street, London EC1Y 8QE, England. Other orders should be sent to the Beverly Hills office.

Advertising: Current rates and specifications may be obtained by writing to the Advertising Manager at the Beverly Hills office (address above).

Claims: Claims for undelivered copies must be made no later than three months following month of publication. The publisher will supply missing copies when losses have been sustained in transit and when the reserve stock will permit.

Change of Address: Six weeks' advance notice must be given when notifying of change of address. Please send old address label along with the new address to insure proper identification. Please specify name of journal. Send change of address to: Journal name, c/o 275 South Beverly Drive, Beverly Hills, CA 90212.

EDWARD S. MILENKY
U.S. Department of Energy
Washington, D.C.

ARMS PRODUCTION AND NATIONAL SECURITY IN ARGENTINA

Since 1950, 28 developing countries have produced tanks, ships, aircraft, other major weapons systems, and infantry and artillery weapons for their own use and for export. Local input has ranged from assembly of imported components to completely indigenous design and manufacture. In 1967 exports from less-developed countries (LDCs) were worth $194 million, as compared to exports from all sources of $201 billion. By 1976 world arms exports had increased to $398 billion and LDC exports to $820 million (ACDA, 1978). Even though the role of less-developed countries in world arms production is still small, it is growing and can be significant in some local and regional contexts.

Nascent defense industries in the Third World raise important questions. Terrorists, insurgents, and governments everywhere may find arms more readily available as sources of supply diversify. The spread of weapons manufacture both reflects and promotes the diffusion of power within the international system at large. Aside from the implications for world politics, decisions by less-developed countries to produce some of the requirements of their armed forces provide insight into their respective perceptions of external threats and the national security policies

---

AUTHOR'S NOTE: This article is written in the author's capacity as a private scholar and in no way reflects the opinions of the U.S. government or any agency therein, nor any statement by the U.S. government concerning the accuracy of the data used in this article.

Journal of Interamerican Studies and World Affairs, Vol. 22 No. 3, August 1980 267-288

they adopt in response. Insofar as arms production involves the spread of advanced technology it is one aspect of the drive to industrialize in the Third World, both for the intrinsic benefits involved and as one aspect of the search for the substance and symbols of sovereignty, national power, and international recognition.

Argentina's experience with indigenous arms production provides some useful insights into this general phenomenon. Argentina is an emerging middle power with a long-established role in Western Hemisphere affairs and a growing presence in global diplomacy. Among LDCs it has the longest tradition of manufacturing military equipment, particularly naval ships and aircraft. Its decisions to produce arms have been made in the context of a broad and continuing national debate over foreign policy, national security policy, and economic development. Other developing countries have been concerned with many of the same issues. The balance of this study will be devoted to an examination of the Argentine case, beginning with national security issues and policy responses.

National Security and the Need for Arms Production

THREAT PERCEPTIONS

Argentine civilian and military policymakers identify a series of internal and external threats that forms the basis for national security policy. The country's location and the character of its frontiers form the first set of concerns.

Argentina is remote from world centers of conflict and influence. It gains security from external attack but suffers from a sense of marginality, which has been a favorite theme for historians, social commentators, and political observers (see, for example, Grondona, 1967). Historically, the foreign policy community has resented the dominance of the United States in hemispheric affairs, but has also relied on the United States to ward off any military challenge from the Soviet Union or Soviet-supported client states. Since the overthrow of Perón in 1955, the military has preferred U.S. equipment and training. However, in response to U.S. criticism of human rights practices and U.S. cutbacks in arms sales, the present military government is attempting to diversify its sources of weapons (purchases as reported in ACDA, 1978). In practice the foregoing concerns have been translated into a historic drive to increase Argentina's international role, to maintain an independent foreign policy, and to avoid economic, political, or ideological isolation (Milenky, 1978: 1-16).

Within Latin America, Argentina has been most concerned with maintaining a balance of power in the southern cone of South America. The essential elements of such a balance are military parity with Brazil and Chile, and prevention of any alliance between these two countries against Argentina. Argentine policymakers have also sought a dominant political and economic influence over Uruguay, Paraguay, and Bolivia, which form a buffer zone against Brazil and could provide sanctuary to opponents of an Argentine regime.

Relations with Brazil are the most single important regional issue. Brazil's recent, spectacular economic growth, rapidly increasing population, and growing international recognition as an emerging power have overshadowed Argentina. While both sides regard military conflict as improbable, they have entered into an intense local, regional, and global economic and political rivalry. However, common fears of radical movements in the southern cone and a Soviet naval presence in the South Atlantic, as well as the not inconsiderable benefits of intensified economic relations, bring the two countries together.

Argentina's frontiers are the source of related security concerns. Most of the border areas are remote from major population centers, vulnerable to insurgents, and susceptible to economic and cultural pressures from neighboring countries. There is a long history of disputes with Chile over the long Andean boundary. The Plata River system, shared with Bolivia,

Paraguay, Uruguay, and Brazil, provides easy access to the Argentine heartland, choice hydroelectric dam sites—most of which are shared with other riparian states—and an internal economic and strategic frontier (see, for example, the views of a former junta member, Rojas, 1975).

Maritime frontiers and extracontinental territorial issues remain unsettled. In 1978 Chile and Argentina called full military alerts after negotiations on the delineation of the boundary in the Beagle Channel south of Tierra del Fuego failed. From Argentina's perspective the dispute involves unimpeded sovereign access to its ports on the sourthern coast of Tierra del Fuego and the rights to thousands of square miles of potentially mineral rich continental shelf included in the 200-mile economic zones each side claims around three small contested islands south of the Beagle Channel. Great Britain and Argentina have yet to agree on the ownership of the Falklands-Malvinas Islands, which may also have an oil-bearing continental shelf. Argentina's claim to a sector of Antarctica is contested by other powers and not recognized by many of the signatories to the Antarctic Treaty.

Aside from these territorial questions, the South Atlantic poses growing strategic problems. The 200-mile economic zone Argentina claims must be defended against foreign fishing fleets. Brazil is either a rival or a partner in patrolling waters which carry the bulk of world oil tanker traffic moving between Europe, the United States, and the Persian Gulf. Southern cone countries have apparently discussed defense cooperation among themselves and possibly also with South Africa, but as of early 1980 had not reached any agreements.

These external issues notwithstanding, the military and civilian leadership consider internal security, economic growth and stability, and political reorganization and legitimacy to be their most important political-strategic challenges. A long history of political instability and internal turmoil have seriously weakened the country's capacity for long-range planning and mobilization of resources, as well as tarnished its international standing. Beginning in the early 1960s, internal violence intensified into a virtual civil war between the military on one side and Peronist, Trotskyist, and Marxist guerrillas on the other. Unrest and political protest among disaffected labor and middle-class groups often reached the intensity of spontaneous rebellion, as in the "cordobazo," a mass street battle and general strike that shook the industrial city of Córdoba in May 1969. This source of tension represented a third side to an overall breakdown of national consensus and political authority reflected in the alternation of weak civilian regimes with military juntas and the resort of both types of regimes and their opponents to terror and counter-terror. Since the coup of March 1976, the military appears to have the upper hand, but thousands of Argentines and resident foreigners are still missing and presumed dead by outside observers (de Onis, 1976: 70).

Aside from these more overtly military issues, leaders in the Argentine foreign affairs community recognize economic disorder and underdevelopment as the greatest security problem. Since the nineteenth century the economy has been subject to periodic boom and bust cycles linked to unstable international markets for beef and wheat, the principal export commodities. Import requirements for critical raw materials, technology, capital equipment, and intermediate goods have been comparatively inflexible and severely affected at various times by declining terms of trade. The world's highest rate of chronic inflation, 160% per annum in 1979, compounds these problems. Most groups look back nostalgically to the 1920s, when Argentina was as prosperous as most of Europe and enjoyed steady economic growth fueled by the export of agricultural commodities to relatively open world markets. Since then not only has the country continued to suffer severe economic dislocations, but it has also failed to grow as fast as Europe or even as fast as Brazil, Mexico, or Venezuela. The result is an acute sense of lost status and power which compounds the very real problems of chronic inflation and recurrent balance of payments crises (see, for example, the views of several former presidents writing in Estrategia, 1978).

NATIONAL SECURITY STRATEGIES

Since the 1930s, two distinct approaches to national security policy have emerged in Argentina in response to the internal and external challenges that the country faces. Each represents a general school of thought supported by civilian and military groups.

Classic liberals identify Argentina as Western in alignment and European in culture. They would resolve the country's economic problems by improving prospects for agricultural exports, inviting foreign investment, and by forcing industry to compete on world markets. Supporters include large landowners, businessmen from the larger locally owned corporations and the local subsidiaries of multinational coporations, and the predominant elements of the officer corps of the armed forces. The present government of General Jorge Rafael Videla is drawn mainly from this group. (For typical examples of classic liberal writing, see recent speeches of Economy Minister Martinez de Hoz; and Alsogaray, 1969.)

Statist nationalists see Argentina as a predominantly Latin American or advanced developing country kept subordinate in the world economy by its position as a supplier of raw materials. Only as autonomous as possible a program of heavy industrial development featuring a major role for the state and largely excluding foreign investment is seen as capable of liberating the country from the restraints imposed by a hierarchical and unequal international order (Kaplan, 1969; Frondizi, 1958). The majority of intellectuals, urban professionals, businessmen from smaller companies and firms located in the traditionally poorer interior provinces, union leaders, Peronists, and Radicals (the country's oldest and largest political party) identify with this general approach.

Both groups share some analytical perspectives in common. Each side recognizes economic problems as paramount and believes that political questions will be resolved only after economic growth and stability are established. Each would rely primarily on trade, diplomacy, and internal economic development to recoup Argentina's fortunes in world affairs. External strategic threats will become more manageable if Argentina acquires the wherewithal to hold its own in regional and global political and economic competition. Both statist nationalists and classic liberals also agree that the country has failed to realize its potentially great influence in world politics.

Arms Production

THE DEVELOPMENT OF THE ARMS INDUSTRY

The Argentine arms industry has emerged from the successive responses of various elements of the statist nationalist group within the foreign affairs community to the crises of the Great Depression, World War II, the first Peronist era of the 1950s, and the continuing economic and political malaise that followed it. Statist nationalists have supported a national defense industry as one aspect of extensive government involvement in the development of heavy industry and a general rejection of reliance on outside powers. Classic liberals, by contrast, have been more interested in obtaining arms by purchase as one element in more comprehensive efforts to expand trade and to obtain foreign technology. Aside fom this ideological division, which has been muted by the failure of either group to dominate totally any of Argentina's successive governments, the bureaucratic interests of the armed forces, which focus on security of supply and continuing access to advanced systems and technology, have been crucial.

Arms production is a long-established activity. The first ventures in local manufacture took place in the 1920s. However, the formation in 1941 of the Bureau of Military Factories, the DGFM, established the principle of military-run industrial enterprises and reinforced the link between industrialization and the growth of national power (Potash, 1969: 287). As World War II progressed and Argentina stayed neutral, it found itself unable to obtain arms from either side. By contrast, Brazil accepted Lend-Lease aid from the United States, building up a powerful military which secured combat experience in Italy and the beginnings of a steel industry. The reaction in Argentina was dismay.

In 1943 the United Officers Group (GOU), a secret pro-Fascist military lodge, staged a coup d'état and set out to create the industrial foundations for military power. One of its less prominent members, then Colonel Juan Domingo Perón, declared shortly after the Allied landings in Normandy that Argentina would achieve its aspirations through diplomacy, strong government, and military power whether the Allies or the Axis won the war (Conil Paz and Ferrari, 1966: 118-123). Ultimately the United States replied with diplomatic and economic sanctions and the exclusion of Argentina from all wartime conferences. On January 26, 1945, just as the Russians were taking Berlin, Argentina declared war on Germany.

The wartime experience produced a deep sense of grievance, humiliation, and reactive nationalism which helped Perón into office by free, open election in 1945. Preaching a mixture of integral nationalism and calls for the redistribution of income and power to the lower classes, Perón continued the forced-draft industrialization policies of the GOU. Under the first five-year plan, the DGFM became directly responsible for many areas of heavy industrial development which the military regarded as essential to its needs.

All three services entered the arms business in what for Argentina was a massive fashion. Under the air force a tradition of local aircraft design and manufacture began, often, in the early stages, with the aid of German technicians. Prototype aircraft included an all wood fighter bomber similar to the British Haviland Mosquito, a light jet interceptor-fighter which used a Rolls-Royce engine made locally under license, and the IA-35 Huanquero, a small, multipurpose piston engine transport plane.

Of these designs only the Huanquero went into production, beginning in 1956. Many of the 100 planes produced over the following ten years, including a version armed with a Browning machine gun, are still in service (Military Balance, 1977: 62).

A tradition of indigenous ship design and construction begun in 1938 continued. The navy's yards at Rio Santiago turned out patrol craft and frigates.

The army produced heavy artillery, machine guns, and munitions of various types. With the assistance of German technicians, who apparently helped to establish pilot plants in the 1940s, army arsenals in Rosario developed and manufactured several types of machine guns which are still in use (SIPRI, 1971: 760). However, most tanks, jeeps, and other vehicles were imported.

Perón's fall in 1955 left Argentina with a complex legacy. The economy was in ruins. Autarchic industrialization, subsidized by government diversion of profits from agriculture, created massive balance-of-payments deficits. However, despite the waste, the corruption, and the high cost, Perón left behind the military factories system and the foundations of steel, vehicles, and other heavy industries. The military was permanently in an arms business linked to state industries producing for the civilian economy.

Peronism has continued as an element in the statist nationalist approach to security policy through its civilian and military supporters. However, the governments of the second Peronist period, 1973-1976, did not make major contributions to arms production. Perón himself and then his widow who succeeded him in office, María Estella Martinez de Perón, revived the earlier policy of favoring autarchic industrial development. However, since the military did not offer active support to the regime the government in turn had little incentive to invest in the arms industry.

During the mid- and late 1960s a second element in the statist nationalist approach, the military developmentalists, did contribute to the growth of the defense industry. This group, which emerged from the colonel's course in the Superior War School, the army's educational institution for senior officers, has emphasized the interrelationship of military and economic factors in national security, specifically the need to create the material base for national self-determination through heavy industrial development. One of its most important spokesmen, General Juan E. Guglialmelli (retired), has summed up the doctrine bluntly: "A country which does not have basic industries is a castrated country because basic industries are the virile elements (Revista de la Escuela Superior de Guerra, 1964: 116). In contrast to Peronism, which aspires to the status of a complete social and political ideology, the military developmentalists are more strictly a school of strategic thought.

The military developmentalists reached the peak of their influence under the first two presidents of the Argentine Revolution, Generals Juan Carlos Onganía, in office from 1966 to 1970, and Roberto Marcelo Levingston, in office only briefly in 1970. A military movement that overthrew the ineffectual civilian government of Arturo Illia in June 1966, the Argentine Revolution came to power with a vague program of social and economic reconstruction built on classic liberal principles. However, the failure of the original leadership to achieve social peace or to complete a partially successful economic stabilization program allowed the developmentalists to come to the fore after the anti-Ongania coup of June 1970. The new junta's first proclamation and a comprehensive development plan for the 1971-1975 period, which was published in December 1970, set out their program—the growth of heavy industry, greater control over foreign investment, and diversification of Argentina's international economic relationships, limited at the time to the United States and Western Europe—as steps toward national autonomy and greater international status (Plan Nacional, 1970).

Even though General Alejandro Agustín Lanusse's March 1971 military coup swept the December 1970 development plan and its supporters aside, the period of the Argentine revolution did see additional steps toward national weapons production under military auspices. Under Onganía the Army instituted Plan

TABLE 1
Arms Production Agreements Under Plan Europa

DATE	VENDOR	SYSTEM	PRODUCTION AGREEMENT
1969	France	AMX Light Tank	Local assembly of imported components
1970	Britain	Two Type-42 Destroyers	Coproduction, with first two built in Vickers Yard in England and second at AFNE in Rio Santiago
1973	West Germany	Two Salta Class Submarines (1180 Displacement)	Assembly in Argentina of imported components, with tentative plans for two more subs

SOURCES: SIPRI, 1971: 864; Jane's Fighting Ships, 1978: 26-33; The Military Balance, 1975-1976: 93.

Europa, a program to obtain license or coproduction agreements for European armaments (Uriburu, 1970, for the story of the program by its architect; SIPRI, 1971: 694-697). Even though reliance on imported technology, technicians, and armaments predates it, Plan Europa was the first long-range attempt to link such acquisitions to a comprehensive security policy in the statist nationalist mode. Table 1 lists systems acquired in Western Europe by a series of Argentine military missions.

Since the end of the Argentine revolution period in 1973, the military developmentalists have been important as one faction in the armed forces and as unofficial members of the foreign affairs community. *Estrategia*, published by the Argentine Institute of Strategic Studies and International Relations, a private organization, has many retired military developmentalists, including General Guglialmelli, on its board of directors and among its published authors. This journal is now the most influential national publication in its field, a sort of local equivalent of *Foreign Affairs*, serving as a medium of communication for members of the elite with interests in foreign affairs and national security. Given the strong vested interest represented by the military factories system and the continuing appeal of an autarchic approach to economic growth and national security, a resurgence of the developmentalists is possible.

ECONOMIC BASE OF THE DEFENSE INDUSTRY

Argentina has limited but important potential for the production of moderately sophisticated weapons. With 28% of its GNP of industrial origin and a per capita income of $2100, the country approaches the economic level of the lower-ranking OECD nations. Steel, vehicles, and capital equipment are strong sectors but depend heavily on imported technology, multinational corporations that may at any time decide to shift production elsewhere, and foreign capital for major projects. State-owned industries in petroleum, aluminum, vehicles, railroads, and other areas suffer from featherbedding, massive deficits, and generally inefficient operation. The present government has decided to sell many of these operations to the private sector. The transition period may temporarily increase inefficiency. The locally owned private sector tends to be fragmented into small, undercapitalized firms with obsolete equipment. However, the government has been able to encourage formation of consortia or consolidations to encourage local participation in the development of nuclear and hydroelectric power.

The energy base is secure. In 1978 Argentina imported only 10% of its petroleum and may have the potential for self-sufficiency. Important reserves of coal and hydroelectric power are only now being developed. Atucha I, Latin America's first nuclear power reactor, went on line in 1974. A second power reactor is nearing completion in Cordoba Province. By the year 2000 nuclear power, supported by large indigenous uranium reserves, is supposed to supply 7500 megawatts, or 23% of electricl generation (Banco de Boston, 1978; Nuclear Engineering International, 1978).

National scientific and technological resources are uneven. Less than 1% of GNP has been allocated by government for research and development. Universities are still recovering from the political purges of four recent presidents. Since 1958 CONICET, the National Research Council, has been the principal source of grants for research. However, its funds are limited, and coordination with other government bodies is poor. A National Institute of Industrial Technology, INTI, exists, but in the past has allocated less than $5 million annually for research support. Most patent registrations come from foreign companies or from companies with licensed foreign technology. Trained professionals in science, engineering, and management continue to emigrate in great numbers to the United States and Western Europe (Banco de Boston, 1978).

Despite these limitations Argentina has been able to achieve some results when it has concentrated its economic and technological resources. Argentines have won international recognition for medical research. CNEA, the National Atomic Energy Commission, acquired its first research reactor in 1958, has constructed many of its own facilities, and recently signed an agreement to export a research reactor of its own design to Peru. The National Commission for Space Research, CNIE, has carried out experiments with sounding rockets for several years and contributed to the International Geophysical Year (see CONACYT, 1971: 5; Confirmado, 1978).

Administrative skills is the ability to transform economic and technological resources into military resources (Knorr, 1970: 26). While such abilities are difficult to evaluate on an absolute or comparative basis, Argentina's history of political instability presents serious obstacles to long-term planning and execution of projects. National commentators have remarked on their countrymen's low propensity to cooperate or to function effectively as managers or workers (Fillol, 1966: 21-26, 61, 94-95; Murena, 1957: 1-16).

In some developing countries the military can function more effectively as a managerial and technical organization than other elements in society because of its hierarchical command structure, the often superior training of its officers and enlisted men, and some degree of institutional insulation from social and political turmoil. This appears to be only partly the case in Argentina. The military has no monopoly or even preponderance of trained manpower and professionals. It also has a long history of involvement in national politics as well as its own tendency toward internal factionalism manifest in the presence of secret lodges, interest cliques, and personal followings (Imaz, 1970: 57; Milenky, 1978: 76-78). At times factions in the three armed services have even fought each other in the streets. On the other hand, the armed forces have maintained more institutional continuity than civilian government bureaucracies. They have been able to undertake some long-term military hardware development projects. Military officers have also played prominent roles in civilian ministries, state industries, and private firms. Therefore, although the Argentine military is subject to many of the political conflicts which beset the country at large, it has retained greater administrative skill than most civilian institutions.

If all of the foregoing factors are taken into account, then Argentina is capable of producing fairly sophisticated major weapons systems, particularly if it is able to obtain critical electronics and avionics technology from abroad. The country's record in developing nuclear energy indicates that scarce administrative, technical, and scientific talent can be rationed and directed toward long-term projects with some degree of insulation from political interference. However, limited capabilities and resources for basic research and manpower development impose stringent constraints.

CONTEMPORARY ARMS PRODUCTION

In its present form the Argentine defense industry is a product of the successive developments described above and the limits imposed by the country's industrial and technological base. Its facilities function as dependencies of the three armed services under the leadership of the DGFM, the Bureau of Military Factories, which appears to be under the army's control. Links to state-owned steel, aluminum, and vehicle production firms, which often have military officers in key management positions, appear to be close, as indicated by support of the armed services for new state projects in such areas as aluminum (for aircraft production), and in the production by the DGFM of some goods for the civilian economy, such as railroad cars and trains for the Buenos Aires metro (Ceresole, 1968: 95; SIPRI, 1974: 241).

DINIFIA, the National Bureau of Aeronautical Manufacturing and Research, under air force control, is responsible for aircraft production and design. Under Perón in the 1950s it was most active when the air force attempted to design and fly several types of jet fighters using British Rolls Royce engines made under license (SIPRI, 1971: 763). However, by the 1960s DINIFIA had cancelled development of nearly all of its jet fighter aircraft and was concentrating on transport and counterinsurgency aircraft, most notably the IA-50 Guarani II light, twin-engine transport and the IA-58 Pucara counterinsurgency plane. As of 1977, 15 Pucaras and 22 Guarani II's were in service with the Air Force (Military Balance, 1977-1978: 67). Fifteen additional Pucaras were on order. Three new planes were under development, the IA-60 Pucara jet attack fighter; a trainer based on the Pucara airframe; and the Cicare CH-11 Cobri Helicopter, a trainer which would apparently use an engine imported from the United States (SIPRI, 1977: 289).

Following the pattern set by the DGFM, DINIFIA has produced civilian aircraft. Prototypes include the IA-45 Querandi, a twin-engine light executive transport, and the IA-46 Ranquel, a light agricultural monoplane. As of 1971 the Ranquel was in production, but the Querandi had been cancelled (SIPRI, 1971: 763).

In conclusion, the Argentine Air Force has been successful in meeting some of its needs for light transport and counterinsurgency aircraft. The Huanquero and the Guarani have remained on active status for up to 20 years (based on survey of Military Balance, 1960-1978). However, the maximum recorded production run for an indigenous design is 100 Huanqueros. Nearly all Argentine designs have used some licensed or imported components such as tires, machine guns, or in the case of jet aircraft, engines. Since there are no recorded export sales, all planes have been used domestically. The combination of imported components and short production runs probably means that costs per unit are quite high, although the savings in foreign exchange and technological experience gained constitute offsetting benefits.

AFNE, the State Naval Shipyards and Factories, is capable of producing locally designed naval ships as large as frigates. Recent output has included three "Lynch" class large patrol craft with 100 ton displacements built in the mid 1960s and the Cabo Antonio, a 4300-ton landing ship (tank). Two fast missile-carrying attack craft with 234-ton displacements are under construction as of early 1980 (Jane's Fighting Ships, 1977: 26). As is the case with aircraft, ship production runs are short.

Of all of the services, the army is the most secretive about its local manufacturing activities. As noted earlier, arsenals in Rosario have produced indigenously designed machine guns and ammunition for infantry and artillery needs. In the past the French AMX-13 light tank has been assembled. A family of vehicles using the same chassis, including light and medium tanks and an armored personnel carrier, is under development in West Germany in cooperation with the Thyssen-Henschel firm, apparently for mass production in Argentina (Defense Interarmees, 1979).

Most of this production has been destined for domestic consumption, but the Argentine defense industry retains an interest in exporting. Between 1967 and 1976 a total of $22 million in weapons was exported, most of which was probably ammunition and small arms (ACDA, 1978: 121). The Lanusse government did provide modest aid to Uruguayan President Bordaberry's struggle against the Tupamaro urban guerillas in 1972 and otherwise unconfirmed reports by Argentine leftist groups claimed that then President Perón shipped tear gas and small arms to the Pinochet government in Chile in 1974 (La Opinión, 1974).

However, attempts to market major systems have thus far been unsuccessful. The Pucara has been offered to Peru, Bolivia, Libya, and South Africa (SIPRI, 1977). An improved version, the Pucara B, was exhibited at the Le Bourget Air Show in Paris in 1979, reportedly attracting some interest from Venezuela and the Dominican Republic (Defensa, 1979: 64). Despite these failures, the potential for lowering per unit costs, earning hard currency, bidding for influence in Latin America, and rivaling Brazil's growing arms industry will keep Argentina in the export business.

Conclusion

THE ARGENTINE EXPERIENCE

Arms production decisions in Argentina are the product of responses to external threats and internal security needs as determined by national security policy, pressures for arms production which have grown out of internal political relationships between civilian and military elites, and the capabilities and limitations inherent in the country's industrial-technological base. A review of each of these three elements leads to conclusions useful in understanding the more general phenomenon of Third World defense industries

Since neither classic liberals nor statist nationalists contemplate major external military threats or an external role for the armed forces, local weapons production is geared to needs which are modest on a global scale. The primary missions of the Argentine military are internal security, frontier defense and patrol, coastal naval patrol, and service as a political-strategic counterweight to the armed forces and ambitions of neighboring countries. Foreign weapons purchases are necessary primarily to supply highly sophisticated equipment, such as jet fighters, or the needs of a rapid buildup in response to local tensions, as in the confrontation with Chile over the Beagle Channel. Aside from these needs the local defense industry can supply some of the needs of the army for basic infantry and artillery weapons, moderately sophisticated ships and planes for the low intensity threats faced by the air force and navy, and counterinsurgency aircraft for more specialized purposes.

Aside from meeting these specific defense needs, arms production in Argentina is a product of the debate between classic liberals and statist nationalists. Statist nationalists, particularly the military developmentalists, have identified national security with heavy industrial development. Powerful feelings of lost status stemming from the trauma of the Great Depression, the humiliations of the wartime period, and powerful nationalist reactions to the role of foreign capital in the economy have fed this impulse periodically since the 1940s. Felix Luna, a prominent Argentine historian, echoes other intellectuals who decried the country's close integration into British imperial markets prior to World War II with this description of the national economy in 1943: "Argentina was molded into a vast granary at the service of its exports" (Luna, 1972: 18). This image of passivity and domination contrasts powerfully with General Guglialmelli's characterization of heavy industry as "the virile elements" of the nation (Revista de la Escuela Superior de Guerra, 1964).

Internal political struggles involving the bureaucratic interests of the armed forces have also shaped the present arms industry. Weapons manufacture can be a useful public works pork barrel. The GOU and Presidents Perón and Onganía apparently bid for support with project decisions in a manner understandable to defense contractors everywhere. Building railroad cars and airplanes for the civilian economy in the military factories system has provided additional career opportunities and reinforced the image of the armed forces as patriotic contributors to national development. In the context of continuing political instability, the military has been among the few institutions with the administrative skill and continuity to manage long-term projects.

The Argentine experience also illustrates the upper limits of arms production. Key technologies such as jet engine manufacture and electronics are missing. Licensing or coproduction agreements can fill some of the gaps, but foreign sources can still supply high performance systems more cheaply and rapidly. Furthermore, arms purchase agreements can form an important part of an overall strategy to develop markets for Argentine products and to secure access to advanced foreign technology. Therefore, self-sufficiency in basic weapons as a hedge against foreign cutoffs is the most likely course of action.

ARMS PRODUCTION IN DEVELOPING NATIONS

As the Argentine experience indicates, the obstacles to local defense industries in Third World countries operating above the rifles-and-ammunition stage are formidable. Weapons production can have a boot-strap effect on industrialization once the beginnings of basic industry have been acquired. However, a country must also have a cadre of civilian or military technocrats capable of directing the enterprise over a long period and a supply of either highly talented designers or foreign prototypes. Argentina seems to have received some assistance in the formative stages of its arms industry from German technicians. The less demanding requirements of many Third World military establishments may ease the task, but only rising middle powers such as Argentina, Brazil, India, or Yugoslavia can realistically aspire to any degree of domestic defense production.

A security-equals-development, particularly heavy industrial development, philosophy and a politically active military are a common combination in the Third World. Under such conditions arms production may be undertaken as one of many prestige projects or to satisfy the military's bureaucratic interests. A shortage of foreign exchange, political problems in acquiring foreign equipment, and a general preference for import substitution and a greater degree of national economic and strategic independence may provide more practical reasons.

Aside from these internal factors, widely shared perceptions of the international system promote weapons manufacture in developing countries. These include deep-seated feelings of dependence, resentment of international inequalities in wealth and power, and a declining faith in the value of great power security guarantees. The symbols and substance of national sovereignty and the classic nation-state—a sense of autonomy, independence, impermeability to external pressures, and a sense of distinctive identity—are harder for rising developing nations to achieve in a hierarchical and interdependent world order. Under these conditions arms production along with military forces may help to provide symbols of national identity and virility, an affirmation of independence, and some tokens of modernity.

In a very important fashion defense industries combine ideological and political gratification with some potentially realizable strategic, economic, and technological gains. For this reason a number of rising middle powers among developing nations may choose to arm themselves. As a result, it is likely that military technology will diffuse more rapidly and that arms will become more readily available to governments, insurgents, and terrorists, with potentially significant impacts on local, regional, and perhaps some global conflicts.

REFERENCES

ACDA [U.S. Arms Control and Disarmament Agency] (1978) World Military Expenditures and Arms Transfers, 1967-1976. Washington, DC: Author.

ALSOGARAY, A. (1969) Política y economía en Latinoamérica. Buenos Aires: Editorial Atlantida.

Banco de Boston [Buenos Aires] (1978a) The Situation in Argentina. Monthly newsletter: October 4.

——— (1978b) The Situation in Argentina. Monthly newsletter: May 4.

CERESOLE, N. (1968) Ejército y política nacionalista. Buenos Aires: Editorial Sudesta.

CONACYT [Consejo Nacional de Ciencia y Tecnología] (1971) Potencial científico y técnico nacional. Buenos Aires: Government of Argentina.

Confirmado (1978) Interview with Carlos Castro Madero, President of CNEA [Comisíon Nacional de Energia Atómica]. August 3: 18-21.

CONIL PAZ, A. and G. FERRARI (1966) Argentina's Foreign Policy, 1930-1962. Notre Dame, IN: Univ. of Notre Dame Press.

Defensa [Madrid] (1979) Untitled article. August-September: 10-21.

Defense Interarmees [Paris] (1979) Article. March: 26-30.

DE ONIS, J. (1976) "Isabelita's terrible legacy." New York Times Magazine (March 24): 70.

Estrategia (1978, 1979) Series of short articles by former Presidents Onganía, Frondizi, Levinson, Lanusse, Luder, and Videla. November, December, January, February.

FILLOL, R. (1966) Social Factors in Economic Development: The Argentine Case. Cambridge, MA: MIT Press.

FRONDIZI, A. (1958) Argentina y América Latina. Buenos Aires: Presidencia de la Nación.

GRONDONA, M. (1967) Argentina en el tiempo y en el mundo. Buenos Aires: Editorial Primera Plana.

IMAZ, J. (1970) Los que mandan (Those Who Rule). Albany: State Univ. of New York Press.

Jane's Fighting Ships (1977, 1978) Annual yearbook. London: Jane's Yearbook, Calton House.

KAPLAN, M. (1969) Formación del estado nacional en América Latina. Santiago, Chile: Editorial Universitaria.

KNORR, K. (1970) Military Power and Potential. Lexington, MA: D. C. Heath.

LUNA, F. (1972) De Perón a Lanusse, 1943-1973. Buenos Aires: Editorial Planeta Argentina.

MARTINEZ DE HOZ, J. (1976) Speech in La Nación. April 3: 1.

MILENKY, E. (1978) Argentina's Foreign Policies. Boulder, CO: Westview.

Military Balance (1960-1979) Annual yearbook. London: International Institute of Strategic Studies.

MURENA, H. A. (1957) "Notas sobre la crisis argentina." Aur 248: 1-16.

Nuclear Engineering International (1978) November: 10.

La Opinión [Buenos Aires] (1974) May 12: 4.

Plan Nacional (1970) Plan Nacional de desarrollo y seguridad, 1971-1975. Buenos Aires: Presidencia de la Nación.

POTASH, R. (1969) The Army and Politics in Argentina, 1928-1945: Yrigoyen to Perón. Stanford, CA: Stanford Univ. Press.

Revista de la Escuela Superior de Guerra (1964) "Palabras del señor general de brigada Juan E. Guglialmelli, director del centro de altos estudios y escuela superior de guerra, al calausurar el 17 curso de coloneles." November-December: 116.

ROJAS, I. (1975) Intereses argentinas en la Cuenca del Plata. Buenos Aires: Ediciones Libera.

SIPRI [Stockholm International Peace Research Institute] (1977) World Armaments and Disarmament. Stockholm: Almqvist & Wiksell.

——— (1974) World Armaments and Disarmament. Stockholm: Almqvist & Wiksell.

——— (1971) The Arms Trade with the Third World. Stockholm: Almqvist & Wiksell.

URIBURU, J. (1970) El Plan Europa, un intento de liberación nacional. Buenos Aires: Cruz y Fierro Editores.

Edward S. Milenky is a Foreign Affairs Officer with the U.S. Department of Energy and holds a Ph.D. in International Relations from the Fletcher School of Law and Diplomacy. He is the author of Argentina's Foreign Policies *(Westview Press, 1978),* The Politics of Regional Organization in Latin America: The Latin American Free Trade Association *(Praeger, 1973), and numerous articles.*

JOHN D. MARTZ
Department of Political Science
Pennsylvania State University
University Park, Pennsylvania

THE REGIONALIST EXPRESSION OF POPULISM
Guayaquil and the CFP, 1948-1960

> In any general discussion of populism, Latin America is the odd man out [Hennessy, 1969: 28].

Even a cursory review of recent writings on Latin American politics suggests an inclination by many to have done once and for all with the concept of populism. Either it is defined so broadly as to be useless or is relegated to a historical era presumably never again to be seen in the region. Yet the term shows a vitality and stubborn resilience in refusing to disappear, notwithstanding periodic revisions and redefinitions. This is scarcely unique to Latin Americanists. As a pair of European authorities contended more generally:

> There can, at present, be no doubt about the *importance* of populism. But no one is quite clear just what it *is*. As a doctrine or as a movement, it is elusive and protean. It bobs up everywhere, but in many and contradictory shapes. Does it have any underlying unity, or does one name cover a multitude of unconnected tendencies? [Ionescu and Gellner, 1969: 1].

AUTHOR'S NOTE: This research was assisted by a grant from the Joint Committee on Latin American Studies of the Social Science Research Council and the American Council of Learned Societies.

Journal of Interamerican Studies and World Affairs, Vol. 22 No. 3, August 1980 289-314

If this sense of frustration and uncertainty is to be accepted, there may be little recourse but to follow the wry advice of another interested scholar, who suggested "to each his own definition of populism, according to the academic axe he grinds" (Wiles, 1969: 166). Yet perhaps it should not be left at that.

Students of the politics of Ecuador are among those finding it most difficult to escape the tentacles of populism, however defined. For Ecuador we are told, among other things, that two populistic tendencies have been dominant since 1934 (Del Campo, 1977: 3-4); that populism has long nourished and seduced the masses (Hurtado, 1969: 229); that it constitutes the first effort to elaborate a national ideology in response to the country's objective conditions (Hurtado, 1977: 208); that it must be studied relative to the semiproletariat and to caudillistic movements (Cuvi, 1977: 183); that such movements seek active incorporation of the popular masses into political life (Ortiz, 1977: 213); or that populist forces are destined historically to fail in equitably arbitrating diverse sectoral and class interests (Quintero, 1978: 271). How, then, can populism be dismissed out of hand?

Whatever their philosophical outlook or ideological predisposition, Ecuadorean analysts generally agree that two movements should be labeled populistic: *velasquismo* and *cefepismo*. The first mirrors the extraordinary career of José María Velasco Ibarra, the five-time president who bestrode the political scene from the early 1930s until his death in March 1979 at age 86. The latter emanates from the Concentración de Fuerzas Populares (CFP), which seized control of Guayaquil and the coast from 1948-1960, receded for some years, and then rose from the ashes in a quest for national power that culminated in its April 1979 electoral triumph. It is the first historical period of the CFP which concerns us here, constituting as it did a special and rare manifestation of populism at the local and regional level. But first, a broader consideration of Latin American populism is in order. Space dictates that our overview be selective rather than exhaustive.

PERSPECTIVES ON POPULISM

The most widely cited source is Di Tella (1965: 47), who defines populism as "a political movement which enjoys the support of the mass of the urban working class and/or peasantry but which does not result from the autonomous organizational power of either . . . [and] is also supported by non-working-class sectors upholding an anti-*status quo* ideology." From consideration of potential sources of strength he identifies four types of populist parties: multiclass integrative, *aprista,* "nasserite" or military reformist, and social revolutionary. By so doing Di Tella thus attaches the generic rubric to organizations ranging from Mexico's PRI through Acción Democrática of Venezuela and Liberación Nacional of Costa Rica, from Columbia's ANAPO and the Unión Odriíta in Peru to Castroism in Cuba. Such terminological breadth provides limited guidance to the scholar, even granting the quadripartite typology. Similar problems are produced by Hennessy's treatment which, in building upon Di Tella, describes three forms of populism: urban, old rural, and new rural. A host of parties and movements are again designated, and a single category—in this instance "old rural"—could contain such seemingly disparate members as *peronismo,* the Mexican Revolution, Peru's Acción Popular, and the Movimiento Nacionalista Revolucionaria of Bolivia (Hennessy, 1969: 36-47).

Further studies have placed Latin American populism within the framework of explicit historical stages. The concept is thereby elevated to greater generality and serves rather different heuristic purposes. Malloy is an acute and articulate exponent of this posture in depicting the emergence of populism as a historical watershed of the 1930s and 1940s, suggesting a generalized regional response to the first crisis of "delayed dependent development." With the exhaustion of the primary product, outward-oriented growth model and a collapse of oligarchic authority, populism "became the guise within which change-oriented segments of the middle class sought to construct multiclass coalitions powerful enough to gain control of the state and underwrite programs of structural transformation" (Malloy, 1977: 9). In its eventual failure to meet contemporary needs, populism had allowed even more pervasive economic penetration by multinational corporations. Eventually, "in confronting this second crisis of delayed dependent development, a large part of Latin America has moved from the implicit and at least potentially democratic corporatism of the populists to the present blatant authoritarian corporatism of the soldiers and technocrats" (Malloy, 1977: 17).

Others have joined in raising populism from the level of party/movement to that of a historical developmental stage. Most have shared the tendency to draw upon the experiences of the most advanced countries, notably Argentina and Brazil. Thus Wynia (1978: 133-148) talks of events following upon both countries' economic expansion of the 1930s and 1940s, describing efforts to attract urban working-class support in the wake of post-depression industrialization. A student of Brazil understands populism as "nationalist political movements that arise when incipient industrialization brings on rapid social change" (Erickson, 1979: 157). Drawing upon the same political system, Mendes (1977: 20) argues that "Latin American populism . . . sought to substitute for the dynamic process of social demands and collective pressures the extended use of state mechanisms for resource allocation." Eschewing a definition of populism while describing and justifying the changes from populism to "post-populism," he therefore shares the perspective of historical-structural approaches to Latin American development at the macro level.

This orientation is qualitatively distinct from the view that regards populism as a discrete and identifiable type of political organization. Its potential contribution rests on an analytic plane which seeks protean understanding in global and universalistic terms. In order to move toward the specificity of parties and electoral movements, less sweeping and more narrowly drawn conceptualization is required. For example, consider the Dix study of *gaitanismo* and ANAPO in Colombia. Citing Di Tella but proceeding along less ambitious lines, he defines populism "as a political movement which challenges established elites in the name of a union between a leader and 'the people' (undifferentiated by group or class)" (Dix, 1978: 334). Four facets of the phenomenon are studied and compared: sources of support, leadership composition, organization and leadership style, and ideology and program. From these he concludes that gaitanismo and ANAPO constituted populist challenges to the traditioal political order, flourished in response to frustration with the system from an increasingly mobilized population, and were fundamentally reformist rather than revolutionary.

A recent biography of Gaitán, while acknowledging a debt to Di Tella, nonetheless runs along lines more akin to Dix. Sources of populist strength, organization, and programmatic appeals receive extended treatment, and the personalism of the civilian caudillo is heavily underlined. As the primary ingredient of Columbian populism, Jorge Eliécer Gaitán symbolized the movement in a fashion suggestive of counterparts in other countries.

> The masses were displaced from the old culture without having become absorbed totally by the new urban, industrial culture. They lacked autonomous institutions of self-defense, such as independent trade unions, a coherent ideology based upon their new economic and social environment, or the means for articulation of their interests. Their lack of political sophistication made them susceptible to the combination of personalism and mass mobilization techniques [Sharpless, 1978: 115].

Such a statement contains resonant echoes of Ecuadorean politics where, as Hurtado writes (1977: 208-209), populist caudillos seek political mobilization by the subproletariat, employing its own language and avoiding abstractions while presenting easily intelligible ideas and reducing political appeals to slogans designed for broad popular consumption.

For our present purposes, we will accept Jaguaribe's description of populism as a political movement characterized by direct charismatic appeal to the urban masses.

> That appeal is made more by his personal actions than through the mediation of a party, and it conveys to the masses that they can have strong hopes for the relatively fast improvement of their condition if that leader can obtain enough power to carry out important socioeconomic reforms, promote the national development of the country (checking the abusive influence of foreign groups), and undertake welfare programs and substantial redistributive measures [Jaguaribe, 1973: 441].

In considering the regional populism of the CFP during its 1948-1960 period, three aspects will be stressed: sources of support, leadership style and organization, and political doctrine. To these must be added the peculiar impact of regionalism, for the literature is scarcely rich with studies of political movements at the subnational level, whether populist or otherwise. Several questions require examination: are there uniquely local characteristics; what is the relationship to the national arena; and what factors favor or mitigate against the extension of regional success to the country at large? To place these within the Ecuadorean context, a brief excursion into local and regional traditions will be instructive.

REGIONALISM AND GUAYAQUIL

The regional and subregional fragmentation of Ecuador has underlain cultural, socioeconomic, and political divisions persisting throughout the country's recorded history. Although geographically segmented into coast *(costa),* highlands *(sierra),* and the Amazonian east *(oriente),* the sparse population of the last has meant that the costa-sierra rivalry has been paramount (Martz, 1972: 1-41). There is no manifestation as pervasive as the stubborn resistance of the major coastal city, Guayaquil, to national authority and to the hegemonic aspirations of Quito, the highland capital. As early as 1820 the Province of Guayaquil issued a declaration of independence, and ever since, the *guayaquileños* have opposed centralism while advocating local autonomy and federalist patterns of government. Thus its struggle against highland domination has been relentless, although Guayaquil "began to make significant headway against the claims of Quito only in the early twentieth century when commercial prosperity created a new-rich aristocracy whose members were often far wealthier than the elites of the capital city" (Pike, 1977: 74).

It is little exaggeration to say that residents of the port city have traditionally viewed inhabitants of the highlands as scarely less strange and alien than Colombians (Hurtado, 1977: 147ff). Another Ecuadorean has explained:

> Tradition is not the marrow and soul as in the sierra. The coast is open to the outside world, to what is new, is foreign and is in vogue. The function of the coast is economic because of its very location. A perennial restlessness agitates it, a perennial change of ideals and enthusiasm [Pérez Guerrero, 1960: 62-63].

Such attitudes have gained an increasing pervasiveness as Guayaquil has progressively outgrown and outstripped Quito. Surpassing it in population by 1880, the port city increased some 30% from 1890 to 1930 (from 45,000 to 116,000), and the post-World War II urban explosion propelled it further ahead. Perhaps the major impetus came with the coastal agricultural boom in bananas and, following in the decade of the 1950s, the deliberate intensification of import-substituting industrialization.

From 1950-1974 the population tripled, and by the start of the 1980s had reached the million mark. From 1962-1974 the annual growth rate had been 5.9%, while for the 1950-1962 intercensal period—the years about which this study revolves—it was among the highest in Latin America at 7.3%. Of particular significance was the uncontrolled growth of Guayaquil's peripheral squatter zones, collectively termed the suburbio. Constituting only 12% of the population in 1950, the *suburbio* was 57% of the city total a quarter century later. Here again the 1950-1962 period was most dramatic, with the annual growth rate of 15%; from 1962-1974 it registered 9.1%. Accompanying the demands and requirements of the suburbio residents, moreover, were those of the central city urban poor (whose slums are known as *tugurios*). As a consequence, the fruits of the new economic prosperity, uneven though they were, included the pronounced wave of national migration to the cities—especially to the coast and most significantly to Guayaquil. In relative terms, it was the port city that seemingly promised the greatest opportunities for employment and for higher wages.[1]

As a prominent Ecuadorean sociologist has observed, a by-product of this postwar phenomenon was the rapid growth of a marginal *subproletariado* which provided the basis for the regional emergence of populism—a personalistic, messianic, and clientelistic populism presenting itself as the voice of the people. The socioeconomic and political frustrations of the marginal lower class reflected the Catholic, ruralized political culture prevalent in the newly settled suburbios. Political participation ceased to be the exclusive preserve of the elites, and the marginal urban subproletariat was by its very nature susceptible to spontaneous electoral mobilization by populist movements (Cueva, 1972: 81ff). A North American scholar concurred in similar language:

> Populist parties, by responding periodically in a personalistic, charismatic, and therefore comprehensible fashion to the discontents and demands of the newly participant, but economically marginal masses, also act as a depressurizing mechanism. As mass political participation rises, populist leaders—promising jobs, public services, and a government responsive to the forgotten people of society—come to dominate the electoral arena at the expense of both the traditionally and ideologically oriented parties [Fitch, 1977: 170].

Such was the milieu and the opportunity in Guayaquil by mid-century. The response was organized and articulated by Carlos Guevara Moreno and, with his Concentración de Fuerzas Populares, would dominate Guayaquil and much of the coast for a decade. In more recent years the movement has negotiated the leap to fully national prominence and, in 1979, to control of the central government under a new president, *cefepista* Jaime Roldós Aguilera. These events go beyond our present boundaries, however, for while the 1948-1960 experience provides an essential backdrop to the more contemporaneous CFP successes, the party's origins and initial phase under Guevara Moreno also comprise a discrete historical phenomenon directly pertinent to the regionalist variant of populism. The locus of political activity was Guayaquil where, then as now, the basic problem—preeminently urban—was "the incomplete integration of *suburbio* into city life" (Moore, 1978: 200). It was toward a promised resolution of urban ills that the CFP avowedly directed its energies.

The Rise and Fall of The CFP

PERSONALISM AND PARTY ORIGINS

On 29 May 1944 widespread demonstrations toppled the government and resulted in the second presidency of José María Velasco Ibarra. The preceding years had been notoriously unstable: fourteen presidents had served from 1931 to 1940, and none would complete his term during the period 1924-1949. Velasco himself was to remain until September 1947, serving first as provisional president and then ruling under both the 1945 and the 1946 constitutions. The latter period of *velasquista* government was notable for a series of repressive measures in defense of the regime, enacted and implemented by the young Minister of Government, Carlos Guevara Moreno. From this position of national visibility he was shortly to found the CFP.

Born in the highland city of Riobamba to a family of modest means, Guevara Moreno was raised largely in Guayaquil, where his father founded and directed the Liceo Ecuador, a private school. He studied chemistry at the University of Guayaquil, became leader of a leftist student bloc,[2] and was expelled for participation in a campus strike. Traveling to Europe, he joined the International Brigade in the Spanish Civil War, for which opponents would later attack him as a Marxist sympathizer. Temporarily teaching secondary school in Bogotá, he then returned home and soon gravitated to politics. After serving briefly as Velasco's Secretary General of Administration, in 1945 he was named Minister of Government amidst widening turbulence, labor demonstrations, and student protests. For the president, who blamed the agitation on Marxists but also regarded Guevara Moreno as a Communist, it was a masterful political stroke.

Recalling the moment three decades later, Velasco told an interviewer "From the outset there was great enthusiasm. . . . Everybody said 'congratulations on the communist Minister!' Telegrams from everywhere praised me for the communist Minister" (Cuvi, 1977: 103). Guevara Moreno was given carte blanche to suppress dissent, and he accepted the charge in the spirit intended. Protests were forcibly quelled with little regard for civil liberties, and the Communist and Socialist parties were banned. "The 'bolsheviks' were extirpated; university students were beaten and jailed; factory workers were bloodily attacked and punished; the shops and papers of the socialist daily *La Tierra* were destroyed . . . journalists or radio broadcasters who criticized and grumbled were intimidated, insulted, or jailed" (Reyes, 1960: 790). With the Left decimated but centrist and conservative sectors antagonized, Velasco then requested his resignation. On August 12, 1946 Guevara Moreno accepted the ambassadorship to Chile.[3]

This early experience was instructive. Guevara Moreno had shown few scruples in his reliance on violence and shock tactics; these would later be emulated by the CFP. Political opportunism was also evident in ignoring earlier leftist sympathies while winning favor with the president. Years later Velasco would characterize him as one of only two "magnificent" ministers during his five presidencies.[4] Further opportunity beckoned upon Guevara Moreno's return to Guayaquil and, after Velasco's removal from office, he undertook the creation of a political party. The vehicle at hand was the Unión Popular Republicana (UPR), organized in 1947 by Rafael Mendoza Avilés and a group of reform-minded fellow faculty members from the University of Guayaquil. Mendoza had narrowly lost the November 1947 mayoral race (Blanksten, 1951: 166-168),[5] and with his colleagues welcomed the arrival of a rising political star.

At a rally in the Plaza Victoria in October 1949, an enlarged UPR was christened the Concentración de Fuerzas Populares, with Guevara Moreno proclaimed *Director Nacional.* In a short time he imposed iron control upon the nascent hierarchical structure. While the II National Convention subsequently adopted a ten-point doctrine which described the party as democratically constituted—"the masses are deliberative rather than merely obedient"—there was also recognition of the role of the leader. According to Point 9:

> The *Cefepé* and its *cefepista* ideology is not a movement of a personalistic or caudillistic type, for it is profoundly impregnated with Ecuadorean popular sentiment. But it recognizes the importance of the leader or caudillo as an historic motor and as a human factor, for in the final analysis such men are those who symbolize spiritual currents . . . those who personify the faith of the Ecuadorean majorities in the redemption of the Motherland [CFP, n.d.: 9]

Whatever the extended impact of personalism, party strength was not immediately sufficient to seize control of Guayaquil. In the elections of November 6, 1949 Mendoza Avilés again lost to the incumbent, dissident Liberal Rafael Guerrero Valenzuela. However, the margin was small (42.3% to 41.4%) and the CFP won one of the five contested seats on the Municipal Council. In November 1950 the party won two of six seats and plans were readied for Guevara Moreno's November 1951 mayoral candidacy. In the meantime, organizational bases were being strengthened and popular support aroused.

ORGANIZATION, MOBILIZATION, AND PROTEST

Despite official lip service paid to the allegedly decisive influence of the rank and file, the *Director Supremo,* as described in the organization statutes, was supreme indeed. Notwithstanding his nominal accountability to the National Convention (article 24), the *Director* through the *Comando Nacional* issued decisions to which the membership was bound (article 11). And although the Convention was designated the "Supreme Authority" of the CFP (article 3), in practice it remained subject to the will of the party caudillo. So too were the advisers with whom Guevara Moreno surrounded himself acquiescent to his wishes, although he carefully chose men with talent and acumen.[6] Given the decision to direct its appeals to the urban lumpenproletariat, this leadership developed a cellular organization in Guayaquil erected on *barrio* committees which joined together in the urban parish and then at the municipal level. As units grew outside the city, a *Comando Provincial* was also formed, reporting to the Comando Nacional and, ultimately, Guevara Moreno (Galarza Arízaga, 1963: 138ff). Funds were received from a small but influential group of wealthy coastal businessman, and the drive for power was under way.

Proclaiming itself from the inception a movement of insurgence against the privileged groups, the party set forth a series of reformist programmatic points. At the founding in Plaza Victoria the Director Supremo defined cefepista popular action as "the active incorporation of the popular masses into political life and the control of public services, in order to prevent the latter from degenerating into the simple usufruct of influential oligarchies; because only the reversion of State actions concerning public service and social service can place the *pueblo* in a condition of satisfaction and security." (Ortiz, 1977: 213). In the process of mobilizing the masses, Guevara Moreno and his lieutenants proved themselves masterful propagandists and manipulators of public passions.

For the first time modern techniques of mass mobilization were widely employed in Ecuador; Guevara Moreno proved a master in the use and manipulation of slogans, pamphlets, marches and assorted political symbols. Characteristic were its denunciatory proclamations from the pages of the party weekly *Momento,* the cover of which showed a man carrying hammer and whip, fighting "reaction, demagoguery, and corruption." Consider, for instance, the unalloyed audacity and verbal vehemence of the issue celebrating its first anniversary. The lead editorial of October 28, 1950, entitled as always "Comentarios del Momento," set its sights on Galo Plaza Lasso, the elected president. It read, in part:

> "Membrate S.A." [its customary pejorative nickname for Plaza] is a person born and educated abroad, without the slightest contact with our popular elements . . . without a personality vigorous enough to create a true tyranny of castes or of the oligarchy under his direct initiative, without any ideological political conceptions, one who is but a gelatinous jellyfish of blanching fears, in whose name others govern. The two words "Galo Plaza" are nothing but a letterhead under which a gang of high-level deformities operate. It pursues nothing but robbery, draining abundant funds from the Treasury, *trafficking in great political influence* and the financing of the antinational privileged of the caste of landowning, semi-feudal property owners possessing a fossilized conservative patina.

Such verbal bludgeoning, accompanied by the provocation of overtly antigovernment incidents by the CFP, sorely taxed Plaza—himself a representative of the *serrano* landowning bourgeoisie who was deeply devoted to the maintenance of constitutionality and the democratic process. It was inevitable that he would eventually retaliate, as Guevara Moreno doubtless intended.

Following a government defeat in 1950 congressional elections, Guevara Moreno undertook a popular revolt. An irregular force of civilians and cefepistas joined with a rebellious infantry battalion to seize Guayaquil's airport, radio, and telephone system. Local military leaders loyal to Plaza subdued and crushed the uprising within 24 hours. Security forces occupied CFP headquarters, suspended publication of *Momento,* and silenced the party's Radio Continental. Guevara Moreno was arrested and sent to Quito's García Moreno penitentiary, where he remained for some fourteen months. Rebel officers were dishonorably discharged and sentenced to a year in prison. Guevara Moreno, playing his role to the hilt, subsequently used the date of the rebellion—July 15—as a symbolic occasion to celebrate annual party conventions and to inveigh against the "oligarchy." Plaza, speaking in 1954 to a North American audience in praise of Ecuadorean democracy, described the episode thusly:

> A group that had the support of most of the lower elements in the city, which had been terrorized by them for months, took over control of the municipal palace one night and broadcast the news to the rest of the country that the local garrison had surrendered to them; but as soon as they came in contact with the first army men they were promptly overpowered and put in jail [Plaza, 1955: 38].

Comparable verbal vendettas were provoked with Velasco Ibarra when he succeeded Plaza in 1952 and began his third presidency. Guevara Moreno in his role as newly elected mayor of Guayaquil had supported the 1952 candidacy of his erstwhile former chief. Cefepista backing on the coast had been instrumental in the comfortable velasquista margin of victory. The rapport between the older and younger caudillos was short-lived, however. As a contemporary noted, "Cefepismo . . . was one of the most efficient contributions to the electoral triumph of Dr. Velasco Ibarra, but did not obtain its quota of influence and, on the contrary, was persecuted to the point of ostentatiously displaying the halo of martyrdom" (Maldonado Estrada, 1954: 135). Characteristically defensive over the emergence of a possible successor, jealous of Guevara Moreno's own popularity and concerned about the latter's unchallenged authority in Guayaquil, Velasco in barely three months was charging insurrectional conspiracy and a misuse of funds in the Guayaquil municipality. When the CFP swept November 1952 municipal elections, leaving Mayor Guevara Moreno with control of seven of eleven seats, the die was cast.

In early December the *Jefe Máximo,* his wife, and four ranking cefepistas were exiled to Columbia. Announced the President, "Sr. Guevara brought to Ecuador all the cynicism and opportunism of the totalitarians. . . . There was imminent danger of a period of bloodshed and ruin" (Linke, 1955: 43). In an effort further to cripple the CFP a year later, Velasco cancelled Guayaquil elections, named a new majority to the Guayas State Council, and imposed the ardent velasquista Pedro G. Menéndez

Gilbert as mayor. Speaking to the press on 13 October 1953, Velasco said in part:

> For me, the CEFEPE is one of the worst evils surviving in Ecuador. It is a party of completely immoral people . . . a party without program, without any programmatic positions . . . a party that directs the most vile passions of man: vengence and economic concupiscence. This party intends to inaugurate terrorism on a large scale in Ecuador [Maldonado Estrada, 1954: 206].

As with Plaza before him, however, Velasco was unable to deflect the cefepista drive for power, and the allegiance of its followers was not to be denied. Before chronicling the party's electoral trajectory, however, an examination of its orientation and outlook is in order. What were the appeals that resisted the powerful interventions of two popularly elected presidents? At base, they were fundamentally antisystem outcries against the heightening social malaise of Guayaquil of the 1950s.

DOCTRINE AND PROGRAM

The basic cefepista orientation, as set forth in the "Ten Doctrinal Points," emphatically stressed its "purely Ecuadorean" character. There was immediate repudiation of "foreign doctrines or ideologies . . . which are no more than a verbalistic or simply theoretical repetition of philosophical postulates that form the marrow of European and, in general, international tendencies" (Point 1). Furthermore, party doctrine was described as distinctly Ecuadorean. In the language of Point 8:

> The ideology of the *Cefepé*. . . is neither conservative, totalitarian, liberal, socialist, nor communist; that is, it is not based on a collection of abstract and imported philosophical principles removed from our reality; the ideology of the *Cefepé* is popular, because it looks to the people as a national and historic phenomenon; it is Ecuadorean, because its reason for being is the Ecuadorean people, who live in Ecuadorean territory and within the tradition of history. Thus its essence is profoundly democratic, progressive, antifeudal, opposed to the bonds of bossism and men

> of influence. . . . *Cefepismo* is a totally new political movement in the Ecuadorean milieu, because it breaks with the tradition of political bands of leaders and incorporates the plebeians (in the sense of Rome, that is, of an actively engaged people) into transcendent political decisions [CFP, n.d.: 8-9].

Attached to this characterization of uniquely Ecuadorean perspectives was the basic call for a major recasting of power relationships within the country. Point 4 spoke of a great historical crossroads demanding a smashing of the oligarchies which represented the most backward elements of the feudal national structure. "Semicolonial feudal *latifundistas*" and "usurious commercial plutocrats" were denounced as denying equality before the law. In the same spirit the seventh point emphasized the need to honor juridical norms in erasing immorality and corruption from the system. While freedom of individual enterprise was praised, it required the tutelage of the state for effective social action. The basic message of the doctrinal principles, in short, was a populistic appeal to the downtrodden rather than a philosophical exposition of ideology.

Doctrinal tendencies were further articulated in "C.F.P.: Conciencia de un Pueblo," a prefatory statement appended to later editions of the party principles and statutes. Describing itself as having arisen from the hearts of the people of Guayaquil—"the capital of popular rebellion in behalf of our nationality"—the CFP spoke of the search for truth, for a more just socioeconomic order, and for the dignity of man. In order to understand and to serve the true moral collectivity of Ecuadoreans, the party sought "a radical and profound revolutionary transformation of the methods and goals of the Ecuadorean State . . . a spiritualization of the people, their cultural elevation, their coming of age with regard to political conscience and moral perspectives" (CFP, n.d.: 3). The declaration concluded with a characteristic rhetorical flourish in addressing the health of the Motherland; the requisite was not "a formula in books nor a secret possessed by the vain, nor the business of some brutal gang of bosses insensible to human suffering. It is the work of the people in their magnificent intuition and heroism" (CFP, n.d.: 4).

If the cefepista orientation was provocative and aggressive in tone, the specific programmatic objectives were nonetheless reformist rather than revolutionary. Individual chapters of the program dealt with such topics as finance, credit, and commerce; agriculture and industry; communications and transportation; labor and social welfare; the tax system and administration; national defense and the police; international policy; education and culture; and suffrage and democratic guarantees. The party proposed a somewhat impreise redefinition of systemic centralization and administrative decentralization as a means of extending government resources to all citizens. The basic image was that of a powerful and activist state. The banking system was to be brought under control of the central government, while agricultural planning would establish cooperatives, mechanize productivity, reform the rural legal system, and nationalize lands not cultivated by the owners. Industry was also to be guided by the state, with extractive activities in particular to be controlled scientifically and productively. Technification was advocated for all major economic sectors.

Thus the party combined radical, often intemperate attacks on the existing system with a statist program designed to strengthen rather than to supplant it. Developed and articulated by Guevara Moreno and a handful of close associates, it was linked to skillful manipulation of political symbols, astute methods of mobilization, and the unchallenged rule of the Jefe Máximo. Our task now becomes that of tracing the electoral course of the party during the 1950s.

THE ELECTORAL QUEST

Barely two months after his release from prison by the Plaza government, Carlos Guevara Moreno—cloaked in the mantle of persecuted martyrdom—swept to victory in the November 1951 mayoral race. Polling 47.4% of the vote against three opponents, he also carried cefepistas into three of the five contested seats on the municipal council, giving the party five of the eleven seats.[7] A year later another victory raised its total to seven, which event was soon followed by Velasco's expulsion order and subsequent intervention of Guayaquil city government. When Guevara Moreno was permitted to return in early 1954 he remobilized his forces and headed the provincial slate for congress. In June 1954 the cefepistas polled 46.8% of the vote in a multiparty.[8] The ineffable Velasco again stepped in, barring Guevara Moreno from congress on the grounds that his absence from Ecuador (although decreed by the regime) disqualified him from meeting residency requirements.

The president subsequently threw government funds and influence into the Guayaquil electoral arena, but to little avail. In November 1954 the party again ran first with 42.6% of the vote. A year later even more blatant and massive velasquista intervention, enhanced by a lavishly funded alliance with the Liberals, enabled the officialist candidate to win a narrow victory for mayor over Guevara Moreno; the margin was 30,172 for Emilo Estrada Icaza to 28,783 for Guevara Moreno. Yet the CFP won three of the five contested council seats, restoring its representation to five. The momentum clearly lay once again with the cefepistas, and the stage was set for the Jefe Máximo's 1956 presidential bid. The contest was to prove heated, combative, and bitter (see Table 1).

Three candidates entered the competition with Guevara Moreno. Camilo Ponce Enríquez, Velasco's Minister of Government during much of his term, represented the Conservatives and his own personalistic Movimiento Social Cristiano (MSC); the Liberals nominated Raúl Clemente Huerta Rendón, a prominent guayaquileño; and the 1952 Liberal standard bearer, former Quito mayor José Ricardo Chiriboga Villagómez, ran on his own. Each of the three entertained hopes of winning Velasco's backing and, after considerable uncertainty, he finally opted for Ponce. After a two-month postelection delay in tabulating the ballots, Ponce was declared the victor over Huerta by 3,000 votes (29% to 28.5%), with Guevara Moreno trailing by 30,000 votes while polling 24.4%. Given the weight of officialist influence and never-resolved indications of extensive fraud, Ponce clearly owed his victory to Velasco. The regional quality of cefepismo was writ

TABLE 1
Valid Voters in Presidential Elections for Guayaquil, Guayas, and Ecuador, 1952-1960

YEAR	VALID VOTES Guayaquil	Guayas	Ecuador	PERCENTAGES VALID VOTES A	B	C
1952	40,000	59,000	357,000	69	11	17
1956	104,000	141,000	614,000	74	17	23
1960	120,000	170,000	767,000	71	16	22

SOURCE: Consejo Supremo Electoral (1952 through 1960). Figures are rounded off by thousands. A = % Guayaquil votes of Guayas; B = % Guayaquil votes of Ecuador; C = % Guayas votes of Ecuador.

large, as Guevara Moreno swept Guayas province with 52.6% and won three of the four remaining coastal provinces. Despite the historical coastal strength of the Liberals, he led the region with 41.8%, followed by Huerta with 36.3%. He polled only 10.6% of the highland vote, however, and ran a distant fourth in Quito. It remained to be seen whether he and the CFP might later negotiate the leap from regional political domination to national power.

In retrospect, the 1956 race was the apex of Guevara Moreno's career, although there seemed little reason to think so at the time. He had seemingly cemented his control of the coast and, given the fragmented party system, could reasonably aspire to ultimate mobilization of the sierra masses as well. Furthermore, the costa remained loyal. On November 4, 1956 the CFP won five of six seats in Guayaquil, giving it an unprecedented eight of eleven council members as the party received 50.7% of the total. A year later came the greatest victory of all as Luis E. Robles Plaza, a longtime confidante of Guevara Moreno, swept to the mayoralty with 72.5% over three opponents. The CFP won all five council seats, thereby giving it ten of the eleven members. Robles initiated a new and expanded program of public construction that at first augured favorably for both the city and party (Orellana, 1957: 147-154). Adding to this the manifest weakness of the Ponce government, prospects for 1960 appeared bright. Events, however, were soon to prove otherwise.

The Robles administration became disastrously scandal-ridden. The Mayor was unable to withstand or to control the party's voracious lust for power and public funds that came in the wake of the 1957 landslide. He was also ineffectual in confronting a disruptive strike by health and sanitation workers in Guayaquil, which dragged on for seven months. Pressures for positive action mounted, yet projected new public works were productive more of swollen contracts and payoffs than of material progress. At the same time, the relative withdrawal of Guevara Moreno from party leadership had opened the way to internal disputes and bickering. As noted, he had constructed the CFP with "energetic discipline and an axis of rigorously hierarchical echelons [running] from top to bottom, maintaining the concept of indisputable authority at the apex of the hierarchy—the Jefe Máximo—although the principal political resolutions were adopted with the apparent participation of sectoral leaders and the declarations of the rank and file" (Galarza Arízaga, 1963: 137-138). Without his constant presence, internal party unity was impossible.

The charismatic appeal of personal leadership was not transferable, and the adherence of cefepista supporters diminished as the Robles administration continued to founder. In June 1958 congressional elections the CFP vote in Guayas dropped over ten points, although securing five of the twelve seats.[9] By November the party fell to 32.6% of the municipal vote, with council representation reduced by two. At this juncture Robles moved to replace Guevara Moreno as party chieftain, further sapping cefepista vitality. The latter belatedly returned from the unexplained isolation of his home, Las Peñas, to contest with Robles the mayoralty in 1959. The defecting mayor secured less than 3% of the vote, finishing fourth in a field of six. The crippled and divided party, however, could not be instantaneously repaired, and Guevara Moreno ran second to the velasquista ex-mayor Menéndez Gilbert. In what proved to be the final candidacy of the Jefe Máximo, he lost by 50.4% to 36.5%. Losses on the council left the CFP with only a minority of seats.

Guevara Moreno's earlier drive for power was diminished, and later forays into politics were episodic and quixotic. As the CFP approached 1960 presidential elections, by then a mere shell of its 1956 organization, the party unexpectedly signed an agreement with the Socialists and Communists at Riobamba in January. There the once bitter antagonists subscribed to the Uníon Democrática Nacional Anticonservadora (UDNA); the alliance soon produced an electoral movement supporting a ticket headed by the Marxist Antonio Parra. Guevara Moreno professed optimism and briefly campaigned with his old zeal, but then withdrew totally from the process, ignoring the urgent pleas of his followers. The UDNA polled under 6% of the vote and the once powerful cefepista congressional delegation was reduced to two. Guevara Moreno officially resigned as Director Supremo and left Ecuador for voluntary exile. The remnants of the party were turned over to José Hanna Musse, under whose leadership the last gasp of *guevarismo* as a force of consequence won 18.5% of the vote and two of six council seats on 6 November 1960.

In late 1961 Guevara Moreno returned home and briefly attempted to regain control of the party. By that juncture, however, it was beginning a dramatic renaissance under the leadership of Asaad Bucaram, and the guevaristas led by Hanna Musse were a negligible splinter group. The former Jefe Máximo again withdrew to Las Peñas. In 1968, after five years' exile, he sought to reunite the CFP with the guevaristas but soon recognized its impossibility. His final political act was to endorse Velasco as presidential candidate that year: "I trust that this time Dr. Velasco Ibarra will triumph in the elections and will maintain his dynamic contact with the people, and will not let himself be deceived by the same trincas and the same obligarchs" (El Año Ecuatoriano, 1968-1969: 51). Thus he had come full circle from his 1940s service as a velasquista minister.

As late as 1979 Hanna Musse continued with his "CFP guevarista" splinter, but as a meaningful force it had expired in 1960; today's CFP is that of Bucaram and Roldós. The startling demise of the movement under Guevara Moreno, while precipitated by the mismanagement of the Robles administration in Guayaquil, owed its fate to a loss of the ferocious appetite for political battle which the party caudillo had long epitomized. While the causes remain obscure, the outcome offers telling testimony to the centrality of his personalistic role in the CFP. The later resurgence of the party under Bucaram was also dependent upon charismatic leadership. As before, the conditions of subproletariat life in Guayaquil remained, its residents susceptible to populistic appeals and authoritarian guidance.

Conclusions: Regionalist Populism in Ecuador

The record of the Concentración de Fuerzas Populares under the rule of its founder would seem to coincide with the characteristics often ascribed to populist political movements in Latin America. Certainly it was consistent with Jaguaribe's emphasis on direct personalistic appeals to urban masses in pledging welfare programs, redistribution of goods and services, and a rapid improvement of the human condition for the dispossessed. Furthermore, the sources of cefepista support were predominantly the newly participant, economically marginal inhabitants of Guayaquil's suburbio and of the tugurios. The leadership style was personalistic, messianic, and authoritarian. Guevara Moreno and his camarilla of lieutenants were, with few exceptions, members of the petit bourgeois in rebellion against the traditional socioeconomic and political elites. Organization was cellular and hierarchical, with shock brigades providing the spearhead of attack and functioning under conditions of rigorously disciplined militancy. The movement lacked clear ideological self-definition and despite its antisystemic rhetorical zeal, represented nationalistic reformism. The major tenets of the cefepista program advocated a strengthened role of the state, but one which was by no means revolutionary.

The regional component was not necessarily sui generis but, at the least, constituted an exaggerated manifestation of the qualities customarily associated with populism. Ecuador's stage of historical development, while by no means comparable to that of Argentina and Brazil in the 1930s and 1940s, did bear a superficial resemblance. Economic growth after World War II and the extraordinary rapidity of migration to Guayaquil created the conditions under which a populist movement might readily develop and flourish. It was the unemployed and underemployed —truly the subproletariat—that provided a reservoir of supporters and voters. The primitive character of organized labor in Ecuador ruled out any meaningful role for the unions. Similarly, the backwardness of rural Ecuador mitigated against the impact of the peasantry, which has been viewed in some countries as significant to populism. The traditional ban against suffrage for illiterates was a corollary to the relative uninvolvement of the country dweller.

Such was the demography of mid-century Ecuador that the natural core for populism lay in Guayaquil. The city's history of restlessness, rebellion, and resistance to national authority further heightened the circumstances within which the CFP could organize and thrive. Given the debility of a fragmented party system and the lack of cohesion among its members, the opportunity for a well-organized and disciplined movement was favorable. With Guayaquil and Guayas respectively the most populous city and province, and with the coastal population increasingly outstripping that of the sierra, the electoral basis for success was evident. So meteoric was the rise of the CFP that its failure to win the presidency in 1956 came less than a decade after its founding. With a concentrated effort to extend its organization to the highlands after 1956, ultimate success might have been achieved. That the attempt was not undertaken remains a mystery eternally locked in the enigmatic Jefe Máximo.

On another occasion it will be valuable to compare the 1948-1960 era with that of Bucaram's CFP since 1962, for the latter, after seventeen years, did ultimately achieve a sweeping national electoral triumph. At least one circumstantial factor was the presence of velasquista populism until recent years—the "Gran Viejo" of national politics was to win election in 1960 and 1968 to his fourth and fifth presidencies. After his ouster in 1972, he soon ceased to be a major political actor as the ravages of age belatedly took their roll on the octagenarian. But be that as it may, the guevarista era of the CFP remains a striking example of populism at the regional level. Its characteristics were not unlike those ascribed to other such movements in Latin America, but reflected the demographic and socioeconomic realities of Ecuador in the 1950s. Guayaquil provided the legions of followers; economic conditions the circumstances favorable to mobilization of the subproletariat; and Carlos Guevara Moreno the messianic zeal to voice and personify the protests of the downtrodden against the prevailing ills of a deeply conservative and traditional society.

NOTES

1. Much of the data in this paragraph comes from Moore (1978). For easy access to further demographic materials see Martz (1972).

2. He was joined by Pedro Antonio Saad and Rafael Coello Serrano. The former was to become the dominant leader and longtime Secretary General of the Partido Comunista del Ecuador (PCE) while the latter, after some years with the Socialists, joined Guevara Moreno at the inception of the CFP.

3. Velasco carefully timed the resignation decision to precede the opening of a Constituent Assembly which would write the 1946 constitution. Guevara Moreno, denying that the move was politically motivated, simply told the press that he was "convinced of the utility and good sense of a renovation of men and wills within our Cabinet . . . ." (El Año Ecuatoriano, 1971-1972: 65).

4. The other was Camilo Ponce Enríquez, who served Velasco as Minister of Government before winning the presidency in 1956 (Cuvi, 1977: 129).

5. The victor was Rafael Guerrero Valenzuela, son of a former provisional president but himself a popular local radio broadcaster. He defeated Mendoza with 6085 (21.5%) to 5227 (18.5%) votes in a multicandidate contest.

6. Among his closest and most trusted confederates were former Socialist Rafael Coello Serrano; Miguel Macías Hurtado, one-time collaborator of Liberal president Carlos Arroyo del Río (1940-1944); Amalio Puga Pastor, the brilliant parliamentarian and orator Luis E. Robles Plaza; the spokesman of Guayaquil's *turco* commercial community, José Hanna Musse; Gonzalo Almeida Urrutia; mayoral aspirant Rafael Mendoza Avilés in the early years; Alejandro Castro Benítez; and Rafael Dillon Valdez, director of the party weekly *Momento*.

Guevara Moreno also attracted the sympathies of a number of artists and intellectuals, among them Agustín Vera Loor, Alfonso Zambrano Orejuela, Elías Gallegos, Hugo Maldonado Dueñas, and—most strikingly—the internationally famed author of *Huasipungo* and other works, Jorge Icaza.

7. The former CFP-backed candidate for mayor, Mendoza Avilés, ran with Liberal backing and finished a distant second. The elected cefepista councilmen were Robles Plaza, Pablo Estrada Valle, and J. Febres Cordero. The joined Macías Hurtado and Trujillo Monlís, who had been elected in 1950.

8. The delegation led by Guevara Moreno also included Robles Plaza, Puga Pastor, Simón Cañarte Barbera, Julio Acevedo Vega, Manuel Villavicencio, and Salvador Lofredo Rodríguez.

9. Listed fourth on the cefepista delegation was Asaad Bucaram, the party caudillo in the post-1962 era.

REFERENCES

BLANKSTEN, G. I. (1951) Ecuador: Constitutions and Caudillos. Berkeley and Los Angeles: Univ. of California Press.

CFP [Concentración de Fuerzas Populares] (n.d.) Qué es el CFP? Guayaquil: n.p.

Consejo Supremo Electoral (1952-1960) Informe(s). Annual bulletins. Quito: Gaceta Oficial.

CUEVA, A. (1972) El proceso de dominación política en Ecuador. Quito: Ediciones "Crítica."

CUVI, P. (1977) Velasco Ibarra: el último caudillo de la oligarquía. Quito: Facultad de Ciencias Económicas, Universidad Central del Ecuador.

DEL CAMPO, E. (1977) El populismo en Ecuador. Quito: Facultad Latinoamericana de Ciencias Sociales.

DI TELLA, T. (1965) "Populism and reform in Latin America," in C. Veliz (ed.) Obstacles to Change in Latin America. London: Oxford Univ. Press.

DIX, R. H. (1978) "The varieties of populism: the case of Colombia." Western Pol. Q. 23 (September): 334-351.

El Año Ecuatoriano (1971-1972) Yearbook. Guayaquil.

——— (1968-1969) Yearbook. Guayaquil.

ERICKSON, K. (1979) "Brazil: corporatism in theory and practice," in H. Wiarda and H. Kline (eds.) Latin American Politics and Development. Boston: Houghton Mifflin.

FITCH, J. A. (1977) The Military Coup d'Etat as a Political Process: Ecuador, 1948-1966. Baltimore, MD: Johns Hopkins Press.

GALARZA, ARÍZAGA, R. (1963) Esquema político del Ecuador. Guayaquil: Editorial Alborada.

HENNESSY, A. (1969) "Latin America," in G. Ionescu and E. Gellner (eds.) Populism: Its Meaning and National Characteristics. New York: Macmillan.

HURTADO, O. (1977) El poder político en el Ecuador. Quito: Pontificia Universidad Católica del Ecuador.

——— (1969) Dos mundos superpuestos; ensayo de diagnóstico de la realidad ecuatoriana. Quito: INEDES.

IONESCU, G. and E. GELLNER [eds.] (1969) Populism: Its Meaning and National Characteristics. New York: Macmillan.

JAGUARÍBE, H. (1973) Political Development: A General Theory and a Latin American Case Study. New York: Harper & Row.

LINKE, L. (1955) Ecuador, Country of Contrasts. London: Royal Institute of International Affairs.

MALDONADO ESTRADA, L. (1954) Una etapa histórica en la vida nacional. Quito: Editorial "Rumiñahui."

MALLOY, J. [ed.] (1977) Authoritarianism and Corporatism in Latin America. Pittsburg, PA: Univ. of Pittsburgh Press.

MARTZ, J. (1972) Ecuador: Conflicting Political Culture and the Quest for Progress. Boston: Allyn & Bacon.

MENDES, C. (1977) Beyond Populism (L. Gray Cowan, trans.). Albany: Graduate School of Public Affairs, State University of New York at Albany.

MOORE, R. (1978) "Urban problems and policy responses for metropolitan Guayaquil," in W. Cornelius and R. Kemper (eds.) Metropolitan Latin America: The Challenge and the Response. Beverly Hills, CA: Sage.

ORELLANA, J. G. (1957) Resumen histórico del Ecuador; apuntaciones cronológicas complementaries 1947-1957, vol. 3. Quito: Editorial "Fray Jodoco Ricke."

ORTIZ, V. (1977) La ideología burguesa en el Ecuador; interpretación socio-política del hecho histórico en el periódo (1924-1970). Quito: n.p.

PEREZ GUERRERO, A. (1960) Ecuador. Quito: Publitécnica.

PIKE, F. B. (1977) The United States and the Andean Republics; Peru, Bolivia, and Ecuador. Cambridge, MA: Harvard Univ. Press.

PLAZA, G. (1955) Problems of Democracy in Latin America. Chapel Hill: Univ. of North Carolina Press.

QUINTERO, R. (1978) "Los partidos políticos en el Ecuador y la clase terrateniente en las transformaciones del estado." Ph.D. dissertation, University of North Carolina.

REYES, O. (1960) Breve historia general del Ecuador. Quito: Editorial "Fray Jodoco Ricke."

SHARPLESS, R. (1978) Gaitán of Colombia: A Political Biography. Pittsburgh, PA: Univ. of Pittsburgh Press.

VAN NIEKERK, A. (1974) Populism and Political Development in Latin America. Rotterdam: Universitaire Pers Rotterdam.

WILES, P. (1969) "A syndrome, not a doctrine: some elementary theses on populism," in G. Ionescu and E. Gellner (eds.) Populism: Its Meaning and National Characteristics. New York: Macmillan.

WYNIA, G. (1978) The Politics of Latin American Development. Cambridge: Univ. Press.

John D. Martz is Professor and Head of Political Science at the Pennsylvania State University. His most recent book, with Enrique A. Baloyra, is Political Opinion in Venezuela. *He served as Editor of the* Latin American Research Review *from 1974 to 1979.*

MAX AZICRI
Department of Political Science
Edinboro State College
Edinboro, Pennsylvania

THE INSTITUTIONALIZATION OF THE CUBAN STATE
A Political Perspective

Departing from other approaches in the literature of Cuban studies (Azicri, 1979) this article does not examine the current phase of institutionalizing the revolution as an unforeseeable event due to fortuitous circumstances, such as the regime's blunder of the 1970 sugar harvest. Indeed, ten years later, it seems simply inaccurate to explain so many epoch-making events that have dominated revolutionary politics as if they occurred just because the regime was unable to produce the remaining 1.465 million tons of its goal of 10 million tons of sugar. However, this is not to construe the 1970 sugar harvest and its surrounding events to be void of any significance in what followed later; more properly, it is meant as a rejection of the notion that the institutionalization of the revolution is the direct outcome of that single historical happening.

The Legitimacy-Institutionalization Question

THE INCOMPATIBILITY OF AUTHORITY AND FORCE

The Institutionalization of the Cuban state and the events that prompted it have been the object of social science analyses which

---

AUTHOR'S NOTE: Gratitude is expressed to Elsie Deal, Jorge I. Dominguez, and William L. LeoGrande for their comments and suggestions on an earlier draft.

Journal of Interamerican Studies and World Affairs, Vol. 22 No. 3, August 1980 315-344

conveyed different and, in some instances, conflicting interpretations. According to some Cuban analysts (González, 1974, 1976a, 1976b; Mesa-Lago, 1978), this current phase of political change came about as a consequence of the

> neglect and disarray which adversely affected so many sectors of the economy due to the excessive amount of resources used preparing for the 1970 sugar harvest at the expense of other national interests, [which] resulted in confusion and a temporary sense of loss of direction and goals [Azieri, 1978: 258].

The thrust of this interpretation is that owing to an existent centralized policy-making institutional setting, which lacked channels providing an input to a wider range of concerns and interests, these mistakes were not only possible but almost inevitable. Failure to achieve the production goal set for the 1970 sugar harvest, therefore, became the turning point for the revolutionary regime. In other words, the government could no longer delay coming to grips with a central dysfunctional systemic failure. The flaws in its decision-making mechanism, the product of an authority structure supporting a *centralized system controlled by a charismatic leader,* could always lead the nation astray in the future with such ill-conceived policies, as it had done in the past.

Nevertheless, and in spite of the apparent persuasiveness of this commonly held interpretation, for other analysts the major problems in Cuban policy-making patterns are not those stemming from a centralized, charismatic authority but from a *coercive exercise of power* which is mainly determined by the very nature of *Castro's repressive leadership* (Horowitz, 1965, 1977; Fagen et al., 1968). Interestingly enough, these two notions—charismatic leadership and forceful, coercive leadership—are in conflict with one another, since they are mutually exclusive within the logic of their theoretical premises. This theoretical inconsistency, however, has failed as a deterrent to contradictory interpretations of this political phenomenon.

The incompatibility between legitimacy (authority) and force (coercion) has been clearly stated (Easton, 1958: 180): "Authority stands in contrast to coercion. In a political system in which . . . large elements of force must be used to bring about obedience [compliance], then the holders of political power are coercers." Moreover, states Easton, "[in such a case] they rule through coercion and cannot be said to hold political authority in the system." On the other hand, authority and legitimacy are recognized as being so closely related in their meaning that they should be regarded as being almost equivalent terms or, at the very least, as having a common distinct character, distinguishable from other political modalities:

> What clearly distinguishes authority from coercion, force, and power on the one hand, and leadership, persuasion and influence on the other hand is *legitimacy*. Superiors feel that they have a right to issue commands; subordinates perceive an obligation to obey. If the character of the communication is questioned, then authority is diminished. [Peabody, 1968: 474].

In short, while charismatic authority is widely recognized as the main source of legitimacy for the regime, this notion runs contrary to the characterization of revolutionary power as constituting the application of force by a repressive leadership. However, it is generally agreed in the literature of Cuban that Castro is indeed a charismatic leader (as expressed among others by González, 1974; Mathews, 1961; Mesa-Lago, 1978; Morton, 1965) and that force has been used as a necessary mechanism of social control under Castro's rule, particularly as a means of preserving public order, curtailing antisocial behavior, and more specifically, combating counterrevolutionary actions (Azicri, 1975, 1978; Domínguez, 1978; Rivero Collado, 1977). Therefore, the charismatic basis for the regime's authority, as well as its use and application of force, should be recognized as different political phenomena which are central to the main thrust of this analysis.

From both a theoretical and empirical perspective, the discussion above seems to indicate that the value of a notion such as charismatic authority, while still valid as a proper characterization of revolutionary legitimacy, fails, nevertheless, as a sensible explanation of why force has been present in the exercise of revolutionary power; that is, a distinction needs to be established as to what is accepted as the regime's charismatic legitimacy (authority) and its actual exercise of power, which includes force. As the record demonstrates, on certain occasions coercion has been used as a means of gaining the population's compliance with certain policies and programs (Azicri, 1975, 1977, 1978); on the other hand, the regime has pursued other governmental strategies in which force was absent in an attempt to maximize its political effectiveness and to heighten public compliance. Hence in this context, force was one among different modalities which served to formalize the regime's patterns of exercising power.[1]

Nonetheless, an empirical-systematic study of the first ten years of revolutionary rule, from 1959-1968, demonstrates that among the dominant governmental strategies, or patterns of exercising power, pursued by the regime, there were: (1) a charismatic pattern indicating a centralized authority structure in which power has not been delegated; (2) a participatory pattern signifying instances and/or a trend toward some degree of decentralization of power; (3) an instrumental pattern relying on material incentives to gain compliance for official policies; (4) a normative pattern gaining compliance through moral incentives that are based on revolutionary values and cultural system; and (5) a coercive pattern utilizing force to secure compliance for policies with a low level of acceptability, or combating counterrevolutionary actions.

The substantive differences listed above among the patterns of governing strategies used and representative of the regime's actual exercise of power were determined not by the character of the existent source of legitimate authority—Castro's charismatic leadership—but by a cluster of pragmatically chosen and empirically recognizable political indicators. These include the content of the policy pursued, population group involved, type of incentives used to gain compliance, and finally, the kind of governmental structures, including mass organizations, that were considered more suitable to accomplish specific developmental goals. Thus, governmental patterns of exercising power did represent centralized modalities, in agreement with a charismatic authority structure and decentralized patterns involving a participatory process in which acceptance and support for official policies were sought. Some input from medium and lower levels of the political system was allowed, i.e., Communist party organs below the Secretariat, Political Bureau, or Central Committee, or party members at large in some form or capacity, and mass organizations such as the Committees for the Defense of the Revolution, the Federation of Cuban Women, and others (Azicri, 1975).

FROM CHARISMATIC TO INSTITUTIONALIZED AUTHORITY

Max Weber's threefold classification of legitimate authority (1964: 324-392), including charismatic authority as a personalized type and legal-rational authority as institutionally based, provides a conceptual framework germane to the kind of changes brought upon the regime's authority structure by the institutionalizing process (Valdes, 1976). Regarding the applicability of Weber's typology to examine the Cuban institutionalizing experience, however, it seems pertinent to follow a cautious route before reaching any conclusions. On the affirmative side, it should be stated that

> the generally recognized notion of Castro's charismatic leadership being the main sustainer of the revolution's authority structure—by providing its source of legitimacy—gives some credence and common-sense basis to this particular approach [Azicri, 1979: 67].

Nevertheless, like such contradictory concepts as authority and force applied by different analysts to examine the nature of the revolution's authority and leadership, Weber's theoretical framework may have a potential to obscure rather than to clarify the Cuban experience. Weber establishes a developmental continuum along his typology of authority structures, with the implication that a transitional shift should take place in those cases when charismatic authority becomes routinized, turning them into either legal-rational or traditional authority (Blau, 1963: 309; Eisenstadt, 1968: 44-65). Significantly, recognizing that this transition is not yet final, it has been stated that formalization rather than institutionalization is what has taken place in Cuba so far (Domínguez, 1978); thus, it seems necessary to clarify the meaning of these concepts.

First, as was indicated earlier, in a political system with a leader possessing charismatic authority, as in Castro's case, the actual exercise of power by such a regime is not always similar to the legitimizing role exerted by the charismatic leader. That is, what would be termed a charismatic governing strategy would not apply to every political situation.[2] Second, throughout the seventies, the establishment of new political institutions that have continued functioning and developing further in the eighties, does not prove that a definite, final modification of the regime's basis of legitimacy has already taken place either. That is, this institutional development should not be approached as a stage in which a transition from a charismatic to an institutionalized legal-rational authority has become final. (The third type in Weber's classification of legitimate authority, traditional, is obviously not applicable at the present time to the Cuban case.)

Nevertheless, the basis for the revolution's authority has always been broader than the legitimacy provided by Castro's charismatic leadership (Fagen, 1969). The revolutionary political culture has played a significant role since the early years in legitimizing the revolution. The political culture transformation initiated in 1959 (Fagen, 1969, 1972; Moreno, 1971) still continues today, albeit with substantive changes in its intensity and directions; all along, it has provided a system of values which not only legitimizes revolutionary power and elicits compliance and acceptability for the regime's policies, but also defines individual and collective behavioral patterns (Kozol, 1978). Consequently, revolutionary ethics either support or condemn acceptable or unacceptable behavior, depending to a great extent on whether such actions are beneficial or inimical to the revolution.

All in all, the original basis for the regime's authority was substantively enlarged and to some extent modified with the new political structures that were added during the institution-building phase of the 1970s—i.e., the 1976 constitution, and the National, Provincial, and Municipal Assemblies of the Organs of People's Power. Given the comprehensiveness of the institution, state-building phase undertaken in Cuba, institutionalization is being approached here as:

> the process by which organizations and procedures acquire value and stability. The level of institutionalization of any political system can be defined by the adaptability, complexity, autonomy, and coherence of its organizations and procedures [Huntington, 1968: 12].

Thus, determining the degree of institutional "adaptability, complexity, autonomy, and coherence" attained by the new political structures, as examined in this study, may provide a valuable insight into both the present status of the regime's authority and its overall institutionalizing experience. An additional conceptualization of this political phenomenon brings to our attention that it should also be seen as a process whereby "amorphous, discontinuous, erratic political activity gives way to more coherent, continuous, stable activity channeled through . . . ongoing political institutions" (Williams and Wright, 1975: 7). The newly created political institutions, therefore, and their relationship to the political system as a whole—i.e., their functional capability in terms of working as stable and autonomous political conduits broadening the scope of political participation in the decision-making process—are the main political indicators used in this evaluation of the Cuban political system.

The New Political Institutions

THE 1976 SOCIALIST CONSTITUTION

The popular approval of the new constitution through a national referendum held on February 24, 1976 was a carefully calculated political step by the regime. In addition to the previous nationwide discussion of the constitutional draft which took place in a myriad of meetings held by mass organizations and collective legal offices *(bufetes colectivos),* and in work centers and informal gatherings, and beyond the fact that it satisfied legal formalities, the referendum was held to bring popular participation into the institutionalization process. This participatory process allowed for a channel of grassroots recommendations requesting changes in the final draft. However, it is difficult to ascertain with fairness how many of these recommendations were actually heeded by the drafters of the constitution.

With the new constitution, the regime sought to increase the institutional cohesiveness of the state by integrating it further into the newly established political structures as well as with the recently institutionalized socialist legal system. The 1976 charter formalized the socialist character of the Cuban polity, its society and economic system; it also broadened the basis for the regime's legitimacy by providing a legal sanction to earlier social change that was being integrated into a comprehensive constitutional framework. In short, the Cuban state had become formally structured under a socialist constitution which would stand as the supreme law of the land.

The 1976 constitution also put an end to sixteen years of provisional revolutionary government. Throughout this period the Council of Ministers exercised ample, practically unlimited, executive and legislative powers according to the Fundamental Law of the Republic of 1959, which had been modified on numerous occasions as dictated by circumstantial needs and political expediency. In agreement with the constitutional mandate and under the institutionalized political stage inaugurated on December 2, 1976, the National Assembly of People's Power—with its powerful Council of State—was called to session to hold its first historical meeting and exercise legislative power. Also under the new constitutional arrangement, the administrative and executive functions fell under the jurisdiction of the Council of Ministers and its strategically important executive committee. However, a decentralization of state functions was instituted. Henceforth, the central government would share its control of social services and other administrative functions with the Organs of People's Power. Moreover, integrating the politico-administrative and governmental-administrative organs of the state under a single head, the same person would preside over the Council of State and the Council of Ministers and become the President of the Republic; as was expected, the National Assembly elected Fidel Castro as the first president under the new constitution.

A school of socialist jurisprudence that developed under the revolution provided the general principles upon which the 1976 charter and the socialist legal system were established; therefore, these principles were present in the guidelines followed in the organization of the state (Alvarez Tabio, 1977: 305). This socialist legal doctrine prescribes: (1) who will exercise political power; (2) the kind of organic principles to be applied; (3) the type of political methods to be used; and (4) legal and political limitations to be followed. A proper response to these issues, claims Alvarez Tabio, would provide the main thrust of socialist constitutional law. According to him, and in contradistinction to liberal-democratic systems, under socialism the "thesis of check and balance and division of power is rejected," and rather than confronting each other, the "organs of the socialist state . . . collaborate among themselves within the framework of the Constitution and the laws." These legal norms should not be limited to Cuba; they should be applied to every socialist state. Otherwise, states Alvarez Tabio, "any policy opposing [such principles] would fail inevitably."

These juridicial concepts are equally present in political statements. For example, as explained by Blas Roca, president of the National Assembly of the Organs of People's Power, the twelve chapters and 141 articles of the new constitution are essential in order to build "'a new society under the direction of the working class headed by its Marxist-Leninist communist party'," especially since the pre-revolutionary "'1940 Constitution is a bourgeois constitution [designed] to govern a bourgeois system characterized by neocolonialism'" (Black et al., 1976:

268). Nevertheless, the 1976 constitution preserved some of the 1940 constitution, while it incorporated features from other socialist state constitutions (de la Cuesta, 1976).

The political ideology and institutional characteristics of the Cuban state are clearly defined in the first article of the 1976 constitution (pp. 2-3): "[Cuba is] . . . a socialist state of workers and peasants and all other manual and intellectual workers." Earlier, in its preamble, it states that "revolutionary power . . . started the construction of socialism and, under the direction of the Communist party, continues said construction with the objective of building [a] communist society."

Political and societal institutions and belief systems which received legal recognition by the socialist charter, therefore becoming institutionalized, include: (1) the Communist party, the country's single leading political institution (Article 5); (2) the existent mass organizations, an integral part of the socialist state because of their important social and political functions (Article 7); (3) Marxism-Leninism, the official ideology of the revolution (Preamble of the Constitution); (4) democratic centralism, the principle defining intrastate relations among, and within, political and administrative structures (Article 66); (5) the reward system, from each according to his ability, to each according to his work, corresponding to a socialist stage of development (Article 19); (6) the dictatorship of the proletariat, the operational principle supporting the power wielded by the working class in alliance with peasants and other urban workers (Article 4); (7) public ownership of the means of production, the foundation of a socialist economy (Articles 14-27); and (8) proletarian internationalism, the cornerstone of the country's foreign policy in its relationship with other socialist nations, Third World countries, and anti-imperialist movements (Article 12).

Moving beyond the liberal social reformism of earlier Cuban constitutions, the 1976 charter established the first socialist political, social, and economic system in the Western Hemisphere. It also provided goals to be implemented and normative guidelines to be followed which go beyond the changes already implemented by the regime. However, social change as such has never been a major problem for the revolution before, nor is it likely to be one in the future. The real challenge lies in having to conform now to the norms and procedures created by its own institutionalization process and to accept the fact that the era of improvisation with political structures and decision-making mechanisms is finally over, that the revolution has to live up to its own constitutional commitment.

INSTITUTIONALIZING THE COMMUNIST PARTY

The present Cuban Communist Party (PCC) was founded in 1965 with approximately 50,000 members and candidates.[3] However, it was not until ten years later, from December 17 to 22, 1975, when its First Congress was finally held, that the institutionalization of the country's single political party was seriously pursued; by that time its membership had increased to 202,807 members and aspirants. (Currently it is estimated at 250,000.)

The first Congress represented more than an assembly of political leaders and party delegates to discuss a number of theses and resolutions which would decide the course of forthcoming governmental policies. As one of the three institutional power pyramids in the political system, the party's functions and structures were being formalized so it would perform properly the central political role expected of a Communist party in a Marxist-Leninist state, particularly when Cuba was undergoing its own institutionalization process.

Thus, for the party to function under the 1976 constitution within the context of the new state governmental and politico-administrative organs established therein—i.e., the Council of Ministers (government) and the National Assembly and the Provincial and Municipal Organs of People's Power (politico-administrative)—the proper place and role of the party in the new scheme of things had to be defined. Altogether, the First Party Congress was a momentous occasion counterpointed by political undercurrents stemming mainly from the magnitude of the political changes that were being decided upon (First Congress of the Communist Party of Cuba, 1976; Tesis y Resoluciones, 1976).

The 1960s were years representing high doses of voluntarism and idealism that led in many instances to mistaken positions assumed by the party leadership. This included the fact that the "line of demarcation between the Party and the state [became] blurred . . . [hence] the Party [was] devoting itself mostly to administrative duties . . . the Party had to run everything" (Casal, 1976: 24). To overcome this problem, the institutionalization of the party involved a two-stage process. First, the party itself became recognized and strengthened by improving its "internal cohesion and coordination . . . [which made it] the dominant [political] institution in post-1970 Cuba" (LeoGrande, 1979: 478-479). Second, and running contrary to well-established revolutionary tradition, the party would have to be extricated from its former involvement in the administration of government (Casal, 1976).

The intensive preparation leading to the First Party Congress started in April 1975 with assemblies held throughout the country to elect, or in some cases reelect, delegates representing the rank and file membership. The significance of the electoral procedure followed, however, on such an important occasion has been questioned for being "unrepresentative as usual"; that is, lacking in effective political participation (Domínguez, 1978: 331).

Notwithstanding the skills and determination demonstrated by Fidel and Raúl Castro in their long tenure as power holders (González, 1976a: 1-19), in today's Cuba the actual seat of power is purposely, if only gradually, becoming institutionally oriented. In terms of the PCC's share of political power, two of the major centers of decision-making are located in the party itself, its Political Bureau and Secretariat. This political reality underlines the party's strong standing in relation to the other two institutional power pyramids in the political system. Meanwhile, the third and fourth power centers are represented by the executive committee of the Council of Ministers—the top layer of the central government institutional power pyramid—and the Council of State of the National Assembly, the head of the Organs of

People's Power—the politico-administrative power pyramid. This welcome separation of political power between the party and the governmental and politico-administrative state organs is somewhat lessened in reality by the fact that the regime's leadership is characterized "by overlapping membership in these key decision-making institutions" (Domínguez, 1978: 307).

The institutionalization of the party represents a major revision not only of past practices but also of structural arrangements, including such demanding tasks as: (1) making viable democratic procedures within the party a reality, as well as strenthening its institutions; (2) increasing the number of party members [women amount only to 17% of its total membership and 5.5% of its national leadership];[4] (3) improving the level of education among its members [in 1975 "20% of the party members (had) not yet attained a sixth-grade education, 42% only a sixth-grade education, 25% (had) a secondary level in adult education, 9% an intermediate-higher education, and only 4% (had) a university education"] (First Congress of the Communist Party of Cuba, 1976: 240); and (4) clarifying its political role by separating all party functions from any administrative tasks. Also, at the time of the First Congress, the party elected its new Central Committee (112 full members in 1975 from a total of 100 in 1965), which in turn elected the members of the Political Bureau (13 members in 1975 from 8 in 1965), the Secretariat and Control Commission, as well as the First and Second Party Secretaries—Fidel and Raúl Castro, respectively (Casal, 1976: 25).

The last of the four party tasks, stopping it from further encroachment into governmental and politico-administrative functions, represents a major and long-overdue goal which, given the degree of involvement that existed in the past, seems difficult to accomplish in its entirety. Equally pressing is the issue of determining the relationship between the party and the new state political organs. As agreed by the First Party Congress, such relations should take place "on the basis of properly delimiting the authority, responsibility and functions of each institution," insofar as it is "recognized that the Organs of People's Power are the supreme authority in those areas under its jurisdiction." However, it is still the party which would "guide, promote, and control the tasks of the state organs . . . [but] without substituting them in their authority and functions" (Tesis y Resoluciones, 1976: 184).

The question of who rules in the political and institutional hierarchy constituted by the party and the governmental and politico-administrative state organs has been the subject of revealing comments by Raúl Castro (1976: 84-75). He states that even if it is true that "the Party *directs,* the state *directs,* and the mass organizations *direct,*" the level of importance in these directives is not always the same; thus, the directives of the state organs "do not have a general character as the directives from the higher organs of the Party; furthermore, [the state organs] do not *direct* the Party and the mass organizations." Therefore, the party directives stand above those from other political, governmental, and social institutions throughout the system, even though the state organs and even the mass organizations possess a jurisdiction of their own which is not to be violated by party interference. Evidently, party potential to intrude into other institutional domains is a danger which, if allowed to run unchecked, may very well hinder the overall drive for the institutionalization of the state. The existence and development of viable and autonomous state institutions is at stake.

As indicated throughout this narrative, many of these changes were long overdue. Nevertheless, achieving and securing them at this present stage of development would mean growth for the party in particular and the political system in general. Implicit in this analysis is the notion that Cuba's socialist system would be able to increase its level of responsiveness to popular expectations and demands beyond its previous record. Also, in this regard, the institutionalization of the party requires that a more articulated and efficient political institution perform those functions usually associated with political parties in liberal-democratic systems—i.e., interest articulation and aggregation, political mobilization, and the curbing of social and political alienation while enhancing integration within the system. Given the character of a socialist polity, however, these functions become rather sensitive and critical to the regime, which explains in part the centrality of the PCC in contemporary Cuba.

At this time the party is supposedly on its way to celebrate its Second Congress in 1980, assuming that the five-year cycle between congresses is followed closely. Meanwhile, in recognition of this major event during its second session for 1979—December 26-27—the National Assembly approved naming 1980 as the year of the Second Party Congress. This is in keeping with revolutionary tradition of naming every year after an event of national significance (Granma Weekly Review, 1979a).

THE ORGANS OF PEOPLE'S POWER, THE COUNCIL OF STATE, AND THE COUNCIL OF MINISTERS

Beyond the Matanzas Experiment

The second of the institutional power pyramids in the political system, the Organs of People's Power (OPP), was activated when its National Assembly met for the first time on December 2, 1976. The creation of this new "supreme organ of the state" gave birth for the first time under revolutionary rule to a socialist democratic legislative and administrative forum—i.e., institutionalizing political representantion under the dictatorship of the proletariat, the actual cornerstone of Cuban socialist democracy. Heretofore the practice had been to have the cabinet, established in 1959, exercise a centralization of executive, legislative, and judicial functions.

The adoption of deliberative and administrative assemblies at the national, provincial, and municipal level was made possible by the earlier experiment held in Matanzas province, where provincial and municipal OPP assemblies operated on a trial basis in 1974 and 1975. After the evaluation and final approval of this pilot project at the First Party Congress, the Organs of People's Power were instituted on a nationwide basis in agreement with the provisions of the 1976 constitution.

The Matanzas experiment, however, did not lack its share of problems—quite the opposite (Sobre los Organos del Poder Popular, 1976: 9-10). Among the difficulties encountered during this experimental period was the absence of administrative expertise and know-how on the part of party and OPP cadres, which in some way accounts for the ensuing backlash when people often failed to participate in the new decision-making opportunities available through People's Power. As admitted at the First Party Congress, this situation demanded urgent corrective measures if the new system of political representation was going to function on a national scale better than it had in Matanzas. Also, synchronization and planning of needed personnel and utilization of available manpower were administrative responsibilities demanding substantive improvement in post-1975 OPP operations. Nonetheless, deficiency and improvisation dominated these early years, aggravating an already serious situation of scarcity of consumer goods in general, and in particular, the perennial shortages of housing and cement with its sequel of additional production and social problems. "The delegates of Popular Power . . . that work in those organs did not have any previous experience . . . it would only be with time . . . that they [would] learn the full extent of their responsibilities" (Sobre las Dificultades Objetivas de la Revolución, 1979: 5, 11). However, and contrary to so many objective obstacles, with the enthusiasm, ingenuity, and dedication provided by so many people across the island, it seems as if in the long run the learning, and mastering, of these new politico-administrative roles would prevail with more pluses than minuses, thereby insuring the viability and permanence of the Organs of People's Power (Casal, 1979: 6; Sobre la Constitución del Poder Popular, 1978).

The Organs of People's Power

The new legislative and politico-administrative institutions are organized with one legislative National Assembly headed by a president, a vice president, and a secretary, fourteen politico-administrative Provincial Assemblies, each with an executive committee of 7 to 21 members, and 169 politico-administrative Municipal Assemblies, with executive committees of 5 to 15 members. The delegates to the Municipal Assemblies are elected for a 2½ year term by their neighbors by secret, popular vote on the basis of one municipal delegate for each electoral circumscription, and it is not necessary to be a party member to be elected. Following an indirect, electionary process, the municipal delegates elect their provincial counterparts for a term similar to their own. There is one Provincial Assembly for each of the 14 provinces established under the new politico-administrative division of the country. The number of provincial delegates is determined by the population of each province on the basis of one delegate for every 10,000 citizens, or fraction greater than 5,000. Also, the municipal delegates elect the deputies to the National Assembly with one national deputy for every 20,000 citizens, or fraction greater than 10,000 (Bengelsdorf, 1976: 3-18; Granma Weekly Review, 1979b). Approximately 55.5% of all national deputies come from the ranks of the municipal delegates. At the national level, 90% are members of the PCC; at the municipal level, approximately 50% of the delegates are party members.

The 1976 constitution establishes the jurisdiction of the Organs of People's Power at its three different levels—national, provincial, and municipal. The Provincial and Municipal Assemblies "govern in all that concerns them . . . [directing] economic production and service units which are directly subordinated to them . . . [providing] economic, cultural, educational, and recreational services" (Article 102). The Municipal Assemblies have authority "over the operations of schools, of hospitals and clinics, of stores, movie theatres and . . . transportation," while the provincial level is the "supreme authority for the services and production units which cross over municipal boundaries, but which operate within provincial boundaries" (Bengelsdorf, 1976: 12-14).

The administrative functions exercised at both levels, municipal and provincial, are complex. They include: (1) enforcing laws and regulations coming from superior state organs; (2) electing the members of their executive committees and revoking their mandate if the need arises; (3) determining the organization, functioning, and tasks of the administrative units in charge of the socioeconomic activities under their control; (4) appointing and recalling the judges of the people's courts in their jurisdictions in agreement with the 1977 reorganization of the judicial system; and (5) enhancing socialist legality and internal order.

The OPP provincial level works as an intermediate unit between the National and Municipal Assemblies and as a centralizing agency between different municipalities. However, in some instances, as when national deputies are rendering to their Municipal Assemblies, the provincial level is circumvented. The parallel governmental and politico-administrative system is oriented toward internal integration and double subordination in agreement with democratic centralism: while an agency may be under the jurisdiction of its corresponding provincial or municipal assembly, it also functions under the control of the central government. Thus, even though the OPP has brought about considerable decentralization of the central government by placing administrative agencies under its control, these agencies are still subordinated to the central government as well.

Elections and Political Participation

Two national elections for delegates of Municipal Assemblies have been held, October 1976 and April 1979. At the forthcoming election in October 1981, the newly elected municipal delegates will elect both the new provincial delegates and the deputies for the National Assembly.

The electoral procedure, allowing only for direct election at the municipal level, reduces the impact of national elections on the political system as a whole. Also, the limited form of campaigning allowed—posting a picture and a biography of the candidate on a bulletin board at the electoral circumscription for everyone to see—is narrowed even further since provincial delegates and national deputies do not campaign seeking popular support, since they are chosen by municipal delegates. However, the national deputies are accountable to the Municipal Assembly that elected them, and must render periodical accounts of their work.

Given the usual political involvement by all population groups under the revolution, the electoral system has produced some distorted political results. In 1976, after having a turnout of 95.2% of the total number of electors, 520 women were elected representing only 6.6% of the total number of electors. Some sources put it as 8% in 1976 and slightly less in 1979, with 7.2%. On the other hand, this may be more indicative of a traditional rural bias against accepting women's political participation than a flaw in the electoral system itself.

Women received more votes in urban than in rural areas: the highest percentage of women elected was in Havana province, 13.1%—followed by city of Havana, 12.6%, and Matanzas, 9.9%. By contrast, in such remote places as the special municipality of Isla de Pinos, now renamed Island of Youth, no women were elected in any of the 73 circumscriptions (Granma Weekly Review, 1976b). Altogether, however, including both urban and rural areas, women are underrepresented at the state politico-administrative organs; presently, they constitute only 22% of the deputies at the National Assembly.

Nevertheless, it seems that the accountability exerted by the Organs of People's Power has induced increasing popular participation in OPP's decision-making processes. This is felt at the local level, particularly when national deputies and provincial and municipal delegates render accounts *(rendición de cuentas)* of the way they handled different proposals and requests while still receiving further demands from the people. The complexity of learning the new roles of People's Power—including both ends of the spectrum, the representative delegate and/or deputy and the represented citizen—became critical in the 1979 election when 50% of the 10,752 municipal delegates elected in 1976 were not returned to office. Before that, 1% had been recalled for reasons hinging on their qualifications and performance as delegates, with the percentage of recalled male delegates higher than that of female delegates, while 900 had been replaced for such involuntary reasons as sickness, moving to another circumscription, and others. This direct and almost immediate popular verdict, however, has been mainly limited to the local level with the exception of two deputies recalled by the National Assembly out of a total membership of 481 deputies. One of the latter was an agricultural worker caught cheating in a school examination and, therefore, expelled from the National Assembly on the charges of demeanor inappropriate to his responsibilities (Arañaburo, 1979; Granma Weekly Review, 1979b, 1976a).

The National Assembly

According to Article 67 of the 1976 constitution, the National Assembly stands at the top of the pyramidal structure of the Organs of People's Power, representing the "supreme organ of state power" and expressing the "sovereign will of all the working people." Besides being invested with legislative and constitutional reform authority, its powers include revoking the decree laws issued by the Council of State (this powerful body functions when the National Assembly is not in session); approving the national budget; declaring a state of war in the face of military aggression; appointing the members of such organs as the Council of State, the president, vice president, and other judges of the People's Supreme Court, and the attorney general of the Republic; and exercising control over the organs of state and government (Article 73).

The National Assembly holds regular sessions, usually for two days, twice a year, in July and December; also, whenever the need arises it is called to hold an extraordinary session. During its first three years, from 1976 to 1979, the National Assembly approved approximately 30 laws, reached more than 35 agreements, and held several elections. This heavy legislative load includes the annual state budgets, yearly economic and social development plans, and civil, penal, administrative, public, military, and other laws. The laws are drafted by the Commission on Juridical and Constitutional Affairs of the National Assembly, but they are put together in coordination with any of the 20 standing commissions which function throughout the year conducting business in preparation for the regular sessions. The deputies are normally assigned to one or more commissions, which are staffed with advisory and clerical personnel. Regardless of how demanding working as the people's representative could be, the national deputies continue holding the same jobs they had before being elected with no additional pay other than being reimbursed for their expenses while discharging their responsibilities; however, they are freed from their daily jobs whenever they need to attend National Assembly sessions or commission meetings. The commissions hold their meetings in different cities throughout the year, rather than limiting them to the National Assembly headquarters in Havana (Arañaburo, 1979).

The legislative process can be examined in some detail by looking at the steps followed by the 1979 Penal Code. After more than ten years on the drafting board—which at that time started with the Juridical Committee of the PCC and was later replaced by the National Assembly Commission on Juridical and Constitutional Affairs—the Penal Code was finally approved in the second session for 1978, on December 28-30, but it did not come into effect until November 1, 1979 (Azicri, 1980; Tigar, 1979). However, before it was approved by the National Assembly, the original draft was subjected to the long participatory process of examination and discussion by the people, a process customary with major revolutionary laws. Nevertheless, once the stage for people's participation was over, who would make the critical decision of what goes into the final text of the law and which of the suggestions made at the grassroots or intermediate level would be accepted or rejected remained unanswered.

The record of the National Assembly seems to indicate that the deputies take in earnest their political representative roles, discussing their constituency's concerns as well as their own. After more than three years, the trend followed is of serious, open, and thorough discussion of issues and proposed legislation. Laws can be proposed not only by national deputies, but by the Council of State, the Council of Ministers, the commissions of the National Assembly, the trade unions and mass organizations, the

People's Supreme Court, the Attorney General, and through a petition signed by at least 10,000 citizens who are eligible to vote. In spite of such strides, it does not appear as though the moment in which the national deputies can demonstrate their willingness to reject a major policy, or propose new alternatives departing substantively from what is officially recommended, has arrived yet. From the standpoint of liberal democracy, the coming of age of the National Assembly as a truly independent, even autonomous parliament is still down the road.

The Council of State

The Cuban state and governmental institutions have been found by González (1976b: 8) and de la Cuesta (1976: 20-21) to match the Soviet Union's; the National Assembly has been paired with the USSR Supreme Soviet and the Council of State with the Presidium of the Supreme Soviet. In actuality, Cuba has departed in some cases from other socialist experiences, particularly in the case of a single person heading both the state and government.

The deputies of the National Assembly elect from their own ranks the members of the Council of State—31 members including a president, first vice president, five vice presidents, and a secretary—who will serve throughout the duration of the assembly, a five-year term.

The President of the Council of State, elected among the members of this body, becomes then, the head of state and government, a position currently held by Fidel Castro. By law, the president of the Council of State is simultaneously the president of the Council of Ministers, which is the actual government of the country. The members of the Council of Ministers are appointed by the Council of State in consultation with the president.

The power of the Council of State to represent the National Assembly in the long period between sessions becomes rather significant with the list of additional powers—20 entries—granted in Article 88 of the constitution, which turns this office into a major decision-making center in today's Cuba. Moreover, whatever balance existed between the National Assembly and the Council of State was tilted toward the latter during the second 1979 session of the National Assembly: henceforth, "the decree-laws issued by the Council of State have equal standing and judicial validity as the laws approved by the Assembly" (Granma Weekly Review, 1980b). This additional power was used swiftly: the Council of State issued Decree-Law No. 31 of January 10, 1980, in a major overhaul of the central administration agencies, modifying the system established by Law 1323 of November 30, 1976, which was a major law in the institutionalization process of the Cuban state.

The circumstances and motivations for these changes are not completely clear yet. However, it is known that there were difficult times in Cuba toward the end of 1979 and the first months of 1980; these have been coupled with both human and institutional changes, touching ministers and ministries. Besides serious economic difficulties, forceful entries in Havana into diplomatic Latin American missions by disaffected Cubans seeking political asylum has prompted the regime to ratify its compliance with the right of asylum, but to state that it cannot accept extending "the utilization of that right to *common criminals*" (Granma Weekly Review, 1980a).

Not to downgrade the seriousness of these events, they may constitute one more passing episode in the long and troubled history of the revolution; in all likelihood the regime will survive them and move forward, as it has done in the past. The most lasting effect of this period, however, may very well be the shifting of the balance of power between the Council of State and the National Assembly. The unchecked predominance of the former could only hinder the future political and institutional growth of the latter.

The Council of Ministers

Recognized as the "highest-ranking executive and administrative organ" of the regime, the Council of Ministers constitutes "the Government of the Republic." Together with all the bureaucratic structure of the central government, this is the third institutional power pyramid in the system. Articles 93-99 of the 1976 Constitution cover the organization, power, and accountability of this executive body, as well as other matters related to it. The composition of the Council of Ministers includes: a president, who is head of state and government; first vice president; several vice presidents, at least seven; the president of the Central Planning Board; the ministers, the secretary, and other members determined by law. Covering a broad area of governmental control, Article 96 determines in twenty entries the powers invested in this executive and administrative organ.

The president, the first vice president, and the remaining vice presidents of the Council of Ministers constitute its executive committee, which is one of the four major power centers in the country. Strategically located, this powerful committee exercises control over the administration. Also, in emergency situations, according to Article 95, the executive committee "may rule on matters normally under the jurisdiction of the Council of Ministers." Thus, by concentrating within itself executive and administrative functions at the highest level, the executive committee becomes the highest layer of governmental decision-making in the pyramidal structure of democratic centralism. However, its immediate task is to oversee and direct the work of the also powerful Council of Ministers.

Interlocking at different levels, and interacting in governmental (bureaucratic administration and decision-making) and politico-administrative (administrative policy-making, supervision of services and agencies, and legislation) actions, the highest governmental organ, composed of the Council of Ministers and its executive committee, and political organs of the state, composed of the National Assembly and its Council of State, stand next to one another in a system of horizontal collaboration and vertical subordination, or democratic centralism. Likewise, and under this layer, the administrative structure composing the medium and lower levels of the central government works on the same basis and principle with the politico-administrative Organs of People's Power, or Provincial and Municipal Assemblies.

Finally, the structural features of the Cuban state have been defined and established by the process of institutionalization.

Conclusions

Throughout this narrative, the institutionalization of the political and administrative structure of the Cuban state has been examined by following its three major, interrelated institutional pyramids. This analysis included the provisions of the 1976 Constitution determining the statutory characteristics of these political institutions. Institutionalizing the four major power centers in the political system, the three pyramidal structures include: (1) the central government, which includes the maze of bureaucratic agencies, institutes, and ministerial offices headed by the Council of Ministers and its executive committee, one of the regime's four power centers; (2) the new politico-administrative and legislative state organs consisting of the Organs of People's Power, with Municipal, Provincial, and National Assemblies crowned by the Council of State, another major power center; and (3) the central political institution leading the entire political system, the Cuban Communist Party, which with its Political Bureau and Secretariat includes two major power centers.

The immediate and long-range expectations of this institutional arrangement are based on the twofold nature of these structures: their administrative-bureaucratic and politico-representative roles and functions. Moreover, their system of double subordination is based on the principle of democratic centralism. This principle conveys the notion that each one of these major structures should preserve its own identity while performing its institutional functions. Also, they should become integrated horizontally, in order to channel decisions from one to the other, and vertically, so decisions made by higher organs are binding for lower ones. However, insofar as they are interlocking and interacting with one another, the regime should prevent any power center from reigning over others; no institutional pyramid should become subordinate to another. That is, notwithstanding the significance of the political leadership provided by the Communist party, the National Assembly is not meant to be just a ratification board for the policies dictated by the party or the Council of State, but a deliberative organ that makes decisions and legislates on its own right.

The challenge faced by a developing political system to achieve integration while still allowing institutional and functional differentiation (Pye, 1966) is particularly pressing in Cuba today. The integration/differentiation challenge brings back to this analysis Huntington's conceptualization of institutionalization, discussed earlier. Thus, achieving a close integration or institutional coherence among state organs and the Communist party within the political system, while still preserving institutional identity throughout this process (or structural autonomy) and the performance of specific but interrelated functions (or complexity/adaptability), poses a "crisis of development" to an institutionalizing regime such as the Cuban. Interestingly enough, this problem was recognized by Jose Arañaburo (1979), secretary of the National Assembly. He believes that national deputies who are party militants do not seek to impose the party's policies on the National Assembly—or the Provincial or Municipal Assemblies, for that matter. Their purpose, states Arañaburo, is to convince their fellow deputies of the wisdom and correctness of such policies and not to dictate to them. From the perspective of this analysis, however, the question still remains of the feasibility of a national deputy who is also a party member taking a critical position and, therefore, voting against what is already official party policy. Such an action, in a strict sense, would constitute a violation of the principle of democratic centralism; on the other had, behavior similar to this under a liberal democratic parliament would certainly mean a reprehensible breach of party discipline.

In short, is it true both now and in the future for this stage of the institutionalization process that power pyramids—individually and collectively—could exercise their functions and political responsibilities without either imposing themselves on others or being imposed upon by such societal institutions as the mass organizations? The response to this question is central, not only for the present institutionalization of the state, but also for the future growth and development of its system of socialist democracy. Nonetheless, as of now the system has scored decisive strides, moving from earlier stages characterized by "erratic political activity" into a process of institutional stability, coherence, continuity, and decentralization of decision-making responsibilities, such as making the OPP responsible for the administration and supervision of services which heretofore were the responsibility of the central government alone.

Finally, regarding the legitimacy-institutionalization question discussed above, this writer's position on this subject is that the alleged revolution's source of legitimacy, or charismatic authority, is neither a limitation nor a complete definition of its actual exercise of power. Thus, the explanation mentioned before—that the initial charismatic type of authority was eventually widened into a broader legitimizing category—seems more credible with, for example, the revolutionary value and cultural system sustaining and providing additional legitimacy to the regime. Hence, the newly created political institutions become legitimized as long as they emerge and are the product of this very revolutionary value system. Meanwhile, Castro's charismatic leadership was and is at the very center of the revolutionary process, still providing a legitimizing influence in the process of institutionalizing the revolution.

NOTES

1. The idea of governing strategies (patterns of exercising power) includes three basic elements present in governmental attempts to maximize goal attainment: (1) the choice of an approach to goal attainment, such as mobilizing the population for specific results; (2) the choice of a method of communicating policies and programs to the people, which includes centralized forms when the government communicates policies directly to the people, and decentralized forms when the mass organizations, instead of the government, communicate governmental policies or agree on their own within the framework established by the regime; and (3) the choice of a method of gaining the population's

compliance with governmental policies and programs, which includes material and moral incentives, political participation, and coercive methods (Azicri, 1977: 6).

2. A charismatic pattern of exercising power represents a centralized governing strategy such as when the charismatic leader addresses the masses when seeking their compliance with official policies on the basis of moral incentives—i.e., the leader's personalized appeal and the revolutionary value system. In spite of commonly held beliefs, such as the popularized image of Castro speaking at a mass rally, a charismatic pattern had a much lower rate of frequency during the first ten years of revolutionary government than other governmental strategies available to the regime—i.e., decentralized patterns of exercising power based on material or moral incentives or even the use of coercive methods combined with centralized patterns (Azicri, 1975).

3. The present Cuban Communist Party (PCC) was preceded by two earlier attempts to form a revolutionary political party. Initially, the 26 of July Movement, the Revolutionary Student Directorate, and the Partido Socialista Popular (PSP), which is the old, prerevolutionary Communist party, were all amalgamated into the Integrated Revolutionary Organizations (ORI) from 1961 to 1963. The ORI was changed into the United Party of the Socialist Revolution (PURS) from 1963 to 1965, and in 1965 became the Cuban Communist Party of today.

4. The party membership is predominately middle age or younger, with 46.2% under 35 years of age and 76.7% under 45 years. However, there was a decline in the age group under 27 years from 22.7% in 1967 to the much lower rate of 4% in 1975. This decline was caused by the decision that younger members and aspirants should stay longer in the Union of Communist Youth (UJC) and then join the PCC. Nevertheless, 45 years of age seems to be the critical point in the chronology of party membership; thus, after reaching this age the percentage of older members declines drastically. The party leadership, however, seems to follow a different trend, with its senior members retaining their position(s) and status in spite of their old age (Tesis y Resoluciones, 1976: 29-30).

REFERENCES

ALVAREZ TABIO, F. (1977) Política y Legalidad. La Habana: Editorial de Ciencias Sociales.

ARAÑABURO, J. (1979) Report given at the panel on "Decentralizing decision-making: the role of popular power." New York: National Conference on Cuba, Center for Cuban Studies.

AZICRI, M. (1980) "Crime and law under socialism: the 1979 Cuban penal code." Rev. of Socialist Law 6 (March).

——— (1979) "The institutionalization of the Cuban revolution: a review of the literature." Cuban Studies/Estudios Cubanos 9 (July): 63-78.

——— (1978) "The *institucionalización* of Cuba's revolution." Revista/Review Interamericana 8 (Summer): 247-262.

——— (1977) "The governing strategies of mass mobilization: the foundations of Cuban revolutionary politics." Latin American Monograph Series 2. Erie: Northwestern Pennsylvania Institute for Latin American Studies.

——— (1975) "A study of the structure of exercising power in Cuba: mobilization and governing strategies (1959-1968)." Ph.D. dissertation, University of Southern California.

BENGELSDORF, C. (1979) Report given at the panel on "Cuba in the 1970s: evaluating the institutionalization of the revolution." Pittsburgh, PA: Eighth National Meeting, Latin American Studies Association.

——— (1976) "A large school of government." Cuba Review 6 (September): 3-18.

BLACK, J. K., H. I. BLUTSTEIN, J. D. EDWARDS, K. T. JOHNSTON, and D. S. McMORRIS (1976) Area Handbook for Cuba. Washington, DC: Government Printing Office.

BLAU, P. M. (1963) "Critical remarks on Weber's theory of authority." Amer. Pol. Sci. Rev. 57 (June): 305-316.

CASAL, L. (1979) "Cuba on the transition to socialism: the evolution of socialist democracy." New York: National Conference on Cuba, Center for Cuban Studies.

——— (1976) "Cuban communist party: the best among the good." Cuba Review 6 (September): 23-30.

CASTRO, R. (1976) Fidel Castro, Raúl Castro. Selección de Discursos Acerca del Partido. La Habana: Editorial de Ciencias Sociales.

Constitution of the Republic of Cuba. (1976) New York: Center for Cuban Studies.

DE LA CUESTA, L. A. (1976) "The Cuban socialist constitution: its originality and role in institutionalization." Cuban Studies/Estudios Cubanos 6 (July): 15-30.

DOMÍNGUEZ, J. I. (1978) Cuba: Order and Revolution. Cambridge, MA: Harvard Univ. Press.

EASTON, D. (1958) "The perception of authority and political change," pp. 170-196 in C. J. Friedrich (ed.) Authority. Cambridge, MA: Harvard Univ. Press.

EISENSTADT, S. N. [ed.] (1968) Max Weber on Charisma and Institutionalization. Chicago: Univ. of Chicago Press.

FAGEN, R. R. (1972) "A perspective on the transformation of political culture in Cuba," pp. 187-219 in S. A. Halper and J. R. Sterling (eds.) Latin America—The Dynamics of Social Change. New York: St. Martin's.

——— (1969) The Transformation of Political Culture in Cuba. Stanford, CA: Stanford Univ. Press.

——— and R. A. BRODY, T. J. O'LEARY (1968) Cubans in Exile—Disaffection and the Revolution. Stanford, CA: Stanford Univ. Press.

First Congress of the Communist Party of Cuba (1976) Collection of Documents. Moscow: Progress Publishers.

GONZÁLEZ, E. (1976a) "The party congress and poder popular: orthodoxy, democratization, and the leader's dominance." Cuban Studies/Estudios Cubanos 6 (July): 1-14.

——— (1976b) "Castro and Cuba's new orthodoxy." Problems of Communism 25 (January-February): 1-19.

——— (1974) Cuba Under Castro: The Limits of Charisma. Boston: Houghton Mifflin.

Granma Weekly Rev. (1980a) February 10: 1.

——— (1980b) January 20: 5.

——— (1979a) December 31: 1.

——— (1979b) February 25: 2-3.

——— (1976a) November 14: 6, 11.

——— (1976b) October 24: 11.

HOROWITZ, I. L. (1977) "Military origins of the Cuban revolution," pp. 66-87 in I. L. Horowitz (ed.) Cuban Communism. New Brunswick, NJ: Transaction.

——— (1965) "The stalinization of Fidel Castro." New Politics 4 (Fall): 16-19.

HUNTINGTON, S. (1968) Political Order in Changing Societies. New Haven: Yale Univ. Press.

KOZOL, J. (1978) "Growing up dogmatic: conversations in a Cuban classroom." Saturday Rev. (September 2): 19-23.

LEOGRANDE, W. L. (1979) "Party development in revolutionary Cuba." J. of Inter-american Studies and World Affairs 21 (November): 457-480.

MATHEWS, H. L. (1961) The Cuban Story. New York: George Braziller.

MESA-LAGO, C. (1978) Cuba in the 1970s—Pragmatism and Institutionalization. Albuquerque: New Mexico Univ. Press.

MORENO, J. A. (1971) "From traditional to modern values," in C. Mesa-Lago (ed.) Revolutionary Change in Cuba. Pittsburgh: Univ. of Pittsburgh Press.

MORTON, W. M. (1965) Castro as Charismatic Hero. Lawrence: Center for Latin American Studies, University of Kansas.

PEABODY, R. L. (1968) "Authority," pp. 473-477 in International Encyclopedia of the Social Sciences. New York: Macmillan and Free Press.

PYE, L. W. (1966) Aspects of Political Development. Boston: Little, Brown.

RIVERO COLLADO, C. (1977) La Contrarrevolución Cubana—Los Sobrinos de Tío Sam. Madrid: Akal Editor.

Sobre la Constitución del Poder Popular (1978) Ciudad de la Habana: Dirección de Divulgación y Relaciones Internacionales, Poder Popular.

Sobre las Dificultades Objetivas de la Revolución (1979) Lo que el Pueblo Debe Saber. La Habana: Editora Política.

Sobre los Organos del Poder Popular (1976) La Habana: Departamento de Orientación Revolucionaria del Comité Central del Partido Comunista de Cuba.

Tesis y Resoluciones. (1976) Primer Congreso del Partido Comunista de Cuba. La Habana: Departamento de Orientación Revolucionaria del Comité Central del Partido Comunista de Cuba.

TIGAR, M. E. (1979) "The educative function of criminal law: popular participation and public educational aspects." New York: National Conference on Cuba, Center for Cuban Studies.

VALDES, N. (1976) "Revolution and institutionalization in Cuba." Cuban Studies/Estudios Cubanos 6 (January): 1-37.

WEBER, M. (1964) The Theory of Social and Economic Organization. (T. Parsons, ed.). New York: Free Press.

WILLIAMS, E. J. and J. WRIGHT (1975) Latin American Politics—A Developmental Approach. Palo Alto, CA: Mayfield.

Max Azicri is Professor of Political Science at Edinboro State College, Edinboro, Pennsylvania. He received a Doctor of Law degree from the University of Havana and an M.A. and Ph.D. in Political Science from the University of Southern California. He has authored several articles and essays on contemporary Cuba, revolutionary politics, the women's movement, and socialist legal system. His current book-length project is on Women in Cuba: The Revolutionary Experience.

RICHARD CRAIG
Department of Political Science
Kent State University
Kent, Ohio

OPERATION CONDOR

Mexico's Antidrug Campaign Enters a New Era

In recent years Mexico has demonstrated the capacity to cultivate, process, ship, and transship vast quantities of illegal narcotic drugs. Such activity has traditionally been geared to the realities of domestic poverty, enormous profit, and American demand. Mexican marijuana dominated the U.S. market until quite recently. More importantly from the American viewpoint were the tons of Mexican heroin which saturated U.S. cities in the mid-1970s. Furthermore, Mexico is still the source of vast quantities of psychotropics and an increasingly popular conduit for South American cocaine.

According to Craig (1978), U.S. officials long sought to convince their Mexican counterparts that the key to any effective antidrug program lay in eliminating the illicit product at the source. Until such time that herbicides were applied on a massive scale against marijuana and opium poppies, they argued, the annual Mexican campaign would prove an exercise in futility. The Mexicans listened, studied, and experimented for several years, but it was not until the fall of 1975 that they decided to change the character of their program fundamentally by employ-

---

AUTHOR'S NOTE: This article is a revised and updated version of a paper delivered at the annual meeting of the Latin American Studies Association on April 5, 1979 in Pittsburgh. Mexico's antidrug campaign was known as Operation CANADOR (Combate Contra el Narcotrafico) until 1975; after that date it was called Operation Condor.

Journal of Interamerican Studies and World Affairs, Vol. 22 No. 3, August 1980 345-363

ing defoliants. The decision did not come easily, and there were two primary reasons for the delay. Officials and laymen alike feared the potentially harmful effects of such chemicals. Furthermore, they simply refused to acknowledge publicly what others had long known—that their country had become one of the world's largest heroin producers. To compound matters the problem was growing worse with each passing month. Something drastic had to be done.[1]

In November 1975, following a secret meeting between Mexican Attorney General Pedro Ojeda Paullada and Sheldon Vance, senior adviser to the secretary of state and coordinator for international narcotics affairs, Ojeda Paullada informed the United States that beginning immediately the antidrug *campaña* would include the use of defoliant chemicals. One year later, in the fall of 1976, Operation Condor became the core of this accelerated program. Located in the heart of Mexico's opium-growing region, it has become a domestic and international showpiece. Yet while the unprecedented program has registered very impressive results, it has not terminated the Mexican "connection" entirely. Operation Condor, its accomplishments, promise, and problems, constitutes the focal point of this analysis.

The 1975-1976 Campaign: A Macrocosm

The decision to employ herbicides as the core of Mexico's eradication effort was made public in stages. At a press conference in Mexico City on November 13, 1975, Ojeda Paullada described his government's new approach. It would involve twice the number of federal police, several thousand additional soldiers, numerous aircraft, and the extensive use of sophisticated technology. However, when questioned about herbicides, Ojeda Paullada hedged, observing "the Government of Mexico will under no circumstances conduct or condone operations that could have an adverse effect on the country's ecology. . . . But it does not mean that we should not use herbicides" (Drug

Enforcement, 1975-1976: 11). Early in January 1976, Dr. Alejandro Gertz Manero, the man chosen to head the new *campaña,* was even less subtle when he explained that "there were simply too many fields to destroy on the ground. . . . We're hopeful that the herbicide will make a radical difference" (New York Times, 1976). Two days later, Defense Secretary General Hermenegildo Cuenca Díaz responded to a reporter's query by admitting that herbicides were being used "experimentally" in the states of Sinaloa and Guerrero. Amidst growing debate on the question, Gertz Manero cleared the air. "Yes, we are using herbicides," he declared on January 7, "and before mid-year we are going to completely end the cultivation of narcotic drugs" (Excelsior, 1976b).

Gertz Manero, like subsequent Mexican officials, was somewhat overly optimistic in his prediction. His frankness was refreshing, however, as it clarified a cardinal point: the 1975-1976 antidrug effort would be unparalleled. In effect, the Mexican government had decided to remove the kid gloves with drug traffickers by: (1) making the campaign truly *permanent;* i.e., year-round, (2) pouring $35 million into the effort, (3) coordinating the program vertically between national and subnational authorities and horizontally between the Justice Department (Procuraduría) and the Army, (4) cooperating more effectively with the United States and other foreign governments, (5) vigorously addressing the problem of drug-related corruption, and (6) using modern technology which featured the aerial application of herbicides.

Primary responsibility for the revitalized campaign was again lodged in the Procuraduría, which coordinates the narcotics activities of the Mexican army and other state and municipal law-enforcement officials. Although often inseparable in practice, we may divide the antidrug efforts of the Procuraduría into two parts: halting cultivation and manufacture of opium poppies, marijuana, and psychotropics; and preventing domestic and international traffic in these and other drugs. Of the two, eradication presented the more direct challenge.

The extent of opium and marijuana cultivation in the fall of 1975 was indeed vast, with the government admitting that 600,000 square kilometers were being utilized, directly or indirectly, for such illicit farming. More importantly from the American perspective was the existence of some 30,000 opium plots, a total that simply could not be destroyed by traditional stick-beating tactics. Instead, the Mexican government employed the most modern aerial technology. Remote sensors, multispectral and infrared photography, and even satellites were used to discover and plot the fields. Some 40 aircraft, the majority of which were helicopters provided by the United States, were used to locate and spray the plots or to ferry soldiers into position to perform the eradication chore. Eleven advanced base camps were established in heavy opium-growing zones to facilitate the rapid transport by helicopter of these troops. The soldiers themselves were better equipped with modern light weapons that often proved the differences between life and death during armed clashes with heretofore better armed growers and traffickers.

Drug-related corruption involving military officers, politicians, and judges received particular attention. To counteract such graft within the army, the secretary of defense sought to remove his men from the enormous temptations inherent in a multimillion dollar drug environment by constantly rotating zonal commanders and lesser officers. While not wholly successful—one would be extremely naive to impose such a standard—it would be difficult to document any major corruption cases involving the officer corps during the revitalized campaña.

The emphasis on greater coordination and cooperation that typified the eradication program also characterized the interdiction phase. Particularly crucial was the excellent working relationship that evolved between Mexican and U.S. drug officials. "This is my third year here," remarked an American narcotics official in January 1976, "but never have we had the working relationship with Mexican officials that we've had since the launching of this year's campaign. In this respect it's a new and much better ball game" (Interview, 1976b). More information was exchanged, extensive use was made by Mexican officers of the expertise of 30 U.S. Drug Enforcement Administration (DEA) agents, and greater cooperation was evidenced in the building of conspiracy cases involving drug offenders in the two countries. The addition of some 250 federal police agents proved indispensable to the dismantling of narcotic laboratories, arrest and prosecution of traffickers, and interdiction of drugs being shipped within and through Mexico. These specially trained, well-paid, and wholly dedicated young men provided the key element in the resounding success of Mexico's revived antidrug effort. Sheldon Vance and DEA head Peter Bensinger summed up the opinion of most observers when they stated that "no single international effort now underway is doing more to combat heroin trafficking than the Mexican Government's eradication program" (U.S. Department of Justice, 1976).

Comparative statistics furnished by the Procuraduría tended to support such praise. Mexican soldiers and federal police destroyed 21,405 opium plots from September 1, 1975 to August 31, 1976, as compared to 13,580 plots during the preceding twelve months; eliminated 16,686 fields of marijuana vis-à-vis 6,762 in 1974-1975; arrested a total of 4,399 individuals on drug charges as compared to 2,752 during the previous period; seized 215 kilograms of cocaine in transit; and dismantled 16 drug processing laboratories. Perhaps even more indicative of the accomplishment and outlook of Mexican narcotics officials during the first year of Operation CANADOR (Combate Contra el Narcotrafico), as the overall antidrug program has since been tabbed, was the opinion of a high-ranking federal police agent in February 1976: "We're really attacking the poppy fields in Oaxaca, Guerrero, and other states; and when we finish wiping them out we're going to launch an all-out drive against the critical triangle, because that is where it's at" (Interview, 1976a).

Operation Condor: A Microcosm

The agent's words reveal two salient aspects of the 1975-1976 program. It was unprecedented in comparison to all preceding campaigns. Yet despite impressive results, it really revealed only the tip of a massive opium-heroin iceberg located in the northwestern states of Sinaloa, Durango, and Chihuahua. The *triángulo crítico,* or Zone VI as it is officially designated, was indeed "where it's at." And there was a lot more of *it* than even the "realists" had imagined: more opium plots, more processing laboratories, more weapons, more desperate campesinos, more corruption, more lawlessness, and more money. The fact was that no serious interruption in the Mexican heroin connection could be expected until the opium nucleus of Sinaloa and its neighboring states was brought under control. In late 1976 the question thus became: "What is the new López Portillo administration going to do about it?" The answer was not long in coming.

The 1976-1977 campaña began in the fall with little fanfare or publicity. Initially, it appeared to be merely a stepped-up, expanded version of the preceding year. Such impressions vanished, however, in January 1977 when Operation Condor was officially launched in the heart of Mexico's opium citadel. If the first year of Operation CANADOR was best described as "unprecedented," Condor was better termed "war." Frankly admitting that "we will have lost the war" if thousands of opium plots are not destroyed in the triángulo within a three-month period, Mexican authorities promised results to back up words. "It's better to do it than to say it," declared Oscar Flores Sánchez, the new attorney general. "People are already tired of that which has been repeated so many times and yet not fulfilled in actual practice. The results will be better than the words" (Excelsior, 1977). Ultimately, the accomplishments equalled the words, but they were not registered without a prolonged and controversial struggle which is continuing.

Two appointments by President José López Portillo have proved crucial to the continuing success of Operation Condor—Flores Sánchez as procurator and General Félix Galván López as secretary of defense. Longtime friends, both are *norteños,* men well aware of the extent of Mexico's drug situation, and totally dedicated to complying with their president's charge to rid Mexico of the "drug curse." American narcotics officials have been particularly impressed with Florez Sánchez, the man ultimately responsible for the progress of Operation Condor and the overall Mexican effort against drug traffic.

The new attorney general surprised even the most optimistic officials early in January 1977 when he requested the presence of key Americans, including the ambassador, to discuss the administration's new approach. "The man was amazingly open and enthusiastic," observed a high-ranking American narcotics official; "he opened the meeting by informing us he'd read up on all the treaties relating to drugs between our two states, and asked if *we* would draw up a historical review of such cooperation and include in it *our* current thoughts on improving Mexico's campaign." His goal was "the total elimination of opium poppy cultivation and maximum cooperation with the United States and other countries in the endeavor" (Interview, 1977).

Enthusiasm, commitment, and cooperation notwithstanding, the total elimination of Mexican opium poppy cultivation was, and is, a virtual impossibility. Achievement of such a goal in Sinaloa alone poses a monumental chore. Not only is the state the core of Mexico's heroin industry, it is also a classic microcosm of the good and bad of Mexico's "economic miracle." Sinaloa is the nation's leading agricultural state, the site of Mexico's most advanced farming for export, a major mining center, and the locale of two beautiful yet quite different cities, Mazatlán and Culiacán. On the other hand, it is also the center of grinding poverty, repeated land seizures, open and armed defiance of authority, notorious corruption, martial law, and until very recently the hub of one of the world's largest concentrations of opium-heroin production. The capital city, Culiacán, literally had to be seen and experienced in the 1970s to be believed. Comparisons with the Chicago of the "roaring twenties" have often been offered. Those who put them forth, however, either did not see the Chicago of Al Capone, or the Culiacán of *los traficantes y pistoleros.* The author's personal experience in Culiacán during 1976 leads him to readily concur with Pyes (1977) who observed: "but Culiacán has only 350,000 inhabitants and the equivalent of a St. Valentine's Day Massacre every two weeks."

The extent of lawlessness, corruption, and de facto power of *narcotraficantes* was legend. Even the state's governor, a man often accused of sanctioning such an environment, called the problem "insoluble." In early January 1976, following a particularly noteworthy daytime gun battle between rival gangs in downtown Culiacán that left at least a dozen dead, Alfonso G. Calderón lamented that "the mafiosos don't show any respect." He went on to describe an area of 21,161 square kilometers, or 49.8% of the state, in which many of the 200,000 campesinos were involved in drug traffic. Why do they do it? "Because," he said, "they want to have a nice pair of pants, a nice hat, and a nice shirt." Like thousands of their countrymen, the Sinaloa campesinos are desperate, and they seek desperate solutions to their problems. The culmination of their plight is clearly reflected in the governor's words: "Even if we bring the entire army to Culiacán, it would not be enough" (Excelsior, 1976a). Perhaps in the long run his prophecy will prove correct, but early in 1977 the new administration set out to prove him wrong. With the inauguration of Operation Condor the inhabitants of Sinaloa must have thought the entire Mexican army had indeed been transferred to the triángulo crítico and headquartered near Culiacán.

The assignment of these 2,500 soldiers, 250 federal police, units of the Mexican air force and navy, state and local police, and an undisclosed number of DEA agents was formidable to say the least. With the launching of Condor I it was revealed that some 11,000 fields of opium and marijuana had already been located in the entire 80,000 square kilometer area of Zone VI. At least 20,000 of the region's campesinos were involved in raising and/or shipping the drugs; each was very well armed and more than willing to defend his illicit product, which brought up to ten times the annual income he had traditionally received from legitimate crops. Two primary tasks thus faced the civilian and military commanders of Condor I: eradication of the illegal crops and pacification of the countryside.

Eradication of thousands of illicit plots, some of which exceeded 40 acres, was to prove no mean task even with the most dedicated men utilizing advanced technology. Without the highest level of cooperation and coordination between federal police and the army it would have proved impossible. And coordination has proved the *sina qua non* of Condor's success. In the words of an American military attaché (Interview, 1978a): "Condor I was truly remarkable for two reasons—its massive, concentrated use of herbicides and the unprecedented coordination between the Procuraduría and the Army. When Mexico City said 'frog' the Army really jumped."

The eradication process began with high level multispectral reconnaisance photographs, which when developed revealed the numerous marijuana and opium plots. Following confirmation by low-level flights, the opium fields were sprayed by helicopter with 2, 4-D, and the marijuana plots with Gramoxone. Squads of soldiers were then ferried in by helicopter to secure the area and destroy those plants missed from the air. The location of many opium plots in extremely hazardous terrain meant that soldiers did some of the spraying or destroyed the poppies through traditional stick-beating methods. The process often proved hazardous for pilot, soldier, and campesino.

While the total number of federal police and soldiers killed has never been made public, it surely approaches 100; the campesino-trafficker total is certainly much greater. Pilots flying low-level reconnaissance, spraying illicit plots, and transporting soldiers often encountered heavy ground fire. Some crashed while attempting to spray defoliants at acute angles, while still others were killed when their helicopter blades struck wellhidden cables strung from one hillside to another. Numerous lives were lost in pitched battles once the soldiers were discharged from helicopters, as the campesinos occasionally chose to defend their precious plots instead of disappearing into the woods and returning to replant their fields as soon as the soldiers departed.

Pacification of the countryside proved even more difficult than eradication of opium and marijuana fields. Soldiers were charged with restoring law and order in the three-state area of Zone VI. Without a massive military presence the task would have been patently impossible; with it the chore has become only slightly less onerous. The *municipio* of Cosalá, for example, which lies some 100 miles north of Culiacán, discovered a whole new industry in the 1970s: cultivation of the opium poppy. For many if not most of Cosalá's campesinos, opium gum became the first and only source of cash income they had ever known. Of course it was illegal, but the farmers were adamant, and the mayor was helpless before the hordes of soldiers arrived. "We've got 1,500 square miles of wilderness to cover," he explained to a reporter. "Our police force is six men with three old M-1 rifles among them" (Christian Science Monitor, 1976).

Reaction to the soldiers by residents in other Sinaloa highland *municipios* such as Choix, El Fuerte, Sinaloa de Leyva, Elota, Mocorito, and the legendary Badiraguato was uniformly negative and generally hostile, for despite the sincere desire of many high-ranking officers to win over the campesino, he all too often equates the soldier with the government, an institution that had forgotten he ever existed until he began to live with some degree of dignity. His distrust of all outsiders is well known throughout Mexico, and the army's tactics have done little to change his outlook.

When army units located a known or suspected drug center their orders were clear: "Clean it out!" And they did, completely. In so doing they occasionally went beyond the call of duty. And the word soon spread. According to a well-placed American diplomat in Mexico City (Interview, 1978b): "Look, when these units make ground sweeps through known or suspected drug-producing areas they are occasionally too clean. Houses are ransacked, men beaten, women violated, and belongings confiscated. These tactics, even though they are definitely rare, don't exactly endear the military to the campesinos."[2]

Similar accounts too numerous to be discounted reveal a fundamental problem for national officials. The campesino's plight is obvious to even the most casual observer. With inflation, and apparently even with an increased flow of petrodollars, his problem is growing worse, not better. Figures from the National Bank of Mexico (Excelsior, 1980) depict a disaster for rural Mexico during the 1970s. The agrarian sector grew at only a 2% annual rate in comparison to an overall annual economic growth rate of 6%. In 1970, 58% of Mexico's population lived in rural areas; by 1980 the figure had dropped to 40%. Simultaneously, annual per capita farm income declined from 651 to 575 pesos, as the total area under cultivation dropped 20%.[3] Between 1973 and 1975 Mexico went from net agrarian exporter to importer. Early in 1980 the farm sector's decline had reached a crisis stage, prompting the government to purchase 10.7 million tons of food grains abroad in order to avert politically explosive food shortages.

Unable to survive off the land, desperate campesinos are flooding the cities, abandoning *ejido* and private plots, seizing haciendas, executing local *caciques,* streaming across the border as illegal immigrants, and becoming drug entrepreneurs. All these activities are disconcerting to Mexico City. But only one of them to date, involvement with narcotics, has caused deep official concern *and* determined action. This had led some writers (McConahay, 1976; Pyes, 1977; Wright, 1976) to conclude that Mexico's war against the poppy may be more accurately termed a war against the peasant and the real or imagined guerrillas of the sierras.

While the army's continuing effort to pacify the countryside has been both difficult and controversial, the restoration of law and order in Culiacán proved equally troublesome and journalistically sensational. Any improvement in the city's ambient was noteworthy, given the situation prior to the inauguration of Operation Condor. Life was cheap, very cheap, in Culiacán. Murders and funerals were so commonplace that local residents came to accept them as normal. Depending on the source, there were between two and three drug-related homicides daily during 1976, "surely a nongovernmental peacetime record for a western city with fewer than 200,000 [sic] inhabitants" (Miami Herald, 1977). Following a year of martial law the figure had been reduced to *only* one killing every three days! Then, and now, many law-abiding citizens lived in fear of *narcotraficantes;* as a result, most carried handguns on their person and high-powered rifles in their automobiles. Vividly recalling her life at the time as a Culiacán teenager, a female student at the University of Veracruz remarked:

> Never, never will I forget those days. Everyone in my family, including my ten-year-old brother, carried a pistol when they left

> the house—even in broad daylight! There simply was no law and order, and it was especially bad for young girls like me. My father dictated that I could never go out alone or even with a boyfriend unless I was accompanied by an older male with a pistol. Two of my girlfriends were gang raped, and in one case my cousin was killed by thugs when he tried to aid his sweetheart. Things really changed when the Army took over, and by 1978 it was pretty safe to go out, even at night [Interview, 1980].

Unfortunately, honest reporters did not share such feelings of security. The Mexican public was shocked and outraged early in February 1978 by the blatant assassination of Roberto Martínez Montenegro, a prize-winning reporter for Culiacán's *El Noroeste* and Mexico City's *Excelsior.* Unlike many of his contemporaries on trafficker payrolls, Martínez Montenegro had continued to expose the extent of drug-related corruption in the city and state. Because of this he was eliminated by two hired *pistoleros.* His murder, the third such killing of a reporter during one five-month period, highlighted the plight of citizens and caused the governor well-deserved embarrassment and discomfort.[4]

When a journalist asked what kind of guarantees he would provide honest reporters in the assassination's wake, Governor Calderón caustically replied: "Guarantees? What kind of guarantees? Do you want me to look after you, little boy?" (Excelsior, 1978). In subsequent weeks the state's chief executive withstood a series of challenges to his authority and integrity. During this time he came to admit that (1) undoubtedly some state and federal officers were protecting traficantes; (2) drug money, in effect, dominated the city and countryside; (3) there were more millionaires and a higher inflation rate in Culiacán than any Mexican city; (4) narcotics traffic was the primary cause of regional violence and lawlessness; (5) a large part of the buildings and hotels in Guadalajara may have been financed by drug money; (6) industrialists, merchants, and professionals wanted to leave Sinaloa because of the violent atmosphere; (7) campesinos became involved with drugs out of dire necessity; and (8) Sinaloa's tourism industry was being severely damaged by the publicity, dangers, and inconveniences resulting from narcotics traffic.

The Martínez Montenegro affair embarrassed not only the governor but Mexico City as well. Operation Condor's accomplishments were slighted in the aftermath, and this was unfortunate because they were most impressive. Wholesale drug prices doubled in Mexico as supplies were constricted. Army soldiers and federal police in Zone VI destroyed 43,915 plots of opium and 14,801 marijuana fields during calendar 1977. They confiscated 192 kilograms of opium, 81 kilograms of heroin, and 6 kilograms of morphine while simultaneously dismantling 20 heroin/morphine laboratories.

Such figures clearly illustrate two facts. First, Condor I was a resounding success by all statistical standards. While granting that statistics are relative indicators, they are nonetheless crucial. The number of opium fields destroyed is particularly important from an American perspective. Second, they vividly depict the contribution of the Sinaloa area to Mexico's overall narcotics problem. Note, for example, the following comparative figures for calendar 1977. Zone VI witnessed the liquidation of 43,915 poppy fields, while the national total was 45,909. The 192 kilograms of confiscated opium dominated the national figure of 226, as did the 20 heroin laboratories dismantled vis-à-vis the grand total of 27.[5] Obviously, when it comes to opium, morphine, and heroin, the triángulo crítico enjoys a monopoly. Or perhaps in the wake of Condor II-IV it would be more accurate to say that it enjoys a changing monopoly.

The phalanx of Mexico's campaña permanente, now in its fifth year, has radically altered both national and international drug scenes and dramatically affected the American heroin and marijuana market. Such has been the incessant, massive application of herbicides that opium and marijuana fields are becoming smaller, widely dispersed, and more difficult to discover. Sinaloa still remains the opium epicenter, but the size of its plots has shrunk to one-tenth acre on the average. More importantly, there are far fewer plots in the state and throughout Mexico. Fields are now being discovered in such heretofore unheard of locales as Querétaro, near Cuernavaca, and in the states of Chiapas and Veracruz. They are smaller in size and far more difficult to detect.[6] Heroin-processing laboratories are more widely dispersed. Traffickers are wiser and less bold. Some have shifted operations to handling Mexican psychotropics or cocaine being processed in Colombia and shipped through Mexico. Others, like their American counterparts, have retired from the drug business altogether, either voluntarily or as guests of the government in federal prisons. Still others, new faces, have taken their place.

In the aftermath of increased defoliant usage, the imprisonment of several major international traffickers and disruption of their networks, seizures of vast quantities of cocaine in transit, and the removal or imprisonment of corrupt judges and politicians, all but two statistical indicators of an even more intensive Operation CANADOR 1978 declined vis-à-vis 1977.[7] Note, as a case in point, the following comparisons: (1) Opium plots destroyed: 1977 - 45,909, 1978 - 24,190; (2) Marijuana fields eliminated: 1977 - 23,449, 1978 - 9,630; (3) Heroin confiscated: 1977 - 283 kilograms, 1978 - 153 kilograms; (4) Heroin laboratories dismantled: 1977 - 27, 1978 - 22 (Procuraduría, 1979).

Only the hard-core skeptic could discount these figures and even he would concede *the* crucial success indicator of Mexico's program from Washington's viewpoint—its impact on the U.S. drug scene. DEA sources in Mexico City report that the percentage of the American heroin market captured by "Mexican brown" has declined steadily and markedly as follows: 1974 - 85%, 1975 - 74%, 1976 - 60%, 1977 - 53%, 1978 - approximately 50%. In 1976 approximately 7-8 tons of heroin entered the United States. Three years later the amount was estimated at less than 4.5 tons. The retail price of one milligram of pure heroin increased from $1.26 in 1976 to $2.25 in 1979. Purity of Mexican heroin seized at the border dropped from 70% in 1975 to 25% early in 1979. Purity of all retail heroin on American streets declined from 6.6% in 1976 to 3.5% in the second quarter of 1979, a 47% decrease. Finally, deaths resulting from heroin overdose dropped from 1800 in 1976 to a projected 360 during all of 1979, a resounding 80% decrease. And what is true of heroin as a result of Mexico's campaña is even more evident in the case of marijuana.

Even though more marijuana is being smoked in the United States today than was the case in the early 1970s, the Mexican share of that market has shrunk from approximately 90% in 1974 to an estimated 20% with this writing. It would appear the government's use of Paraquat has dramatically reduced Mexican marijuana acreage while severely tarnishing its popularity north of the border. As regards the marijuana "connection," Colombia has undeniably replaced Mexico.[8]

Concluding Observations

Mexico's national campaign against narcotic drugs entered a new phase in the fall of 1975 when the government decided to eradicate opium and marijuana fields with herbicides. One year later Operation Condor became the core of this unparalleled program. Launched in the heart of Mexico's triángulo crítico, Condor has dramatically affected the Mexican and American drug scenes and earned international acclaim for its architects.

Still lacking, however, is an adequate explanation of why Mexican authorities decided to revamp, modernize, and accelerate their antidrug program. Why, in particular, did they opt for the extensive use of herbicides and the massive military presence that has epitomized Operation Condor and the campaign in general since 1975? Unicausal explanations abound, depending on one's source. Individually, none can fully explain the policy change. In combination, they go far in answering the fundamental question: What's in it for Mexico?

First, government officials were embarrassed by the fact that their country had become a major source of heroin. Marijuana is one thing; tons of opium and heroin are something else for a country that has long taken pride in its reputation as a leader in international efforts to contain drug traffic. Not only was Mexico's international image being tarnished, but politicians and laymen alike had become seriously concerned over increased domestic drug use. The use of solvents and glues by poor urban youth remains the foremost national drug problem. However, marijuana smoking is rapidly growing in popularity in a country that shows no intention of decriminalizing its usage. Opium and heroin addiction, while still in the nascent stages, is increasing, particularly in northern border cities. The potential for greater abuse of marijuana and opium/heroin was obviously enhanced by their massive in-country presence. Apparently convinced that herbicides posed no threat to folk and fauna, a frontal assault against drug cultivation, manufacture, and trafficking was clearly in Mexico's own national interest. The same could be said when it came to pleasing a very important neighbor.

Operation Condor and the entire revitalized campaña are inexorably linked with Mexico-United States relations. Vast quantities of oil notwithstanding, friendly relations with Washington are politically and economically crucial to Mexico City. When Mexico replaced Turkey as the prime source of heroin for the U.S. market in the early 1970s, narcotics became a priority item for American diplomats in Mexico City, who, without exception, see American pressure as the deciding factor in Mexico's 1975 decision to employ defoliant chemicals on a massive scale. Again without exception, these same diplomats are unanimous in praising the program's recent results. Mexico has thus not only pleased the Carter administration with Condor, but it has also acquired another valuable chip in the current diplomatic poker game with Washington.

International imagery, domestic drug problems, and diplomatic pressure are undeniably important in analyzing Mexico's decision to revamp its antidrug program. Individually and collectively, however, they still leave the analyst somewhat puzzled and skeptical. Each existed in varying degrees prior to 1975, yet Mexico, it is contended, did not act until then, primarily because the entire drug production-trafficking phenomenon failed to pose a serious threat to regional stability in the minds of Mexican officials until the mid-1970s. By that time several ingredients combined to produce concerted action from the top: (1) campesino desperation and the resort to drug cultivation and trafficking; (2) arming of the campesino and professional trafficker with weapons often superior to those of local and national law enforcement officers; (3) open and increasingly violent defiance of law and authority; (4) infusion into the sierras of enormous sums of money from narcotics sales that came to dominate local and regional economies, politicians, judges, and police; and (5) the merging of these trends in areas that have traditionally been the breeding grounds for rural guerrilla movements. Together they posed a threat to the control by the government and the all-pervasive Partido Revolucionario Institucional (PRI) over the entire country from Tijuana to Mérida. Analyzed in combination with U.S. pressure, a tarnished international image, and a burgeoning drug problem at home, the development of a clandestine, well-armed, and very well-financed nexus in the countryside goes far in explaining why Mexican officials launched Operation Condor and why they show no signs of easing their antidrug offensive. On the contrary, their commitment appears stronger than ever. The campaña is, in their own words, permanente!

NOTES

1. Another factor in Mexico's decision may have been, oddly enough, the U.S. government. "I think the Mexicans probably would have started spraying earlier," the author was told early in 1977, "had we not been so persistent in cautioning them about the possible negative effects on other crops. We were really concerned that they not harm other crops and thereby place the whole eradication program in jeopardy" (Interview, 1977).

2. For analysis of these and other possible human rights violations during Operation Condor, see Craig (1979).

3. The per capita income figures, if accurate, are truly astounding. Perhaps it should have read "dollars." If so, *Excelsior* erred twice by also editorializing the figures in pesos.

4. To my knowledge none of the murderers of Martínez Montenegro or his journalistic colleagues has ever been brought to justice. In all likelihood the pistoleros were themselves eliminated. One of them may well have been Culiacán's Chief of Police, Jaime Alcalá García, who was himself ultimately assassinated on December 4, 1978 in Guadalajara.

5. A word of caution is in order concerning these comparative data. The 1977 totals for Condor were given to an *Excelsior* reporter by Carlos Aguilar Garza, the civilian coordinator in Zone VI. The national figures, on the other hand, were provided by the Procuraduría. I have encountered some bewildering problems with Mexican narcotics statistics. For example, *Excelsior* listed six kilograms of confiscated morphine during

Condor 1977, while Procuraduría figures total only three kilograms for the entire national campaign of that year.

6. The shrinking size of opium poppy fields was clearly depicted by an American narcotics officer in Mexico City (Interview, 1979): "There are apparently no sizeable opium plots left out there. Three guys from NASA have been working all over Mexico for three months trying to devise a close-up aerial spotting system for miniplots. They informed us just this morning that the fields are so small that they've been unable to train their computer to understand what a poppy is at close range. It simply hasn't been able to follow the command 'find poppies.' When they finished their report, one of my staff asked somewhat in jest: 'Do you think the American taxpayer is getting his money's worth out of you guys if you spend several weeks down here without being able to statistically verify the existence of any poppies?' Now, my friend, that's what I call a successful campaign."

7. The two exceptions were psychotropics removed from circulation and persons arrested on drug-related charges. The number of stimulants confiscated, for example, was three times larger than the 1977 total.

8. Still unclarified in the game of marijuana statistics, however, is the percentage supplied to American smokers by domestic producers. It may well be (Dowdy, 1979) that the amount is far larger than many government analysts realize.

REFERENCES

Christian Science Monitor (1976) March 31.

CRAIG, R. B. (1979) "Human rights and Mexico's antidrug campaign." Presented to the Rocky Mountain Council on Latin American Studies, May.

——— (1978) "La Campaña permanente: Mexico's antidrug campaign." J. of Inter-american Studies and World Affairs 20 (May): 107-131.

DOWDY, J. [pseudonym] (1979) "Spice Valley, U.S.A.: marijuana moonshiners." Atlantic Monthly 243 (January): 6ff.

Drug Enforcement (1975-1976) "Mexico." Volume 1 (Fall): 9-13.

Excelsior (1980) January 22.

——— (1978) February 15.

——— (1977) January 16.

——— (1976a) February 4.

——— (1976b) January 8.

Interview (1980) Jalapa, Veracruz: University of Veracruz (January 12).

——— (1979) Mexico, D.F.: U.S. Embassy (February 19).

——— (1978a) Mexico, D.F.: U.S. Embassy (February 14).

——— (1978b) Mexico, D.F.: U.S. Embassy (February 13).

——— (1977) Mexico, D.F.: U.S. Embassy (January 10).

——— (1976a) Mexico, D.F.: Procuraduría General de la República Mexicana (February 13).

——— (1976b) Mexico, D.F.: U.S. Embassy (January 16).

McCONAHAY, M. J. (1976) "Mexico's war on poppies—and peasants." New Times 7 (September 3): 33-38.

Miami Herald (1977) August 28.

New York Times (1976) January 2.
Procuraduría [Mexico, D.F.] (1979) February 16. (mimeo)
PYES, C. (1977) "The war of the flowers." Oui (October 10): 94ff.
U.S. Department of Justice (1976) Press Release, June 8. Washington, DC: Department of Justice.
WRIGHT, L. (1976) "Mainlining the Mexican revolution." New Times 7 (September 3): 21-32.

Richard Craig is Associate Professor of Political Science at Kent State University. His research on international narcotics traffic in the Americas has resulted in his writing The Bracero Program: Interest Groups in Foreign Policy, *published by the University of Texas Press in 1969, as well as numerous articles.*

CAROLINE O.N. MOSER
Development Planning Unit
University College
London, England

WHY THE POOR REMAIN POOR
The Experience of Bogotá Market Traders in the 1970s

The persistence of long-term poverty among sectors of the urban and rural population in less-developed countries (LDCs), as well as in the so-called developed world, has resulted in the formulation of a diversity of interpretations by theoreticians and policy-makers seeking to comprehend the life of the poor, and for political, economic, and moral reasons to develop solutions to alleviate poverty. Recognition of the failure of the Accelerated Growth Model to produce adequate redistribution of resources and income throughout society through the "filter down" effect has led to changes in emphasis in poverty-related research during the past two decades. There has been a shift in focus away from measurements of absolute poverty, the insufficiency of basic needs to ensure survival, toward the clarification of the determinants of relative poverty, the social inequality experienced by those in the bottom segment of the income distribution within a given society. A well-known theoretical debate in the 1960s concerned Oscar Lewis's (1961) "culture of poverty" concept—that the poor have a self-perpetuating subculture with an autonomous dynamic of its own, transmitted from one generation to the next through the process of socialization. This was

---

AUTHOR'S NOTE: The author would like to thank Peter Lloyd, Peter Sollis, and Desmond McNeill for their critical comments.

Journal of Interamerican Studies and World Affairs, Vol. 22 No. 3, August 1980 365-387

widely refuted by, among others, Leacock (1971) and Valentine (1968) who in his alternative interpretation of a "situation of poverty" located the chief source of relative deprivation suffered by poor people in their structural position in the wider social system and in the actions and attitudes of the nonpoor. A more recent and very different approach that has received particular attention from Lipton (1977) emphasizes rural-urban imbalances as the most important source of class conflict in poorer countries.

This article focuses on one particular aspect of the lives of the poor, their strategies for economic survival, and is concerned with the specific case of self-employed urban market sellers. Since it examines the dynamics, growth potential, and constraints on economic expansion of the small-scale retail enterprises at which they work, the most useful theoretical basis would seem that provided by the informal sector/petty commodity production debate.[1] At a theoretical level the informal sector concept with its a priori dualist division of the urban economy has been widely dismissed as of limited utility. From a policy perspective, however, this has not as yet been acknowledged; the ILO and the World Bank, which have been most important in popularizing the concept, still use it as a model for their policies designed to alleviate urban poverty.[2] It was a recognition by the late 1960s that "accelerated growth" models were not solving the problems of income redistribution, poverty, and unemployment in LDCs which resulted in the ILO World Employment Program, committing governments to "active employment policies," with strategies focusing on employment as a major policy objective in its own right. In a series of studies at country, city, and sector level (including the 1970 Colombia Plan), employment rather than unemployment was identified as the problem, and the "working poor" emphasized as a "target group" requiring particular attention. Since the majority of these tended to find their livelihood outside wage employment, the productive role of the informal sector was emphasized.[3]

From a dualist perspective, recognition of the potential for an "evolutionary" low-income sector has led it to be considered the key to the solution of Third World employment problems.

However, while sophisticated measurement techniques continue to categorize and enumerate the characteristics of the two sectors and policy-oriented studies advocate the direct intervention of the state in implementing reforms and fiscal measures to increase informal sector growth, critics increasingly question the informal sector's ability to generate employment. Thus it is maintained that the informal sector does not have an autonomous dynamic of its own and that the level of capital accumulation possible is constrained by structural factors in the total socioeconomic system, so that small-scale activities tend to participate in economic growth in a "dependent subordinate" way with the resulting tendency toward "involutionary" rather than evolutionary" growth.[4]

At a theoretical level, an alternative approach conceptualizes the urban economy in terms of a continuum of productive activities, with complex linkages and dependent relationships between production and distribution systems. A framework with greater utility for handling the complexities of internal differentiation, diverse and dependent linkages, the social as well as technical relations of production has been developed, based on petty commodity production, a form of production that exists "at the margins" of the capitalist mode of production, but nevertheless is "integrated" into it and subordinate to it. Studies such as those by Gerry (1974), Williams and Tumusiime-Mutebile (1978), and King (1974) have clarified the important function of petty commodity production within the capitalist mode of production for the maintenance of low levels of subsistence and the low cost of labor reproduction, through a variety of mechanisms such as the provision of goods and services at highly competitive prices below their real value.

In view of the proliferating body of critical literature on the "informal sector" concept, it might seem of limited relevance to refer to it yet again. However, it must be emphasized that the bulk of criticism remains largely at the level of macro a priori theoretical assertions and counter-assertions with limited empirical data over any time period on how far structural linkages between different scale enterprises are exploitative or benign or on the extent to which they change. Until there is sufficient concrete evidence on the subordinate nature of small-scale enterprises, international agencies such as the ILO and World Bank, as well as regimes in LDCs seeking palliative ameliorating measures to reduce poverty, may continue to use the "informal sector" as a policy tool.

In the evaluation of macro theory and the policies that emanate from them, individual macro studies can provide no more than examples of "apt illustration"; a series of studies is necessary if general conclusions are to be made. Therefore, the intention in this article is no more than to attempt to contribute evidence at the micro level which will enable conflicting theories and their attendant policy measures to be assessed. This it aims to do through the presentation of longitudinal comparative data on the dynamics of small-scale marketing enterprises in Bogotá, Colombia, the constraints on expansion, and the levels of accumulation possible over time.[5] It seeks to help determine the degree to which enterprises such as these are capable of autonomous growth and identify both the nature of the structural linkages between different levels of marketing and their changes over time, and in this way the degree to which wider outside constraints determine the involutionary nature of the market and consequently why these poor remain poor.

The Plaza San Juan and Its Sellers[6]

Within the urban centers of Latin America, market systems with complex structures exist, comprising various categories of individual market places, wholesale and retail, daily and periodic. One such market place within the Bogotá market system, which I call the Plaza San Juan, is a small daily retail outlet mainly for fresh foodstuffs and situated in one of the residential suburbs of the city. It is one of the poorest markets in Bogotá and performs a dual function as a center for commodity distribution and a means of employment for certain sectors of the urban population.

The Bogotá market system is controlled and administered by the *Empresa Distrital de Servicios Públicos* (EDIS), a public corporation responsible for such other public works as slaughterhouses and street cleaning. In 1970 the market system consisted of the wholesale marketing complex, called *Plaza España* (stretching over an area of 6 square miles and including up to 700 wholesalers and several thousand bulk breakers and retailers), 14 daily retail markets, and 22 periodic markets. The Plaza San Juan is one of the older smaller markets, consisting of a disorderly arrangement of homemade *puestos* (stalls). It was built in 1935 and by 1970 was divided into two parts—a dark and cold interior market with 25 puestos, and behind it an uncovered area with 65 puestos. It is situated in a long-established but rapidly changing neighborhood located about 15 blocks from the commercial city center on the lower slope of the Montserate mountain. Until recently it was a predominantly low-class area with multioccupied dwellings rented by the room, a fact reflected in the buying patterns of customers, the vast majority of whom buy on a daily basis. The recent rapid growth of the city has made the suburb, with its proximity to the city center, increasingly attractive to the professional middle classes and there has been an accompanying large increase in the construction of owner-occupied houses and apartment blocks. In 1970 a total of about 100 people worked in the Plaza daily—puesto owners, *cargeros* (load carriers), family and nonfamily assistants. The 90 puestos comprised small numbers selling goods such as meat, fish, nonperishable grains, clothing, and cooked foods. The largest category was composed of the 60 puestos selling fresh produce, fruit, vegetables, and staples, which formed a distinct group situated in the external market and on which the following comparative discussion is based.

THE ORGANIZATION OF MARKET STALLS

The sellers are not peasant producers selling their own produce but are what Mintz (1964) calls "professional sellers," middlemen who depend on marketing for their living. Neither are they itinerant traders buying rurally to sell in the city; rather they are entirely involved in the urban market system, buying wholesale in order to retail in the local market. They do not operate their puestos with a random hodgepodge of different produce but make rational decisions in the choice of what they sell, within the limitations imposed by personal (i.e., specific) and wider (i.e., generalizable) constraints. Each particular fruit, vegetable, or staple has specific selling characteristics with different demand and supply factors and related risks and profit margins. In 1970, I identified five distinct categories of puesto operations and ranked puesto size from largest to smallest (only of relative value and not related to any size structure outside the Plaza San Juan). A significant correlation emerged between the size of puesto and type of produce sold. As Table 1 shows, distinct patterns were identified in the relationship between these two factors which together determined the economic basis of the enterprise. The evidence showed that the larger the scale of operation, the greater the tendency to sell fruit, or fruit and staples, with their greater capital requirements and higher risks but larger profit margins.

Conversely, the smaller the seller, the greater the tendency to sell only vegetables with their low capital requirements and risks but also lower profit margins. In between the two were the medium-scale sellers who tended toward combinations of staples (potatoes, *yuca* [sweet manioc], or *plátano* [plantain]) and vegetables or fruit and vegetables. The sellers were by no means a "homogeneous group" but formed a continuum from very small peddlers of vegetables to the large-scale operations with a wide assortment of fruit and staples.

Diversity in the scale of puesto operation was ultimately the result of differences of capital resources available to individuals. All the sellers aimed to maximize profits, but larger-scale operators, who were more advantageously placed in terms of their capital and personal constraints and consequently able to take larger risks, were able to make regularly larger profits both per unit of capital and in total than smaller-scale sellers. The result, simplified into two polar types, was articulation of two

TABLE 1
Numbers of Sellers in Each Category of Produce Sold
in Terms of Size and Operation

SIZE OF OPERATION		Numbers of Sellers in Each Category of Produce Sold: Fruit only	Staple & Vegetables	Fruit & Vegetables	Vegetables only	Total
Large	2(potatoes) 2(plátano)	4	1(potatoes) 1(plátano)	2		12
Medium	1(plátano)	3	3(plátano) 3(yuca) 1(potatoes)	11	7	29
Small		1	1(yuca)	4	13	19

differing incentives, with sellers utilizing the market for two very different ends: Large-scale sellers operated puestos geared to the maximization of profit and expansion and were upwardly mobile in that the possibility existed of breaking out of the market. Small-scale sellers, who were caught in the vicious circle of small amounts of capital, uneconomic wholesale buying, and very low profit margins, operated below the level at which expansion was possible and operated to maintain the status quo and not become insolvent.

THE SOCIAL CHARACTERISTICS OF SELLERS

Sellers of different scale *puesto* operations not only tended to retail different products but showed marked differences in their social characteristics. Depending on the age and sex of the individual seller at the time of his entry into the market, so depended the constraints under which he was forced to operate and his goals in undertaking this type of work. From extensive data general characteristics can be summarized. Old men unable to continue as rural agricultural laborers or urban manual laborers were attracted to marketing at the end of their working lives. With heavy family financial commitments they set up with limited accumulated capital and little hope of expanding their enterprises. Most were small-scale sellers, as were old women, of many of whom were widowed or deserted and also without capital. However, the majority of women sellers entered when young, often because they were the sole supporter of a number of dependents. Many started their working lives in domestic service, but had been forced out by the time their second child arrived. Large family commitments limited the likelihood of accumulating sufficient capital to increase the size of their enterprise, so they tended to be medium- or small-scale sellers. Younger men entered the market with a different intention reflected in their larger scale of operation and shorter length of stay. With high unemployment and low wages they chose marketing as the best career option, generally after trying out other jobs. On entry into the market many were able to use family contacts and borrow credit. They saw it as "settling down" but with smaller family commitments and the possibility of accumulating capital, they also saw it as a "stepping stone" into more lucrative areas of marketing.

The Plaza San Juan 1978

Categorization of the sellers in the Plaza San Juan as a heterogeneous group of workers with differential access to resources made it possible in 1970 to identify, amid the overall involutionary situation, those "healthy" entrepreneurs with the potential for growth most likely to accumulate sufficient resources to expand their enterprises either in the market or into other economic enterprises.

In 1978 slightly less than half of the original 60 fruit, vegetable, and staple sellers remained in the market. Of the 34 sellers no longer there, 13 had died from natural causes or were murdered and killed in accidents, most of whom were elderly women. Of the remaining 21 sellers who left the market for other reasons (one-third of the original market work force), more men than women and more small-scale sellers than large-scale sellers had left. Although there is close interdependent relationship between their different motives for leaving, so that it is not always possible to distinguish clearly the causal determinant, as Table 2 shows, 38% left because of insolvency (none of whom were large-scale sellers), 19% left because of ill-health, and 28% because of alternative or better jobs.

In this last category all were men, mainly large-scale sellers who went to work in other retail markets or in wholesale marketing. one of these is Miguel who now rents a cigarette kiosk down on *Septima*, the large main road below the market. He left not because of insolvency but because he found the logistics of running a market puesto too taxing in his old age. Another seller, Tomás, left simply to see if he could have better luck as a *fritango* (a cooked-food seller) in another retail market. So it is only in the case of the remaining four sellers that there is clear evidence of upward mobility and it must be emphasized that this is based on information of those still in the market.

But what had happened to the old sellers still in the market, 26 of whom still operate their puestos? Puesto operations had declined in 42% of the cases and a further 42% had remained static, while only in the remaining 15% was there any indication of expansion of marketing enterprise. Significantly enough none of these were large-scale sellers. This suggests that there is only a limited level of expansion possible in the market, after which sellers have to move out of this level of economic activity.

Three very brief case studies provide contributory micro evidence by showing, at the individual level, some of the constraints on expansion.

JOSÉ

In 1970 José was one of the largest-scale sellers in the market, operating a centrally located puesto in which he sold fruit and potatoes—a combination with large operating capital require-

TABLE 2
Characteristics of Sellers Leaving the Market Between 1970 and 1978

	Male			Female			
MOTIVE	15-29	30-49	50+	15-29	30-49	50+	TOTAL
Death			3		3	7	13
Ill-health			1			3	4
Insolvency		1	1	2	1	3	8
Alternative or better job	1	1	4				6
Thrown out		1			1		2
No information		1					1
Total							34

ments but also large profit margins. After an extremely diverse job history both rurally and in other urban areas in agricultural wage labor, contraband, factory work, and marketing he had come into the Plaza San Juan eight years previously. He was 40 years old, married with three children under 7, and lived in two rented rooms near the market. In 1970 José seemed in an ideal position to expand his enterprise with large numbers of fixed clients and a prestigious reputation. By 1978 his situation had changed drastically. His puesto had declined; he now sells a mixture of fruit and vegetables requiring less capital inputs but with decreased profit margins. Although complaining of increased competition in the market and inflation and the effects of the increasing cash flow necessary to stock his puesto, nevertheless the most important changes have been personal ones. He now has five children, his puesto was very badly robbed 18 months before by nightwatchmen, and both he and his wife have had a number of serious illnesses. His wife is still in the hospital while he continues to save for a serious spleen operation. The enormous drain of medical expenses has meant that he no longer has sufficient operational capital to stock a large-scale puesto, and is downwardly mobile.

ROSA

In 1970 Rosa was a medium-scale fruit seller who had been in the market for five years, after working in domestic service. She was 39, her husband was a house painter, and they had six children, five of whom were studying. In 1978 her position had remained unchanged despite the fact that she had moved her puesto to a more strategic position and was now selling vegetables and staples instead of fruit. Although two of her children are now working and contributing to the household income and a third is helping her in the market, with two children still at school and a third enrolled at one of the city's universities, she is still investing considerable resources in education. In addition, her husband had been unemployed, owning to ill-health, for the last two years. Consequently her puesto operation had remained static neither expanding nor contracting.

MANUEL

In 1970 Manuel was a medium-scale *yuca* seller who, after working as a rural agricultural laborer and a cigarette *ambulante* (street seller) in Bogotá, had been in the market ten years. He was 55, lived locally in rented rooms, and was married with 15 children. Six of these were still living at home while three others had been left to be educated in his home town in Santander. Manuel had prospered, and in 1978 was operating a larger thriving *puesto* with diversification into additional staples. In the market his success is attributed to the fact that he works hard, saves, and neither drinks nor smokes. However, in addition, his outlay on education has been considerably reduced in the intervening period, with only three children at school and the rest working, mostly married with their own families. With the proceeds from selling a smallholding he inherited in Santander, Manuel had bought a house in the neighborhood and set himself up as a landlord. Not only is he upwardly mobile in the market but he has used these additional resources to diversify into other investments, again suggesting the limits on expansion in the market.

These three case studies provide examples of personal constraints at different points in individual life cycles which prevent sellers from expanding their enterprises. The crucial role that good fortune or bad luck appears to play in the lives of people who live so close to the margins of survival means that they do not have sufficient capital base to cushion themselves against crises and are pushed into insolvency by any small incident. Education and medical expenses, as well as rent (which I have not detailed here), are the biggest drains on the resources of the poor, which in turn influence the amount of running capital available and consequently the potential for generating autonomous growth of their enterprises.

Information at the market level concerning the long-term survival of this level of economic activity in the city—the low-income retail market—is provided by a comparison of the socioeconomic characteristics of sellers and categorization of market puestos between 1970 and 1978. With 37 new fruit, vegetable, and staples sellers, this group of sellers in the market now totals 63. Comparative statistical data show that younger, more educated men are increasingly moving into this type of self-employment, the number of sellers under 35 having doubled in 8 years. Therefore the traditional role of small-scale marketing as a "refuge occupation" that absorbs the labor surplus—the unskilled, old and women—is changing. These sellers are increasingly rendered uncompetitive and forced out through insolvency, to be replaced by the younger more "skilled" professional seller. EDIS information supports this view with their data on the increasing insolvency rates and puesto turnover in the market over the past few years. Although wage employment in Bogotá has remained static during this period, showing cyclical rather than long-term trends, these statistics are generally very unreliable in terms of self-employment, subemployment, and underemployment as the 1970 ILO report on Colombia showed.

The evidence from the Plaza San Juan certainly suggests that younger, more skilled men are finding it increasingly difficult to find wage employment. The increased use of family networks to find jobs is another indicator of this trend. In 1970, 36% of the sellers had relations in the market; by 1978, this number had increased to 54%, many with two or three members of nuclear or extended families but almost always operating individual puestos. Also over the eight-year period there has been considerable increase in the use of child labor with many more sellers relying on the assistance of their children, particularly during the highly competitive peak selling periods of the week. Traditionally this type of residual unpaid family labor has been called upon when economic conditions deteriorate.

During the 1970-1977 period, Colombia underwent massive inflation. Despite a 40% increase in Gross Domestic Product with exports tripling, the cost of living rose by 350% and the national food index by 470% during the same period. middle- and upper-income groups certainly benefited from economic expansion and the relative numbers of the very poor may well have declined, but "the absolute number of people without access to services and living near subsistence income levels increased" (Gilbert, 1978a, 1978b). Statistical evidence shows that real income of manufacturing workers in 1977 was worth only 84% of its value in 1970, and there is comparable data for other areas of wage sector employment. Without longitudinal statistical information relating to those outside wage employment it remains impossible to state categorically the degree to which they have succeeded in profiting from the inflationary situation. There are indicators in the case of the Plaza San Juan to suggest that these small-scale retailers have suffered from inflation because of increases in, for instance, market puesto rents, transport costs, and house rents as well as comparable food price increases. An important change has been in the categories of puesto operation, reflecting both sellers' increasingly restricted access to operating capital and consumer purchasing power in the neighborhood. There has been a marked shift in demand away from fruit sales, especially those high profit "opportunist" products which in low-income areas are bought as weekend luxuries. Increasingly sellers are now selling only vegetables and staples (with expansion in demand for potatoes and decline in plátano, no longer a low-income staple). With increasing competition for limited resources in the market, another trend has been the decline in the specialist seller with known reputation and fixed clients, more concerned with quality than small differences in competitive prices; the vast majority of sellers are now merely *"lichigo"* sellers who stock a little of everything.

Despite cases of individual mobility the overall picture is one of increasing poverty, with sufficient indicators to show that sellers in the market are poorer than they were eight years ago. Of the original 60 sellers, 39 are still in employment either in the market or elsewhere. Tabulations from various sources based on weekly turnover figures, personal observation, and life history information suggest, as an optimistic assessment, that in terms of their enterprises half are downwardly mobile, a quarter remain static, and only the last quarter have in any way increased their scale of operation in the intervening eight years. Generally, age-income profiles for those with less than secondary education show declining income with increased age. This is certainly the case here because the demanding logistics of running this type of enterprise is one important mechanism of income decline. As Table 3 shows, however, the situation is more complex since there are also more upwardly mobile sellers in the 50-plus category than in other age categories, while at the same time there are also younger sellers who are downwardly mobile.

Productive Enterprise Dynamics

The persistence of long-term poverty among low-income workers such as these can therefore be explained in terms of general causal factors such as lack of access to capital, increased competition resulting from unemployment and rural urban migration of unskilled workers, and the prohibitive drain on resources of house rent, medical expenses, and education. These then can be identified as important constraints limiting the potential for autonomous growth of small-scale enterprises and consequently for increasing employment. But does this provide us

TABLE 3
Mobility Characteristics of Sellers Still Working in 1978
in Terms of Age

MOBILITY CHARACTERISTICS	AGE IN 1978 15-29	30-49	50+	TOTAL
Upwardly Mobile				
Still in Plaza San Juan	-	1	3	4
Working Elsewhere	-	2	2	4
Static				
Still in Plaza San Juan	-	7	4	11
Working Elsewhere	-	-	1	1
Downwardly Mobile				
Still in Plaza San Juan	1	4	6	11
Working Elsewhere	-	1	7	8
TOTAL				39

with a sufficient explanation of the dynamics of productive enterprises at this level and the extent to which the relationship between these and larger-scale enterprises are exploitative or benign? This is of particular interest in Bogotá during this period, coinciding as it partially does with President Pastrana's Four Strategy Development Policy which, among other policy measures, specifically prescribed the use of construction programs to solve unemployment and redistribute income. Since small-scale enterprises such as those in the Plaza San Juan are not autonomous entities (as a dualist informal-sector approach would suggest) but part of a continuum of productive activities, an examination of the changes over the past eight years in their direct and indirect linkages with large-scale retail enterprises and their dependent relationship within the wholesale marketing system of Bogotá must also be included in the analysis. Obviously a complexity of factors are significant and I can only refer briefly to three of the most important here.

THE WHOLESALE MARKETING SYSTEM

For twenty years up until 1972 the *Plaza España* was the principal wholesale market in Bogotá. A commercial and residential complex stretching over a six-mile radius in the city center, it included large numbers of *bodegas* (warehouses) as well as ten principal *plazas*. It was principally controlled by EDIS and had evolved gradually along with the growth of the city without any government planning. Inherent in its development were such problems as inefficient distribution of merchandise and severe transport and circulation congestion.

In order to "modernize and revolutionize the entire wholesale marketing system in the city," in 1972 the new Wholesale Market—the *Central de Abastos*—was opened in Ciudad Kennedy. It was a vast modern complex partially based on the Paris wholesale market and consisted of some 22 warehouses, administrative buildings, banks, and so on. It is controlled and administered by Corobastos, a semipublic agency and its subsidiary, Cabsa. During the reform policy of the late 1960s, President Lleras' administration increasingly encouraged state intervention to promote large-scale capitalist development, with centralized agencies established to limit local level control. Corobastos, which has taken over from EDIS in running the Bogotá wholesale marketing system, provides one such example. Here is found the penetration of state and finance capital along with merchant capital in the distribution sector. Corobastos is defined as a Mixed-Economy Corporation, but with 84% of its capital provided by Cofiagro, Banco Ganadero, Idema, Incora, and Banco Cafatero, there is a fundamental investment by the public sector.[8] It is, however, intended that by 1979 private sector capital should constitute 45%. However, private-sector representatives, mainly large-scale wholesalers, in fact already have excessive power relative to the low percentage of capital subscribed because of their unified front in relation to those of the atomized public sector (Silva, 1976). Rationalization of the wholesale marketing system promotes the interest of large-scale capital with an inevitable developing tendency for economic concentration of the wholesale market in the hands of certain groups. In the simultaneous development of monopolistic and oligopolistic pricing practices, it is the small-scale producer and retailer who is increasingly placed in a disadvantageous position.

The effects of this new wholesale marketing system on the Plaza San Juan have been considerable. While sellers have benefited from a more efficient wholesale market in terms of produce quality and speed of buying, they have had to contend with resultant increase in traveling time and transport costs, both bus and haulage. In addition it would appear that their complaints of increasing price fixing by mafia-like *"Lagartos"* (lizards) wholesalers are justified. Other complaints such as those that monopolistic buying practices by supermarkets are cutting off their access to particular products, are however, more difficult to assess. Nevertheless, there is obviously increasing appropriation of surplus by large-scale capitalist enterprises in the wholesale market. With the linkages between them and small-scale sellers essentially exploitative, the effect is to reduce the profit margins of the latter.

SUPERMARKETS

Despite the fact that sellers in small-scale markets assess prices without including labor costs, their prices are becoming increasingly uncompetitive in comparison with other retail outlets. Lack of access to capital and the consequent small-scale split buying make them unable to compete with corporate chains, such as Ley, and with hypermarket and supermarket chains such as Carulla, which tend to operate with direct contractual linkages to rural producers, bypassing much of the Bogotá wholesale complex. Increasingly the competitive prices and hygienic displays of supermarket fresh produce has attracted the upper income groups who represent considerable spending power in the city. But they have long been deterred from shopping in markets because of their reputation for violence and fluctuating prices. Of far greater importance over the past eight years has been the growth and development of consumer-owned cooperatives and above all of *Cajas de Compensación Familiares* (Family Subsidy Funds). In Bogotá, the two most important are Colsubsidios and

Cafam. Labour legislation requiring large companies to invest 4% of their payroll into a fund which in turn pays a family subsidy to workers has resulted in the development of a private sector welfare system, clinics, recreation centers, and particularly in the large-scale development of so-called nonprofit making super-market consortiums which now control over 30% of foodstuff retailing to Bogotá. They not only provide competition for private sector supermarkets but more importantly provide cheaper retail outlets for industrial wage laborers who previously would have used small independent neighborhood stores and a plaza such as the San Juan. This provides another example of the increasing penetration of merchant capital into the distribution sector which, because of efficiency and access to large-scale capital, is increasingly taking over large areas of the market.

LAND VALUES

Petty commodity production can continue to exist only where it is not considered profitable for large-scale capital to do so. Thus, the Plaza San Juan continues to exist as long as it provides an outlet for low-income groups who, since they cannot afford the transport costs or the scale of buying involved in supermarket purchases, buy uneconomically on a daily basis. However, close proximity of the San Juan suburb to the city center is increasingly changing the class composition of the area and consequently the spending power in the market. With a well-known international hotel down the road and high-rise flats around, land speculation in the areas is increasing. EDIS recognizes that the market is declining as more low-income inhabitants of the area are forced, through rent increases or forced eviction, to move to the south of the city. At the same time it is interesting to note that EDIS also admits to an increasing proliferation of "illegal" markets in the south. This indicates that like King's (1974) "moving frontier," small-scale enterprises will continue to mushroom in areas where it is still unprofitable for large-scale enterprises to penetrate. Overall, however, the long-term process is first one of growth and then of destruction as it is forced out by large-scale capital enterprises (Bienefeld, 1975).

It is recognized that there are several limitations in a general description such as this in which the nature of the dependent linkages have not been traced out in detail and the various factors have not been weighted according to their differing particular effect on declining puesto sales. Nevertheless, it would appear that the dependent subordinate relationship between this level of petty retailing and the wider capitalist marketing structure, both wholesale and retail, has meant that with decreasing access to resources and the growth of monopolistic practices, the level of economic activity that occurs in the Plaza San Juan has become increasingly involutionary. It is unable to generate growth but only to reproduce the existing conditions and scale of operations frequently at the expense of its cost of labor (such as the increased use of unpaid family labor) and standard of living (such as working longer hours). The informal sector approach, which categorizations two separate sectors, assumes they each have an autonomous potential for growth and is primarily concerned with the flow of labor between them; it tends to underestimate the importance of the articulation of subordination/domination relationships within the capitalist system.

Conclusion

In this article it has been shown that the lack of upward mobility of the sellers in Bogotá's Plaza San Juan between 1970 and 1978 must be analyzed in terms of both individual and more general reasons. At the individual level three causal factors were identified as crucial in determining the level of accumulation possible: first, those relating to *life crises* (illness, legal problems as against uncommon windfalls such as inheritance of property); second, those relating to the different stages in the *life cycle* (children at some points a help, at others a hindrance, old age and declining health reducing the physical ability to operate a market stall), and third, those relating to *alternative investments* (where capital necessary for accumulation is withdrawn from the enterprise and, for reasons of future security, is invested in such areas as children's education, ownership of property, or the diversification in to other risk-spreading enterprises).

However, individual constraints such as these occur at all times and on their own provide inadequate explanation of why during the period under discussion in particular these poor remained poor. Examination of more general reasons indicates that inflation and the decline in real wages were time specific insofar as the assumption cannot be a priori be made that they were always present, whereas changes in the wholesale marketing system and growing competition from supermarket outlets were both time and place specific and were related to the particular development policies undertaken by the government at the time. Therefore, it is ultimately in the light of these more general reasons that the individual failures of the sellers in the Plaza San Juan to accumulate sufficient resources to expand their enterprises, must be reviewed if the experiences in one market are to have any wider significance.

The overall decline in prosperity in the Plaza San Juan during the period 1970-1978 was accompanied by an increase in the number of workers both in this market and in retail marketing generally (such as the illegal markets in southern Bogotá) during the same period. Few of the sellers who left the market for other employment had been absorbed into the wage-earning proletariat of, for instance, supermarket or factory work, while at the same time those sellers recruited into the market were increasingly younger, better educated men who had been unable to get into wage-sector employment. These conclusions concerning the experiences of sellers in only one of Bogotá's many markets must remain at the level of an individual micro-study until other longitudinal studies of the urban labor force are undertaken. Nevertheless there is sufficient evidence to indicate that the underlying processes affecting this type and scale of petty commodity enterprise is not unique but common to other enterprises in the city, as well as in other Third World cities.

As it becomes increasingly profitable for large-scale capital to penetrate into the different areas of wholesale and retail marketing of fresh foodstuffs (including supermarkets), fewer petty producers make the transition to small capitalist production. For a small number the process is one of proletarianization (Gerry, 1974) as they enter wage employment within the marketing sector. For the vast majority, however, no alternative to independent selling exists. Some manage to survive by working harder and existing on less, while others (at a greater rate than ever before) are forced out by insolvency and join the proliferating numbers of street hawkers, augmenting their income by begging, prostitution, and theft. In both cases the process is one of further impoverishment and marginalization.

NOTES

1. For a detailed critique of the informal sector/petty commodity production debate, see Moser (1978).

2. Among a large number of publications see in particular ILO (1972a, 1976).

3. See in particular ILO (1972b).

4. See, for instance, Bienefeld (1975) and Scott (1979).

5. The empirical data was collected through participant observation, in a Bogotá retail market throughout 1970, which was then revisited in March-April 1978. This provided an opportunity to examine the lives of a group of low-income urban workers with an eight-year interval.

6. This section is no more than a brief abstract from very detailed material on the sellers and their market operations, which is necessary as comparative background information (see Moser, 1975, 1977).

7. In a world of increasing scepticism over the validity of detailed statistical information, the importance of anthropological observation should not be dismissed as unscientific. In the case of the San Juan sellers, an extremely detailed knowledge of the sellers, and their puesto operations and marketing procedure meant that on revisiting the market after eight years, significant changes could be quickly assessed and then confirmed or denied by the sellers themselves.

8. (The figures on capital composition were cited in Corobastos in December 1977.) *Cofiagro* (33.16) is the *Corporación financiera Agropecuaris y de exportaciones,* a mixed-economy bank in charge of providing credit for food production distribution and exports, Banco Ganadero (21.69) and Banco Cafatero (5.46) are both state controlled banks linked to two of Colombia's most important primary exports, cattle and coffee. Idema (13.52) is the *Instituto de Mercadeo Agropecuario,* a public agency controlling prices and direct-intervention programs on food. Incora is the *Instituto Colombiano de la Reforma Agraria,* a public agency in charge of agrarian reform programs.

9. In a detailed survey in 1974, Silva (1976) calculated that "independent plaza retailers" share of the food market had declined from 28.1% to 24.8% between 1970 and 1974 (p. 203) and projected that it would decline to 14% by 1990 (p. 252).

REFERENCES

BIENEFELD, M. (1975) "The informal sector and peripheral capitalism: the case of Tanzania." IDS Bulletin 6 (February): 53-73.

Corobastos (1977) Informe de Actividades de 1977. Bogotá: Corporación de Abastos de Bogotá S.A.

GERRY, C. (1974) "Petty producers and the urban economy: a case study of Dakar." ILO World Employment Programme Working Paper 8. International Labor Office, Geneva.

GILBERT, A. (1978a) "Bogotá: politics, planning and the crisis of lost opportunities," pp. 87-126 in W. A. Cornelius and R. V. Kemper, Metropolitan South America: The Challenge and the Response. Beverly Hills, CA: Sage.

——— (1978b) mmm mmm 09.32

——— (1978b) "Carrar la brecha or business as usual? The Colombian economy under Alfonso López Michelson." (unpublished)

ILO [International Labor Organization] (1976) World Employment Programme: Research in Retrospect and Prospect. Geneva: Author.

——— (1972a) Scope, Approach and Content of Research Oriented Activities of the World Employment Programme. Geneva: Author.

——— (1972b) Employment, Income and Equality: A Strategy for Increasing Productive Employment in Kenya. Geneva: Author.

——— (1970) Towards Full Employment: A Programme for Colombia. Geneva: Author.

KING, K. (1974) "Kenya's informal machine makers: a study of small-scale industry in Kenya's emergent artisan class." World Development 2 (March): 9-28.

LEACOCK, E. B. [ed.] (1971) The Culture of Poverty: A Critique. New York: Simon & Schuster.

LEWIS, O. (1961) The Children of Sánchez. New York: Random House.

LIPTON, M. (1977) Why Poor People Stay Poor. London: Temple Smith.

MINTZ, S. (1964) "Market systems and wholesale societies." Econ. Development and Social Change 12: 444-448.

MOSER, C. (1978) "Informal sector or petty commodity production: dualism or dependence in urban development?" World Development 6 (September/October): 1041-1064.

——— (1977) "The dual economy and marginality debate and the contribution of microanalysis: market sellers in Bogotá." Development and Change 8 (October): 465-489.

——— (1975) "Differentiation and mobility in a Bogotá retail market." Ph.D. dissertation, University of Sussex.

SCOTT, A. M. (1979) "Who are the self-employed?" pp. 105-132 in R. Bromley and C. Gerry (eds.) Casual Work and Poverty in Third World Cities. London: John Wiley.

SILVA, A. (1976) "Evaluation of food market reform: Corobastos, Bogotá." Ph.D. dissertation, Michigan State University.

VALENTINE, C. (1968) Culture of Poverty: Critique and Counter Proposals. Chicago: Univ. of Chicago Press.

WILLIAMS, G. and E. TUMUSIIME-MUTEBILE (1978) "Capitalist and petty commodity production in Nigeria: a note." World Development 6 (September/October): 1103-1104.

Caroline O.N. Moser, currently a lecturer at the Development Planning Unit, University College, London, is a social anthropologist who gained her doctorate from a study of low-income urban market sellers in Bogotá, Colombia. Recently she spent eight months in a slum community in Guayaquil, Ecuador, where she carried out research on the politics of access to housing and infrastructure and the subordination of marginalized female workers. Her articles have appeared in numerous periodicals.

STEVEN ELLNER
Department of Economics
Universidad de Oriente
Puerto La Cruz, Venezuela

Comment

LEONARDO RUIZ PINEDA
Acción Democrática's Guerrillero for Liberty

Charles D. Ameringer's article "Leonardo Ruiz Pineda: Leader of the Venezuelan Resistance, 1949-1952," published in the May 1979 issue of the *Journal of Interamerican Studies and World Affairs,* examines Acción Democrática's (AD) deification of its deceased leader after the party returned to power in 1959. According to Ameringer, Ruiz Pineda, as "pacific hero" (1979: 210) and disciple and admirer of Rómulo Betancourt, was ideal material for transformation into a martyr "in the style of Martin Luther King, not Malcolm X" (1979: 230); this glorification was partly in response to the party's breakaway youthful faction which had opted for guerrilla violence. Additional information, however, is needed to complete the picture presented by Ameringer and modify somewhat his basically accurate conclusions. It should be noted that these observations are based on published works which postdate the completion of Ameringer's article.

In the three and a half years that Ruiz Pineda headed the AD clandestine movement, a rivalry developed between him and the party's exile leadership under Rómulo Betancourt. This breach has been commented upon by leading members of other parties (including Jóvito Villalba, president of the Unión Repbulicana Democrática) who maintained regular contact with Ruiz Pineda, as well as by his closest associates in AD (Peña, 1977). Eligio Anzola Anzola, who was the Minister of Interior in the AD government in 1948 and then became a

Journal of Interamerican Studies and World Affairs, Vol. 22 No. 3, August 1980 389-392

leading member of the resistance, vividly described this estrangement as follows:

> Between president Rómulo Betancourt and the secretary general of AD, compañero Leonardo Ruiz Pineda, there was a great separation, not only separation but great discrepancies in the way in which they conducted the movement. Leonardo practically did not communicate with president Betancourt, to the extent that one night . . . I asked him when was the last time he had received a correspondence from Rómulo, and he told me that he did not write to the man and that from now on I should respond to communications from Rómulo because he [Ruiz Pineda] did not want anything to do with Betancourt [Acuña, 1977: 477].

The discord described above in part stemmed from Ruiz Pineda's determination to build a broad-based movement which would encompass the entire opposition, including the Communist party (PVC) (Rangel, 1973: 139; Luzardo, 1961: 6; El Nacional, 1979: D-9). This strategy was reflected in the pact between AD and PVC oil worker leaders, who in May 1950 called a strike with the intention of overthrowing the military government (Dáger, 1979: 129; Mesa, 1978: 210). Betancourt, on the other hand, favored giving priority to the efforts to work with sympathetic elements in the armed forces. In addition, ever since AD's founding in 1941, he had staunchly opposed all forms of cooperation with the Communists (Moleiro, 1978: 151).

In the decade following Pérez Jiménez' overthrow in 1958, AD was racked by three major divisions, the antecedents of which dated back to the previous two decades. Each one of the emergent factions claimed Leonardo Ruiz Pineda as one of their own (Peña, 1979: 129). Of course, it is a futile exercise for historians to attempt to surmise what Ruiz Pineda would have done had he lived to participate in these internal party struggles. Nevertheless, it is a shortcoming of Ameringer's article that the author fails to question AD's contention that Ruiz Pineda belonged to the more conservative pro-Betancourt faction, which retained control of the party through each of the three divisions. The argument that Ruiz Pineda's opposition to violence would have led him to contend against AD's *fidelista* faction is a distortion of his real position. Ruiz Pineda was hardly a Martin Luther King. Ruiz actively participated in plans for an armed insurrection and in fact just weeks before his death he was expecting a massive shipment of arms to the eastern part of Venezuela where the uprising was to begin (Acuña, 1977: 510-511; Rodríguez, 1978: 124).

Ruiz Pineda's willingness to work closely with Communists would have placed him at odds with AD's Betancourt wing, which excluded the PCV from inter-party agreements on national unity in 1958. That Ruiz Pineda would have sided with the *betancourtistas* in the party's subsequent schisms cannot be accepted as a foregone conclusion. The breakaway factions raised the charge of caudillismo—that Betancourt had maintained an iron grip on the party at the expense of internal democracy. This accusation echoed Ruiz Pineda's objection to Betancourt's efforts to control the party's underground through emissaries sent from abroad (Linares, 1978: D-5). Ameringer is certainly correct when he says that "if he [Ruiz Pineda] did not exist, AD would have had to invent him." What needs to be added is that the AD-induced Ruiz Pineda myth, like so many myths, clouds historical reality and must therefore be critically judged by historians writing on the subject.

REFERENCES

ACUNA, G. (1977) Cuando mataron a Ruiz Pineda. Caracas: Ediciones Rafael Arévalo González.

AMERINGER, C. (1979) "Leonardo Ruiz Pineda: leader of the Venezuelan resistance, 1949-1952." J. of Interamerican Studies 21 (May): 209-232.

DÁGER, J. (1979) Testigo de excepción: En las trincheras de la resistencia, 1948-1955. Caracas: Ediciones Centauro.

LINARES, L. (1978) "Metródico y organizado Alberto Carnevali destacó en la resistencia a Pérez Jiménez." El Nacional, May 20: D-5.

LUZARDO, R. (1961) Alfredo: Breve historia con notas marginales. Caracas: Tipografía Chacao.

MESA, S. (1978) Por un caballo y una mujer. Valencia: Vadell Hermanos.

MOLEIRO, M. (1978) El partído del pueblo: Crónica de un fraude. Valencia: Vadell Hermanos.

El Nacional (1979) "Raúl Ramos Giménez: un ejemplo de dignidad en la política venezolana." April 26: D-9.

PEÑA, A. [interviewer] (1979) Conversaciones con Carlos Andres Pérez. Vol. 1. Caracas: Ateneo de Caracas.

——— (1977) "Cuando los tanques aplastan las instituciones democráticas." Interview with Jóvito Villalba. El Nacional. Nov. 30: 1-C.

RANGEL, D. A. (1973) [written in 1958] "Leonardo, el de la estupenda hazaña," pp. 131-140 in José Agustín Catalá (ed.) Leonardo Ruiz Pineda: Guerrillero de la libertada. Caracas: Ediciones Centauro.

RODRÍGUEZ ITURBE, J. (1978) Crónica de la década militar: I, 1948-1953." Nueva Política 28-29 (April-September): 87-206.

Steven Ellner is Assistant Professor in the Department of Economics at the Universidad de Oriente at Puerto La Cruz, Venezuela. He received his Ph.D. from the Department of History at the University of New Mexico in 1979.

THIS ISSUE IS DEVOTED TO:
PUBLIC ENTERPRISE IN LATIN AMERICA
guest editors ALFRED H. SAULNIERS
THOMAS J. TREBAT
JAN PETER WOGART

Vol. 22 No. 4
November 1980

JOURNAL OF INTERAMERICAN STUDIES

and WORLD AFFAIRS

A Publication of the Center for Advanced International Studies,

The University of Miami

SAGE PUBLICATIONS

Journal of INTERAMERICAN STUDIES
and WORLD AFFAIRS

The editors and publisher wish to acknowledge with gratitude the assistance and encouragement of the Center for Advanced International Studies, University of Miami, in providing ancillary services and support for this journal.

Journal of
INTERAMERICAN
STUDIES
and WORLD AFFAIRS

Vol. 22
No. 4
November
1980

CONTENTS

THIS ISSUE IS DEVOTED TO:
PUBLIC ENTERPRISE IN LATIN AMERICA
Guest Editors ALFRED H. SAULNIERS
THOMAS J. TREBAT
JAN PETER WOGART

Introduction
THOMAS J. TREBAT and JAN PETER WOGART 395

State Enterprise in a Liberal Regime: The Banco do Brasil, 1905-1930
STEVEN TOPIK 401

The Changing Nature of Development Banking in Brazil
WERNER BAER and ANNIBAL V. VILLELA 423

ENCI: Peru's Bandied Monopolist
ALFRED H. SAULNIERS 441

Public Enterprises in Latin America: An Annotated List of Recent Research Papers
ALFRED H. SAULNIERS 463

Decision-Making in a Public Marketing Enterprise: CONASUPO in Mexico
MARYE THARP HILGER 471

REVIEW ESSAY

Integration and Regional Development: The Case of the Commonwealth Caribbean
RALPH PARAGG 495

BOOKS RECEIVED 501

Index to Volume 22 509

SAGE PUBLICATIONS / *Beverly Hills* *London*

Policy: The **JOURNAL OF INTERAMERICAN STUDIES AND WORLD AFFAIRS** reflects the interests of the scholarly community and interested public concerned with the social, economic, political, and cultural aspects of life in Latin America (including the Caribbean), particularly in those instances where the subject is of concern to more than one of the traditional disciplines. As these concerns change, so will the content of the journal.

Articles which have special relevance for interrelationships between American nations and of those nations with the rest of the world will be given special consideration. An effort will be made to include occasional articles that state an unusual or even discordant position on a subject of broad interest to be supplemented by critical comments of authorities representing differing positions on the topic. The editors continue to welcome articles by scholars from all parts of the world.

Manuscripts should be submitted in duplicate to: Editor, **JOURNAL OF INTERAMERICAN STUDIES AND WORLD AFFAIRS,** Box 24-8134, University of Miami, Coral Gables, Florida 33124. Manuscripts should be typewritten, double-spaced, with footnotes, references, tables, and charts on separate pages, and should follow the current journal style. A brief biographical paragraph describing each author's current affiliation, research interests, and recent publications should accompany the manuscript.

Correspondence regarding book reviews should be sent directly to: Book Review Editor, **JOURNAL OF INTERAMERICAN STUDIES AND WORLD AFFAIRS,** Box 24-8134, University of Miami, Coral Gables, Florida 33124.

JOURNAL OF INTERAMERICAN STUDIES AND WORLD AFFAIRS is published four times annually—in February, May, August, and November.

Subscriptions: Regular institutional rate $36.00 per year. Individuals may subscribe at a one-year rate of $18.00. Add $2.00 for subscriptions outside the United States. Orders from the U.K., Europe, the Middle East, and Africa should be sent to the London office (address below). Noninstitutional orders **must** be paid by personal check.

Second class postage paid at Beverly Hills, California. ISSN 0022-1937

This journal is abstracted or indexed in **Historical Abstracts, Human Resources Abstracts, Sage Urban Studies Abstracts, International Political Science Abstracts, Public Affairs Information Service, Curren. Contents, Social Sciences Citation Index, Social Sciences Index, ABC POL SCI,** and **United States Political Science Documents.**

Back Issues: Information about availability and prices of back issues may be obtained from the publisher's order department (address below). Write to London office for sterling prices.

Inquiries: Address all correspondence and permissions requests to SAGE PUBLICATIONS, Inc., 275 South Beverly Drive, Beverly Hills, California 90212. Inquiries and subscriptions from the U.K., Europe, the Middle East, and Africa should be sent to SAGE PUBLICATIONS Ltd, 28 Banner Street, London EC1Y 8QE, England. Other orders should be sent to the Beverly Hills office.

Advertising: Current rates and specifications may be obtained by writing to the Advertising Manager at the Beverly Hills office (address above).

Claims: Claims for undelivered copies must be made no later than three months following month of publication. The publisher will supply missing copies when losses have been sustained in transit and when the reserve stock will permit.

Change of Address: Six weeks' advance notice must be given when notifying of change of address. Please send old address label along with the new address to insure proper identification. Please specify name of journal. Send change of address to: Journal name, c/o 275 South Beverly Drive, Beverly Hills, CA 90212.

THOMAS J. TREBAT
Bankers Trust Company
New York, New York

JAN PETER WOGART
World Bank
Washington, DC

INTRODUCTION

Latin American development during the postwar period has been characterized by increasing government intervention in the economy. In addition to its direct impact on the economy through higher expenditures on social goods and services, the state has undertaken—either single-handedly or jointly with private domestic and even foreign investors—a large number of investment projects. Most of these investments have been planned and operated by public sector enterprises, whose growing importance has become a topic of increasing concern to social scientists interested in Latin America. While interdisciplinary public enterprise studies have a well-established tradition among observers of Western Europe and certain developing countries, notably India, the literature on the important Latin American experience with public sector firms has only begun to develop in recent years.[1]

State enterprises throughout Latin America occupy strategic positions in basic industries, utilities, transportation, commerce, and finance. The essays collected here are from case studies of financial as well as marketing and consumer-oriented state enterprises in Brazil, Peru, and Mexico.[2] While each essay deals with public enterprises involved in different pursuits and national settings, they have in common a case study approach and a

Journal of Interamerican Studies and World Affairs, Vol. 22 No. 4, November 1980 395-399

focus on the decision-making process as handled in Latin American public enterprises. While emphasis differs, each of the studies demonstrates the changing nature and evolving characteristics of these institutions. The historical analysis of functions and performance reveals close links between these public firms and the development strategies pursued by the various governments during the relevant periods. As national economic goals change, the shifting priorities on the macroeconomic level are often reflected—for better or worse—in the orientation and output of the public enterprise. Public enterprises emerge from these studies as flexible instruments of government policy.

Steven Topik deals with the case of the Banco do Brasil which, while privately owned and operated over extended periods of time, has functioned as a government bank for more than seventy years. Even during the first thirty years of this century, when the liberal-privatist development model prevailed in Brazil, the nature and tasks of the bank changed significantly. A decisive turn occurred during and after World War I, when a financial crisis, brought on by the dislocations of the world economy, led the Brazilian state to expand its participation in the economy and to use the Banco do Brasil increasingly as its financial agent.

While assuming expanded functions as a commercial bank, the Banco do Brasil did not evolve into a development bank, i.e., an institution specializing in long-term loans for the construction of economic and social infrastructure. This task was entrusted to another public enterprise, the Banco Nacional de Desenvolvimento Economica (BNDE), which was founded in 1952. In their case study, Werner Baer and Annibal Villela show clearly how the changing role of the BNDE over time reflects changes that occurred in Brazil's underlying economic development strategy.

Through the mid-1960s, the BNDE's main function was to aid the import-substitution process by financing public sector investments in basic industry, including steel, and in power, transportation, and other economic infrastructure. Against the backdrop of steady growth of public and multinational enterprises in Brazil, the major task of the BNDE since the late 1960s shifted to that of providing long-term credit at favorable rates to domestically owned private enterprises. While the BNDE has grown over the years to become less dependent on the central government for its own resources, Brazilian authorities at the macroeconomic level were responsible for the bank's shift in focus toward concentration on long-term financing of the private sector.

While almost all governments of developing nations support industrial and agricultural development with public financial institutions, the Peruvian and Mexican case studies in this volume provide examples of public enterprises involved in marketing, an activity usually dominated by private enterprise in mixed economic systems. Alfred Saulniers is concerned with ENCI, a Peruvian firm involved in the import of key commodities. ENCI is a relatively new firm, and a definitive assessment of its nature and operations is not yet possible. However, Saulniers' description of the origins of ENCI is an example of the often difficult passage from private to public ownership and control that occurred in the Peruvian economy during the 1970s. His study details ENCI's evolution out of periods of growth and decline caused by poor enterprise organization and excessive—as well as contradictory—control by the central authorities.

Public enterprise has played a more important role in Mexico than in many other Latin American countries. CONASUPO, a diversified public marketing and distribution enterprise, has pursued government goals of supporting domestic agricultural prices while keeping food prices low for urban consumers. In her essay, Marye Hilger concentrates on the decision-making process in CONASUPO and illuminates the role played by politics in the firm's operations. While CONASUPO has been a more successful firm than ENCI, its Peruvian counterpart, Hilger's study demonstrates that in Mexico, as in Peru, external influences on public enterprise decision-making contribute to inconsistencies in organizational purpose and marketing objectives and in the tactics and programs designed to meet these goals.

In presenting these four case studies of public enterprise in practice, along with an annotated list (prepared by Saulniers) of recent unpublished studies—in the traditional sense—on Latin American public enterprises, the editors hope to encourage additional empirical research on the emerging role of the state in Latin American development. In particular, more case studies of individual public firms, or groups of firms, will help us to answer the key questions of how Latin American public enterprises behave and how this behavior differs, if at all, from that of private enterprises engaged in similar economic activities.

Another interesting research theme concerns the effect of different national settings on Latin American public enterprise functions and performance. Comparative cross-national studics of experience with public sector firms in, say, Brazil and Mexico, or Argentina and Chile, would point out differences in the uses and results of public enterprise, but might also reveal common socioeconomic pressures, independent of particular historical circumstance, which shape a shared mode of public enterprise behavior.

NOTES

1. Examples of recent work include ECLA (1971: 1-70), Baer (1974: 263-281), Baer et al. (1977: 69-91), FitzGerald (1976), and Villareal and de Villareal (1978: 213-245).

2. The four articles appearing in this issue, along with three others, were originally presented as part of a panel during the Latin American Studies Association meetings in Pittsburgh, April 1979.

REFERENCES

BAER, W. (1974) "The role of government enterprises in Latin America's industrialization," pp. 263-281 in D. T. Geithman (ed.) Fiscal Policy for Industrialization and Development in Latin America. Gainesville, FL: University Presses of Florida.

——— et al. (1977) "On state capitalism in Brazil: some new issues and questions." Inter-American Economic Affairs 30 (Winter): 69-91.

ECLA [Economic Commission for Latin America] (1971) "Public enterprises: their present significance and their potential in development." Economic Bulletin for Latin Amerca 16: 1-70.

FITZGERALD, E.V.K. (1976) The State and Economic Development: Peru Since 1968. Cambridge: Cambridge Univ. Press.

VILLAREAL, R. and R. R. de VILLAREAL (1978) "Las empresas públicas como instrumento de política económica en México." Trimestre Económico 45 (April-June): 213-245.

Thomas J. Trebat is presently Chief Latin American Economist at Bankers Trust Company, a commercial bank with headquarters in New York City. He was formerly a Visiting Assistant Professor of Economics at the University of Texas, Austin. Trebat has done extensive field research on the economic performance of public enterprises in Brazil and is the author of a forthcoming book (Cambridge University Press, 1981) on this subject.

Jan Peter Wogart, Associate Editor of the Journal of Interamerican Studies and World Affairs, *is an economist in the Latin American country program of the World Bank. In addition to working on macroeconomic issues of fiscal and monetary policy, he has concentrated on industrial economics. His publications include* Price Stabilization in Brazil *(1976) and* Industrialization in Colombia *(1979).*

STEVEN TOPIK
Department of History
Universidade Federal Fluminense
Rio de Janeiro

STATE ENTERPRISE IN A LIBERAL REGIME
The Banco do Brasil, 1905-1930

The growth of public enterprise is generally viewed as a product of the post-World War II developmentalist state. In late-developing capitalist countries, however, many important firms already came under state control during preceding liberal regimes. Because of the liberal context in which they operated, such companies frequently adopted policies that differed in important ways from those followed under the developmentalist state. The purpose of this study is to focus on the Banco do Brasil—the single most important publicly controlled firm of Brazil's First Republic (1889-1930) and today the seventh largest bank in the world—in order to examine the nature of state enterprise in a liberal regime.

Background

The current Banco do Brasil came into existence in 1905 when a banking crisis brought its direct predecessor, the Banco da República, to the brink of bankruptcy. Because of the important

AUTHOR'S NOTE: The author would like to thank Werner Baer, Winston Fritsch, Paulo Neuhas, Alfred H. Saulniers, and Annibal Villela for their comments.

Journal of Interamerican Studies and World Affairs, Vol. 22 No. 4, November 1980 401-422

position that the Banco da República occupied in the country's financial system and its semiofficial role as the government's banker, the federal Treasury intervened to prop it up. When the measures failed to resuscitate the bank, the federal government took stronger action; the reorganized bank, now named the Banco do Brasil (BB), came directly under the control of the Union. The Treasury purchased almost one-third of the shares of the new institution, by far the largest single block of votes. In addition, the bank's new statutes authorized the President of the Republic to appoint the BB's president and one of its four directors (Ministério da Fazenda, 1905: 74, 98). The federal government held further leverage as the bank's largest client, as well as through its power to offer or rescind special privileges. Although the Treasury would only become the majority stockholder in 1923, when it purchased additional shares, the bank would have already essentially served as a public institution since its reorganization (Ministério da Fazenda, 1924: 136-140). Those of its actions which would prove detrimental to the public's economic welfare stemmed not so much from its pursuit of narrow-minded commercial profit as from misguided federal strategies.

The government's decision to take control of the country's largest commercial bank might seem a contradiction of liberal principles. In fact, it was not. It is true that the country's leaders believed strongly in the efficacy of supply and demand, comparative advantage, and free trade. If the marketplace were allowed free reign, the result would be the maximization of welfare for all persons concerned, as well as progress for Brazil as a nation. Development, they believed, was the result of government restraint, not of state entrepreneurship. For the market to allocate resources, efficiently, however, the country's currency had to remain stable, and, preferably, convertible. One of the government's most important roles in the liberal state was to stand guardian over the currency, guaranteeing its accurate reflection of market forces. The British had long used the semiofficial Bank of England for just such a purpose. The disastrous state of Brazilian finances in the early twentieth century, and, indeed, throughout the First Republic, forced the federal government to take extraordinary actions for just such a reason.

The Bank Before World War I

When the federal government took control of the Banco do Brasil, it did so in order to use it to stabilize exchange. The Treasury deposited its funds in the BB, which became the government's sole agent in foreign exchange transactions, and, as a result, the largest dealer in the lucrative market. Although it thereby undercut foreign banks' domination of exchange operations, the BB had not been intended as a nationalist weapon. The Minister of Finance originally sought to sell one-third of the shares to European financiers; only their reluctance forced the BB to be wholly Brazilian-owned (Pena, 1905). Congress further demonstrated the government's liberal bent by refusing to grant the bank any special legislated powers. As a special agent of the U.S. Congress (U.S. Department of Commerce, 1915: 101) reported in 1914:

> Not only is there a marked absence of laws directly applicable to banking concerns, but there is also an equally noteworthy absence of control exercised either by the Government or by associations among the banks . . . even the large governmental or semigovernmental banks in Brazil, Uruguay, Argentina, Chile and Bolivia are competitive with the other banks. Whatever influence they exercise is secured through their active and direct competition, not through any special authority over the other banks conferred upon them.

The bank's financial power proved too limited to prevent more than relatively small oscillations in the milreis. While the exchange rate remained steady between 1906 and 1914, the Caixa de Conversão was much more responsible than the BB for the feat. The Caixa was a federal institution that fought the upward trend in the Brazilian currency by selling convertible notes redeemable in gold. Once the Caixa ceased operation in 1914, when World War I provoked a drain of gold, the BB could only dampen a secular trend toward depreciation of the milreis. It was able to avoid drastic oscillations in the exchange rate market created by speculators; however, because its ownership was still principally private, it could not afford to take consistent losses by sustaining a rate markedly different from the prevailing one. The Treasury's finances were such that, once the war broke out, it refused to provide the BB with special funds to manipulate the exchange rate except in extreme emergencies. In the words of one of its presidents, the bank had to "conciliate the interests of the bank with those of the National Treasury" (Banco do Brasil, 1918: 15). It fulfilled this aim well, returning healthy profits in its exchange operations (which were often responsible for about 20% of total profits) while smoothing fluctuations in the exchange rate and eventually stifling speculation (Jornal do Commercio, 1911: 31; Banco do Brasil, 1910, 1911, 1912: Anexos).

At the same time, the Banco do Brasil continued its other commercial operations after coming under state command. In this capacity, its directors conceived of it as "the constant and beneficial regulator of public credit" (Banco do Brasil, 1911: 10). It was not, however, a development bank. Indeed, its 1905 statutes prohibited loans or note discounts of more than six months' duration, forbade rediscounts altogether, and precluded the purchase of stocks in other companies (Ministério da Fazenda, 1905: 77, 78). While it did control Lloyd Brasileiro Shipping Line for a short time, it had inherited the line from the Banco da República. The BB never operated Lloyd—the largest merchant fleet in Brasil—and anxiously sought to recover its investment in the company (Jornal do Commercio, 1912: 144, 145).

The bank's directors believed that its function was not so much in supplying capital as in regulation circulation and, therefore, credit. It frequently remedied credit shortages by lowering interest rates; it extended some aid to coffee during the first valorization program and to rubber during its crisis in 1910 (Banco do Brasil, 1911: 11, 12; 1914: 4). At the same time, however, the bank remained cautious, as it was still primarily privately owned and received limited federal funds to use for loans. When World War I provoked a liquidity crisis, the BB actually increased its discount rate, cutting operations almost in half (Banco do Brasil, 1915: 7, 13; 1916: 18). Indeed, the bank tended to be more conservative than its competitors. During the 1906-1913 period the BB's loan-to-deposit ratio was less than .7, while the other banks recorded a ratio greater than 1.0 (Banco do Brasil, 1924: Anexon: IBGE, 1940: 1355).

In discussing the role of the BB in the overall economic development of Brazil at the time, it should be noted that Brazil's banking system was limited, regionally concentrated, foreign-dominated, and conservative. Cameron (1967) has established a rough criterion by which to judge the relative importance of a banking system. Using the number of financial establishments (headquarters and branches) per 10,000 people in the population for an index, he maintains that less than .5 is a low bank density and less than .1 is very low. Rio de Janeiro, which dominated national finances, had a density rating in 1912 of .15. The state of Minas Gerais, the second richest in Brazil, had a rating in 1921 of only .1. In comparison, Great Britain, when it began its industrialization surge more than 100 years earlier, had had a density of .77, while the United States in 1920 enjoyed a density of 2.94 (Cameron, 1967: 20-24; IBGE, 1917: 56; IBGE, 1940: 1295, 1296; Wirth, 1977: 56).

Another indication of the limited scope of the Brazilian financial market is that in 1921 the per capita bank deposit was about $17.50, and in 1928 it was just a little higher—about $20.00. At the same time, average deposits in the United States stood at $152.08 in 1921 and $235.79 in 1928 (IBGE, 1940: 1356; U.S. Department of Commerce, 1965: 7640). Brazil's low deposit figure reflects not only the country's poverty, but also the shortage of formal financial institutions. In 1912, fully 82% of all mortgages were extended by individuals, not by lending institutions, and the informal money market was not only in the countryside—fully 54% of all the mortgages were for urban or suburban land (IBGE, 1917: 47).

In the areas relatively well supplied with lending institutions, foreign banks played a large role. Until 1920 they controlled almost half of all deposits and extended almost half of all loans (Wileman's Brazilian Review, 1930: 479, 480). This was important not only because lending policies were formulated outside Brazil, but also because the foreign houses provided even fewer loans that could be termed developmental than their Brazilian competitors; foreigners committed their funds almost entirely to financing international commerce. Brazilian banks concentrated more on domestic financing: for the 1922-1929 period, native banks provided 92% of all mortgages in terms of value (Jornal do Commercio, 1930: 217-220; Joslin, 1963: 25, 67, 163).

The Effects of World War I on the Bank

World War I had serious repercussions in Brazil and led to important changes in the Banco do Brasil's role in the economy. The traditional export economy faltered and the influx of foreign capital stopped. At the same time, the European conflict sparked nationalist passions and convinced many in Brazil's ruling class that the state needed to take a more active role in protecting and developing the economy. As a result, federal economic interventions, particularly those employing the Banco do Brasil, increased rather dramatically during and after the war. World War I provoked a 40% decrease in Brazil's capacity to import, seriously unbalancing the federal government's finances. Because its revenues derived principally from import duties, the Treasury's budgetary deficits mounted, averaging more than one-third of the value of total expenditures (Villela and Suzigan, 1973: 140, 441). The war also cut off Brazil from European capital markets, so that the government printed unbacked money to cover its operating expenses. The total amount of currency issued grew 75% during the war years. This, in turn, spurred an inflation rate of almost 200% between 1914 and 1919 (Villela and Suzigan, 1973: 418, 419, 424).

Isolation from their traditional markets and suppliers made many of Brazil's leaders aware of their country's vulnerable economic and defensive position and brought into question the efficacy of free trade. The absence of foreign investment during the war further inclined them to believe that the state should play a larger role in encouraging development. As Cincinato Braga, later a president of the BB, argued: "The State cannot remain indifferent to Brazil's disastrous economic situation" (Braga, 1915: 9). The country's newly organized and highly vocal nationalist groups called for more than ad hoc interventions. They championed more systematic and institutionalized aid to key economic sectors (Gil Blas, 1921, 1922a, 1922b). Both the federal Treasury's financial woes and the new current of economic thought encouraged the federal government to extend new powers to the Banco do Brasil.

The sharp decline in international commerce provoked a liquidity crisis in the Brazilian economy. To ease the credit shortage, Congress authorized the Treasury to lend 100,000 contos (approximately $28,000,000 at the 1914 exchange rate) to the country's banks in 1914. The Banco do Brasil received the largest share, 22%, which was slightly more than the percentage it held of total deposits. The funds were short-term loans (with an original term of six months, later extended to two years) to avert a bank crash and facilitate commercial transactions. It was the first such public loan to banks since an 80,000-conto industrial bonus was issued by the Banco da República in 1893 (Ministério da Fazenda, 1920: 49-53).

The next year Congress provided an example of countercyclical monetary policy. Because the Brazilian economic situation in general, and the federal government's finances in particular, had worsened, the Treasury printed 350,000 contos. The Banco do Brasil received 50,000 contos of the total to use in rediscounting. This, too, was a substantial departure from previous policy. The BB's rediscounting possibilities had been greatly circumscribed by statute, because it was considered to be a somewhat risky and inflationary practice. Now, to stimulate the velocity of currency and thereby extend more short-term credit to agriculture, commerce, and industry, Congress encouraged BB rediscounts. Moreover, unlike the situation in 1914, the BB was the only bank to which this loan was extended. Other banks could take advantage of it only by rediscounting through it (Brasil, 1915: Decreto 21986). Thus, it reconfirmed the Banco do Brasil's privileged position, a position that the bank continued to assert through market operations, rather than through special legislated powers.

The special conditions created by the war thus led Congress, for the first time, to provide the BB with almost $12,000,000 to be used for the development of the domestic economy. The following year, the new relationship between the bank and the Treasury was reconfirmed: Congress had provided 50,000 contos to assist the rubber industry, and the government's bank received the bulk of the funds (Jornal do Commercio, 1918: 93). These measures were part of a new federal orientation to agricultural aid. Beginning in 1906, Congress had provided a L3,000,000 loan to prop up the price of coffee; in 1917, also in defense of coffee, the Treasury funneled another 110,000 contos (approximately $26,610,000) through the BB. During the 1920s the federal government would expand its activities even further, funding the third valorization of coffee almost entirely. Loans continued to be aimed at facilitating commercialization, however, rather than production.

The war years, then, witnessed Brazil's government offering important new favors to the Banco do Brasil, strengthening the ties between the two. However, because of the economy's poor performance, the bank's average profits for 1914-1918 were about 10% below the 1913 figure, and deposits fell off 15%. The only bright spot was the extension of credit, as loans grew 10%. More tellingly, the Banco do Brasil, despite the government's aid, lost much of its dominance in the financial market. Before the war it had controlled about 25% of all deposits. This dropped to 18% in 1914 and then to about 10% until 1921. The other commercial banks, during the same time, recorded impressive gains in their sight deposits (see Table 1). The BB fell behind its competition despite a vigorous expansion program that saw its number of agencies grow from a meager 4 in 1914 to a respectable 42 in 1919 (Ministério da Fazenda, 1920: 132; Banco do Brasil, 1914: 17).

fited from the rediscount service, as foreign banks tended to use their home offices. Among Brazilian financial houses, the BB itself took advantage of 80% of all rediscounts (Souza, 1928). Brazilian's share of total loans, note discounts and deposits rose from about 55% in 1920 to about 70% in 1923 (Wileman's Brazilian Review, 1930: 478, 480).

The Carteira's operations demonstrated that while the federal government was moving to ever greater economic intervention, it still maintained its faith in the market place. Rediscounts were extended for only a four-month period. Congress sought to mobilize savings for development in the private sector by maximizing the turnover of public funds. The state would not itself foster nascent industries except in a few exceptional cases, despite the absence of long-term capital in the private financial market.[2]

The federal government discouraged the Banco do Brasil from extending long-term loans, largely because it wanted the bank to maintain a high level of liquidity in order to be able to lend to the government. Thus, the Carteira employed a large portion of its funds in rediscounting Treasury notes, which substantially limited the section's multiplier effects in the economy. The bank's president in 1924, Cincinato Braga, estimated that the federal government drained about 500,000 contos a year from the capital markets for nonproductive uses (Banco do Brasil, 1924: 21-25). The government's bonds were probably responsible for the estimated 2½% yearly decrease in the velocity of money between 1920 and 1945 (Peláez and Suzigan, 1976: 189).

The Carteira's other shortcoming was its regional concentration. The Federal District alone received 62% of the rediscounts. Together with the state of Sao Paulo it received 77% and, out of a total of 20, the country's four largest states plus the Federal Districts consumed fully 93% of the rediscount funds (Banco do Brasil, 1922: 11; 1923: 9). This was the case despite the bank's own claim that one of its main concerns was "the intensification of banking in the country's interior" (Banco do Brasil, 1923: 9).

In 1923 President Arthur Bernardes abolished the Cateira de Redescontos as a part of a larger banking reform intended to remedy a soaring inflation rate and a precipitous fall of the milreis. Between 1922 and 1923 the country experienced its second highest one-year jump in inflation (34%) and the lowest exchange rate (44.6 milreis to the pound sterling) of the First Republic. Bernardes blamed the decline on the 43% increase in currency issued the previous 3 years. He partly blamed the Cateira for the inflation of money. The bank continued to dominate the rediscount market after 1923 despite not being able to issue notes specifically for that purpose.

Despite losing the Carteira, the Banco do Brasil gained from the reform because it received a monopoly of issue of currency. It served, in a limited sense, as the country's central bank between 1923 and 1926, finally fulfilling the role foreseen for it in 1905. The move was part of an international wave of efforts to return to the gold standard; after the Geneva meetings of 1922 and England's return to the gold standard in 1925, 1926 saw 34 countries stabilize their currency in relation to gold (Mauro, 1976: 356). In Latin America, Colombia, Ecuador, Mexico, and Chile founded central banks during the 1920s (Aranha Archives, n.d.). The Brazilian experiment was financed with L10 million which the Treasury loaned the BB. The bank was supposed to return Brazil to the gold standard by retiring inconvertible Treasury notes and eventually replacing them with convertible ones when the exchange rate reached par (Banco do Brasil, 1924: Anexo).

When President Arthur Bernardes granted the BB a monopoly of currency issue, he viewed it principally as a vehicle through which to restrict the money supply and return to convertibility rather than to meet the needs of commerce, agriculture, and industry. The bank's policy was to raise its discount and rediscount rates and extend loans for only 30-day periods. As a result, the BB's loans and deposits declined markedly. By 1926, deposits had fallen 22% and loans 4% from their 1923 high. Deposits did not regain their 1923 level until 1928 (Banco do Brasil, 1931: Anexo). The economy also felt the pinch. During the 4-year experiment currency issues actually declined 2%—the largest decline of the century up to then (Villela and Suzigan, 1973: 412).

Although the bank in the end did adhere to the President's policy, a controversy arose in 1924 that put into question whether the institution was primarily private or public. Bernardes wanted to reduce the money supply. The president of the Banco do Brasil, Cincinato Braga, issued 727,000 contos by the end of 1924, about 25% of the money supply. Bernardes, outraged, claimed that Braga was disobeying him in order to extend commercial loans to his fellow Paulistas. Braga defended himself, maintaining that he had reluctantly undertaken the action only because the bank faced a liquidity crunch. The Treasury owed—and refused to pay—826,000 contos, which equaled all of its capital, reserves, and most of its private deposits. Braga issued currency to cover withdrawals, not to make commercial loans. In either case, the image of independence that the BB's president asserted was quickly shattered; Bernardes fired him. Braga's successor withdrew most of the bank's issue (Braga, 1931: 10, 20, 26-30, 55).

The incident illustrated the role of the bank's president: he was supposed to defend the government's interests over the bank's. The people appointed to direct the BB virtually guaranteed that the institution would respond to the dictates of the president of the Republic. The bank's presidents were chosen by the national commander-in-chief and, as we have seen, were at his beck and call. These men were generally politicians who held no stock in the bank and were devoid of other ties to it, such as previous employment there; as a result, they had no personal interest or independent power base in the BB. They remained at the helm at the most four years; the average tenure during the First Republic was less than two years (Banco do Brasil, 1910 through 1930). This further undermined their personal authority. The directors also depended on the federal government for their positions, as they were either appointed by the president of Brazil or elected—and the Treasury's voting bloc allowed it to sway all elections.

The bank greatly centralized authority and decision-making. The BB's president and close subordinates in the Rio headquarters directed the loan and employment policies of all branches. Officers within the Rio office also enjoyed little freedom of action. Therefore, the authority of career employees, who might have had the bank's interests more at heart, was circumscribed by men who were political appointees (Souza, 1927).

The federal Treasury's interests dictated a tight money policy, because a weak milreis increased the already considerable burden of the foreign debt. In 1923, the Bernardes Administration dedicated 29% of its budget to servicing the debt and another 61% to operational expenses (Villela and Suzigan, 1973: 415). Although the government could theoretically support a policy of deficit spending to stimulate economic growth, both the reigning economic theory and the country's credit rating militated against it. The government needed to encouraged foreign investment, because Brazil faced a yearly service charge on past debts and dividend repatriation of L25 million-29 million, which the trade surplus alone could not cover (Banco do Brasil, 1924: 6, 7). To maintain a good credit rating and to encourage foreign capital, the milreis had to remain stable. The value of the national currency was an especially pressing concern of the Bernardes Administration, because the moratorium on amortization payments extended by the second Funding Loan (1914) was due to end in 1927. The Banco do Brasil stood at the center of Bernardes' financial program.

Indeed, during the 1905-1930 period, the Banco do Brasil's policy generally coincided with that of the federal government. The BB's president observed in 1923: "In its exchange section the bank has always been much more concerned in serving the general interests of the country than its own" (Banco do Brasil, 1923: 8). The Treasury was the bank's primary exchange customer. In 1918, for example, 72% of the BB's operations were for the Treasury (Banco do Brasil, 1918: 22). It should be pointed out, however, that despite purchasing or selling foreign currency at prices that differed from the prevailing market prices, the bank realized substantial profits from this function.

The BB also tended to operate countercyclically to achieve the government's dual goals of preventing inflation and avoiding sharp reductions of credit (Ministério da Fazenda, 1926: 42). For the period 1921-1930, the correlation between the bank's ratio of cash on hand to deposits and that of the other commercial banks was a significant –.47 (calculated from Banco do Brasil, 1931: Anexo: Neuhaus, 1975: 67). With its rediscounting and currency issuing capacity (1923-1926) the BB exercised considerable sway over the credit market.

After the alterations in the bank's statutes in 1923, there remained even less reason to characterize it as a private company. Because it "delivered services to the federal government considered to be public" it was exempt from all taxes. In addition to selecting the bank's president and now two of its directors, the federal government would henceforth own a minimum of 50% of the bank's stock. (Congress set aside the money to purchase the necessary number of shares to reach that total.) And the BB would act as "agent of the federal government in exchange operations and all others of a banking nature." The bank was awarded a monopoly of currency issue and the sole right to issue gold-backed checks for payment of customs duties (a privilege it had enjoyed since 1905). Bank employees even worked as an extension of the federal bureaucracy, transferring tax and customs payments from federal offices all over the country to the Ministry of Finance in Rio (Banco do Brasil, 1924: 136-140).

The Banco do Brasil took no further steps in the direction of long-term loans during the First Republic, even once it lost its monopoly of issue in 1926. President Washington Luís suspended the bank's issue of unconvertible paper currency in order to seek a formula through which the bank could eventually come to issue convertible currency. The BB continued its conservative credit policy despite the fact that it was no longer a central bank. In fact, in 1928 the BB's directors prohibited borrowing for initiating new companies or for fixed capital investments in existing ones. They so limited themselves because they still perceived the BB as a potential central bank; as such, they believed it should devote its funds to controlling commercial credit rates by maximizing the velocity of its funds (Banco do Brasil, 1928: 7; Banco do Brasil, 1929: 14).

Conclusions

After its reorganization in 1905, the Banco do Brasil attempted to fulfill numerous and somewhat contradictory roles. As a commercial bank, it attempted to aid commerce, industry, and agriculture and turn a healthy profit at the same time; in this capacity, it sometimes acted procyclically. In attempting to become or act as a central bank, it sought to control the means of payment through the manipulation of discount and rediscount rates, through issues of currency (1923-1926), and through direct loans. In this role, the BB tried to expand the money supply during economic downturns. However, the bank was also custodian of the exchange rate. As such, it had to raise interest rates during emergencies so that internal inflation would not drive down the milreis. Finally, as the Treasury's banker, the BB had to maintain a high liquidity level and devote substantial portions of its resources to the federal government. This limited its capacity to carry out its other duties. The federal government simply did not provide the Banco do Brasil with sufficient resources or powers to accomplish all of the tasks it had been assigned.

The Treasury failed to provide the funds for a truly dynamic central bank partly because it did not have the resources to do so. Its poverty was particularly acute during recessions, when its funds were most needed, because 65% of its revenues derived from import duties; they generally fell when the economy was troubled. The faith of politicians in the doctrines of hard currency and laissez faire further inhibited Congress from granting the bank sufficient resources or more legislated powers. In fact, it was the government's shortage of revenue, its ideological proclivities, and its need to direct the nation's financial and exchange markets that led it to its arrangement with the Banco do Brasil in the first place. By employing a semiprivate commercial institution, such as the BB, rather than establishing public ones, the state was able to capture deposits and benefit from commercial profits while keeping at bay political opposition to state economic interference.

Probably the most important advantage of the relationship for the Treasury was the large quantity of deposits to which it now had access. The bank's influence in national financial markets came more from the weight of its deposits than from the smaller state privileges it received. Of course, the deposits flowed in because of the bank's ties to the government, which were interpreted by the general public as a federal guarantee. As a result of that security, the federal government could tap 25% of the nation's bank savings without resorting to such unpopular means as taxation, printing money, or high interest rates. (When one includes the 10% of total deposits housed in the federally controlled Caixas Econômicas, the government controlled more than one-third of the nation's savings deposits [IBGE, 1940: 1356].)

As the government's banking agent, the Banco do Brasil lent a considerable portion of its deposits to the Treasury. In fact, the statutes of 1923 mandated that the bank would lend Congress up to 25% of the projected revenues. In 1925, for example, one-quarter of the bank's loans were to the Treasury (Jornal do Commercio, 1926: 24). The bank also served as a source of federal loans to the states, and, therefore, as a source of centralization; in 1926, seven states owed a total of 40,000 contos (Ministério da Fazenda, 1926: 70-74). In addition, the deposits provided the bank with a potent tool with which to implement the monetary policy Congress had assigned to it. Given the lack of legislated powers such as establishing reserve requirements, the added market force supplied by the public's deposits was essential.

State capitalism was also profitable for the Treasury. In dividend payments alone, it received about 80,000 contos between 1923 and 1930; these funds went to retiring Treasury notes. More importantly, the BB was able to earn sufficient profits that it could retire about 180,000 contos in Treasury notes in 1923 and 1924 alone. It also placed a considerable amount of its profits in reserves, as its statutes forbade the distribution of more than a 20% dividend. This stipulation prevented private stockholders from benefiting as much as they might have from the bank's monopoly position and guaranteed that the Treasury would profit disproportionately to its shares of stock. By 1930 its reserves stood at 208,000 contos (about $22,000,000). A large portion of the reserves were channeled into Treasury bonds, so that the bank became the largest holder of the floating federal debt. Another part of the reserves went to an amortization fund that purchased gold with which to redeem unbacked Treasury notes (Banco do Brasil, 1924: 27; Banco do Brasil, 1925: 22; Banco do Brasil, 1926: 20; Banco do Brazil, 1931: 39, Anexo). Thus, the bank not only lent money to the government, it paid off part of the government's debt.

The arrangement with the BB also saved the Treasury some money. The bank essentially lent its employees to the federal government to perform such functions as exchange and rediscount transactions and even more administrative tasks such as funneling revenue from tax collectors and customs houses to the Ministry of Finance. In addition to being more efficient than if the government had to establish its own network, the arrangement meant that half of the expenses were assumed by the bank's private stockholders. Reducing the federal government's operating expenses was politically important, because there were loud complaints being voiced by citizens and politicians about the size and cost of the state bureaucracy. The more direct control of operations that the government could have exerted had it directly taken over and merged the bank into the government would not have compensated for the political opposition such a move would have engendered.

Thus the relationship with the Banco do Brasil proved a felicitous solution for a government controlled by an economically liberal rural oligarchy and suffering financial difficulties. It is important to emphasize that federal politicians were not simply guided by an economic theory. Rather, the demands of the rural export-oriented oligarchy and European investors largely shaped the policies. Within the constraints set by these factions, the arrangement worked relatively well. By extending, at no cost to itself, privileges to a commercial bank that it controlled, the government acquired ready access to a substantial volume of public deposits for loans, profits for revenues, and market power to carry on its financial policies.

Although the government's financial measures stimulated the growth of the national banking system, it failed to provide developmental loans. Because of federal oversight and greater rediscount services, the banking network grew faster than the economy as a whole. Between 1913 and 1930 the issues of mortgages grew 30% faster than the real GNP. Native financial institutions also expanded their share of total banking to a considerable degree because of the BB's rediscounts. Their percentage of total loans and discounts grew from 54% in 1913 to 72% in 1929.[3] Not only was the system larger, it was healthier. Because of the government's participation and the larger resources of the Banco do Brasil, the 1929 crisis did not have the serious repercussions that the crises of 1864, 1875, and 1900 had had.

On the other hand, the banking system continued to be lamentably small, concentrated, and conservative. The index of banks per 10,000 people was still .15 in 1930, and Rio and São Paulo continued to dominate; in 1930 they assumed 74% of all mortgages (IBGE, 1940: 1356). Although a few states established mortgage banks, such as Minas Gerais (in 1889), Paraíba (1912), Rio Grande do Sul (1928), Paraná (1928), and most importantly São Paulo (1927), long-term institutionalized loans remained relatively scarce. The annual average value of mortgages of all Brazilian banks in the 1920s was only 80% of the annual mortgages issued by Argentina's Banco de la Nación alone (Jornal do Commercio, 1930: 217; Banco de la Nación, 1925: 9; Baer, 1975: 262). And this was at a time when, according to an estimate by First National City Bank, the net wealth of both countries was approximately equal (Jornal do Comercio, 1925: 127). While the BB made some effort to provide regional credit—by 1930 it had over 80 branches—its principal effect was to concentrate resources in Rio. The headquarters actually drained funds from the branches, even from the prosperous São Paulo agency, rather than providing them with loan capital (Souza, 1928). The bank also did not remedy the concentration of international banking in foreign hands. No Brazilian bank had a foreign branch during the First Republic.

State enterprise, as represented by the Banco do Brasil, failed to make a substantial contribution to industrial and agricultural development during the First Republic. But, then, that was not its immediate goal. The BB performed its functions of maintaining the exchange rate, discounting and rediscounting, and lending to the government as well as its resources and statutes permitted. Moreover, it realized impressive profits; had it extended long-term loans, it would have been a much less successful capitalist enterprise. Given the government's continuing reliance on private enterprise and export-led growth, and considering the precariousness of national finances, any sharp departure from such policies was extremely unlikely.

But despite the continuing hegemony of the liberal model, the Banco do Brasil of 1930 was considerably different from that of 1905. Through it, the state haltingly expanded the range of its economic participation. The increasing complexity of the economy and the financial crises created by dislocations in the world market demanded extraordinary government measures. Bureaucratic momentum meant that the special powers created to meet specific emergencies tended to continue to take on new attributes once the emergency subsided. Although the Banco do Brasil's powers grew intermittently and haphazardly, it was suitably prepared by the end of the First Republic to fulfill the larger role the state would assign it once the Depression and World War II put the liberal model to rest.

NOTES

1. On another occasion he credited the sharp jump in the bank's deposits from the general public to the Carteira's "immense prestige" (Banco do Brasil, 1921: 13).

2. The exceptions were generally important to the national defense. Decree 3316 of August 16, 1917 cites coal, iron, steel, railroads, and shipping as privileged sectors.

3. Calculated from IBGE (1940: 1350, 1351, 1359) and Cantador and Haddad (1975: 430, 431) deflated by the price index of Cantador and Haddad (1975: 432-436). Data on foreign participation comes from *Wileman's Brazilian Review* (1930: 479-480).

REFERENCES

Aranha Archives [Rio de Janeiro] (n.d.) "Principais etapas de estabilização" in Bancos, pasta I.

BAER, W. (1975) A Industrialização e o Desenvolvimento Econômico do Brasil. (Paulo de Almeida Rodrigues, trans.). Rio de Janeiro: Fundação Getúlio Vargas.

Banco de la Nación (1925) Memoria y Balance General del Ejercicio 1925. Buenos Aires: Talleres Gráficos de la Compañía General de Fósforos.

Banco do Brasil (1910-1917) Relatório [annual publication]. Rio de Janeiro: Jornal do Commercio.

——— (1918) Relatório [annual publication]. Rio de Janeiro: Leuzinger.

——— (1919-1922) Relatório [annual publication]. Rio de Janeiro. Jornal do Commercio.

——— (1923-1931) Relatório [annual publication]. Rio de Janeiro: Leuzinger.

BRAGA, C. (1931) Brasil Novo II. Rio de Janeiro. Imprensa Nacional.

——— (1915) Discurso Sobre Cafe e Borracha. São Paulo: n.p.

Brasil (1915) Leis do Brasil, Decree 21986. [Rio de Janeiro] August 28.

——— (1907) Leis do Brasil, Decree 1841. [Rio de Janeiro] December 31.

CAMERON, R. (1967) Banking in the Early Stages of Industrialization. New York: Oxford Univ. Press.

CANTADOR, C. and C. HADDAD (1975) "Produção real, moeda e preços: a experiência brasileira no período 1861-1970." Revista Brasileira de Estatística 36: 407-441.

Gil Blas [Rio de Janeiro] (1922a) May 26.

——— (1922b) January 6.

——— (1921) November 17.

IBGE [Instituto Brasileiro de Geografia e Estatístical] (1940) Anuário Estatístico 1939-1940. Rio de Janeiro: Typ. de Estatística.

——— (1917) Anuario Estatístico 1908-1912. Rio de Janeiro: Typ. de Estatística.

Jornal do Commercio (1911, 1912, 1918, 1925, 1926, 1930) Retrospectivo Comercial. Rio de Janeiro: Author.

JOSLIN, D. A. (1963) A Century of Banking in Latin America. New York: Oxford Univ. Press.

MAURO, F. (1976) História Econômica Mundial, 1790-1970. Rio de Janeiro: Zahar Editores.

Ministério da Fazenda (1930) Movimento Bancario do Brasil. Rio de Janeiro: Imprensa Nacional.

——— (1905, 1906, 1920, 1924, 1926) Relatórios. Rio de Janeiro: Imprensa Nacional.

NEUHAUS, P. (1975) História Monetária do Brasil, 1900-1945. Rio de Janeiro: IBMEC [Instituto Brasileiro de Mercado de Capitais].

PELAEZ, C. M. and W. SUZIGAN (1976) História Monetária do Brasil: Análise da Política, Comportamento e Instituições Monetárias. Rio de Janeiro: IPEA/INPES [Instituto de Planejamento Econômico e Social/Instituto de Pesquisas].

PENA, A. (1905) Leopoldo Bulhões to Afonso Pena, 6-1-2, 551, in Afonso Pena Archives (March 6). Rio de Janeiro: Arquivo Nacional.

SOUZA, C. I. (1928) "A stituação do Banco do Brasil e a sua próxima reforma." OA 28.12.00 in Oswaldo Aranha Archives, December. Rio de Janeiro: Fundãco Getúlio Vargas. (mimeographed)

——— (1927) "Estudo sobre o Banco do Brasil." OA 27.06.00 tt. in Oswaldo Aranha Archives, June. Rio de Janeiro: CPDOC [Centro de Pesquisa e Documentação]. (mimeographed)

U.S. Department of Commerce (1965) The Statistical History of the United States. Stamford, CT: Fairfield.

——— (1915) Banking Opportunities in South America. Washington, DC: Government Printing Office. (Prepared by William H. Lough, Special Agent Series.)
VILLELA, A. V. and W. SUZIGAN (1973) Política do Governo e Crescimento da Economia Brasileira, 1889-1945. Rio de Janeiro: IPEA/INPES.
Wileman's Brazilian Review [Rio de Janeiro] (1930) April 10.
WIRTH, J. D. (1977) Minas Gerais in the Brazilian Federation, 1889-1930. Palo Alto, CA: Stanford Univ. Press.

Steven Topik is a visiting professor in the Department of History, Universidade Federal Fluminense, Niteroi, Rio de Janeiro, Brasil. His current research interest is the role of the liberal Brazilian state in banking, coffee, industry, and railroads.

WERNER BAER
Department of Economics
University of Illinois—Urbana

ANNIBAL V. VILLELA
Consultaria Economica Ltda.
Rio de Janeiro

THE CHANGING NATURE OF DEVELOPMENT BANKING IN BRAZIL

Prior to the mid-1960s, there was little concern in Brazil for the relative size of different ownership sectors—state, domestic private and multinational (Baer et al., 1973; Baer et al., 1977). The main policy objective had been the promotion of import-substitution-industrialization (ISI). Because the Brazilian domestic private sector did not have the technological and financial means to create new industries with a high technology content or to help expand public utilities, multinational firms and state enterprises were relied upon to carry out those tasks. The National Bank for Economic Development (BNDE) was created in order to finance the state's direct participation in Brazil's economy.

By the second half of the 1960s, Brazil's policy makers became concerned with the relative weakness of the domestic private sector, which was increasingly overshadowed by the two other members of the "tripe."[1] Because they wanted to prevent the emergence of an economy dominated by state and multinational firms, they devised programs to strengthen the domestic private

AUTHORS' NOTE: The authors wish to thank Mario Gelli, Raimundo Nonato Ramos, and Eugene White for many useful suggestions and for their help.

Journal of Interamerican Studies and World Affairs, Vol. 22 No. 4, November 1980 423-440

sector. The BNDE was chosen as one of the principal instruments for that task and by the second half of the 1970s, most of its activities were devoted to it. By our examination of the growth and evolution of the BNDE, we hope to shed some light on the differences in the problems facing a development bank which turned from a financier of the public sector to one which concentrates on the private sector.

Origins of the BNDE

BNDE was created as a result of the recommendations of the Joint Brazil-United States Mission (1950-1952). The mission had come to the conclusion that in order to prevent infrastructural bottlenecks from slowing economic growth, a massive investment program would be needed. It recommended that 41 projects be undertaken, involving primarily transportation and power generation. The program, which came to be known as the National Plan for Economic Reequipment, had an estimated total of $8 billion, or the then-equivalent of Cr 22 billion. The Export-Import Bank and the World Bank were to provide $500 million for the foreign exchange component of the program.[2] The Brazilian government was to pass three laws in order to provide the basis for local financing of the investments: one set up the bases for raising domestic funds; a second allowed the Treasury to guarantee foreign credits to private firms; and a third provided for the creation of the BNDE.[3]

Although the bulk of the recommended programs consisted of government investment projects, Finance Minister Lafer insisted on the creation of a new institution to finance them. His main argument was that

> at the outset we wondered whether it was really necessary to create a new agency for the purpose, or whether it would be sufficient to distribute the new functions throughout the existing bureaucratic structure. The former solution was preferred due to the entirely new types of operations to be carried out, as well as for the flexibility and independence the new agency would need, which

> was not found in the existing government departments nor in the autonomous government agencies which the government participates in [BNDE, 1964: 222].[4]

Given its need to raise new resources every few years plus the appointive power of the executive (Pinto, 1969; Martins, 1977), the BNDE could not be expected to develop as an institution that could be independent of either the executive or the legislative branch of the government. It has been pointed out, however (Pinto, 1969: 34), that as an "autarquia," "the BNDE would enjoy a substantial amount of insulation from the inflexible administrative practices, for which the Brazilian Federal bureaucracy is known."

The 1952-1956 Period: The BNDE and the Program for Economic Reequipment

The BNDE was officially installed in November 1952, but did not start its operations until September 1953. During its first few years of operation, it tried to follow the recommendations of the Joint Mission. This became a difficult task, as neither the Export-Import Bank nor the World Bank continued to provide the originally promised foreign resources. Until 1954, less than one-third of those funds were turned over. By 1958 they were totally suspended.[5] In addition, the original cruzeiro cost estimates for the various projects proved to be inadequate because of accelerating inflation. Another problem was the delay in receiving approved public funds. The BNDE's annual reports in the mid-1950s often expressed the fear of having to divert new resources from supplementary funds to projects already under way.

The scarcity of funds kept the BNDE's share of gross capital formation below 3% prior to 1956, and only the projects having top priority were funded. The demand for funds was far greater than the supply, and many industrial firms which solicited funds from the BNDE were not assisted. Of total lending operations in those years, less than 10% went to the private sector. But the

BNDE affected investments by other means. Being empowered to guarantee foreign loans contracted by domestic firms, it backed several million dollars' worth of loans during its first 5 years.

Because the BNDE's financing activities were relatively small in its first years of operation, its staff spent a large proportion of its time developing the type of research activities on the Brazilian economy which had been started by the Joint Brazil-United States Mission. The resulting accumulation of information and capacity for analysis of the BNDE made it an influential institution in the planning of future governments.[6]

In general, however, the bank was dissatisfied with what it considered to be the limited means it had available to promote economic development. Although it was permitted to subscribe to the capital of firms, it lacked the funds to do so in its early years. Its report of 1955 (BNDE, 1955: 126-127) expressed the hope that in the future the BNDE would be able to enter into this area and, through its investments, inspire the confidence of other investors and thus build up the national capital market.

The 1957-1963 Period: The BNDE and Industrial Development

The position of the BNDE improved considerably under the Kubitschek government. A Development Council was created which relied on the bank for its planning functions. In fact, Kubitschek's well-known Targets Plan (Programa de Metas) was formulated by the BNDE staff. According to Pinto (1969: 47) it presently fell on the BNDE "to judge, on behalf of the federal government, which types of economic enterprises were eligible for government support." Thus, the BNDE was "by its legal nature, the official controller of decisions, and not just a manipulator of incentives. This subtle but significant clash between the bank's roles may have been responsible for a major change in the bank's loan policies, which later came to favor manufacturing industries to the detriment of infrastructure projects."[7]

The Kubitschek government made an effort to strengthen BNDE's finances. The situation in 1956 was precarious, and when a congressional commission examined the bank's financial status, it found that the failure to provide adequate funding was seriously undermining the completion of the Program for Economic Reequipment. On the commission's recommendation, a new law was passed altering the previous legislation regulating the bank. It created a progressive additional income tax, and a 4% tax was placed on undistributed profits. In addition, insurance and investment companies were still required to contribute 25% of their funds to BNDE projects, although they were now given the option of directly investing their funds with BNDE approval. The law also stipulated that the BNDE could not provide more than 60% of a firm's capital. The law was capped by a requirement that 25% of its resources from the Fund for Economic Reequipment (at that time almost all of its revenue) had to be invested in the Center-West, North and Northeast. (BNDE, 1956: 12-20). As far as the latter provision was concerned, it turned out that "these areas were incapable of coming forward with projects for enterprises which were in line with the industrial expansion contemplated by the Target Plan, or which would meet the feasibility requirements set by the BNDE" (Pinto, 1969: 51).

At that time, the BNDE also found it easier to obtain foreign funds. A major source was the U.S. Wheat Accords, the first of which was signed in 1955. These placed the money from the sale of U.S. grain in a special account at the BNDE, and the funds provided the Bank with a substantial fraction of its resources. Also, after special negotiations between the U.S. and Brazil, the Export-Import Bank and the World Bank agreed to expand their loans to Brazil (BNDE, 1958: 300-302).

In spite of these changes, the BNDE's resources did not increase sufficiently to provide it with adequate finances for all its projects. One of the principal problems was the government's withholding of funds specifically earmarked for the BNDE. In 1956, for example, it should have received Cr 13.2 million from the Fund for Economic Reequipment, but it obtained only Cr 3.5 million. For the period 1952-1958 Cr 67.4 million should have been allocated to the bank, yet only Cr 34.6 million were released. The situation began to improve in 1959, when only 18% of the funds were withheld. Nevertheless, there was still a tendency for the government to use funds allocated for the BNDE for other purposes (BNDE, 1959: 38).

Demand, measured by loan applications, was strong throughout the period, but the bank's nominal interest rates were almost constant. Those entities receiving loans were thus receiving an increasing subsidy, i.e., negative rates of interest as the rate of inflation accelerated. The BNDE hoped to get a return of 9% on average from its investments in order to cover expenses and the 5% guaranteed on forced loans. The interest rates it charged during those years were 8% for railroads; 9% for warehouses, ports and power projects; 10% for transportation projects other than railroads; and 11% for industry. In 1958 the average expected return rose to 9.5% and stayed at that level for several years. In contrast, the average annual inflation rate in the 1957-1961 period was more than, 28% reaching 47.7% in 1961.

The focus of the BNDE's activities shifted from transport and related activities to electricity and steel production. This change is evident from the summary of authorized financial operations in the two periods contained in Table 1.

The shift to industry was also accompanied by a new approach towards financing. In May 1956 the Administrative Council of the BNDE approved a resolution enabling the bank to engage in equity financing. This type of operation would turn the bank into the principal shareholder of the steel enterprises USIMINAS and COSIPA, and minority shareholder in firms involving paper and cellulose, shipbuilding, tires, and other products. It was felt that this type of financing would protect the BNDE from the erosion of its funds through inflation (Baer, 1969: 79-83). This, of course, would depend on the degree of price controls the government would force on the firms in which the BNDE had placed its funds.

Evaluation: The BNDE as Financier of the Public Sector

The emphasis on power and industry during the late 1950s and early 1960s was justified by the fact that power shortages were still threatening the future growth of the economy and that the

TABLE 1
BNDE: Authorized Financial Operations

	1952–1956	1957–1963
Transport	68.3%	7.5%
Power	19.5%	40.8%
Industry	9.8%	48.6%
Other	2.7%	3.1%
TOTAL	100.0%	100.0%

SOURCE: BNDE, 1963: 10.

expansion of such basic industries as steel was essential to sustain the import substitution industrialization strategy.

BNDE's raison d'etre as a financier of the public sector was its independence from any specific government sector needing finance. It was thus in a position to demand from and/or provide to its clientele projects justifying proposed expenditures. This presumably led to more rational investment planning. Individual investment projects were also related to overall national development programs which, as already mentioned, were often prepared by the staff of the bank. The degree of power the BNDE had was limited, however. As we saw before, it frequently had to struggle to obtain new resources, and even the funds allocated to it were often not released in full by the government. No research to date gives us much of an indication on the influence the BNDE may have had on the routine functioning of its client institutions—either the ones to which it extended credit or the ones where it was a shareholder—that is, whether it had any influence on the internal organization of firms, on their pricing and employment policies, or other internal policies and functions.

The Evolution of the BNDE since 1964: Financier of the Private Sector

BNDE's finances were reformed in 1964. The additional tax was eliminated and replaced by giving the institution 20% of all income tax receipts (BNDE, 1964: i-ix). This arrangement lasted until 1967, when a constitutional amendment was enacted to allow for a tax on financial transactions which became the new income base of the bank. In addition, BNDE received an annual allocation from the federal budget and money from special funds, and, by the mid-1960s, the return on capital investment was also becoming a significant additional source of revenue (BNDE, 1967: 43).

In 1967, BNDE underwent an institutional reform. It was transferred from the Finance to the Planning Ministry and its internal organization underwent a considerable number of changes (BNDE, 1967: 49-51).

At the same time, BNDE's activities began to change rapidly as new funds began to flow in. Its investments increased and its share of gross capital formation rose from 2.7% in 1964 to 6.6% in 1965. Steel still absorbed 68% of the loans in 1965, but this was less than the high of 80.9% in 1963, and its share continued to fall—to 45.6% in 1966 and 10.2% in 1969. Loans were increasingly made to firms in nonferrous metals, chemicals, petrochemicals, paper, machinery, and other industries. Accompanying the change in the mix of BNDE's investments was also a trend towards greater support of the private sector. In 1964, 94% of financing was destined for the public sector, but in the following years this proportion fell continuously (see Table 2).

Most of the increased assistance to the private sector was achieved by the creation of new funds within the bank. The Fund for Economic Reequipment continued to be used for supporting the traditional type of public sector financing, while new funds gave loans to private enterprises. FINAME (Fund for the Acquisition of Machinery and Equipment) a subsidiary of the BNDE, was founded in 1964 to assist firms in financing the purchase of machinery. Its operations are carried out through a system of financial agents and commercial banks. In 1965 FIPEME (Financing for Small and Medium-Sized Firms) was created to assist small and moderately sized firms to reequip and expand their operations. It functioned through a network of agents and helped firms in the textiles, metals, cellulose, paper,

TABLE 2
Distribution of BNDE Financing between Public and Private Sectors (Percentage distribution)

YEARS	PUBLIC SECTOR	PRIVATE SECTOR	TOTAL
1952-1956	90.3	9.7	100.0
1957-1961	82.7	17.3	100.0
1962-1966	81.3	18.7	100.0
1967-1971	44.0	66.0	100.0
1972	21.8	78.2	100.0
1973	24.2	75.8	100.0
1974	33.5	66.5	100.0
1975	22.7	77.3	100.0
1976	18.9	81.1	100.0
1977	20.8	79.2	100.0

SOURCE: Calculated from BNDE, 1977.

wood products, plastic, and automobile parts sectors. Another fund was created at the time to help firms in need of working capital.

The bank's form of financing also underwent changes. More use was made of stock subscriptions. In 1965 this already accounted for one-third of BNDE's operation. A program to provide impetus to the development of the capital market was created. PROCAP (Program for the Stimulation of the Capital Market) was supposed to assist firms in placing stocks. It was hoped that firms would thus raise more funds through expanding equity participation than through borrowing (BNDE, 1970: 4, 15).

The bank also expanded into technical assistance and training. FUNTEC (Fund for Technical and Scientific Development) was founded in 1964 to support graduate instruction, especially of industrial engineers, chemists, and physicists, and to finance research projects. It obtained a considerable amount of outside support. The Inter-American Development Bank gave a $4 million loan to develop graduate programs, and the BNDE was joined by USAID and some other Brazilian entities in contributing scholarships for study abroad.

Finally, the BNDE also established funds to conduct special studies to increase plant efficiency in various industries, eliminate bottlenecks, assist in the selection of technology, improve accounting practices, and examine sectoral and regional problems. These were consolidated in 1970 into a Fund for the Modernization and Reorganization of Industries (FMRI), which was created as a result of the government's concern about the ability of Brazilian firms to compete in internal and world markets. By centralizing all the bank's programs for technical assistance, the government hoped to improve that type of activity (BNDE, 1970: 3).

In the second half of the 1960s, the bank paid more attention to regional problems. Accords were signed with regional development banks and development agencies in which the BNDE committed itself to pass on part of its financial resources. In 1965, 88.2% of BNDE's financing occurred in the Southeast; by 1976 this proportion had declined to 51.3%. The Northeast's share increased from 3.9% in 1965 to 17.5% in 1976 and the South's from 3.4% to 14.6% (Revista do BNDE, 1977: 29).

One study found that this type of cooperation brought about a better allocation of resources. Decision-making was passed on to the regions where local problems were better known. Through this financial collaboration, there was increased coordination of state and regional planning, there was an improvement in the level of technical program evaluation, and the BNDE was able to increase its national coverage without enlarging its organization. Some negative aspects, however, were also uncovered: the system lacked coordination of agents within regions, it increased the possibility for local political influence in the choice of projects, and it suffered from a lack of qualified personnel in local agencies to make adequate loan evaluations and to monitor projects.

The Mid-1970s

The National Development Plan of 1974 gave the BNDE the task of developing the basic resources and high technology capital goods sectors. In order to coordinate its new programs with its already diverse activities, it drew up a Plan of Action for 1974-1978 to ensure that its operations were consonant with the National Development Plan.

These actions were possible because, after the change of regime in 1964, the influence of the BNDE on economic policy-making grew substantially. It became one of the primary instruments through which the state directed the economy's investment activities. Martins (1977: 63-64) has claimed that from the mid-1960s to the present the BNDE experienced "not only a growth of its resources, but also its activities were extended to all industrial sectors . . . the Bank became a key tool in the financial intermediation of the public sector." The BNDE's role in the economy grew substantially. Its share of gross capital formation rose from 2% in 1963 to 9% in 1976. Its staff and number of subsidiaries expanded rapidly to handle its enormous increase in activities.

To develop the intermediate and capital goods industries, two BNDE subsidiaries were created in 1974: FIBASE (Insumos Básicos S.A.-Financiamento e Participacões) and EMBRAMEC (Mecánica Brasileira S.A.). The former was to help supply basic industrial imputs by aiding the private sector to produce fertilizers, nonferrous metals, paper, pulp, and organic and inorganic chemicals. EMBRAMEC was designed to promote basic capital goods firms. Most of the financing of these subsidiaries was granted through minority equity participation. A third subsidiary was IBRASA (Investimentos Brasileiros S.A.), which was to provide support for firms in the private sector by subscribing to ordinary or preferential shares and debentures. Most loan operations of these and previously established funds were supposed to be on a real interest basis in the second half of the sixties and the seventies, i.e., all had indexing clauses.

During the seventies, the BNDE also created agencies to finance and guide small and medium-sized private firms, reorganized its programs to develop capital markets, and established a Program for Basic Consumption Items, which supported the expansion of the production of basic foodstuffs of high nutritive value and low costs for lower income groups.

A Brief Summary of BNDE's Growth Since 1964

The overall growth of BNDE's activities since 1964 has been impressive if only from a quantitative point of view. The value of total domestic operations grew from approximately \$60 million in 1964 to \$381 million in 1970, and to about \$5.7 billion in 1976. During the early 1970s BNDE's financial operations amounted to about 4% of the loans of the financial system to the private sector; this had grown by 1978 to about 12% (BNDE, 1977; Banco Central do Brasil, 1979).

By the second half of the 1970s, 80% of BNDE's activities were directed towards the private sector. It was, in fact, the domestic private sector's principal source of external financing, as only a small amount of capital was being raised through the sale of new shares or bonds (the private sector was wary of issuing indexed bonds, which were therefore dominated by the state). Simultaneously, there were significant changes in BNDE's sources of funds. The most striking change is the decline of government resources from about 60% prior to 1964 to 2.2% in 1977. The principal source of funds by the second half of the 1970s was social trust funds (see Table 3).

Implications of BNDE's Institutional Transformation

The change of the BNDE from an investment financier of the public sector to the main source of outside investment funds of the private sector was due to two developments. First, it was the logical outcome of the growing independence of state enterprises within the Brazilian public sector. By the second half of the 1960s, state enterprises in steel, power generation, and petrochemicals were going concerns which had the capacity to generate internal investment funds, especially given the fact that they were allowed to follow adequate pricing policies for such purposes. This also enabled them to borrow funds directly from international institutions and from the private foreign capital markets. Therefore, there was little need for them to rely on a development bank.

TABLE 3
Origin of BNDE Resources

RESOURCES	PERCENTAGE DISTRIBUTION 1952-196		
INTERNAL RESOURCES	22.0		
Capital & Reserves	18.4		
Returns on Investments	3.6		
RESOURCES FROM GOVERNMENT	59.5		
Additional Income Tax	50.4		
Compulsory Insurance Co. Deposits	3.6		
National Investment Fund*	5.5		
SPECIAL RESOURCES - AID-BNDE ACCORD**	13.6		
EXTRAORDINARY RESOURCES***	4.9		
TOTAL	100.0		
	1973	1976	1977
Internal Resources	38.9	21.9	21.8
(Returns on Investments)		(12.8)	(10.5)
Government Resources	16.2	0.1	2.2
Repass Operations	29.8	17.1	17.7
PIS/PASEP@	-	54.3	47.1
Foreign Resources	15.1	6.6	11.2
TOTAL	100.0	100.0	100.0

SOURCES: XIII Exposicao Sobre o Programa de Reaparelhamento Economico of BNDE, 1964; also BNDE, 1977.
*Created in 1963.
**PL 480 Agreements.
***Special Transfers from National Treasury.
@Private and Government Workers' Retirement Funds.

Second, by the mid-1960s, there was an increasingly felt need by policy makers to strengthen the domestic private sector, which did not have the financial means to maintain its relative size vis-à-vis state and multinational enterprises. As a result, the BNDE found a new role for itself as the principal instrument to support and strengthen private Brazilian firms. This new role not only provided the BNDE with a justification for its continued existence, but also for access to new sources of finance, especially the social trust funds such as PIS/PASEP (Programa de

Integracao Social/Programa de Formação do Patrimonio do Servidor Publico). The increased reliance on the latter, however, poses a dilemma because these funds are indexed. This makes it increasingly difficult for the bank to provide subsidized loans, i.e., at negative rates of interest, unless the government is willing to make available special additional funds or is willing to allow a decrease in the indexing applied to the PIS/PASEP deposits (Baer, 1979; Baer and Beckerman, 1980).

BNDE was forced to make subsidized loans for investment projects in 1975 and 1976—the maximum indexing for loans was 20% which was less than the rate of inflation of about 30% and 40% in each of these years. This type of operation would not be possible in the long run without greater access by the bank to subsidized funds. In fact, the use of indexed funds was forcing the BNDE to act increasingly like a traditional investment banker—looking for real earnings. This might explain the rise in the relative importance of FINAME, which finances the sale of domestically produced machines at indexed rates. The BNDE subsidiary accounted for 60% of the bank's activities in 1977. It also explains the difficulties the bank was having in 1978 in placing long-term indexed loans. Individual firms were not willing to assume the burdens of indexation. They did not want to risk having their debt increase according to an index applied to government bonds, while the prices of their products might rise at a smaller and their costs at a greater rate (Baer and Beckerman, 1980).

This increased difficulty in loan-making could substantially weaken the bank. The declining earning capacity of its portfolio could ultimately threaten its ability to pay for the interest and for the indexing of its deposits. By the late 1970s this was becoming a major dilemma, which was, ironically, brought about by the BNDE's initial coup in securing the giant social trust funds for itself.

There can be little doubt that FINAME's activities have strengthened the domestic private sector by allowing firms to sell their equipment with adequate credit. This type of activity has been quite automatic; that is, little effort was made to emphasize one or another sector. Until 1979, the BNDE was subordinate to the planning Ministry,[8] and FINAME's credits were ample and not affected by the Finance Ministry's credit policies. Sooner or later, however, a test of power over priorities might occur—in other words, whether in the interest of stabilization FINAME's activities should be curtailed, thus resulting in a deemphasis on the strengthening of the private sector.

One of BNDE's methods of assisting private firms has been through the purchase of minority shares of enterprises. As we saw above, that is how a number of the bank's subsidiaries inject funds into firms. This method could cause some future problems if the earnings from such investments are not high enough to cover the interest and indexing payments obligations of the BNDE. There arises a further complication, moreover, if the firm in which the BNDE owns minority shares (or to which it has made substantial loans) is in financial difficulties. Should such a firm be allowed to go into bankruptcy, or should the BNDE help by buying more shares, and thus acquire control? (In the case of a debtor firm, the question would be whether the debt should be converted into BNDE ownership shares.)

In a number of cases the BNDE has taken control of firms. The motivation was the preservation of jobs and the possibility of losing less by reorganizing a firm than by liquidating it. The intention is to sell the firm back to the private sector once its earning powers have been restored. This "unintentional" nationalization ("estatização") has not occurred on a wide scale to date, but might increase if Brazil should enter a more prolonged phase of slow economic growth. Thus there always lurks in the background the possibility that the BNDE's instruments designed to strengthen the private sector could actually result in a substantial amount of state take-overs.

BNDE's Power Over Resource Allocation

In an economy where the state is as powerful an economic agent as in Brazil, the allocation of resources is determined to a large extent outside of the market. This is especially the case of savings which are generated by the government (either directly or through forced savings) and which represent over 50% of national savings. In order to understand the forces which are behind the allocation of resources, it becomes necessary to study the decision-making units of the state, of which the BNDE is an important entity.

Much research remains to be done to understand the role of the BNDE within this allocational mechanism. It is still not clear what role the bank played in its phase as a government financier. We mentioned that it was influential at times in the formulation of general development plans. It is not certain, however, whether it had much influence in those state firms to which it was the principal creditor (as in transportation and power generation) or shareholder (as in steel firms). It might have been influential in shaping the basic investment plans of those firms—though even that is not certain—but it may have had little influence in other micro policy decisions such as pricing or wages.

As a financier of the private sector, the BNDE has acted through a large number of affiliated or subsidiary organizations and funds. A large portion of resources available are channeled to the private sector in a fairly automatic manner (e.g., FINAME). This has not given the bank much control over the allocation of such resources, except for the disciplinary function it assumes over the manner in which funds were distributed by financial agents. With other funds, the BNDE probably has exerted more influence through the requirements of projects which preceded the granting of finance. Firms are forced to plan and justify their expansion and therefore more rationality has been introduced in the allocation of resources. More research is needed, however, to discover the importance of project planning requirements. With the availability of indexed funds, which have to be applied without delay in order to provide the bank with the necessary earnings, there might be a tendency for analysts to overlook the difficulties in granting loans or equity participation funds. Demand projections and cost estimates for projects might be overly optimistic in order to justify funding. Once this comes to light, however, the BNDE might be so committed to such projects that it is forced to invest more funds than originally intended.

NOTES

1. "Tripe," meaning tripod, refers to the three dimensional ownership structure of Brazil's productive and financial sectors—private domestic, state, and multinational.

2. Funds were to be distributed in the following way: railroads—48%; highways—1%; ports—7%; coastal navigation—5%; power generation—33%; miscellaneous—6%. (See BNDE, 1965: 4).

3. Law no. 1474 (November 26, 1951) raised domestic funds through an additional assessment of 15% on taxable income and 3% on undistributed profits. This levy was in the form of a 5-year forced loan on natural and juridical persons, with an interest of 5% per year and a bonus of government bonds equal to 25% on the loan. The BNDE's resources were augmented by compulsory deposits of 4% of the Federal Savings Banks' reserves and 3% of the Social Security agencies' reserves. Finally, insurance companies and investment corporations were to leave 25% of their funds invested in the bank.

4. For the economic and political background of the creation of the BNDE, see Martins (1977: vii).

5. Pinto (1969: 41) cites a confidential source who stated that a number of events—such as Vargas' New Year's eve speech of 1952 (which denounced foreign governments for plotting to obtain massive profit remittances from foreign enterprises in Brazil) and the creation of Petrobras—caused a cooling of the U.S. and the World Bank towards financing Brazilian growth.

6. Much research was carried out jointly with an ECLA group and with researchers of the Instituto Brasileiro de Economia/Fundação Getúlio Vargas (Pinto, 1969: 41; Martins, 1977: 55-56).

7. Because the Conselho do Desenvolvimento was also responsible for the Grupos Executivos, which were important instruments for developing new priority sectors of the economy, the BNDE also became heavily involved in the industrial planning of the period (Pinto, 1969: 47).

8. The government taking office in March 1979 shifted the BNDE into the Ministry of Industry and Commerce.

REFERENCES

BAER, W. (1979) The Brazilian Economy: Its Growth and Development. Columbus, OH: Grid.

——— (1969) The Development of the Brazilian Steel Industry. Nashville: Vanderbilt Univ. Press.

——— and P. BECKERMAN (1980) "The trouble with index-linking: reflections on the recent Brazilian experience." World Development (August).

BAER, W., R. NEWFARMER and T. TREBAT (1976) "On state capitalism in Brazil: some new issues and questions." Inter-American Economic Affairs 30 (Winter): 69-91.

BAER, W., I. KERSTENETZKY and A. V. VILLELA (1973) "The changing role of the state in the Brazilian economy." World Development (November): 23-34.

Banco Central do Brasil (1979) Boletim (April).

BNDE [National Bank for Economic Development] (1955, 1956, 1958, 1959, 1963, 1964, 1967, 1970, 1977) Relatório das Atividades. Rio de Janeiro: Author.

——— (1965) Origins, Resources and Operations. Rio de Janeiro: Author.

——— (1964) XIII Exposição Sobre o Programa de Reaparelhamento Econômico. Rio de Janeiro: Author.

MARTINS, L. (1977) A Expanşão Recente do Estado no Brasil: Seus Problemas a Seus Atores. Rio de Janeiro: IUPERJ [Instituto Universitario de Pesquisas do Rio de Janeiro].

——— (1976) Pouvoir et Developpement Economique. Paris: Editions Anthropos.

PINTO, R.F.S. (1969) The Political Ecology of the Brazilian National Bank for Economic Development (BNDE). Washington, DC: Organization of American States.

Revista do BNDE (1977) [annual publication]. "25 Anos de BNDE: Avaliaçáo." Rio de Janeiro: BNDE.

——— (1964) [annual publication]. Rio de Janeiro: BNDE.

Werner Baer is Professor of Economics at the University of Illinois—Urbana. He has written many books and articles on Brazilian economic problems and on Latin America in general, the most recent one being The Brazilian Economy: Its Growth and Development *(Grid Publishing, Inc., 1979).*

Annibal V. Villela, a member of the consulting firm Consultaria Economica Ltda. in Rio de Janeiro since 1978, has been secretary for Economic and Social Affairs of the OAS in Washington, DC, a professor in the Economic Development Institute of the World Bank, and a professor at numerous universities in the United States. His postgraduate studies were conducted at the Universities of Stockholm and London. He has published extensively on economic development in Latin America.

ALFRED H. SAULNIERS
Institute of Latin American Studies
University of Texas, Austin

ENCI
Peru's Bandied Monopolist

Introduction

Until 1968, state enterprises played a minor role in the Peruvian economy. The list of public sector enterprises was relatively small. It included the Central and sectoral banks, a merchant fleet, railways, a minor petroleum producer, hyroelectric power companies, a steel mill, monopolies over salt, tobacco, and guano, a few tourism projects, and a set of regional development corporations. From 1968 to 1974 the state moved swiftly to expand its role in order to direct and control the course of the country's economic evolution. The public sector increased both in size and scope to include most banking, basic industries, and most international and some domestic trade.

Such a rapid expansion into sectors of the economy hitherto reserved for private enterprise has led to a host of problems which can be analyzed from the perspective of organization and control. Mechanisms for implementing desired government action through public enterprises and for monitoring the operations of such firms in their early years need considerable refinement. In the Peruvian case, changes in government objectives over a short time led to a bewildering set of modifications, not only for the public enterprise portfolio taken as a whole, but also for the management of the individual firm. This article examines the evolution of one of the most bandied of these state enterprises until the end of 1978.

The Empresa Nacional de Comercialización de Insumos (ENCI) was created on August 27, 1974, through Decree Law No.

Journal of Interamerican Studies and World Affairs, Vol. 22 No. 4, November 1980 441-462

20705 with the dual objectives of (a) domestic and foreign marketing of basic inputs for the industrial, mining and agricultural sectors and (b) marketing any other products which could be classified as fundamental to the economy of Peru.[1]

The enterprise was formed through the merger of two public sector firms, the Empresa Nacional de Comercialización Industrial, also known as ENCI, and the marketing activities of the Empresa de Fertilizantes (FERTIPERU). The first section of this article examines the institutional background of the two firms which were merged. The second section details the institutional evolution of the new ENCI from 1974 to 1978. The third section looks at its performance through the growth of imports, sales, subsidies and income; following that, the study will cover basic problems that have marked ENCI's existence. These include import financing control mechanisms, determinants of selling prices, and the legal status of labor. Finally, the article draws conclusions regarding the twin issues of organization and control, and reflects on areas for further investigation.

Background to the Merger

CENTRAL GOVERNMENT

While the Peruvian state had been involved in some minor domestic marketing prior to 1968, its expansion to an increasingly important position came late in the administration of General Juan Velasco Alvarado. His 1971-1975 national development plan sketched out the active role of the state as "promoter, orienter, and direct participant in economic activity," stressing only the following sectors: industry, agriculture, mining, and fishing (Presidencia, de la República, 1971: 26). Marketing was not stressed per se, but rather in a subordinate fashion with respect to other state action.

The following summary of planned action indicates the minor marketing programs contemplated in the first years of military rule. In industry the state was to acquire basic industries by direct investment or nationalization[2] with no explicit provision for marketing production. In agriculture, the state was to manipulate domestic prices and construct such physical market infrastructure as warehouses, silos, cold-storage plants and distribution centers (Presidencia, de la República 1971: 81). An explicit external marketing program was considered for the mining sector, but direct sales by public sector agencies were placed last in the list of overall state marketing policies, following such provision of more comprehensive insurance, and price control (Presidencia de la República, 1971: 143). Given the importance of copper to the Peruvian economy, a different treatment was proposed, with the state expected to take over external marketing by 1971 to mark the third anniversary of the revolution. Strong direct action in an internal marketing system was foreseen only for petroleum products, as PETROPERU was to expand its distribution system (Presidencia, de la República, 1971: 154). In the fishing sector, both internal and external operations were planned. EPCHAP's exports of fishmeal and fishoil were to be stressed, and a joint public-private domestic distribution system for fish products for human consumption was to be organized. The key to the reshaping of, and consequent increase in, the marketing activities of the state in 1974 which resulted in the creation of ENCI was the formation of the Ministry of Commerce (MINCOM). It had been established in December 1973 by splitting the then Ministry of Industry and Commerce and incorporating new activities in an effort to strengthen and rationalize the state's marketing activities. This attempt to bring about major structural changes in the economy was done within the prevailing ideological framework of the enterpreneurial state (Arias, 1975). All marketing administrations of the Ministries of Agriculture, Fishing, Energy, and Mining, along with the Customs service, were incorporated into MINCOM during 1974, in addition to the commercial activities of several public sector firms.

MINCOM was instructed to "define . . . plan, direct, regulate, encourage, control and/or execute" all commercial activities. Its activities covered tariff policies; internal and external trading, including storage, supply, and distribution; plans to increase and diversify nontraditional exports; analyses of Peru's position in international trade; negotiations of trade agreements; and statistical compilation. To meet its goals, MINCOM was given the power to establish decentralized public entities, or to restructure and amplify the scope of operations of existing ones.

MINCOM's formation was reflected in the 1975-1978 national plan, which detailed a more active and direct role for the state in addition to the traditional functions of promotion, regulation, and control. The three principal goals of the sector were to ensure an adequate supply of consumer goods, to provide inputs for economic activity, and to maximize foreign exchange earnings through international marketing (Presedencia, de la República, 1975: 43). The domestic supply of all essentials was to be based on a public enterprise distribution system. Those public enterprises already involved in marketing were to be reorganized, their objectives modified, and their activities amplified to bring them in line with overall sector priorities. ENCI was created as a result of this reorganization.

ENCI, EMPRESA NACIONAL DE COMERCIALIZACION INDUSTRIAL: 1971-1974

A brief overview of one of the firms merged into ENCI in 1974 is provided to demonstrate that many of the operational problems predated ENCI and were simply transferred to it. The Empresa Nacional de Comercialización Industrial (ENCI) was formed in November 1971 to provide greater government control over internal and external markets by selling industrial products considered essential or used as basic inputs for all types of economic activity. Secondary goals were to increase efficiency in foreign exchange use and bring the balance of payments into equilibrium (ENCI, 1973: 7).

ENCI's autonomy was limited in that it could only import merchandise if specifically authorized by government decree. Thus decisions with regard to the types and quantities of goods imported were beyond its control. One week after ENCI's inception, the importation of basic inputs was reserved for the state.[3] However, the entity charged with importing on behalf of the state was not specified.

Instead, ENCI was given that same day a monopoly on newsprint imports. A dual system persisted for some time, as private sector licenses were not abrogated. It was only in March 1973 that ENCI began direct marketing of newsprint for its own account (ENCI, 1973: 12). During 1972 and 1973 a gradual increase in functions took place. ENCI was permitted to import soy oil, special watermarked paper,[4] paraffin, television sets for use in the Selva, PVC, and polyester, and was authorized to import or export cement. In importing soy oil, paraffin and inputs for the plastics and clothing industries, ENCI acted solely as a broker.

ENCI had to follow a cumbersome series of steps to import goods. (To illustrate this, only the quantity decision will be considered.) The Dirección General de Industrias of the Ministry of Industry and Tourism projected domestic demand and supply and determined the shortfall.[5] It further allocated both domestic production and imports among domestic industrial users through a quota system. ENCI had to import the shortfall by strictly following procedures established by the Ministry of Commerce.

ENCI never was given the monopoly over imports of basic inputs, which was reserved for the government. Further, whenever a monopoly was assigned to ENCI by supreme decree, the preexisting private import licenses were allowed to expire at the end of their stated term, delaying the onset of true monopoly power.

By May 1974, ENCI's organic law, which was to detail its functioning, had not yet been issued. In August 1974, less than three years after its creation, ENCI was merged with FERTIPERU.

FERTIPERU, EMPRESA DE FERTILIZANTES

A quick look at the other major component of ENCI indicates the lack of an overall organizational and control framework typical of some public enterprises during the 1968-1974 period.

The Peruvian government had been directly involved in fertilizer production since the 1840s, when private firms exploited the guano deposits under government concession. After the turn of the century, when the guano reserves had been virtually depleted, the Compañía Administradora de Guano, a private company with some government participation, was given a five-year renewable monopoly to exploit the guano and to administer all deposits. In 1963, the state purchased all outstanding shares and expanded the company to include distribution and sales of all types of fertilizers. Its name was changed to the Corporación Nacional de Fertilizantes (CONAFER).

Between 1968 and 1974, the Peruvian government's fertilizer interest underwent a bewildering series of organizational changes. These involved changes in the firm's name, its function, and the ministry or public enterprise to which it was responsible. In July 1968 CONAFER was abolished. All its functions were given to the Servicio de Insumos Agrícolas (SERINA), which was a subsidiary of another public sector firm, the Corporacíon Nacional de Producción Agraria (CONAPA), which operated under the Ministry of Agriculture. The reason given at the time for the integration of public sector activities was to increase their efficiency, thereby saving resources.[6]

In March 1969, when the Ministry of Industry and Commerce was created, the Empresa de Fertilizantes was placed under its control as a decentralized public organization. The Empresa de Fertilizantes was to extract and/or produce fertilizers and market them. Three months later, in July 1969, the Servicio Nacional de Fertilizantes (SENAFER) was attributed to the Empresa Pública de Servicios Agropecuarios y Pesqueros under the Ministry of Agriculture and Fishing, with the functions of mining guano and importing and marketing other fertilizers. In September 1970, to normalize this duplication of functions, SENAFER's functions were transferred from EPSAP, under the Ministry of Agriculture and Fishing, to the Empresa de Fertilizantes, under the Ministry of Industry and Commerce. The change had no effect on its function, but the Empresa de Fertilizantes took the name of SENAFER.

In early 1973, SENAFER received a monopoly on fertilizer imports, with the existing import licenses remaining valid until expiration. On October 30, 1973, the Empresa de Fertilizantes was given the name FERTIPERU and finally had its functions detailed—more than four years after its creation.

Ten months after its form and functions were spelled out, FERTIPERU was dissolved. The part of the company dealing with production was transferred to PESCA-PERU (Empresa Pública de Producción de Harina y Aceite de Pescado) while the marketing operations were given to ENCI.

Structure and Attributes of ENCI, 1974-1978

Following the merger in 1974 with FERTIPERU, ENCI was organized under public enterprise statutes, with an internal governing structure made up of a board of directors and general management. It should be noted that, in Peru, public sector firms may be formed under either public or private enterprise law. The differences lie in the nature and degree of control which the government is able to exercise over the day-to-day operations of the firm. Under the public enterprise statutes, ENCI was subject to greater control at the ministerial level.

Under its statutes of incorporation, ENCI had little autonomy in determining its price and import policies. The yearly import quotas, the projected foreign exchange needs, the import brokers fees and the domestic sales prices had to be approved by the Ministry of Economics and Finance and the Ministry of Commerce, then fixed by Supreme Resolution signed by the Minister of Commerce. Import financing was to be done through the Banco de la Nación.

Between 1974 and 1976 ENCI's position was considerably strengthened. It received monopolies on imports of paraffin, steel wire, raw material for polyesters, paper for newspapers, magazines and books, PVC, fertilizers of all types, beer, wines, and spirits. While a monopoly was not immediately granted for caustic soda, in 1975 it was to import enough to cover the domestic deficit. This was changed to an explicit monopoly in

1976. Crude vegetable oil and jute sacks were to be imported without monopoly to cover existing shortages.

During 1977, ENCI lost some duties and gained others. It received monopoly rights for the export of domestically produced caustic soda, monopoly selling rights both at home and abroad for phosphate rock, and all domestic marketing rights for PVC, both imported and nationally produced. It lost the import and export monopoly for cement, which was given to the four state-owned cement plants.[7]

By 1978, the situation had changed dramatically. In July, the structure of the newly fused Ministry of Agriculture and Foodstuffs was detailed, and ENCI was to be transferred to the agricultural sector by the end of the year, with emphasis placed on ENCI's agriculture-related activities. These included internal and external marketing of agricultural products for human and livestock consumption, agricultural inputs to industry, and industrial inputs to agriculture. ENCI's monopolies on non-agricultural imports and marketing were to be transferred to private sector industrialists and commercial firms and to some public sector enterprises. As a consequence, ENCI lost its monopolies on paraffin imports, steel wire imports, caustic soda imports or exports, PVC imports, and imports and marketing of newsprint and paper for books and magazines.[8]

In addition, major changes were made with respect to another public sector firm which would directly concern ENCI. The Empresa Pública de Comercialización de Harina y Aceite de Pescado (EPCHAP) was divided into two parts. The activities dealing with the marketing of fishmeal and fish oil were attributed to the fishing sector. The rest of its activities, which included the marketing of cotton, wheat, corn, sorghum, soy, barley, milk products, meat, and meat products, was placed under ENCI's control. In February 1979, ENCI was merged with EPSA (Empresa Pública de Servicios Agropecuarios).

Evolution of ENCI's Imports, Sales, Subsidies and Income, 1974-1978

IMPORTS

Table I illustrates the evolution of ENCI's import activities from 1974 to 1977. Importing both directly and as broker for other firms, ENCI accounted for approximatley 4% of the value of Peru's imports. These fluctuated from a high of $123 million to a low of $64 million. Examining the major items, it can be seen that the value of soy oil imports remained relatively stable, with a slight decrease in 1976 which may be attributed to a drop in international prices, as the volume of such imports increased 30% from 1975 to 1976. From 1975 to 1977, the value of fertilizer imports decreased as world market prices fell, and domestic fertilizer production increased 60% as the Talara fertilizer complex began operation (ENCI, 1978a: 13). The value of newsprint imports was relatively stable, with the decrease in 1976 a result of a shift in sources from the U.S. and Canada to Chile and Romania, which resulted in a drop in unit price of almost 20% (ENCI, 1978a: 7).

SALES

Table 2 illustrates the overall growth of ENCI between 1974 and 1978 as attributable both to increases in sales of existing product lines and the addition of new ones. The most notable change is that of fertilizer sales, which increased more than 80% to almost 400 metric tons as a consequence of subsidized prices, an increase in fertilized acreage, and strong promotion by ENCI. In 1976, ENCI was permitted to import and sell cement to meet a short-term deficit on the local market. Caustic soda sales showed strong variations, and polyesters demonstrated a sharp surge from 1977 on. Sales of other products were marked by a weak negative trend.

SUBSIDIES

Fertilizer transport costs from the port of entry or the factory to the point of sale had been subsidized by the government since

TABLE 1
Imports of Principal Inputs by ENCI, 1974-1977
(millions of U.S. dollars)

	1974	1975	1976	1977
Soy Oil	$40.1	$42.5	$36.3	$42.9
Fertilizers	7.2	40.1	5.9	18.2
Newsprint	14.9	14.8	12.8	16.2
P.V.C.	12.1	4.6	3.7	9.5
Paraffin	0.2	3.9	3.2	4.2
Wire Rods	8.0	9.0	0.9	1.6
Caustic Soda	0.6	3.7	0.1	0.3
Cement	--	1.7	0.9	--
Polyesters	3.8	2.2	0.5	8.3
Other*	+	--	0.1	0.6
TOTAL	83.9	122.5	64.4	101.8
ENCI Imports as percentage of total imports	4.39	5.13	3.07	4.86

SOURCE: ENCI, 1978b.
*Alcoholic beverages and jute sacking.
+Less than 0.05.

TABLE 2
Sales of Principal Industrial Inputs by ENCI, 1974-1978
(thousands of metric tons)

	1974	1975	1976	1977	1978
Soy Oil	72.9	57.3	79.5	58.8	62.0*
Fertilizers	--	205.4	323.5	392.6	371.7
Newsprint	39.0	37.3	35.9	41.7	29.6
P.V.C.	10.6	3.6	5.6	10.9	2.4
Paraffin	--	8.6	10.4	9.3	7.8
Wire Rods	--	12.1	13.1	5.7	7.0*
Caustic Soda	1.3	4.3	1.7	3.8	1.6*
Cement	--	--	59.4	--	--
Polyesters	1.1	0.9	0.1	7.8	8.1*

SOURCE: ENCI, 1978b.
The table excludes alcoholic beverages and jute sacking.
*Planned.

July 1975. The subsidy was viewed as a stimulus to farmers in remote areas, providing an incentive to use more fertilizer and thus boost the stagnating domestic agricultural production and diminish the need to import foodstuffs. The subsidy, which in theory was given directly to ENCI by the treasury, amounted to 46% of the total costs of fertilizer sales in 1975. Following price increases, it dropped to 34% in 1976 and 31% in 1977 (ENCI, n.d.: 7). For the last half of 1975, fertilizer subsidies totaled 418.7 million soles, rising to 990 million soles in 1976, and 1,536 million soles in 1977.

Two of the industrial inputs sold by ENCI, cement and caustic soda, were sold at subsidized prices. The goal of the subsidy policy was to lower the price of imported inputs to the level of those produced domestically. An excise tax on caustic soda produced by Química del Pacífico, S.A. was earmarked for ENCI's subsidy. Cement was subsidized both by a transfer to ENCI from the public treasury and by an excise tax on local production. In mid-1976, the tax amounted to 2 soles per sack of domestic cement sold. During 1976, subsidies on cement and caustic soda amounded to 181.3 million soles, or 2.6 million dollars. Revenues from the excise taxes posited directly by producers into ENCI's account in the Banco de la Nícion.

INCOME

Table 3 examines ENCI's income statements. From 1975 to 1978, ENCI's net sales more than doubled, going from 4.8 to 10 billion soles. However, this growth was slower than that of nonfinancial public enterprises as a whole. The cost of goods sold exceeded the value of net sales for all years except 1977, when the firm showed a modest gross profit of 137 million soles. Subsidies increased from 419 million soles in 1975 to 4 billion soles in 1978. Operating expenditures increased 1400% during the same time period. Interests and charges on loans and overdrafts averaged 250 million soles for 1975 and 1976. Foreign exchange losses, negligible in 1975 and 1976, totaled 1.4 billion soles during 1977 and 1978. Both ENCI and its set of public enterprises showed net losses for all years. After subsidies, ENCI showed a profit except in 1975.

TABLE 3
Income Statement for ENCI, 1975-1978 (millions of current soles)

	1975	1976	1977	1978
Net Sales	4796	4037	5643	10081
Less: Cost of Good Sold	4908	4224	5506	11844
Gross Profit (Loss)	(112)	(187)	137	(1763)
Less: Operating Expenditures:				
Sales Expenditures, Promotions, and Publicity	43	160	523	1118
Administrative Expenditures	65	180	170	367
Net Operating Profit (Loss)	(220)	(527)	(556)	(3248)
Plus: Financial and Other Income	27	99	157	60
Less: Interest & Expenditures on Loans & Overdrafts	291	221	-	-
Less: Foreign Exchange Losses	-	-	850	521
Less: Other Expenditures	7	81	-	-
Net Profit (Loss) Before Taxes & Extraordinary Items	(491)	(730)	(1249)	(3709)
Extraordinary Income/or (Expenditures)	-	-	(127)	(132)
Profit (Loss) from Prior Year's Operations	-	-	18	-
Legal Distribution of Net Income	-	-	-	-
Pre-Tax Profit (Loss)	(491)	(730)	(1358)	(3841)
Less: Corporation Income Tax	-	160	72	70
Net Profit (Loss)	(491)	(890)	(1430)	(3911)
Plus: Subsidies	419	1172	1535	4000
Post-Subsidy Profits	(72)	282	105	89

SOURCE: Ministerio de Economia y Finanzas, 1978.
– = Less than 0.5 Million Soles.

ENCI's 1975 losses are attributable in large part to the fertilizer pricing policy imposed by the government for urea. The sale price was fixed on the basis of projected levels of domestic urea production and imports. When production at PETROPERU'S new Talara plant was lower than anticipated, ENCI imported higher-priced urea to meet the shortfall, but the selling price was not changed. Such price rigidity, coupled with the shortfall, produced losses in excess of 115 million soles for urea alone (MINCOM, 1978: 118).

Problems Associated with ENCI

Four problems which strongly influenced ENCI's performance will be examined in this section. They indicate the muddled milieu within which the firm had to operate.

IMPORT FINANCING MECHANISMS

ENCI's financial problems which related to import mechanisms stemmed from the way in which costs were, and are allocated among various public sector entities. Only a few of them will be considered here. As mentioned earlier, ENCI's imports were financed through the Banco de la Nación. A letter of credit was opened, guaranteed by the Banco de la Nación, payable within 180 days in hard currency to the foreign supplier. Prior to the opening of the account, ENCI had to deposit the necessary funds, or, in the case of subsidized products, the nonsubsidized portion, in local currency. This procedure forced ENCI to assume a risk due to exchange differentials. During 1975 and most of 1976, while the sol was relatively stable, no serious problem was posed. However, during 1977 and 1978, as a consequence of the more than 100% devaluation, ENCI's exchange losses were 850 and 521 million soles, respectively. Because previously deposited funds were insufficient to purchase the needed hard currency, ENCI was force either to raise the selling price to cover its increased cost, or, for subsidized goods, to maintain the selling price but charge the cost differential to the subsidy (MINCOM, 1978: 121).

In the latter case, the Banco de la Nación normally paid the foreign supplier at the end of the 180-day period. However, when the subsidy had not been transferred in time by the public treasury, the bank lent ENCI the difference between the amount deposited and the value of the letter of credit. Slowness in transferring funds to ENCI occasioned financial charges.

During the second half of 1976, Peru was faced with a foreign exchange shortage. As a result, when ENCI accounts came due, the Central Bank at times lacked the hard currency to pay them. The Banco de la Nación then refinanced ENCI's unpaid external debts, even though the firm had deposited the local currency equivalent previously. The interest on the new loans was charged to ENCI, even though the firm had met its legal obligation with regard to financing imports. ENCI's board of directors refused to pay, as it had not been informed prior to the issuance of the loans. The Central Reserve Bank refused to pay, even though the additional interest had been the result of its lack of hard currency. The Banco de la Nación had cleared its own accounts at the end of the 180-day period by using loans for refinancing and claimed that it was not involved. This dispute had not been resolved by the end of 1978 (MINCOM, 1978: 122).

A further problem associated with import financing stems from the fact that funds deposited by ENCI in the Banco de la Nación had to be placed in noninterest-bearing accounts. In December 1977, ENCI had slighlty more than 4 billion soles (in excess of 33 million dollars) immobilized in such accounts (BCRP, 1977: 45). This high level of liquidity brought no benefits to the firm. Furthermore, at this time, ENCI was being charged for loans to cover other short-term debts. By mid-1978, the Ministry of Commerce became aware of this inefficiency in the use of the firm's funds. However, no solution had been adopted to remedy the problem (MINCOM, 1978: 126).

PRICING STRUCTURE

ENCI was subject to price rigidity for its product line. The selling price for all domestically marketed goods was to be fixed by Supreme Resolution and was usually changed yearly. Changes in world market prices, adjustments in the exchange rate, increases in transport costs, and changes in other bases used for price calculation all occurred in the short run, and were not easily reconciled with yearly changes. For subsidized items, the residual could be charged to the public treasury, but the maximum subsidy for all product lines was fixed in the biennial budget and not easily adjusted. For nonsubidized items, these unanticipated charges cut into the profit margin.

Centralization of price decision making resulted in long lags between the input of information bearing on prices and the moment of decision. By the time prices were fixed at the ministerial level, the information was usally obsolete (INP, 1978a: 13). This provoked unforeseen losses which were not always covered by the public treasury. By 1978, the subsidies due to ENCI for imports of soy oil in 1972, 1973, and 1974 still had not been paid (MINCOM, 1978: 123). The subsidy for soy oil in 1973 alone would have amounted to 5.6 million dollars (INP, n.d.: 109). When subsidies were not paid by the Ministry of Economics and Finance, they resulted in overdrafts from the Banco de la Nación, further aggravating the firm's financial position.

By mid-1977, forces to decentralize the pricing structure were in operation. Article 58 of ENCI's statues was modified. Prices for all commodities not subject to the system of price control and regulation were to be set by the firm's board of directors. The effect of this was minimal, however, as most of ENCI's product line was subject to price control. By mid-1978, in the expectation of the transfer of EPCHAP's activities to ENCI, a procedure was established to enable ENCI's board of directors to fix cotton prices on a monthly basis. This replaced the prior ministerial resolution, provided for more frequent price variations, and was done to bring Peruvian export prices in line with world market prices. The system was to have been extended to domestic prices for other lines by January 1979.

LABOR

ENCI's labor force was not subject to uniform set of labor laws. The coexistence of various labor laws pertaining to its employees led to inconsistencies. Among these were the application of different wage and salary scales for the same type of work, as well as the existence of different benefits with regard to meals, vacations, scholarly allowances, Christmas and New Years' bonuses, and pension plans. ENCI needed to maintain different legal and administrative procedures for each type of worker (INP, 1978: 16).

ENCI's labor relations were governed by 4 basic laws. Of these 3 pertained to white-collar workers, most of whom came under the labor code pertaining to the private sector. Both ENCI and FERTIPERU were created as public sector firms subject to the private enterprise labor laws. However, at the end of 1975, more than 20% of ENCI's white-collar workers were subject to the civil service code. Most of these came from CONAFER. Through the various mergers involving CONAFER and ENCI, these workers were maintained under the same legal statutes. With the creation of ENCI, they were given the option of switching to the private employee law, but by the end of 1975, 76 white-collar workers were still civil servants (Comisión Multisectorial, 1976: Anexo 14). By the end of 1978, this figure had dropped to 27 workers, primarily through attrition. In addition to the above laws, some white-collar workers were hired on an individual fixed-term contract basis.

Most blue-collar workers at ENCI were covered under private sector legislation. The rest were contracted for a fixed time period and under the provisions of still another legal base (Comisión Multisectorial, 1976: Anexo 14).

Additional obstacles, in the form of strong restrictions on ENCI's authority in personnel matters, were introduced in 1975 when Decree Law 21292 was issued to promote decentralization of decision making within the government. As a consequence of this law, a series of decisions could be taken only at the ministerial level for individuals whose basic monthly wage was in excess of 41,600 soles ($378 in 1977). These included contract hiring and firing, promotion and salary increase, personnel reassignment, change in job description, and retirement. ENCI was faced with a series of slow and costly procedures prior to receiving the ministerial approval. The 1977 Multisectorial Commission recommended a true decentralization of such decision making to the level of the board of directors (Comisión Multisectorial, 1977: 28).

Conclusions

The above summary description of ENCI's activities raises a considerable number of issues in the area of organization and control. This section will attempt to draw tentative conclusions with respect to the recent Peruvian public enterprise experience and to point out further areas where investigation is needed.

The frequent changes in ENCI's institutional form as a result of alterations in ministerial structure or mutations in the attributes of other public enterprises point to the lack of a clearly defined government policy for public sector marketing firms. We can take this one step further, noting strong indications that such policy did not exist for public sector firms in general. The 1971-1975 National Plan, in its first volume, devoted a toal of four lines to public enterprsies, burying them in a section on organizational structure of the central government (Presidencia de la República, 1971: 70). If we accept FitzGerald's conclusion that public enterprises carried "the main burden of enconomic transformation and captial accumulation in the public sector," (FitzGerald, 1976: 47), such an omission on the part of planners is noteworthy. Indepth analysis of ENCI leads to the conclusion that there has been no defined and agreed-upon system for organizing and controlling public enterprises since 1968. While draft versions of a law of public enterprises have circulated since at least 1971, as of October 1979, no such law has been passed. Research is needed on the changing conception of public enterprises, analyzing the system from its period of rapid growth under Velasco to its present consolidation phase. This could focus on the different organizational forms and control mechanisms to be employed by the central government to use public enterprises effectively as tools of national policy.

The increase and subsequent decrease in government-attributed monopoly power, along with the changing ministerial lines of control, should not be interpreted as a totally illogical use of public enterprise as a policy tool, however. Rather, the muddled nature of ENCI's and FERTIPERU's evolution may indicate that the logic should be sought outside the sphere of traditional economic or administrative concerns with resource allocation and efficiency. Recent discussions with knowledgable Peruvians indicate that a high proportion of this functional variation may be accounted for by power plays within the military coalition. This implies that public enterprise was viewed partially as a payoff to maintain key individuals' loyalty to the dominant faction. A second area of investigation strongly related to the first is to determine the validity of this hypothesis.

Our focus on modifications of ENCI's legal structure from 1971 to 1978 is but the first step in the examination of the issue of control. It provides a strong basis for the assessment of compliance with the various decrees and resolutions affecting the firm. The colonial dictum *obedezco pero no cumplo* has a host of modern counterparts which are occasionally revealed by a sequential analysis of the laws themselves. The presence of bureaucratic dissatisfaction concerning transfer to the newly created Ministry of Commerce was evident in Supreme Decree 066-74 MINCOM of March 19, 1974, which declared null and void any changes in organization, budget, personnel, furniture and equipment for those administrative units assigned to MINCOM since its creation. Much of the dichotomy between resolution and practice, which indicates the relative strength of control systems, is not so easy to detect. A third area of fruitful research should be the study of the variance between the laws concerning public enterprises and their interpretations, conducted through in-depth interviews with decision makers within the field. This should provide indications of the depth of control and the possibility of system manipulation from within.

One of the criticisms leveled at state trading organizations is that they are too flexible as policy instruments. They can provide more rapid implementation of secret or imperfectly known central government instructions to restrict trade than they can use of traditional restraints such as tariffs and quotas (Lloyd, 1979: 19). ENCI appears to have been used to provide protection against trade liberalization within the Andean Pact. By giving ENCI an import monopoly and not making foreign exchange available, the government could have sought to circumvent other obligations.

Consider the example of whiskey. For almost 1½ years after having received the monopoly, ENCI did not receive the funds to purchase whiskey. When hard currency was made available, ENCI was constrained to import only from Bolivia. While it may be argued that ENCI was used to strengthen trade relations within the Andean Pact as a result of these constraints, the counterargument may be made that ENCI was being used to protect Peru from the Pact's trade liberalization. Considerable research is needed to determine the effect of public enterprise policies with respect to international agreements, and also to national programs such as agrarian reform, cooperative promotion, income redistribution, and social property.

Finally, the case study approach used here should be extended to other public enterprises to permit in-depth evaluation of the systems of organization and control of public enterprise in Peru. Until now most of the research on the post-1968 Peruvian public sector has been macrofocused. Using such indicators as the relative weight of government in GNP, investment, imports and exports, and the share of government attributed to public enterprises, FitzGerald (1976, 1979), Figueroa and Saberbein (1978), and various groups within the Peruvian government have detailed the rapid change in the size and functions of the state.

Too often, however, such works leave the impression of a continuous, well-organized and superbly controlled growth process. The in-depth study of ENCI demonstrates an intermittent process of growth and setback with little consistency, poor organization and excessive and contradictory control. It is not my intention to extrapolate from the case of ENCI to say that such behavior was characteristic of all Peruvian public enterprise since 1968, but it would be useful to have a set of case studies on which to generate a theory, rather than to develop a theory without a strong micro basis.

ABBREVIATIONS

BCRP	Banco Central de Reserva del Perú
CONAFER	Corporación Nacional de Fertilizantes
CONAPA	Corporación Nacional de Producción Agraria
COPAGC	Comisión Interministerial Permanente de Aceites y Grasas Comestibles
DGI	Dirección General de Industrias
ENAPU	Empresa Nacional de Puertos
ENCI	Empresa Nacional de Comercialización Industrial (1971-August 1974); Empresa Nacional de Comercialización de Insumos (August 1974-present)
EPCHAP	Empresa Pública de Comercialización de Harina y Aceite de Pescado
EPSA	Empresa Pública de Servicios Agropecuarios
EPSAP	Empresa Pública de Servicios Agropecuarios y Pesqueros, now EPSA
FERTIPERU	Empresa de Fertilizantes
INP	Instituto Nacional de Planificación
MINCOM	Ministerio de Comercio
PETROPERU	Petróleos del Perú
PESCAPERU	Empresa Pública de Producción de Harina y Aceite de Pescado
SENAFER	Servicio Nacional de Fertilizantes
SERINA	Servicios de Insumos Agrícolas

NOTES

1. Notes which refer to laws and legislation pertaining to ENCI and its components will be omitted. They may be obtained from the author or found in the following sources: Dirección Genral de Asuntos Legales del Estado (1969-1972), Miranda (1968-1972), and Montengro (1970-1978) for the 1968-1979 period.

2. The absence of an explicit marketing program in the industrial sector is all the more striking becasue the Ministry of Industry and Commerce, which was formed in December 1968, had its functions, organization, and structure set out in March 1969, when the 1971-1975 Plan was in the preliminary discussion stage. It was to promote external trade and to promote and orient internal trade for all products except foodstuffs.

3. These included products of ferrous and nonferrous metals, certain basic chemicals, other organic and inorganic chemicals, fertilizers, cement, and paper.

4. This was destined for the production of *papel sellado*, a necessary ingredient for all bureaucratic transactions.

5. In the case of edible oils, the Permanent Interministerial Commission on Edible Fats and Oils (COPAGC) made the quantity decision in coordination with the DGI.

6. This measure formed part of a package of reform of state institutions under Law 17044, by which Congress delegated extraordinary legislative powers to President Belaúnde. An appraisal of other measures promulgated under this authority given to the president in Law 17044 is found in Kuczynski (1977: 226-243).

7. These were Cementos Lima S.A., Cemento Yura S.A., Cemento Andino S.A., and Cemento Sur S.A.

8. This was given as a monopoly to the Sociedad Paramonga Ltda., a public enterprise concerned with raw material for polyesters.

REFERENCES

ARIAS, L. (1975) Transcript of televised report to the nation by the Minister of Commerce on March 20. El Peruano [Lima] (March 21).

BCRP [Banco Central de Reserva del Perú] (1977) Memoria. Lima: Author. Comisión Multisectorial [Lima] (1977) "Primer informe sobre normas operativas para agilizar la actividad empresarial del estado." (mimeographed)

Comisión Multisectorial de Empresas del Estado [Lima] (1976) Informe Final. (mimeographed)

Dirección General de Asuntos Legales del Estado (1969-1972) Leyes y resoluciones de carácter general de la República del Perúu. Lima: Officina Nacional de Asuntos Jurídicos.

ENCI (1978a) ENCI y las comercialización de fertilizantes en la Perú. Lima: Santiago Valverde.

——— (1978b) Memoria ENCI 1976. Lima: Santiago Valverde.

——— (1973) Memoria. Lima: Santiago Valverde.

——— (n.d.) Informe Sinóptico sobre la Empresa Nacional de Comercialización de Insumos—ENCI. (mimeographed)

FIGUEROA, L. and G. SABERBEIN (1978) "Empresas del estado en el Perú." Presented at the Seminar on the Planning Process in Latin America and Public Enterprises, Lima.

FitzGERALD, E.V.K. (1979) The Political Economy of Peru, 1956-1978. New York: Cambridge Univ. Press.

———(1976) "The state and economic development: Peru since 1968." University of Cambridge Department of Applied Economics, Occasional Paper 49.

INP [Instituto Nacional de Planificasión Lima] (1978) "Apreciaciones generales sobre la problemática de las empresas públicas." (mimeographed)

——— (n.d.) "Análisis económico-financiero de las empresas públicas, Año 1973." (mimeographed)

KUCZYNSKI, P. P. (1977) Peruvian Democracy under Economic Stress. Princeton, NJ: Princeton Univ. Press.

LLYOD, P. J. (1979) "State trading and the theory of international trade." Les Cahiers du CETAI [Montreal], 79-08.

MINCOM [Ministerio de Comercio, Lima] (1978) "Análisis de las actividades financieras de las empresas estatalee de comercio exterior." (mimeographed) Ministerio de Economía y Finanzas [Lima] (1978) "Diagnóstico de la actividad empresarial del estado: 1968-1978."

MIRANDA ITURRINO E. [ed.] (1968-1972) Compendio de legislación Lima: Publicaciones EMI.

MONTENEGRO BACA J. [ed.] (1970-1978) Normas legales: revista de legislación y jurisprudencia. Lima: Editorial Bolivariana.

Presidencia de la República [Lima] (1975) Plan Nacional de Desarrollo, 1975-1978.
——— (1971) Plan Nacional de Desarrollo para 1971-1975, Vol. 1: Plan Global.

Alfred H. Saulniers is a Visiting Assistant Professor of Economics at the University of Texas, Austin, and Coordinator of the Office for Public Sector Studies and the Project Mulhall Data Bank of Economic and Social Data, also at the University of Texas. While conducting dissertation field research in Peru, he also taught courses in economics at the Pontificia Universidad Católica del Perú. He has published extensively on Africa, (particularly on Zaire), as well as Latin America.

ALFRED H. SAULNIERS
Institute of Latin American Studies
University of Texas, Austin

PUBLIC ENTERPRISES IN LATIN AMERICA
An Annotated List of Recent Research Papers

In recent years, a considerable amount of scholarly research has been devoted to the analysis of public enterprise in Latin America. The number of individuals actively engaged in research and their output of materials has increased since the mid-1970s. Partially as a result of this heightened interest, several conferences have been organized to deal with public enterprises, and increasingly detailed information has been made available by governments. Most of this information still receives an extremely limited circulation and is therefore unavailable to the majority of scholars.

In order to make more widely known some of these recent contributions to what is becoming a rapidly growing body of

---

EDITOR'S NOTE: The inclusion of this annotated list of significant recent unpublished research related to the topic of this special issue is an exception to our editorial policy of not publishing bibliographies or bibliographical essays. It was compiled at the request of the guest editors, who felt that, in this instance, it had greater relevance for the topic than a review essay of recently published books. Arrangements for acquiring copies of any of the listed papers may be made in correspondence with Professor Alfred H. Saulniers, Institute of Latin American Studies, University of Texas, Austin, TX 78712.

A statement on current editorial policy is given in the 20-year *Cumulative Index* (1959-1978) of the *Journal of Interamerican Studies and World Affairs*, which is available from Sage Publications.

Journal of Interamerican Studies and World Affairs, Vol. 22 No. 4, November 1980 463-470

literature, this annotated list was prepared. The selection of materials included is by no means complete; indeed, it is deliberately narrow in focus. Only materials dealing primarily with public enterprises in Latin America, unpublished or of an extremely limited distribution, and first available after January 1978 were considered. Not included were published materials, items set within the larger context of the state's role in society, theses and dissertations, case studies prepared for classroom use, government documents, and items about public enterprises in general or those in other world areas. A de facto limitation was to materials recently available either in the Benson Latin American Collection or the Office for Public Sector Studies of the University of Texas at Austin. To have broadened the scope of this work with respect either to time period or to materials covered would have been a more massive undertaking unsuited to a short review.

The present scope has two major advantages. It serves as a guide to the nature of research currently being done, but, more importantly, it serves to identify individuals at present studying Latin American public enterprises from a variety of disciplinary orientations. This clearinghouse function will, it is hoped, lead to increased scholarly interchange and further the development of public enterprise research.

To avoid excessive repetition in references to conference papers, such papers will be identified by a letter designation, as follows:

(A) Presented at the Round Table on Public Enterprise of the Tenth General Assembly of the Latin American Association of Public Administration, Mexico City (mimeographed).

(B) Presented at the International Seminar on Regulation of the Public Enterprise, Mexico City (mimeographed).

(C) Presented at the First Latin American Seminar on Public Policies, Sao Paulo (Fundaçāo de Desenvolvimento Administrativo, mimeographed).

(D) Presented at the Seminar on the Planning Process in Latin America and Public Enterprises, Lima (mimeographed).

(E) Presented at the Second Boston Area Public Enterprise Group Group (B.A.P.E.G.) Conference on Public Enterprise in Mixed Economy LDC's (mimeographed).

ALVAREZ DEL CASTILLO, E. (1979) "Aplicación del régimen constitucional y legal de trabajo a las personas jurídicias de derecho público." 11 pp. (B).

Covers some labor law changes for Mexico's parastatal workers since 1917.

BAER, W. and A. FIGUEROA (1980) "The impact of increased state participation in the economy on the distribution of income: some reflections based on the cases of Brazil and Peru. 41 pp. (E)

Initial attempt to determine the effect of public enterprises on income distribution through prices, technology, employment location, and financing.

BARQUIN ALVAREZ, M. (1979) "El control de ejecutivo y la administración pública federal sobre el sector paraestatal." 41 pp. (B)

Detailed critical typology of Mexico's parastatals with an in-depth analysis of their highly centralized control system and a critical exposition of current efforts to decentralize.

BERLANGA LAURENT, L. (1978) "Control por parte del gobierno federal de las instituciones nacionales de crédito, organizaciones auxiliares nacionales de crédito y las instituciones nacionales de seguros y finanzas." 8 pp. (A)

Covers Mexico's legal mechanisms for controlling public sector credit institutions, noting differences from other parastatal controls.

BOENINGER, E. and E. PALMA (1978) "Empresas estatales: el caso chileno y un análisis general." 142 pp. (D)

Detailed chronology of Chilean public enterprises to 1974. Institutional analysis of the relationship of public enterprises to central government, stressing policy and other instruments available to firms and ministries with examples from Chile.

BONEO, M. (1978) "Las empresas estatales en América Latina." 293 pp. (B)

Comprehensive look at public enterprises and the environment within which they operate. Includes chapters on overall characteristics, origins, and historical growth of public enterprises; their links with central government including the regulatory, planning, budgeting, evaluation and control systems; and a series of proposed solutions to their most typical problems. Contains a series of appendices with partial inventories of public enterprises for selected countries.

BONEO, H. (1979) "Planificación, presupuesto y empresas públicas en América Latina." 62 pp. (C)

View of the public enterprise-government relationship as a conflict between ideal models and reality. Surveys the literature on complex organizations leading to planning and budgeting agencies' ideal model of public enterprise. Differentiates firms as having varied expenditure patterns and access to fiance. Several possibilities for firm-government links are covered and the predominant policies criticized.

BONEO, H. (1980) "Political regimes and public enterprises." 28 pp. (E)

Analysis of Argentinian public enterprises from 1958 to 1977 to demonstrate the affect of political regime on number of firms, value added, prices, and employment.

CARILLO CASTRO, A. (1979) "La regulación jurídico administrativa de la empresa pública en México." 39 pp. (C)

Detailed description of the changing concepts and legal mechanisms of Mexico's public enterprise control system from heavy centralization to attempted decentralization over the 1948-1979 period.

Centro Latinoamericano de Administración para el Desarrollo, Instituto Italo Latinoamericano, Instituto para la Reconstrucción Industrial [Rome] (1978) "Informe final del Seminario sobre la géstion de las empresas públicas de America Latina e Italia." 121 pp.

Report of the February 1978 Rome seminar containing opening and closing addresses and a brief summary of the papers and comments. Topics covered were the origins, concepts and evaluation of public enterprises, systems' characteristics, methods, and problems of control. Presentations about Italy were complemented with discussions on their possible application in Latin America.

CHANES NIETO, J. (1978) "Insuficiencia del marco jurídico de la denominada administración pública paraestatal en México." 27 pp. (A)

Review of the constitutional and legal bases for Mexico's parastatals directly controlled by the government, stressing the negative consequences of a heterogeneous legal framework for efficient government control and suggestions for improvement.

CHUAYFFET CHEMOR, E. (1979) "Formas legales de control administrativo de las empresas públicas en México." 20 pp. (B)

Superficial view of Mexico's public enterprise control system with respect to budgets, purchases, and labor.

CINCUNEGUI, J. (1979) "Objectivos de firma pública: um caso." 16 pp. (C)

Abstract of a larger work on the CVRD (Companhia Vale do Rio Doce) and its region of influence. Rapid overview of microeconomic theories of the firm, their applications to state enterprises, and a short introduction to CVRD.

CORDERO, S. and S. GOMEZ TAGLE (1978) "Estado y trabajadores de las empresas estatales en México." 31 pp. (A)

Describes Mexico's state enterprise labor force by type of occupation, wage income, social services perceived, level of education, and degree of unionization. Conclusions drawn in relation to their importance within Mexico's labor movement. Illustrated with 1975-1976 data.

DAIN, S. (1979) "Empresa estatal e capitalismo maduro." 34 pp. (C)

Think piece on public enterprises which criticizes microeconomic theory, details the dualities of public firms, and suggests a framework based on market position and expansion possibilities.

DECELIS CONTRERAS, R. (1978) "La empresa, la alianza para la producción y el entorno social." 34 pp. (A)

Simplistic linear model of organizations within the Mexican context.

DIAZ MULLER, L. (1979) "Las empresas de integración en el desarrollo latinoamericano." 22 pp. (B)

Cursory look at characteristics, capital sources, origins, objectives, and legal problems of multinational firms established under Decision 46 of the Andean Common Market.

FIGUEROA, L. and G. SABERBEIN (1978) "Empresas del estado en el Perú." 37 pp. (D)

Rapid analysis of Peru's public enterprises with respect to legal forms, relations to central government and management problems.

GARCIA RAMIREZ, S. (1979) "Panorama sobre la empresa pública en México." 18 pp. (B)

Overview of the origins and structures of Mexico's largest parastatal enterprises from 1917 to the present.

GLADE, W. (1979) "The political economy of public enterprise controls: a conceptual view." 44 pp. (B)

Explores the pressures to increase public enterprise efficiency as a result of size of the public sector, impact on capital formation, balance of payments considerations, and internal changes. Covers the pressures to achieve and dangers of several types of control systems.

GOMEZ LARA, C. (1979) "Implantación de carrera para los funcionarios de la empresa pública." 12 pp. (B)

Overview of the institutional and legal reasons that Mexico lacks a civil service system, the need and methods for its implementation.

GOMEZ TAGLE, S. (1978) "La industria eléctrica nacionalizada: bosquejo de un panorama general." 42 pp. (A)

Examination of Mexico's public sector electric industry, covering motives for nationalization, and problems following state takeover. Statistics, some at firm level, on production, consumption, productivity, and financial indicators, from the 1965-1972 period.

GOMEZ TRAPOLA, I. and G. HERNANDEZ VILLALOBOS (1978) "El impacto de las empresas públicas del sector agropecuario y federal en la economía Mexicana." 21 pp. (A)

Overviews aggregate indicators of the 20 largest state enterprises in Mexico's agricultural and forestry sector.

GONZALEZ LOPEZ, G. (1978) "La empresa pública y la política nacional de empleo y capacitación." 20 pp. (A)

Cursory view of the evolution of Mexico's public enterprises, the need for job creation by the public sector, and the benefits of worker training.

GORDILLO, A. (1979) "El control de las empresas públicas en América Latina." 48 pp. (B)

Views the control problem as a result of dynamic tensions within the central government, as well as between government and firm. Examines in detail the sources, methods, and organs of control, with examples taken from many countries.

GRAHAM, L. (1978) "The administration of public enterprises: coordination and control dilemmas for contemporary states." 31 pp. (A)

Rapid literature survey to determine some possible public administration contributions to issues of the control and coordination of centralization.

Instituto Centroamericano de Administración Pública (1978) "La capacitación y el desarrollo del personal de dirección en las entidades públicas autónomas del istmo centroamericano." 42 pp. (A)

Diagnosis of the institutional and economic characteristics of public administration in Central America, followed by a case study of ICAP (Instituto Centroamericano de Administración Pública).

KELLY ESCOBAR, J. (1980) "The comparison of state enterprises across international boundaries: the Corporación Venezolana de Guyana and the Companhia Vale do Rio Doce." 63 pp. (E)

Views public enterprise behavior partly as the outcome of internal coalitions between two employee types: "engineers" and "commissars." Contrasts CVG to CVRD performance on fourteen levels of behavior.

LAVERGNE, N. and D. CAPUTO (1979) "Para una revalorización de las políticas de comercio exterior." 63 pp. (C)

Focuses on state trading enterprises at neglected policy instruments. General reflections on the 1973-1978 Peruvian experience, with a case study of coffee exports.

LOMELIN, J. (1978) "Las empresas eléctricas privadas y públicas en México." 20 pp. (A)

Rapid overview of the development of electric power capacity in Mexico.

LOPEZ ESCALERA, M. (1978) "Relaciones de trabajo en las empresas públicas y su situación jurídico-laboral." 16 pp. (A)

Rhetorical overview of labor's position in Mexico's public sector from 1875 to the present.

MONTEVERDE BUSSALLEU, J. J. (1979) "Informe preliminar sobre las regulación de la empresa pública en el Perú." 30 pp. (B)

Listing of some of the constitutional and legal bases for the creation and control of Peru's public enterprises. Recapitulation of the major legal changes affecting such firms since 1978.

NOVOA MONREAL, E. (1978) "Las empresas públicas y el estado." 14 pp. (A)

Cursory view of legal problems with respect to the origins and goals of public enterprise.

OCHOA CAMPOS, M. (1978) "La municipalización de empresas de servicios públicas." 8 pp. (A)

Covers preconditions and legal bases for the formation of municipal public enterprises in Mexico.

PINI, J. (1978) "Las empresas públicas en el Uruguay." 34 pp. (A)

Covers the internal and external factors which led to a crisis in Uruguay's public sector by 1973 and evaluates the systemic changes made to improve performance.

QUIJANO TORRES, M. (1978) "Los órganos administrativos deconcentrados." 8 pp. (A)

Overview of differnces which mark Mexico's "deconcentrated" firms from central government and from other parastatals.

REICHSTUL, H. and L. CONUTINHO (1979) "Tendencias recientes do investimento empresarial do estado." 25 pp. (C)

Analysis of post-1973 countercyclic Brazilian public investment disaggregated by sectors.

REZENDE, F. (1978) "Las empresas públicas en la economía Brasileña." 45 pp. (D)

Survey of post-1950 Brazilian public enterprises emphasizing efficiency, redistributive effects, and relations to macrogoals of stabilization, growth, and employment. Statistics at the sectoral level for various years from 1966 to 1976.

RUIZ MASSIEU, J. (1979) "Una approximación al control jurisdiccional de las empresas públicas." 35 pp. (B)

Examines in detail the legal complexities of parastatal operations within both the administrative and business spheres. Delineates for the Mexican system areas of current jurisdiction and of indefinite authority.

SACHICA, L. (1979) "Regulación de las empresas públicas en Colombia." 25 pp. (B)

Typology of Colombian public enterprises, discussion of the constitutional and legal foundations for administrative, fiscal and jurisdiction control, and the bases for a firm's autonomy.

SANCHEZ ALBAVERA, F. and J. ESTEVES OSTOLAZA (1978) "Cooperation between state trading organizations in Latin America." United Nations Conference on Trade and Development [Geneva] TD/B/C, July 16. 43 pp. (mimeographed)

Analyzes for selected Latin American countries the forms of participation in foreign trade and the scope of the firms' operations. Discusses the possibilities of cooperation among state trading organizations. Part of an UNCTAD study which covers Africa, Asia, and Latin America.

SARAVIA, E. (1979) "Régimen jurídicio de las empresas públicas gubernamentales Brasileñas." 18 pp. (B)

Brief exposition of Brazilian public enterprise with respect to constitutional bases, legal structure, personnel matters, control systems, jurisdictional aspects, tax status, and profit remittance.

SAULNIERS, A. (1980) "State trading organizations: a bias decision model and applications." 35 pp. (E)

Institutional analysis of sources of bias in estimating the costs and benefits of state trading organizations, and applications to Peru from 1971 to 1978.

SOLARI, A. and R. FRANCO (1978) "La inserción de las empresas públicas en el aparato estatal uruguayo." 132 pp. (D)

Detailed look at the ideological bases and historical evolution of Uruguayan public enterprises from 1904 to the present. Strong concentration on the 1964-1975 period, with analyses of value added, investment, financing, wages, and salaries, and balance of payments effects based on information contained in the statistical appendix.

TORRES GOITIA, H. (1979) "Las empresas públicas en Bolivia." 42 pp. (B)

Rapid survey of the origins and problems of the principal Bolivian public enterprises.

URIOSTEGUI MIRANDA, P. (1978) "La administración de recursos humanos y el sistema de capacitación en una empresa pública: Comisión Federal de Electricidad." 21 pp. (A)

Background to an exposition about the training programs of CFE in 1977-1978.

VASQUEZ, S. (1978) "La necesidad de crear un sistema nacional de capacitación y actualización en administración de empresas públicas." 10 pp. (A)

Polemic on the need to incorporate technical management training for public enterprise within the Mexican educational system.

VILLAREAL, R. de and R. VILLAREAL (1980) "Public enterprises in Mexican development under the oil perspective in 1980." 68 pp. (E)

Rapid overview of pre-1970 public sector. Detailed analysis of public enterprises during the 1970s; simulation model applied to the effects of oil production and exports on GWP, inflation, savings, fiscal deficit, and balance of payments.

WITKER, J. (1978) "El holding como instrumento de control y coordinación de las empresas públicas." 21 pp. (A)

Study of the structure of holding companies and legal bases for an eventual application to Mexico.

MARYE THARP HILGER
College of Business, Division of Management
University of Texas, San Antonio

DECISION-MAKING IN A PUBLIC MARKETING ENTERPRISE
CONASUPO in Mexico

Introduction

CONASUPO (Compañia Nacional de Subsistencias Populares) is a vertically integrated distribution system for staple goods in Mexico. It is an autonomous, public enterprise, and it has broad policy formulation and implementation responsibilities as an agency for development. CONASUPO competes with private sector producers, wholesalers, and retailers, in addition to its special roles in economic and market development.

It is the object of this article to describe how marketing decisions are made in CONASUPO. The environment within which market decisions are made in CONASUPO sets the parameters for its decision processes and influences the types of marketing strategies that it pursues. A model of marketing decision-making will be presented and then used to describe how these processes occur in CONASUPO's structural and environmental context. Lastly, distinctions will be made between decision-making in CONASUPO and in the private sector in Mexico.

Focus on marketing decisions in CONASUPO will be restricted to its retail operations. While there is certainly interdependence in its multilevel operations—from purchaser of commodities to storage, training, manufacturing, wholesaling, and retailing—the multiple and distinct objectives of each of these endeavors confound the issues of marketing decision-making. These interdependencies are discussed, but are not as thoroughly

Journal of Interamerican Studies and World Affairs, Vol. 22 No. 4, November 1980 471-494

analyzed as might be desirable in an overview of CONASUPO decision processes.

The Environment for Decision-Making in CONASUPO

An important facet of marketing decisions within a public enterprise is the organizational environment. Organizational purpose often presents contradictory, multiple goals for such enterprises. In addition, the requisite profit objectives of the private sector may be absent as measures of goal achievement; the "political" profits, or social welfare contributions of the public enterprise that take their place are difficult to assess, yet must guide marketing policy and strategies. Organizational structure also influences the nature of marketing decision-making. The design of a particular enterprise determines to a great extent responsibility and effectiveness for implementing different types of marketing decisions. The consistency between marketing strategy and operational decisions is affected by administrative responsibilities as well. Lastly, the organizational climate places constraints on the "nature" of marketing strategies which an enterprise chooses to pursue. This climate is formed by the enterprises' reward system, values, and training of its personnel and by internal and external environments which impinge on the organization's pursuit of objectives.

CONASUPO'S PURPOSE

CONASUPO has both structural and protective objectives in the Mexican economy. Its structural purpose is to realign markets for commodities and to improve their distribution and availability in Mexico. Its protective goals concern alleviating problems of low-income consumers and producers. These two broad goals are complementary; by introducing rationality into distribution systems for commodities, both the low-income consumer and low-income producers theoretically benefit. These goals relate to CONASUPO's role in overall development policy and illustrate the multiple guidelines within which it attempts to develop marketing policy.

Past Mexican public policies have recognized urban laborers and subsistence-level agricultural workers as the groups most likely to contribute to increases in national demand. Two ways used to achieve this are to reduce prices consumers must pay for living expenses and to increase the benefits of commercial farming. Price controls and subsidies of domestic producers have not been able to break the often monopolistic controls that intermediaries have on distribution channels. As a result, the vertically integrated network offered by CONASUPO can interrupt such speculatively induced barriers to efficient distribution. This efficiency is valued as a means of improving consumer welfare and removing obstacles to development of national market systems, as well as for its potential in freeing resources to be used in other sectors.

Another goal in achieving distributive efficiency is stability in commodity prices and availability. CONASUPO does this through its role as regulator of imports and exports of commodities. When surpluses occur, CONASUPO uses price guarantees to protect low-income producers. During shortages, CONASUPO increases imports of the commodities and assures availability at reasonable prices through its retail outlets.

Another public policy which serves to define CONASUPO's purpose is control over national resources. The development of internal market systems is a necessary accompaniment to industrialization so that increased capacity can be absorbed. In order to foster such market development, more control over command systems is needed. CONASUPO provides such a system by increasing the long-term profitability of small-scale agricultural production and by maintaining its margin and price controls at intermediary levels (CONASUPO, 1973a, 1973b).

Protection of low-income population segments in Mexico has become an imperative of recent public policy. Coupled with inflation, a decreased share of national income has meant a large reduction in purchasing power for low-income groups. What exacerbates the situation is that improved communication and transportation systems allow the least fortunate to become aware of how much less affluent they are than other groups (Reynolds, 1970; Navarrete, 1960).

A past CONASUPO director, Jorge de la Vega Domínguez, stated that the fundamental reason for government regulation

TABLE 1
Outline of CONASUPO Objectives

STRUCTURAL OBJECTIVES:

To exercise control over national resources
To increase self-sufficiency in agricultural foodstuffs
To increase long-term benefits of commercial production
To develop internal, national market systems
To encourage efficiency in wholesaling and retailing
To stabilize commodity prices
To stabilize commodity availability
To reduce speculation and monopolistic-behavior in distribution systems
To foster development of small industry

PROTECTIVE OBJECTIVES:

To provide commodities at reasonable and low prices to low income consumers
To redistribute income
To improve social welfare of low income consumers
To assist the transition from traditional to modern life styles for low income consumers
To increase low income consumers' purchasing power
To provide credit and auxiliary services for low income producers
To increase productivity of low income producers
To provide training for low income producers and consumers

SOURCES: CONASUPO, 1973a; 1973b; Grindle, 1977; Hilger, 1976.

and participation in the market is that standard economic theory of demand-price relationships is not applicable to realities of the marketplace (CONASUPO, 1973b). CONASUPO uses federal funds to subsidize low-income consumers and to transfer resources from society to low-income segments. Policy statements suggest the belief that some consumers have such low purchasing power that private firms simply could not serve their needs profitability. More important, however, CONASUPO provides a means of breaking the low-income groups' dependencies on those private sector intermediaries that exploit them (Grindle, 1977).

An outline of CONASUPO objectives is presented in Table 1. It summarizes this discussion and illustrates the pluralistic goals which marketing strategy in CONASUPO is expected to achieve. For example, pricing must meet the objectives of low-income consumers' economic abilities and, at the same time, serve to increase the incomes of subsistence-level farmers. This article will discuss how such decisions are achieved in a later section.

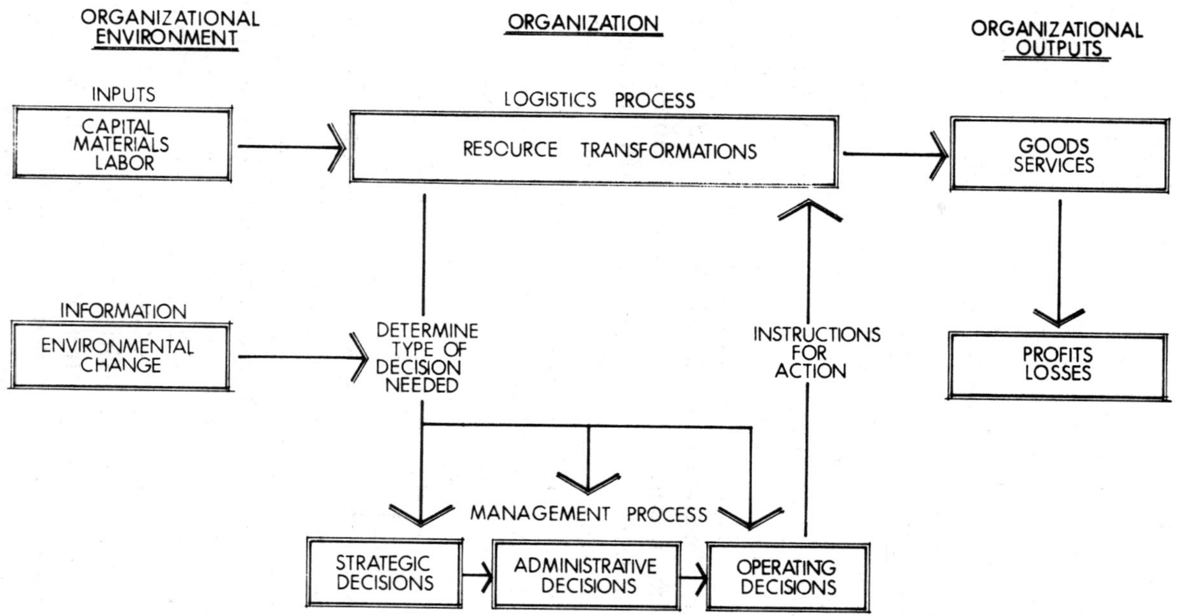

Figure 1: Model of Marketing Decision-Making

ORGANIZATIONAL STRUCTURE AND DESIGN IN CONASUPO

Currently, CONASUPO is a state-owned holding company which supervises and directs the activities of at least sixteen subsidiary companies. An outline of its formal organizational structure is presented in Figure 1. This current structure is the result of several radical changes in the form and nature of CONASUPO responsibilities.

CONASUPO today includes the export-import regulatory functions of CEIMSA (Compañia Exportadora e Importadora Mexicana, S.A.), the storage and purchasing functions of ANDSA (Almancenes Nacionales de Depósito, S.A.), and distribution functions of Nacional Distribuidora y Reguladora, S.A. After several expansive periods, CONASUPO assumed its current scope of activities in 1965. However, beginning at that time and continuing with other major structural changes in the 1970s, decentralization has altered the formal structure of CONASUPO. As illustrated in Figure 1, the subsidiary companies within CONASUPO are relatively autonomous. The holding company's advisory council is composed of representatives of various government ministries, whose function it is to assist in determing CONASUPO's policies. In fact, CONASUPO and its subsidiaries are relatively free to establish their own policies and programs (Grindle, 1977: 17).

Control over the subsidiaries and their programs is exercised in several ways. First, each subsidiary's advisory council includes representatives of the holding company who influence policy. Second, the Operating Division and Subsidiary Company Division of the holding company directly supervise subsidiary performance. Furthermore, the subsidiaries' major function is the implementation of policies that are developed by decision makers in the holding company (Grindle, 1977). Decentralization in CONASUPO means separation between policy makers and those who are responsible for implementing policy. Inevitably, effectiveness and focus varies among the subsidiaries.

ORGANIZATIONAL CLIMATE IN CONASUPO

Several important external factors impinge on the nature of marketing decisions in CONASUPO. One of these is the "sexenio" in Mexico. The majority of CONASUPO personnel are employees of "confianza" (Grindle, 1977). These employees are involved in career patterns in which upward mobility is determined by political alliances. Policy in CONASUPO, as well as other public enterprises and ministries, is responsive to interests of the current president. The change in this office every "sexenio" means substantial personnel changes and changes in emphasis in its policy imperatives every six years. New, high level administrators must quickly familiarize themselves with CONASUPO and its programs, develop policy, and then direct implementation within the six-year constraint (Grindle, 1977). Dependence upon political alliances for career mobility and intergovernmental support also means CONASUPO employees must be sensitive to presidential initiatives and support.

A second element of CONASUPO's organizational climate is the reward structure for employees. Because career mobility depends on personal alliances and membership in "camarillas" (political discussion groups), the decision maker must make decisions and policy within this framework. Motivation for decision-making and policy formulation is determined by these personal alliances and the perceived impact of resource allocations. If a policy is perceived to increase a division's potential resources, it will strengthen the decision maker's political alliances through his ability to distribute rewards (Grindle, 1977). So, for example, a policy that reorients CONASUPO's resources toward rural development would be supported most by those within CONASUPO who see it generating the most resources for their divisions, or by those who have political alliances in other agriculturally related ministries.

Another dimension of the climate for decision-making in CONASUPO is the integration of its policy formulation with political networks within the Mexican bureaucracy. Decisions concerning resource allocations as well as policy are often changed to accommodate existing political hierarchies. For example, support for CONASUPO's rural development program was contingent on the cooperation of other, powerful ministries of the government, such as the Ministry of Agriculture. In addition, policies and programs must consider the interests of the private sector and key political figures (Glade, 1975). Not only do CONASUPO's programs have to build political visibility and serve as positive factors in its employee's careers, but they must also recognize broader political constraints.

Limited participation in determining policy necessarily exclude those who benefit from CONASUPO's outputs from the policy formation stage of decision-making. It was not demand from peasants that caused CONASUPO decision makers to develop a policy of rural development; this policy was in response to presidential initiatives (Grindle, 1977). Employees are not directly rewarded for satisfying the needs of program users, nor are policies determined by inputs from the potential market for its outputs. This is in contrast to business firms, which derive value from their abilities to meet and satisfy market demands. While the political system in Mexico must also be ultimately responsible to all its constituencies, in the short-term those groups that are most effective in presenting their demands are the ones who influence policy. Low-income consumers and produers have not had such influences in the shaping of CONASUPO policy. Policies that might benefit such groups may be implemented in a manner that maintains their status quo, rather than changing it as intended. Conformity between CONASUPO policies and their implementation, as well as formulation of policy, are not contingent upon inputs from its users or their satisfaction with its outputs.

Marketing Strategy and Decision-Making

It is not the intent of this article to provide a comprehensive discussion of marketing decision-making. However, an overview of elements of the planning and decision-making processes can serve as a framework for focusing on decision-making in CONASUPO. Other writers have investigated the impact of marketing decisions and the nature of CONASUPO decision makers (Glade, 1975; Alisky, 1974; Grindle, 1977; Hilger, 1976). The formation of marketing strategies is an integral part of CONASUPO's role in development and is affected by that development. The decision-making process establishes the parameters for policy formulation and implementation.

A MODEL OF ORGANIZATIONAL DECISION-MAKING

Many models of the process of market planning or decision-making exist (Kotler, 1977; Constantin et al., 1976; Rewoldt et al., 1977). In a similar vein as exchange theory, the model postulates that organizational purpose is to deliver goods and services determined to have value in the marketplace. To accomplish this, a firm must organize inputs (land, capital, information, human resources), develop a production process, distribute outputs to the marketplace, and conduct transactions necessary to recover expenditures and investment. If these functions are performed efficiently, surplus value or profits will be created (see Webster, 1974, for further detail).

Ansoff (1971: 11-40) further defines the activities of management as planning, organizing, and controlling combinations of inputs and outputs through two specific processes—logistics and management. The logistics process refers to resource transfers and conversions, that is, the action of changing inputs into outputs. This process is guided by the management process that is information-handling in nature. The management process involves determing what actions are needed in order to accomplish the logistics process, then translating those needs into organization plans and controls for action.

To complete the model, the management process concerns three distinct decision areas—strategic, administrative and operating decisions. Strategic decisions center on the relationship between the firm and its environment. Administrative decisions establish the shape and structure of the firm. Finally, operating decisions include selections of the values of input variables (Webster, 1974).

Marketing management consists of decision-making in all of these areas. In the private sector, the process often takes the form of development of a "marketing plan," which is essentially an outline of strategic, administrative, and operational actions. Further detail on each of these areas should illustrate the nature of such decision-making for marketing.

STRATEGIC MARKETING DECISIONS

Marketing strategy defines the interface the organization will have with its external environment. This interdependence with political, economic, social, legal, technological, and cultural forces determines the resources, opportunities, and threats available to the firm. Obviously, inputs to the logistics process must come from the external environment, and the firm's success depends on responsiveness to changes in those forces. Therefore, a critical strategic concern must be with understanding the nature of the firm's relevant environment and planning how the firm will respond to change in those factors.

Matching a firm's strengths and weaknesses with potential market opportunities requires several tasks. The first of these is to identify profitable market opportunities in the form of market needs not currently being satisfied. Target market selection means choosing those market opportunities that match the firm's resources. Needed input for this process is knowledge of market trends through the tools of marketing research and accurate estimates of the impact of environmental change on the organization.

An objective assessment of strengths and weaknesses, matched with market opportunities, provides the basis for the organization's marketing objectives around which resources will be organized. Marketing objectives consider the effect of competition and other external variables on the organization's particular strengths and weaknesses; growth and viability are based on the basis of the firm's unique strengths. The key to a strategy of differential advantage is a focus on benefits that the market expects rather than the tangible form of the firm's output. A boon of this approach to strategic planning is that it assists operational planning by suggesting the nature of product, pricing, promotion, and distribution tactics that would respond to different benefits expected by purchasers of the firm's outputs. A bicycle satisfies both the needs for transportation and recreation; the physical product designed to satisfy those distinct needs may or may not be the same. Competing makers of bicycles will most likely differ as to style and quality of product, as a variety of products compete to satisfy the need for "recreation" that do not offer the transportation benefit.

A last step in strategic decision-making concerns development of a viable mix of goods and services to be offered to the marketplace. A series of decisions must be made as to how the firm's outputs will mean the criteria set out in prior stages of strategic planning. These decisions concern raw materials, production processes, product designs, distribution, and pricing objectives that will direct the logistics of converting inputs into outputs.

ADMINISTRATIVE AND OPERATIONAL MARKET DECISIONS

As mentioned above, the "marketing plan" is often a tool used by organizations to structure strategic administrative and operational decision-making. The first element of such a plan, the Situation Analysis, corresponds to strategic marketing decisions. The plan itself usually sets out who will do what, and when and how it will be done—in effect, administrative and operating decisions. In addition to the formal marketing plan, other factors affect the nature of administrative and operational decisions.

In the arena of administrative decision-making, formal and informal organizational structures will have a major impact on the integration of strategy and operations. A decentralized firm often allows operational decisions such as actual price levels to be decentralized, while allowing strategic decisions such as pricing objectives to be centralized. Futhermore, administrative decisions concern how marketing decision-makers are evaluated and rewarded. While various tools may be used to evaluate marketing operations, such as market share or levels of consumer satisfaction, a separate decision concerns whether or not decision makers are evaluated on such performance criteria. Other administrative decisions concern communication within the organization—how strategic decisions are communicated to those who make operational decisions, and how the results of operational decisions are communicated to those responsible for evaluation of the marketing plan.

Operating decisions in marketing establish the specific values of input variables, such as materials and processes required to meet a strategic objective. They include issues of product policy (such as width, breadth, and consistency of product lines), distribution policies (service options, intensity and types of intermediary institutions), promotion policies (mix of mass and personal communication media), and pricing tactics (cost-plus or other price setting techniques). Operating decisions are interdependent and cannot be made in isolation from each other or from strategic decisions. A decision to use discount stores and intensive distribution must be consistent with profit margins and pricing of the product, promotion techniques, and product quality. The effective integration of operating decisions determines the potential success of an organization in meeting its strategic objectives.

Marketing Decision-Making in CONASUPO

The model presented in the previous section describes marketing decision-making in private sector firms. Before analyzing CONASUPO decision processes with the structure provided by the model, distinctions between public and private sector decision-making must be made. Decision-making in a public enterprise is expected to be different from that of a private firm; based on ambiguity of its motivation to serve both public and private (organizational) interests. Furthermore, this multiple goal structure leads to conflicting performance standards, multiple behavioral models and values, and polycentric authority and reward systems (McGill and Wooten, 1975). CONASUPO, as previously described, seems to have many of these unique traits of public enterprises.

Decision-making styles in public enterprises have also been described as political, entrepreneurial, or technocratic (Bigler, forthcoming). The technocratic decision maker tends to emphasize the accomplishment of physical tasks and the building of technical expertise within the organization. Performance is often evaluated in terms of getting things done within time and resource constraints. The political management style focuses on distribution of resources to maximize political profits, both individually and organizationally. The "political" decision maker tends to be more open concerning access to the target population but more partisan about internal policies. Further, political managers respond directly to opportunities to enhance publicity or patronage goals, sometimes at the expense of efficient operations. The entrepreneurial manager has perhaps the clearest standards for performance evaluation: creation of economic profits. Economically marginal projects are undertaken only when the public sector is willing to subsidize them (Bigler, 1979).

CONASUPO appears to have been influenced to varying degrees by administrators using all three administrative styles. To date, however, its performance has been measured externally on its ability to meet economic and political criteria. The private sector model may not be totally appropriate for evaluating marketing decision-making in CONASUPO, but it will allow contrast with the private sector in Mexico.

STRATEGIC DECISION-MAKINING IN CONASUPO

Marketing strategy in CONASUPO is reflected in its statements of objectives and in broad policies. Decision-making responsibility for such areas in concentrated in higher levels of the organization. The determination of CONASUPO's mission, as illustrated in Table 1, seems to have evolved as its current structure has—by assuming the objectives of the various public enterprise entities which it now controls. These broad directions for policy, such as "to increase the social welfare of low-income consumers" appear to remain unchanged and uninfluenced by the sexenio. Clearly CONASUPO's overall purpose is to achieve political accommodations with specific sectors of Mexican society.

Administrators in CONASUPO do determine what policies will be used to meet its objectives. Through policy formulation, emphasis on achieving different objectives is varied by different directors of CONASUPO. Policy guidelines appear to be responsive to political forces such as the sexenio, various alliances of administrators with the president and other political figures, and the political potential of the general director. For example, under the directorship of Hank González during the administration of Díaz Ordaz, emphasis was placed on policies to meet the goals of protecting low-income consumers and producers (political style). During de la Vega's directorship, during the Echeverría administration, policies were formulated that focused on structural change in channels of distribution for commodities (technocratic style). In contrast, price regulation objectives predominanted in early CONASUPO days (entrepreneurial/technocratic style).

The policies formulated by CONASUPO administrators depend on their interpretations of the causes of problems they are endeavoring to solve. For example, de la Vega's technical advisors came to the conclusion that agricultural problems in the traditional sector were related to economic relations, rather than to infrastructure and technology. Past CONASUPO policy had centered on providing this sector infrastructure through facilities and price guarantees and through technology, by training farmers in production of high yield crops. Under de la Vega, emphasis was switched to a policy of programs that would restructure low-income produers' relationships with marketing intermediaries (Hilger, 1976).

STRATEGIC DECISION-MAKING AS A PROCESS

Consumer needs are identified by CONASUPO administrators, not by marketing research. Marketing research and forecasting are used as operational tools after strategy has been determined. Because the technical groups study problems in comparative secrecy, it is not known exactly what tools of analysis are used. Input from the external environment comes from administrators' political networks. After policy has been determined, factors such as economic, social, political, and demographic changes are analyzed by the Operations and the Planning and Finance Divisions. This analysis forms the basis for operational decisions. However, because there is an overlap of personnel involved in the informal study groups that determine policy and personnel officially responsible for operational planning, external environmental factors do influence strategy formulation. The overlap of personnel in strategic and other decisions is illustrated in Table 2.

The choice of a target market that matches CONASUPO resources and market needs is predetermined by its statement of purpose. Low-income consumers and producers are specifically identified as beneficiaries of CONASUPO outputs. Nevertheless, there is more flexibility than this implies for administrators to determine exactly which needs of low-income producers or consumers will be met. Such decisions in the past have been the product of politically influenced directives, technical analysis, and assessment of current resources. For example, the Echeverría-influenced support of rural development suggested programs to support low-income producers and to protect the consumer in rural areas. Resource evaluation forced CONASUPO to question its provision of storage capabilities in support of the rural development policy.

CONASUPO administrators use its public sector position to develop strategies of differential advantage. CONASUPO has unique resources with which objectives such as "rationalizing" channels of distribution and protecting low-income consumers can be met. Access to federal subsidies permits CONASUPO to pursue distribution strategies that would not be feasible in private sector retailing. The policies of placing retail stores in low-traffic, low-volume areas and pricing products below cost are seen as essential to fulfilling CONASUPO's mission "to protect low-income consumers."

In determining a mix of goods and services, CONASUPO's strategic decision process again seems to be subject to more political than user inputs. "Products indispensable to the health and well-being of consumers with incomes of less than $1000 MN per month" is the guiding policy. Which goods and services are perceived to be "indispensable" is a strategic decision. At one point, CONASUPO planners decided that dispensaries of medicines would be included in CONASUPO's array of services to low-income producers. However, pressure by the pharmaceuticals industry effectively destroyed support for such a policy, and it was dropped (Grindle, 1977). The location of retail stores in rural rather than urban areas is another such strategic decision. Internal pressures in DICONSA for profitability tend to direct investments in retailing toward urban areas; other policy directives, such as the rural development plans of de la Vega, mandate increased investments in rural areas.

In summary, a pervasive element of strategic decision-making in CONASUPO is composed of multiple influences of political and economic factors. The organizational climate does not reward user-oriented decision-making. And, as is often the case for public enterprises, marketing policies for CONASUPO are determined by forces external to the organization (Ritchie and LaBreque, 1975: 14). Mobility of decision makers is predicated on their abilities to garner increased resources and revenues, not on abilities to increase satisfaction levels of CONASUPO consumers. Therefore, the marketing model of strategic decision-making is less appropriate in the case of CONASUPO than would be one based on political exchange theory, patron-client networks, or similar thinking. The conditions requisite for market-

TABLE 2

Sample Strategic and Operating Decisions in CONASUPO

Sample Marketing Strategies	Determined by:	Sample Operational Decisions	Determined or Implemented by:
Meet the needs of low income urban consumers	P, GD, O, H	Mobile stores	GD, H, S
		Pricing by one piece	GD, H
		Self-service	H, S
		Locations of stores	P, O, GD, H, S, E
		Product mix	GD, H, I, O, E
		Product quality	H
		Promotion of services	H, S
Meet the needs of low income rural consumers	P, GD, O, H	Store locations	P, O, G, D, H, S, E
		Product mix	I, S, H
		Prices charged	GD, S, H
		Services offered	H, S, I
Interrupt dependencies of low income producers on private intermediaries	GD, P, O, H	Store locations in rural areas	P, O, GD, H, S, E
		Provision of services	S, H, O, E
		Training programs	H, O, S, E
		Prices	H, S, E, O
Stabilize internal market prices	P, GD	Pricing not based on costs	GD, H, S
Increase commercial agricultural production	P, GD, H	Price guarantee	H
		Provision of credit	GD, H, S
		Prices of goods below costs	GD, H, S, I
		Free services (sacks for crops)	GD, H, S
		Training Offered	GD, P, O, H, S

P = President of Mexico; O = Other Political Figures; GD = General Director of CONASUPO; H = Holding Company Personnel; S = CONASUPO Subsidiary Personnel; I = Individual Retail Store Managers; E = Other External Sources ing strategies based on maximizing consumer satisfactions for CONASUPO would presuppose meeting other objectives such as the financial or political growth of CONASUPO and its decision makers (Etgar and Ratchford, 1974). Until low-income consumers and producers become more effective as political forces in Mexico, these objectives will supersede maximization of consumer satisfaction.

ADMINISTRATIVE RESPONSIBILITIES FOR MARKETING DECISIONS

As should be clear, marketing strategies are determined with limited participation in CONASUPO. Broad retail policies are mandated by the general director of CONASUPO, its advisory council, and the two divisions of Operations and Planning and Finance. In addition, there is input from other members of the Mexican bureaucracy through its representatives on the advisory council and informal political alliances. The Operations Division, however, tends to focus on resource needs, and therefore has more impact on operational decisions than strategic ones.

The subsidiary companies and their holding company division have responsibility for translating policy into programs. However, programs are sometimes designed by other divisions, and the subsidiaries are required only to put them into operation (Grindle, 1977). Again, however, operating decisions—such as where to place a store or what prices to charge for corn products—may be influenced by external or upper-level political pressures. A store location decision by one of the DICONSA companies might be influenced by private business in the area, the state governor, the state office representative of CONASUPO, the general director, or even the president (Grindle, 1977; Hilger, 1976).

At all levels of CONASUPO, operational decisions are made. Decision rules may exist in order to routinize decision-making based on technical analyses, but they are apt to be preempted by other considerations. Every decision, therefore, is somewhat unique, given its potential consequences on CONASUPO's external environment. While organizational structure leads to decentralized decision-making (whereby strategic decisions are normally made by the holding company and operating decisions are made by subsidiaries), the process is not as distinct as organizational structure implies. Table 2 illustrates these issues.

Evaluation criteria for CONASUPO personnel are based on a combination of traditional and nontraditional rewards. Traditional performance measures are profitability, productivity, or success in meeting organizational objectives; such measures are considered when evaluating personnel at all levels in CONASUPO. Furthermore, personnel of the Finance and Planning and the Operations Divisions of the holding company gather data to report on CONASUPO's overall performance: e.g., revenues, expenses, and subsidies for various operational units. It is unclear whether managers at different levels are held responsible for their performance as indicated by these data. While an individual store manager may be evaluated on the basis of such data, holding company personnel may be rewarded for "political" rather than operational performance.

It is interesting to note that CONASUPO is seen by the public in Mexico to be meeting its goals, even though its reward structure is not always based on success in meeting the needs of low-income producers and consumers. In the Monterrey area, both patrons and nonpatrons of CONASUPO from a variety of income groups believe that it is meeting the needs of low-income consumers and is contributing to development in Mexico (Hilger, 1976). In addition, its products and pricing are seen by low-income consumers to meet their needs when privately owned stores do not (Hilger, 1978).

OPERATING DECISIONS IN CONASUPO

Operating decisions concern such issues as pricing, product mixes, store locations, promotional techniques, sources of supply, and programs of services to meet strategic objectives. As a complex organization, CONASUPO has assigned responsibilities for such decisions to a wide variety of personnel. Operating decisions also vary by the type of subsidiary concerned—manufacturing, storage, retailing, and so on. Sources of supply for DICONSA's are often predetermined by the output of CONASUPO manufacturing companies.

Product quality and mix are essential components of a firm's marketing tactics and of all operational decisions. CONASUPO determines its product quality and mix by its choice of sources of supply and its standards for self-production. Product quality has been variable in the past, leading to low consumer confidence in CONASUPO-brand products (Hilger, 1976, 1978). Many CONASUPO products are supplied by multinational firms whose own products are perceived to be of high quality by the market. The differential perceptions may be due to the overall image of CONASUPO as a "working class" store, to poor specifications, or to corruption in contracts with CONASUPO suppliers. Decisions as to product quality and mix of products available for retail outlets are made by the Operating Division of CONASUPO. Individual stores and DICONSA subsidiaries must choose stock from what is available from this division.

Assortments are individual store decisions but must be made within the available supply constraint. Market feedback on the viability of products chosen by the Operating Division is not automatic; the DICONSA companies are sometimes frustrated that assortments do not match regional needs. Market needs vary radically in rural and urban areas. Overstocking and demand underestimations seem to be taken care of by time as well as by inventory reorder models. Individual CONASUPO stores seem to tailor their assortments, within the above constraints, to local competitive and market environments. A store in Mexico City stocks an average of 4500 items, while one in a rural area stocks about 1500 products.

Distribution tactics concern intensity of outlets, location of outlets, and service policies. The number of outlets in a market area is an operational decision concerning market exposure. In CONASUPO's case, the location of a store and the number of stores in a locality seem to be recommendations made at operating levels whose final decisions are determined by external influences. For example, the Districto Federal had more than 2000 CONASUPO outlets in 1975, while Monterrey had fewer than 30. DICONSA del Norte representatives admitted that every time they planned to open a new store, private food wholesalers in Monterrey would exercise influence in Mexico City to have it stopped. Thus, operating decisions concerning how to effect market penetration are influenced by factors other than market needs. Because store locations can be used as political rewards, they are sometimes placed in areas where CONASUPO has already met a desired level of market penetration (Grindle, 1977). Such influences lead to inconsistency in marketing objectives and implementation tactics.

CONASUPO has two broad directives for its pricing decisions: price stability and prices that meet consumers' economic abilities. In the DICONSA's, prices are determined on varying bases. Rural stores may have product prices that purposefully do not cover costs; urban stores are priced to make profits, often high enough to cover losses in other areas. As in the private sector, competitive effects of prices are also considered. In DICONSA del Norte it was suggested that the lowest possible prices were not always charged for fear of competitive reactions. Yet one of CONASUPO's marketing objectives is considered to be competitive pressure for lower margins and prices. In summary, pricing decisions in CONASUPO seem to be determined with profit objectives in mind, but external influences and policies to "protect" consumers are often interjected into the decision process. Prices are designed to meet a "satisficing" rather than a maximizing objective.

Decisions as to promotional techniques and media are made at two levels in CONASUPO: by DICONSA subsidiaries and by the Public Relations and Press Departments of the holding company. There are no measures of promotional effectiveness except perhaps increased awareness of the agency and its stores. A previous study suggested that the public believes CONASUPO is more visible than private stores due to publicity concerning its operations (Hilger, 1976). Such publicity has, of course, not always been positive.

Few, if any, individual store promotions take place. Extensive use is made of national media, such as television and radio, to build the corporate image. Creative and attention-snaring slogans are often used; attempts are made to standardize these throughout the organization. Whether they are effective within CONASUPO's target market is not known. A promotion director for one of the DICONSA subsidiaries admitted that posters and slogans which company personnel preferred were more likely to be chosen than ones which were tailored to low-income consumers. Because promotion decisions and techniques are generally not tested for effectiveness within local environments, it is less likely that they greatly affect store volume and traffic. In summary, CONASUPO uses institutional promotion rather than product or store-oriented techniques.

Conclusions

While this article has not presented a comprehensive view of marketing decision-making in CONASUPO, some generalizations can be made. One such conclusion is the effect of CONASUPO as an institution of development policy on its marketing decisions. Both strategic and operating marketing decisions are impinged upon by the political context in which CONASUPO exists. The distinction between private sector strategic decision-making and those processes in CONASUPO is not explained by its public policy imperatives alone. The place CONASUPO and its administrators have in the Mexican political hierarchy must also be accounted for when describing the marketing strategies that it pursues.

A second conclusion is that formal organizational structure and decentralization do not mean that decision-making is decentralized. In fact, it appears CONASUPO's structure and reward systems contribute to centralization of strategic, administrative, and operating decisions in marketing areas. In addition, such centralization and external influence in decision-making contribute to inconsistencies in organizational purpose, marketing objectives, and tactics and programs designed to meet those goals.

A further conclusion is that basic marketing concepts are not currently appropriate to or used by CONASUPO management. The central focus on market needs as a basis for marketing strategies is not appropriate to the organizational structure or climate within which marketing strategies are formulated. Where such concepts are appropriate, as in the integration of tactics and programs for meeting overall objectives, decisions appear to be made on an ad hoc basis rather than as part of an integrated strategy.

A final conclusion is that multiple performance criteria (political and economic) reduce the motivation to adopt a model of marketing decision-making appropriate to private sector firms. Performance evaluation is not tied to consumer satisfaction levels. This is explained both by the political inadequacies of its constituency targets and by the immunity that CONASUPO has due to its subsidies. Yet measures of user satisfaction could serve as guidelines for controlling the consistency of strategy and tactics and also as a gauge of success in meeting development objectives.

In addition, the use of marketing tactics at operating levels is limited. Some orientation to basic marketing tools and concepts could strengthen its effectiveness in accomplishing structural goals through competitive tactics. These recommendations also acknowledge the importance of political influence in CONASUPO decision-making; yet if more concrete marketing objectives were set out in response to the political directives, then less inconsistency might occur between operational and strategic decisions.

Several similarities between marketing decision-making in CONASUPO and those processes in the private sector can be noted. First is the aversion to use of marketing strategy based on identification of market needs (Glade and Udell, 1968). Private sector firms in Mexico and Latin America have often been characterized as monopolistic in pricing and distribution behaviors (Halper, 1966; Goldman, 1974). Second, both CONASUPO and private retailers are subject to low consumer outreach in Mexico, which tends to narrow the shopping scope of low-income consumers and thus restricts strategic altenatives (Goldman, 1974). Third, private firms are also subject to political influence within the Mexican economic system. The political impact of marketing decisions can be felt in the form of reduced export permits, blocked credit, or other such government policies.

Political influence on private sector firms, however, is somewhat distinct from that which pervades CONASUPO decision-making. Public policy sets the parameters within which private firms operate, but those parameters do not restrict the nature of marketing strategy or tactics for private firms. Retailers are free to determine target markets and to build marketing strategies that meet their organizational objectives. Tactics tend to be fluid and responsive to environmental changes. Within the organization, private firms have the independence necessary to respond to changing market needs and opportunities. The comparative absence of political influence in private sector strategic and policy decisions is perhaps the fact of most significant contrast to policy formulation in CONASUPO.

Finally, the use of a model of private sector marketing decision-making to evaluate those processes in CONASUPO does not accommodate the pervasive influence of Mexican political networks. A more appropriate model for future studies would have to incorporate political objectives into the analysis of the ways in which economic alternatives are weighed and chosen. The dynamics of this interaction in CONASUPO should alert marketers to the need to adapt techniques for improved effectiveness in achieving economic development goals within the public sector.

REFERENCES

ALISKY, M. (1974) "CONASUPO: A Mexican agency which makes low-income workers feel their government cares." Inter-American Economic Affairs 28: 47-59.

ANSOFF, H. I. (1971) "Toward a strategic theory of the firm," pp. 11-40 in H. I. Ansoff (ed.) Business Strategy. New York: Viking.

BIGLER, G. E. (forthcoming) Ph.D. dissertation, Johns Hopkins University.

——— (1979) "Styles of management in the third sector: some implications of public economic expansion in Venezuela." Presented at the Fortieth National Conference of American Society of Public Administration, Baltimore.

CONASUPO [Compañia Nacional de Subsistencias Populares] (1973a) "Qué es CONASUPO?" (unpublished)

——— (1973b) "Qué hace la CONASUPO?" (unpublished)

CONSTANTIN, J. H., R. E. EVANS, and M. L. MORRIS (1976) Marketing Strategy and Management. Dallas: Business Publications.

ETGAR, M. and B. T. RATCHFORD (1974) "Marketing management and marketing concepts: their conflicts in non-profit organizations," pp. 258-261 in 1974 Combined American Marketing Association Proceedings, Series 36.

GLADE, W. P. (1975) "Entrepreneurship in the state sector: CONASUPO of Mexico." Presented at the Economic Anthropology of Investment Behavior in Latin America Seminar, School of American Research, Santa Fe, NM: August 4-8.

——— and J. C. UDELL (1968) "The marketing concept and economic development in Peru." J. of Interamerican Studies 10 (October): 533-546.

GOLDMAN, A. (1974) "Outreach of consumers and the modernization of urban food retailing in developing countries." J. of Marketing 38 (October): 8-16.

GRINDLE, M. S. (1977) Bureaucrats, Politicians and Peasants in Mexico. Berkeley: Univ. of California Press.

HALPER, D. G. (1966) "The environment for marketing in Peru." J. of Marketing 30 (July): 42-46.

HILGER, M. T. (1978) "Tools for measuring public enterprise goal achievement: consumer attitude research." Presented at the Southwest Council Of Latin American Studies (SCOLAS) meetings, Texas A & M University.

——— (1976) "Consumer perceptions of a public marketer: the case of CONASUPO in Monterrey, Mexico." Ph.D. dissertation, University of Texas.

KOTLER, P. (1977) Marketing Management: Analysis, Planning, and Control. Englewood Cliffs, NJ: Prentice-Hall.

McGILL, M. E. and L. M. WOOTEN (1975) "Management in the third sector." Public Administration Rev. 35 (September-October): 443-477.

NAVARRETE, I. (1960) Distribución del ingreso y el desarrollo económico de México. México City: Institute de Investigaciones Económicas de la Escuela Nacional de Economía.

REWOLDT, S. H., J. D. SCOTT, and M. R. WARSHAW (1977) Introduction to Marketing Management: Text and Cases. Homewood, IL: Irwin.

REYNOLDS, C. (1970) The Mexican Economy: Twentieth Century Structure and Growth. New Haven, CT: Yale Univ. Press.

RITCHIE, J. R. and R. J. LaBREQUE (1975) "Marketing research and public policy—A functional perspective." J. of Marketing 39 (July): 12-19.

WEBSTER, F. E., Jr. (1974) Marketing for Managers. New York: Harper & Row.

Marye Tharp Hilger is Associate Professor of Marketing at the University of Texas, San Antonio. She has taught in Mexico and Peru and is the coauthor of a forthcoming text in international marketing.

REVIEW ESSAY

INTEGRATION AND REGIONAL DEVELOPMENT
The Case of the Commonwealth Caribbean

Chernick, S. (coordinating author). THE COMMONWEALTH CARIBBEAN: THE INTEGRATION EXPERIENCE (A World Bank Country Report). Baltimore: Johns Hopkins Univ. Press, 1978.

Axline, W. A. UNDERDEVELOPMENT, DEPENDENCE AND THE POLITICS OF INTEGRATION: A CARIBBEAN APPLICATION. Ottawa: Univ. of Ottawa, 1977.

It is a commonplace that Third World countries, despite political independence in the postcolonial era, have yet to achieve economic independence and to overcome underdevelopment. This is also true of the Commonwealth Caribbean countries which, despite per capita incomes that are quite high by Third World standards, continue to exhibit the characteristics of dependent underdevelopment. Though both the liberal and radical schools of thought in the Caribbean differ in their explanation of the phenomenon, they tend to agree on regional integration as the appropriate strategy for structural transformation. The studies examined in this essay, basically liberal in their ideological thrust, usefully illuminate the problems of integration from the complementary approaches of economics in the first study and political science in the second.

The Commonwealth Caribbean: The Integration Experience, written under the direction of Sidney Chernick, an old Caribbean hand, is the

---

EDITOR'S NOTE: This review essay, not related to the topic of this special issue or integral to it, is being published at this time by decision of the Journal's editor.

Journal of Interamerican Studies and World Affairs, Vol. 22 No. 4, November 1980 495-500

second World Bank Study to come out of the area. Unlike the first (Chernick, 1973), it is regional rather than local, in focus, and is also broader in scope. Its rationale is to provide a regional framework for aid agencies with interest in the Caribbean and to identify the potentially valuable lessons for those other small developing countries that may wish to seek economic viability through coordinated development and economic integration. However, the lessons are not fully drawn out and remain implicit in the study.

Despite this shortcoming, the work is important because it attempts to evaluate the impact of Caribbean integration on economic development. It is even more significant because it signals the governments of the area concerning the kinds of aid requests that the World Bank is likely to consider favorably, indicates to aid agencies the types of aid that are appropriate to the region, and points the direction in which Caribbean development should proceed.

The central thesis of the authors is that the limited economic progress of the Commonwealth Caribbean states in the contemporary period is bound up with their small size, fragmentation of the market, and the dearth of a meaningful coordinated strategy. In keeping with this prognosis, which is hardly original, the therapy recommended is the deepening of Caribbean integration to include the rationalization of economic activity, specialization on a regional basis, combination of complementary resources, training in skills and research and development. In the substantive chapters dealing with the six sectors of trade and monetary arrangements; population, manpower and employment; transport; agriculture; tourism; and industry, the authors analyze developments, identify problems and constraints, assess the impact of integration, and make specific recommendations.

The Report points out that CARICOM (Caribbean Common Market), formed in 1973, the successor to CARIFTA (Caribben Free Trade Association), formed in 1968, is still very much a disguised free-trade area. Goods which meet the rules of origin (50% value-added in the case of the MDCs and 40% in the case of the LDCs, inclusive of 200 items in the Basic Materials List which are considered "domestic" though imported) qualify for duty-free entry among member states. There is a Common External Tariff (CET) on goods originating outside the area, but the LDCs, because of their differential economic strength, have been permitted a longer time-frame for its adoption. Unregulated capital flows among member countries are implicitly discouraged, and, unlike the EEC, freedom of movement is not part of CARICOM. The Treaty also includes provisions for the harmonization of fiscal incentives, tax-sparing arrangements, functional cooperation, foreign policy coordination, and industrial programming.

On the whole, the World Bank's evaluation is that the impact of regional integration on development has been marginal. The larger market has not yet led to new regionally based industries, to appreciable intersectoral linkages, or to a clearly equitable sharing of benefits. The MDCs continue to dominate intraregional trade (accounting for some 96% of exports and 90% of imports), and within this group Trinidad and Jamaica are the main beneficiaries. This inequitable distribution of benefits continues to be a sore point within CARICOM.

The recommendations of the World Bank for the rationalization of economic activity and the deepening of integration are quite comprehensive, so that any summary can hardly do justice to the wealth of details. No serious observer will deny the appropriateness of the measures to enhance balance-of-payments management on a regional basis, to increase employment and raise productivity, to develop an adequate transport system, to reform agriculture, to improve tourism, and to increase the efficiency and productivity of the industrial sector through regional coordination and programming.

Nonetheless, there are some serious lapses in the analysis. For example, the report concedes that the existence of wide differentials in wages between the organized and unorganized labor markets encourage Caribbean youth to wait for a well-paid, unionized job, rather than accept employment at low wages. But it does not indicate how this problem should be tackled. One would have thought that an income's policy could be helpful in this situation, but the entire issue is evaded.

In the same fashion, the report sees a need for Caribbean governments to foster the repatriation of CARICOM nationals working abroad in order to alleviate the serious skills deficit at home. But is says nothing about the curtailment of the continuing emigration of skilled personnel from the region which creates that deficit in the first place. Equally puzzling is its recommendation for the revival of export agriculture, which has been continuously declinning since the mid-1960s. In view of the report's own admission that the Caribbean is a high-cost producer of sugar (approximately 30% higher than Australia, Fiji, and Mauritius) and in view of the roller-coaster movement of prices, together with the fact that its main export market—the EEC—is normally an exporter of sugar, one would have thought that these are precisely the reasons for getting out of sugar, preferably through an orderly retreat, rather than for an expansion of the industry.

Despite these shortcomings, the need for aid along the lines suggested by the World Bank for assisting the development of Caribbean regional integration can hardly be disputed: technical assistance for the development of a regional system of statistics; manpower analysis and manpower training; educational reform; the upgrading of port management, port development, road transportation and regional shipping; land reform, small-farm development, agricultural marketing and research; feasibility studies in tourism; the establishment of regionally integrated industries; and industrial research and development.

If the merit of the World Bank report is that it underscores the need for the deepening of integration, its weakness is that is does not explain why progress in this direction has, so far, been very limited. The value of Axline's study is that it helps to illuminate the problem. The rationale of *The Politics of Integration* is to provide a political theory of economic integration that is relevant to the Third World because of dissatisfaction with the neoclassical theory of integration, which assumes the conditions which developing countries are trying to create.

The author delineates a three-stage model of integration of increasing complexity, based on the work of Mytelka (Axline, 1977: 43). Stage I is a *laissez-faire* scheme which involves (a) the freeing of trade within the region, (b) adoption and determination of a level of CET, and (c) the freeing of movement of factors of production within the region. However, this scheme exacerbates inequities within the region. Stage II attempts to distribute the benefits of integration by the inclusion of redistributive measures of a compensatory and corrective nature, such as development planning on a regional level, regional development banks, and allocation of industries among countries. Stage III is more *dirigiste* than Stage II, as it includes measures to reduce the pattern of dependence on metropolitan countries (vertical integration) which constitute a major limiting force on the operation of other integrative measures (horizontal integration), such as a regional policy for the regulation of foreign investment. Axline's thesis is that although economic benefits increase as one moves from lower to higher stages of integration, the political difficulties also increase. Thus, Type III, which brings the most benefits economically, is politically the most difficult to achieve.

Caribbean integration evinces some of the characteristics of Stage I and Stage II taxonomies, with free trade, CET, and institutions such as the Caribbean Development Bank (CDB) and the Caribbean Investment Corporation (CIC). The establishment of CARIFTA was made possible, in part, by the realization of the LDCs that revenue losses from the phased freeing of trade could be recouped through consumption taxes and, in part, to various concessions such as the Reserve List, the Agricultural Marketing Protocol, most favorable terms for country of origin, and the reservation of the CDB soft-loans wicket for the LDCs.

Similarly, the Customs Union (CARICOM) was facilitated by concessions such as a large time-frame for the LDC adoption of CET and the establishment of the CIC. However, movement towards more of a Stage III arrangement has been stymied by the issue of the Draft Agreement on Foreign Investment. Despite its gradualistic strategy, the agreement has failed to obtain the support of the LDCs, which fear that they would be frozen out of their fair share of investment. Indeed, they are less apprehensive about the dangers of foreign investment than the MDCs, and it is this ideological cleavage which Axline perceives as the chief obstacle.

However, there is the danger of working too much of the ideological conflict between the MDCs and the LDCs. The latter can hardly be blamed for withholding their consent to the Draft in view of the lackluster performance of the CDB and, to an even greater extent, of the CIC, which is practically a dead letter in providing investment capital. Apart from increasing resources to these two bodies, what is required is a mechanism for the allocation of industries so that the LDCs will become less mesmerized by the illusion of tax havens and free ports as their means of economic salvation. But such a mechanism properly entails the creation of a supranational agency to direct and oversee industrial location. Therein lies the problem: none of the governments are prepared to acquiesce in any diminution of its newly won sovereignty. Furthermore, given the economic difficulties of the post-OPEC world, any MDC government which appears to the electorate to be giving away industries and exporting jobs risks political suicide. Viewed from this perspective, the LDCs hardly seem to be the major obstacle to the integration process.

On the whole, the immediate prospects for the deeping of Caribbean integration are not at all encouraging. Apart from the obsession with national sovereignty, there is the additional difficulty that integration is by no means a nonpartisan issue. Even where the ruling political parties ostensibly support it, there are strong factions—such as Trinidad's PNM—which are not averse to going it alone and leaving Jamaica and Guyana to suffer the consequences of their perceived socialist follies. Neither is the situation helped by opposition parties which are either lukewarm or hostile to integration schemes.

Perhaps the main difficulty is that there is no mass constituency for integration. Support for the movement comes primarily from the West Indian intelligentsia, but even within this group there has been no organized lobby for strengthening integration. Indeed, they have failed to raise public consciousness of the long-term benefits of integration and thus, to prepare the ground for political support from the grass roots. Without such support—even with governments that are not transfixed by sovereignty and are less parochial in their outlook, which are becoming more prevalent as a younger generation of leaders succeeds the old anti-colonial fighters—Caribbean integration is unlikely to progress much beyond its present state.

—Ralph Paragg

REFERENCE

CHERNICK, S. [ed.] (1973) Employment in Trinidad and Tobago. Washington, DC: World Bank.

Ralph Paragg, a researcher in the Department of Politcal Science at Queen's University, Kingston, Canada, is a native of Trinidad and received his degrees from Canadian universities—the University of Calgary (B.A. and M.A.) and Queen's University (Ph.D.). His thesis was entitled "Canada and the Commonwealth Caribbean: the political economy of a relationship in transition."

BOOKS RECEIVED

GENERAL AND REGIONAL LATIN AMERICA

Bernhard, Virginia, ed. ELITES, MASSES, AND MODERNIZATION IN LATIN AMERICA, 1850-1930. Texas Pan American Series. Austin: University of Texas Press, 1979. Notes, viii, 156 pp. $9.95.

Boneo, Horacio. PLANIFICACION, PRESUPUESTO Y EMPRESAS PUBLICAS EN AMERICA LATINA. Estudios Cedes: Vol. 2, No. 4. Buenos Aires: CEDES, 1979. 49 pp. Paper.

Carriere, Jean, ed. INDUSTRIALISATION AND THE STATE IN LATIN AMERICA. Incidentele Publicaties 14. Amsterdam: CEDLA, 1979. 465 pp. Paper.

Chaney, Elsa M. SUPERMADRE: WOMEN IN POLITICS IN LATIN AMERICA. Latin American Monographs No. 50. Austin: Institute of Latin American Studies, University of Texas, 1980. Appendices, bibliography, index. 210 pp. $14.95.

Christensen, Bodil and Samuel Marti. WITCHCRAFT AND PRE-COLOMBIAN PAPER BRUJERIAS Y PAPEL PRECOLOMBIANO. Mexico, D.F.: Ediciones Europamericanas Klaus Thiele, 1979. Bibliografía. 88 pp. Paper.

Eagleson, John and Philip Scharper, eds. PUEBLA AND BEYOND: DOCUMENTATION AND COMMENTARY. Maryknoll, NY: Orbis Books, 1979. Index, abbreviations. xiii, 370 pp. $7.95 paper.

Economic Commission for Latin America. ECONOMIC SURVEY OF LATIN AMERICA, 1977. Santiago, Chile: United Nations, 1978. Evolution of the Latin American economy in 1977; economic trends by countries; two studies on international economic relations. 536 pp. Paper.

Ferber, Robert, ed. CONSUMPTION AND INCOME IN LATIN AMERICA. An ECIEL book (Program of Joint studies on Latin American Economic Integration). Washington, DC: Organization of American States, 1980. v, 484 pp. $15.00 paper.

Fox-Lockert, Lucia. WOMEN NOVELISTS IN SPAIN AND SPANISH AMERICA. Metuchen, NJ: Scarecrow Press, 1979. Conclusions, chapter notes, bibliography, index. viii, 347 pp. $17.50.

Frank, Gary. STRUGGLE FOR HEGEMONY IN SOUTH AMERICA: ARGENTINA, BRAZIL, AND THE UNITED STATES DURING THE SECOND WORLD WAR. Miami: Center for Advanced International Studies, University of Miami, 1979. Notes, bibliography, index. xi, 116 pp. $4.95 paper.

Frenkel, Roberto. DECISIONES DE PRECIO EN ALTA INFLACION. Buenos Aires: CEDES, 1979. Estudios Cedes: Vol. 2, No. 3. 58 pp. Paper.

Hilton, Ronald. A BIBLIOGRAPHY OF LATIN AMERICA AND THE CARIBBEAN: THE HILTON LIBRARY. Metuchen, NJ: Scarecrow Press, 1980. Includes Latin American autobiographical interviews recorded on tape. 675 pp. $29.50.

Journal of Interamerican Studies and World Affairs, Vol. 22 No. 4, November 1980 501-507

Johnson, John J. LATIN AMERICA IN CARICATURE. Texas Pan American Series. Austin: University of Texas Press, 1980. Notes, index. ix, 330 pp. $19.95.

Meyer, Michael C., ed. SUPPLEMENT TO A BIBLIOGRAPHY OF UNITED STATES-LATIN AMERICAN RELATIONS SINCE 1810. Lincoln: University of Nebraska Press, 1980. Abbreviations, key to journals and other serials, index. xxvi, 193 pp. $19.50.

Romano, Ruggiero and Marcello Carmagnani, eds. NOVA AMERICANA, Vol. 2. "Caudillismo, caciquismo e clientelismo." Torino, Italy: Giulio Einaudi Editores, 1979. 391 pp. Paper.

Schnepf, Ryszard and Krzysztof Smolana. BIBLIOGRAFIA DE PUBLICACIONES SOBRES AMERICA LATINA EN POLONIA, 1945-1977. In both Polish and Spanish. Warsaw: Biblioteca Nacional, Instituto de Historia, Sociedad Polaca de Estudios Latinoamericanistas, 1978. Index. 289 pp. Paper.

Thorp, Rosemary and Laurence Whitehead, eds. INFLATION AND STABILISATION IN LATIN AMERICA. New York: Holmes and Meier, 1980. List of tables and figures, index. ix, 285 pp. $34.50.

Veliz, Claudio. THE CENTRALIST TRADITION OF LATIN AMERICA. Princeton, NJ: Princeton University Press, 1980. Bibliography, index. xii, 355 pp. $22.50 cloth, $9.75 paper.

ARGENTINA

Balán, Jorge. URBANIZATION REGIONAL Y PRODUCCION AGRARIA EN ARGENTINA: UN ANALISIS COMPARATIVO. Estudios Cedes: Vol. 2, No. 2. Buenos Aires: CEDES, 1979. Referencias. 42 pp. Paper.

Canitrot, Adolfo. LA DISCIPLINA COMO OBJETIVO DE LA POLITICA ECONOMICA. UN ENSAYO SOBRE EL PROGRAMA ECONOMICO DEL GOBIERNO ARGENTINO DESDE 1976. Estudios Cedes: Vol. 2, No. 6. Buenos Aires: CEDES, 1979. 34 pp. Paper.

Cavarozzi, Marcelo. SINDICATOS Y POLITICA EN ARGENTINA, 1955-1958. Estudios Cedes: Vol. 2, No. 1. Buenos Aires: CEDES, 1979. Referencias bibliográficas. 87 pp. Paper.

Cortes Conde, Roberto. EL PROGRESO ARGENTINO, 1880-1914. Buenos Aires: Editorial Sudamericana, 1979. Colección historia y sociedad. Apéndice estadístico. 291 pp. Paper.

O'Donnell, Guillermo. NOTAS PARA EL ESTUDIO DE PROCESOS DE DEMOCRATIZACION POLITICA A PARTIR DEL ESTADO BUROCRATICO-AUTORITARIO. Documento de trabajo. Estudios Cedes: Vol. 2, No. 5. Buenos Aires: CEDES, 1979. 27 pp. Paper.

Taylor, J. M. EVA PERON: THE MYTHS OF A WOMAN. Chicago: University of Chicago Press, 1980. Notes, bibliography, index, plates. 176 pp. $15.00.

BRAZIL

Hugh-Jones, Stephen. THE PALM AND THE PLEIADES. INITIATION AND COSMOLOGY IN NORTHWEST AMAZONIA. Cambridge Studies in Social Anthropology, No. 24. New York: Cambridge University Press, 1979. Orthography, appendixes, bibliography, index, index of names, illustrations, xvi, 332 pp. $19.95.

Mota, Artur. HISTORIA DA LITERATURA BRASILEIRA. São Paulo, Brasil: Biblioteca Academia Paulista de Letras, Volume 7, 1978. Vol. 3, Tomo I, 277 pp. Tomo II, 253 pp. Paper.

Perlman, Janice E. THE MYTH OF MARGINALITY: URBAN POVERTY AND POLITICS IN RIO DE JANEIRO. Berkeley: University of California Press, 1980. Appendix, notes, bibliography, index. xxi, 341 pp. $5.95 paper.

CARIBBEAN REGION

Equinoccio. EL CARIBE: UN MAR ENTRE DOS MUNDOS. Caracas: EQUINOCCIO, 1978. 297 pp. Paper.

Harrigan, Norwell. THE INTER-VIRGIN ISLANDS CONFERENCE: A STUDY OF A MICROSTATE INTERNATIONAL ORGANIZATION. Gainesville, FL: Center for Latin American Studies, University of Florida, and University Presses of Florida, 1980. Appendices, selected bibliography. vi, 88 pp.

Langley, Lester D. THE UNITED STATES AND THE CARIBBEAN, 1900-1970. Athens: University of Georgia Press, 1980. Bibliographical essay, notes, index. viii, 324 pp. $22.00.

Galvin, Miles. THE ORGANIZED LABOR MOVEMENT IN PUERTO RICO. Cranbury, NJ: Fairleigh Dickinson University Press, 1980. Notes, selected bibliography, index. 241 pp. $16.50.

Pando, Magdalen M. CUBA'S FREEDOM FIGHT, ANTONIO MACEO; 1845-1896. Gainesville, FL: Felicity Press, 1980. Notes, selected bibliography, index. xviii, 144 pp. Paper.

Sender, Ramon J., prólogo. ESCRITO EN CUBA: CINCO POETAS DISIDENTES. Biblioteca Cubana Contemporanea. Madrid: Editorial Playor, 1978. 117 pp. Paper.

Universidad de la Habana. RESUMENES 1979. 2° Evento Científico. Havana: Universidad de la Habana, 1980. Anexo. 941 pp. Paper.

U.S. Department of Commerce. ECONOMIC STUDY OF PUERTO RICO. 2 volumes. Report to the President prepared by the Interagency Task Force coordinated by the U.S. Department of Commerce. Washington, DC: U.S. Department of Commerce, 1979. Vol. I: General Economic Assessment, Federal Programs and Policies. Appendix. 339 pp. Vol. II: Sector Studies (industry, agriculture, tourism, housing & construction, transportation, energy, commercial banking, employment, wage structure, and migration, social conditions, and human services). Appendices. x, 740 pp. Paper.

CHILE

Lecaros Villavisencio, Fernando. LA GUERRA CON CHILE EN SUS DOCUMENTOS. Lima: Ediciones Rikchay Peru, 1979, segunda edición. Apéndices, colofon, índice, índice de ilustraciones. 215 pp. Paper.

Villalobos R., Sergio. LA ECONOMIA DE UN DESIERTO: TARAPACA DURANTE LA COLONIA. Santiago, Chile: Pontificia Universidad Católica de Chile, Ediciones Nueva Universidad, 1979. Abreviaturas, iconografía, bibliografía. 278 pp. Paper.

CENTRAL AMERICA

GUATEXPRO (El Centro Nacional de Promoción de las Exportaciones). Legislación Vigente para el Desarrollo del Sector Industrial. Guatemala, C.A.: GUATEXPRO, 1980. 110 pp. Paper.

Seligson, Mitchell A. PEASANTS OF COSTA RICA AND THE DEVELOPMENT OF AGRARIAN CAPITALISM. Madison: University of Wisconsin Press, 1980. Illustrations, tables, appendices, index. xxxii, 220 pp. $21.50.

COLOMBIA

Arango, Mariano. CAFE E INDUSTRIA, 1850-1930. Centro de Investigaciones Económicas de la Universidad de Antioquia. Bogotá: Carlos Valencia Editores, 1977. Anexos, bibliografía, índice temático, índice de cuadros. 260 pp. Paper.

Berry, R. Albert, Ronald G. Hellman and Mauricio Solaun, eds. POLITICS OF COMPROMISE: COALITION GOVERNMENT IN COLOMBIA. New Brunswick, NJ: Transaction Books, 1980. Index. xii, 488 pp. Paper.

Ospina Vásquez, Louis. INDUSTRIA Y PROTECCION EN COLOMBIA, 1810-1930. Biblioteca colombiana de ciencias sociales FAES, Vol. 1. Medellín: Fondo Rotatorio de Publicaciones FAES (Fundación Antioqueña para los Estudios Sociales), 1979. Bibliografía, cartogramas, cuadros fuera de texto, índice de materias, nombres de personas. 576 pp. Paper.

Restrepo, Vincente. ESTUDIO SOBRE LAS MINAS DE ORO Y PLATA EN COLOMBIA. Biblioteca colombiana de ciencas sociales FAES, Vol. II. Medellín: Fondo Rotatorio de Publicaciones FAES, 1979. (Originally published in 1883.) Apéndice. 260 pp. Paper.

MEXICO

Abreu Gómez, Ermilo, translated; introduction by Mario L. Davila and Carter Wilson. CANEK: HISTORY AND LEGEND OF A MAYA HERO. Berkeley: University of California Press, 1980. Glossary. xii, 68 pp. $8.95 cloth, $2.95 paper.

Alonso, Jorge, ed. LUCHA URBANA Y ACUMULACION DE CAPITAL. México, D.F.: Centro de Investigaciones Superiores del INAH, Ediciones de la Casa Chata 12, 1980. Apéndices, bibliografía. 485 pp. Paper.

Camp, Roderic A. MEXICO'S LEADERS: THEIR EDUCATION AND RECRUITMENT. Tucson: University of Arizona Press, 1980. List of tables, appendices, bibliography, index. xvi, 259 pp. $28.50 cloth, $12.50 paper.

Del Castillo V., Gustavo. CRISIS Y TRANSFORMACION DE UNA SOCIEDAD TRADICIONAL. México, D.F.: Centro de Investigaciones Superiores del INAH, Ediciones de la Casa Chata 10, 1979. Bibliografía. 177 pp. Paper.

De La Peña, Guillermo. HEREDEROS DE PROMESAS: AGRICULTURA, POLITICA Y RITUAL EN LOS ALTOS DE MORELOS. Versión castellana de Pastora Rodríguez Aviñoá y Victoria Miret, revisada por el autor. México, D.F.: Centro de Investigaciones Superiores del INAH, Ediciones de la Casa Chata 11, 1980. Apéndices, índice analítico, bibliografía. 391 pp. Paper.

Glantz, Susana. MANUEL: UNA BIOGRAFIA POLITICA. México, D.F.: CIS-INAH (Centro de Investigaciones Superiores del Instituto Nacional de Antropología e Historia), Editorial Nueva Imagen, 1979. 226 pp. Paper.

Hodges, Donald and Ross Gandy. MEXICO 1910-1976: REFORM OR REVOLUTION? London: Zed Press, 1980. Bibliography, glossary of Spanish words, political glossary, index, map. iii, 194 pp. Paper.

Latapi, Pablo. ANALISIS DE UN SEXENIO DE EDUCACION EN MEXICO, 1970-1976. México, D.F.: Editorial Nueva Imagen, 1980. 256 pp. $12.00 paper.

Lipp, Solomon. LEOPOLDO ZEA: FROM MEXICANIDAD TO A PHILOSOPHY OF HISTORY. Waterloo, Ontario, Canada: Wilfrid Laurier University Press, 1980. Selected bibliography, index. xiv, 146 pp. $8.00.

Schryer, Frans J. THE RANCHEROS OF PISAFLORES: THE HISTORY OF A PEASANT BOURGEOISIE IN TWENTIETH-CENTURY MEXICO. Toronto: University of Toronto Press, 1980. Figures, tables, appendix, notes, bibliography, index. xii, 210 pp. $20.00.

Wolfskill, George and Douglas W. Richmond. ESSAYS ON THE MEXICAN REVOLUTION. Walter Prescott Webb Memorial Lectures. Austin: University of Texas Press, 1980. xi, 136 pp. $9.95.

PANAMA

Anguizola, Gustave. PHILIPPE BUNAU-VARILLA: THE MAN BEHIND THE PANAMA CANAL. Chicago: Nelson-Hall, 1980. Appendices, notes, bibliography, index. x, 472 pp. $25.95.

PARAGUAY

Williams, John Hoyt, THE RISE AND FALL OF THE PARAGUAYAN REPUBLIC, 1800-1870. Austin: Institute of Latin American Studies, University of Texas, 1980. Notes, bibliography, index. x, 286 pp. $17.95 cloth, $6.95 paper.

PERU

Anna, Timothy E. THE FALL OF THE ROYAL GOVERNMENT IN PERU. Lincoln: University of Nebraska Press, 1980. Notes, selected bibliography, index. xi, 291 pp. $19.50.

Bernales B., Enrique, Laura Madalengoitia U. and Marcial Rubio C. BURGUESIA Y ESTADO LIBERAL. Lima: DESCO 1979. Bibliografía, índice onomástico. 372 pp. Paper.

Cavanagh, Jonathan. REFLECTIONS ON CLASS THEORY SUGGESTED BY ANALYSES OF THE PERUVIAN MILITARY REGIME: 1968-1979. Gottingen, Germany: Birte Fries, 1980. Appendices, bibliography. 558 pp. Paper.

CEDEP. PERU: COMERCIO Y DESARROLLO: SEMINARIO NACIONAL PREPARATORIO DE LA UNCTAD V. Serie Encuentros. Lima: CEDEP, 1979. 233 pp. Paper.

CEDEP. PERU: IDENTIDAD NACIONAL. Serie: Realidad Nacional. Lima: CEDEP, 1979. 511 pp. Paper.

Dietz, Henry A. POVERTY AND PROBLEM-SOLVING UNDER MILITARY RULE: THE URBAN POOR IN LIMA, PERU. Austin: University of Texas Press, 1980. Appendices, notes, bibliography, index, list of tables, plates, figures, map, chart. xiv, 286 pp.

Kruijt, Dirk and Menno Vellinga. LABOR RELATIONS AND MULTINATIONAL CORPORATIONS: THE CERRO DE PASCO CORPORATION IN PERU (1902-

1974). Serie: Studies of Developing Countries, No. 25. Assen, The Netherlands: Van Gorcum, 1979. List of tables and figures, appendices, bibliography, index, xviii, 262 pp. Paper. Dfl. 45.

Pease García, Henry and Alfredo Filomeno. PERU 1978: CRONOLOGIA POLITICA, Vol. 7. 1980. Indices temáticos. xiv, 407 pp. Paper. This is the latest volume of the most useful and complete annotated political chronology for any Latin American nation. Coverage began with 1968 and pagination is continuous through the seven volumes.

Rosa Balbi, Carmen and Laura Madalengoitia. PARLAMENTO Y LUCHA POLITICA: PERU 1932. Lima: DESCO, 1980. Anexos, bibliografía, otras fuentes. 199 pp. Paper.

Sánchez, Leon I., Abelardo and Julio Calderón Cockburn. EL LABERINTO DE LA CIUDAD: POLITICAS URBANAS DEL ESTADO 1950-1979. Epílogo, anexos. Lima: DESCO, 1980. 168 pp. Paper.

Wils, Fritz. INDUSTRIALIZATION, INDUSTRIALISTS, AND THE NATION-STATE IN PERU: A COMPARATIVE/SOCIOLOGICAL ANALYSIS. Berkeley: Institute of International Studies, University of California, 1979. List of tables, appendix, notes, glossary of acronyms, bibliography. xii, 273 pp. $5.95 paper.

VENEZUELA

The following books written by ex-President Rómulo Betancourt of Venezuela or related to his political activities were sent to us and to departments of Latin American Studies in American universities at the bequest of the "Fundación Diego Cisneros":

Betancourt, Rómulo. AMERICA LATINA: DEMOCRACIA E INDEPENDENCIA. Obras selectas 2. Barcelona: Editorial Seix Barral, 1978. Documentos complementarios, índice. 235 pp.

Betancourt, Rómulo. EL 18 DE OCTUBRE DE 1945: GENESIS Y REALIZACIONES DE UNA REVOLUCION DEMOCRATICA. Obras selectas 4. Caracas: Editorial Seix Barral, 1979. Indice. 412 pp.

Betancourt, Rómulo. EL PETROLEO DE VENEZUELA. Obras selectas 3. Barcelona: Editorial Seix Barral, 1978. Apéndice documental, índice. 195 pp.

Betancourt, Rómulo. VENEZUELA: OIL AND POLITICS. Boston: Houghton Mifflin, 1979. Epilogue, references, index. xxviii, 418 pp.

Betancourt, Rómulo. VENEZUELA: POLITICA Y PETROLEO. Obras selectas 1. Barcelona: Editorial Seix Barral, 1979. Indice general. 936 pp.

Betancourt, Rómulo. VENEZUELA'S OIL. Boston: Allen & Unwin, 1978. Appendices. 275 pp. Paper.

Liscano, Juan y Carlos Gottberg. MULTIMAGEN DE ROMULO: VIDA Y ACCION DE ROMULO BETANCOURT EN GRAFICAS. Caracas: Editorial Arte, 1978. 450 pp. Paper.

Partido Acción Democrática. VIGENCIA Y PROYECCION DE ROMULO: 50 ANOS DE LIDERAZGO POLITICO. Caracas: Editorial Arte, 1978. 249 pp.

Quintero, José Humberto. EL CONVENIO CON LA SANTA SEDE: CARTAS CRUZADAS ENTRE S. E. CARDENAL JOSE HUMBERTO QUINTERO Y EL PRESIDENTE ROMULO BETANCOURT. Caracas: Colegio de Ingenieros de Venezuela, 1977. 184 pp.

The following book on Venezuela is not part of the Betancourt collection:

Pérez Arcay, Jacinto. EL FUEGO SAGRADO: BOLIVAR HOY. Caracas: Ministerio de la Defensa, República de Venezuela, 1979. Anexos, bibliografía bolivariana, bibliografía general. 347 pp. Paper.

MISCELLANEOUS

Duignan, Peter and Alvin Rabushka, eds. THE UNITED STATES IN THE 1980s: FOREIGN AS WELL AS DOMESTIC POLICY OPTIONS. Palo Alto, CA: Hoover Institution, Stanford University, 1980. Index. xxxix, 868 pp. $20.00.

Dumont, Rene and Nicholas Cohen. THE GROWTH OF HUNGER: A NEW POLITICS OF AGRICULTURE. Ideas in Progress series. Salem, NH: Marion Boyars, 1980. References. 229 pp. Paper.

Feder, Judith, John Holahan and Theodore Marmor. NATIONAL HEALTH INSURANCE: CONFLICTING GOALS AND POLICY CHOICES. Washington, DC: The Urban Institute, 1980. List of tables and figures, selected bibliography, appendix, index. xxi, 721 pp.

Garner, Jane, compiler. ARCHIVES AND MANUSCRIPTS ON MICROFILM IN THE NETTIE LEE BENSON LATIN AMERICAN COLLECTION: A CHECKLIST. Contributions to Librarianship, No. 3. Austin: The General Libraries, University of Texas at Austin, 1980. $10.00 paper.

Hoffman, Stanley. PRIMACY OR WORLD ORDER: AMERICAN FOREIGN POLICY SINCE THE COLD WAR. New York: McGraw-Hill, 1980. Index of persons and subjects. xv, 333 pp. Paper.

Labarca, Guillermo, compilador. ECONOMIA POLITICA DE LA EDUCACION. México, D.F.: Editorial Nueva Imagen, 1980. Glosario. 397 pp. $14.95 paper.

Kegley, Charles W., Jr. and Eugene R. Wittkopf. AMERICAN FOREIGN POLICY: PATTERN AND PROGRESS. New York: St. Martin's Press, 1980. Appendix, references, index. xiii, 512 pp.

Livingston, William S., ed. A PROSPECT OF LIBERAL DEMOCRACY. Austin: University of Texas Bicentennial Committee, 1979. x, 229 pp. $12.95 cloth, $5.95 paper.

OAS. ANNUAL REPORT OF THE INTERAMERICAN COMMISSION ON HUMAN RIGHTS, 1978. Washington, DC: General Secretariat, OAS. 179 pp. Paper.

Robinson, Richard. CONTEMPORARY PORTUGAL. Boston: Allen & Unwin, 1979. List of tables, glossary of political terms, maps, index. 297 pp. $28.50.

Ross, Stanley R. and Wilbert A. Chaffee, eds., with assistance of Beecher C. Ellison. GUIDE TO THE HISPANIC AMERICAN HISTORICAL REVIEW, 1956-1975. (1956-1965 edited by Donald E. Worcester and Walter A. Payne.) Durham, NC: Duke University Press, 1980. vii, 432 pp. $32.75.

INDEX

to

JOURNAL OF INTERAMERICAN STUDIES AND WORLD AFFAIRS

VOLUME 22

Number 1 (February 1980) pp. 1-128
Number 2 (May 1980) pp. 129-264
Number 3 (August 1980) pp. 265-392
Number 4 (November 1980) pp. 393-512

Authors:

AZICRI, MAX, "The Institutionalization of the Cuban State: A Political Perspective," 315.

BAER, WERNER and ANNIBAL V. VILLELA, "The Changing Nature of Development Banking in Brazil," 423.

BOOTH, JOHN, A., "A Guatemalan Nightmare: Levels of Political Violence, 1966-1972," 195.

CRAIG, RICHARD, "Operation Condor: Mexico's Antidrug Campaign Enters a New Era." 345.

ELLNER, STEVEN, "Leonardo Ruiz Pineda: Acción Democrática's Guerrillero for Liberty" [Comment], 389.

FERRER, ALDO, "The Argentine Economy, 1976-1979," 131.

GRABENDORFF, WOLF, "Cuba's Involvement in Africa: An Interpretation of Objectives, Reactions, and Limitations," 3.

HILGER, MARYE THARP, "Decision-Making in a Public Marketing Enterprise: CONASUPO in Mexico," 471.

JAMES, DILMUS D., "Mexico's Recent Science and Technology Planning: An Outsider Economist's Critique," 163.

LEVINE, ROBERT M., "Perspectives on the Mid-Vargas Years: 1934-1937," 57.

MARTZ, JOHN D., "The Regionalist Expression of Populism: Guayaquil and the CFP, 1948-1960," 289.

MILENKY, EDWARD S., "Arms Production and National Security in Argentina," 267.

MOSER, CAROLINE O. N., "Why the Poor Remain Poor: The Experience of Bogotá Market Traders in the 1970s," 365.

MUMME, STEPHEN P., "U.S.-Mexican Groundwater Problems: Bilateral Prospects and Implications," 31.

PARAGG, RALPH, "Integration and Regional Development: The Case of the Commonwealth Caribbean" [Review Essay], 495.

SAULNIERS, ALFRED H., "ENCI: Peru's Bandied Monopolist," 441.

——— "Public Enterprises in Latin America: An Annotated List of Recent Research Papers," 463.

SCHIFF, WARREN, "German-Latin American Relations: The First Half of the Twentieth Century" [Review Essay], 109.
TOBLER, HANS WERNER and PETER WALDMANN, "German Colonies in South America: A New Germany in the *Cono Sur*?" (Ronald C. Newton, trans.) [Review Essay], 227.
TOPIK, STEVEN, "State Enterprise in a Liberal Regime: The Banco do Brasil, 1905-1930," 401.
TREBAT, THOMAS J. and JAN PETER WOGART, "Introduction," 395.
TWINAM, ANN, "From Jew to Basque: Ethnic Myths and Antioqueno Entrepreneurship," 81.
VILLELA, ANNIBAL V., see Baer, Werner.
WALDMANN, PETER, see Tobler, Hans Werner.
WIARDA, HOWARD J., "The United States and the Dominican Republic: Intervention, Dependency, and Tyrannicide" [Review Essay], 247.
WOGART, JAN PETER, see Trebat, Thomas J.

Articles:

"The Argentine Economy, 1976-1979," Ferrer, 131.
"Arms Production and National Security in Argentina," Milenky, 267.
"The Changing Nature of Development Banking in Brazil," Baer and Villela, 423.
"Cuba's Involvement in Africa: An Interpretation of Objectives, Reactions, and Limitations," Grabendorff, 3.
"Decision-Making in a Public Marketing Enterprise: CONASUPO in Mexico," Hilger, 471.
"ENCI: Peru's Bandied Monopolist," Saulniers, 441.
"From Jew to Basque: Ethnic Myths and Antioqueno Entrepreneurship," Twinam, 81.
"A Guatemalan Nightmare: Levels of Political Violence, 1966-1972," Booth, 195.
"The Institutionalization of the Cuban State: A Political Prespective," Azicri, 315.
"Introduction," Trebat and Wogart, 395.
"Mexico's Recent Science and Technology Planning: An Outsider Economist's Critique," James, 163.
"Operation Condor: Mexico's Antidrug Campaign Enters a New Era," Craig, 345.
"Perspectives on the Mid-Vargas Years: 1934-1937," Levine, 57.
"Public Enterprises in Latin America: An Annotated List of Recent Research Papers," Saulniers, 463.
"The Regionalist Expression of Populism: Guayaquil and the CFP, 1948-1960," Martz, 289.
"State Enterprise in a Liberal Regime: The Banco do Brasil, 1905-1930," Topik, 401.
"U.S.-Mexican Groundwater Problems: Bilateral Prospects and Implications," Mumme, 31.
"Why the Poor Remain Poor: The Experience of Bogatá Market Traders in the 1970s," Moser, 365.

Review Essays:

"German Colonies in South America: A New Germany in the *Cono Sur*?" Tobler and Waldmann, 227.
"Integration and Regional Development: The Case of the Commonwealth Caribbean," Paragg, 495.

"The United States and the Dominican Republic: Intervention, Dependency and Tyrannicide," Wiarda, 247.

Comment:

"Leonardo Ruiz Pineda: Acción Democrática's Guerrillero for Liberty," Ellner, 389.

Books Received:

119, 261, 501.